Real English

*The Grammar of English Dialects
in the British Isles*

Editors: *James Milroy and
Lesley Milroy*

LONGMAN
London and New York

Longman Group UK Limited,
Longman House, Burnt Mill,
Harlow, Essex CM20 2JE, England
and Associated Companies throughout the world

Published in the United States of America
by Longman Publishing, New York

© Longman Group UK Limited 1993

First published 1993

ISBN 0–582 08177–7 CSD
ISBN 0–582 08176–9 PPR

British Library Cataloguing-in-Publication Data

A catalogue record for this book is
available from the British Library

Library of Congress Cataloging-in-Publication Data

Real English: the grammar of English dialects in the British Isles/editors,
    James Milroy and Lesley Milroy.
        p. cm. — (Real language series)
    Includes bibliographical references and index.
    ISBN 0–582–08177–7 (CSD). — ISBN 0–582–08176–9 (PPR)
    1. English language—Dialects—Great Britain—Grammar.
    2. Great Britain—Popular culture. I. Milroy, James. II. Milroy,
    Lesley. III. Series.
    PE1711.R4 1993
    427—dc20   92-42775
                                                    CIP

Set in 10/12pt Sabon
Produced by Longman Singapore Publishers (Pte) Ltd.
Printed & bound by Antony Rowe Ltd, Eastbourne
Transferred to digital print on demand 2002

Contents

Contributors   ix
Editors' preface   xi
Acknowledgements   xvi

Part I: Dialect in Education

1   Syntactic variation in non-standard
     dialects: background issues   3
     Jenny Cheshire and Jim Milroy

1.1   The process of language standardization   3
1.2   Written standard English and literacy   7
1.3   The historical development of standard English   9
1.4   Social and regional variation in British English
      today   11
1.5   Attitudes towards regional varieties of English   14
1.6   The social significance of regional syntactic forms   17
1.7   The rule-governed nature of variation   18
1.8   Peer group pressures on language   20
1.9   Language development in older children   21
1.10 Writing   22
1.11 Linguistic assessment   24
1.12 Education   25
1.13 Concluding remarks   31
      References   32

2   Sociolinguistics in the classroom:
     exploring linguistic diversity   34
     Jenny Cheshire and Viv Edwards

2.1   Introduction   34

2.2   The survey of British dialect grammar   35
2.3   Reactions to linguistic diversity   38
2.4   Resources for diversity   46
2.5   Research in the local community   47
2.6   Conclusion   49
       References   50

3   **Non-standard English and dialect levelling**   53
     Jenny Cheshire, Viv Edwards and Pamela Whittle

3.1   Introduction   53
3.2   The Survey of British Dialect Grammar   54
3.3   The questionnaire   57
3.4   Regions included in the Survey   59
3.5   Shared morphological and syntactic features of
       British urban dialects   63
3.6   Conclusion   82
       Notes   83
       References   84
       Appendix 3.1: Questionnaire used in the Survey   87
       Appendix 3.2: Regions represented in the Survey   96

**Part II: Regional variation in English grammar:
             case studies**

4   **The grammar of Scottish English**   99
     Jim Miller

4.1   Introduction: Scottish English   99
4.2   Morphology   106
4.3   Syntax   109
4.4   Organization of discourse   132
4.5   Conclusion   137
       Note   137
       References   138

5   **The grammar of Irish English**   139
     John Harris

5.1   Introduction   139
5.2   The noun phrase   143
5.3   The verb group   151

5.4	The expression of time	159
5.5	Complex sentences	164
5.6	Negation	168
5.7	Prepositional usage	171
5.8	Discourse devices	173
5.9	Conclusion	177
	Notes	182
	Further reading	183
	References	184

6 The grammar of Tyneside and Northumbrian English   187
Joan Beal

6.1	Introduction	187
6.2	The grammar of Tyneside and Northumbrian English	191
6.3	The verb phrase	192
6.4	Interrogative tags	201
6.5	Interrogatives	204
6.6	The noun phrase	205
6.7	Sentence-final elements	210
6.8	Prepositions	211
6.9	Conclusion	212
	References	212

7 The grammar of Southern British English   214
Viv Edwards

7.1	Dialect grammar and South-eastern English dialects	214
7.2	South-eastern English grammar	219
7.3	Negation	226
7.4	Relative pronouns	228
7.5	Personal and reflexive pronouns	229
7.6	Adjectives and adverbs	231
7.7	Demonstratives	232
7.8	Verb particles and prepositions	233
7.9	Nouns of measurement	234
7.10	Conclusion	234

Note   234
Appendix to Chapter 7   236
References and Further Reading   238

Appendix to Part II: Glossary of grammatical terms   239
Jim Miller (with additions by Jim Milroy)

Part III: Resources

8   A directory of English dialect resources: the
    English counties   245
    Viv Edwards

8.1   Introduction   245
8.2   English dialects   248
8.3   The Northern Counties and the Isle of Man   254
8.4   The West Midlands Counties   291
8.5   The East Midland Counties and East Anglia   306
8.6   The Southern Counties   317

Index to Parts I and II   341

Contributors

BIOGRAPHICAL DETAILS

Joan Beal is a lecturer in English Language at the University of Newcastle upon Tyne where she teaches courses on Dialectology, Historical Linguistics and the History of English. She has published several articles on the History of English and on Tyneside English. She is currently carrying out a study of Thomas Spence's *Grand Repository of the English Language*, the first phonetic dictionary of English, which was published in Newcastle in 1775.

Jenny Cheshire is Professor of English Linguistics at the University of Fribourg and the University of Neuchâtel, Switzerland. She is the author of *Variation in an English Dialect* (1982) and co-author of *Describing Language* (1987; 2nd ed. 1992) as well as other books and articles on sociolinguistics, English language and dialect and education. She recently edited *English around the world: sociolinguistic perspectives* (CUP, 1991) and is co-editor of the Longman Real Language series.

Viv Edwards is currently Director of the Reading and Language Information Centre at the University of Reading. Her main research interests are in language and education. Recent publications include *Multilingualism in the British Isles* (co-edited with Safder Alladina, Longman, 1990), *Oral cultures past and present* (co-authored with T. J. Senkiewicz, Blackwell, 1990) and *The world in a classroom* (co-authored with Angela Redfern, Multilingual Matters, 1992). She co-edits *Language and Education: an International Journal*.

John Harris is currently Reader in Linguistics, University College London. His publications include *Phonological variation and* *change* (CUP 1985), *English sound structure* (Blackwell, in press), and articles on phonological theory, language change, and the history of English.

Jim Miller is Reader in the Department of Linguistics and Principal Investigator, Human Communication Research Centre, at the University of Edinburgh. His main research interests are in the relation of spoken to written language, Slavic languages (especially Russian), case, tense and aspect, and transitivity. Main publications include *Semantics and syntax: connections and parallels* (CUP, 1985) and *Syntax: a linguistic introduction to sentence structure*, (with Keith Brown, 2nd edition, Routledge, 1991).

Jim Milroy is Emeritus Professor of Linguistics, and was formerly Head of Department of Linguistics, at the University of Sheffield. His main interests are in sociolinguistics, historical linguistics and the language of literature. Publications include *The language of Gerard Manley Hopkins* (Andre Deutsch, 1977), *Authority in Language* (with Lesley Milroy, 2nd edition, Routledge, 1991) and *Linguistic variation and change* (Blackwell, 1992).

Lesley Milroy is Professor of Sociolinguistics in the Department of Speech, University of Newcastle upon Tyne. Her main interests are in sociolinguistics, conversational analysis and bilingualism. Publications include *Language and social networks* (2nd edition, Blackwell, 1987), *Observing and analysing natural language* (Blackwell, 1987), *Authority in language* (with James Milroy, 2nd edition, Routledge, 1991), and *Linguistics and aphasia* (with Ruth Lesser, Longman, 1993).

Pam Whittle was the research project officer for the survey into British Dialect Grammar from 1986–1989. She is currently a senior health service manager for the Oxford Regional Health Authority.

Real English:
The Grammar of English Dialects in the British Isles

Editors' Preface

This volume is the outgrowth of three recent Economic and Social Research Council-funded projects on the grammar of English dialects in the British Isles. Its aims are to make available, as far as possible, accurate and up-to-date information on regional variation in the use of the grammatical constructions of English, and to direct readers to those resources where further information on regional variation is available. At present, much of this information is not easily accessible; yet, it is likely to be of interest to general readers as well as to professional ones, and we hope that anyone who is inquisitive about language variation will find it useful. But the volume is especially intended to be helpful to those who have a professional commitment to dealing with language in use – for example, teachers, clinical psychologists and speech therapists, and this group now includes overseas teachers of English as a foreign language. It is no longer considered to be sufficient for overseas students to learn the grammar of one highly standardized variety of English, as these students commonly live for a period of time in parts of the country where most of the English they hear – the real English of the title – deviates from the rules of this variety. It isn't the variety that most people speak, and overseas learners are much more clearly aware of this fact than they used to be.

Part I consists of two chapters. Chapter 1 discusses the notion of the standard language and the differences between 'standard' and 'non-standard' varieties. There is also some discussion of the consequences of these distinctions in classroom teaching. Chapter 2 discusses more fully some aspects of linguistic diversity as it affects children in school. Chapter 3 focuses on urban dialect grammar generally. The four chapters of Part II give an account of grammatical variation in four regions of the British Isles: Scotland, Northern Ireland, Tyneside and Southern England. The term *grammar* is used in its technical sense to include both *syntax* (rules of sentence construction) and *morphology* (rules of word formation). An example of a syntactic difference is *the eggs is cracked* as against *the eggs are cracked*: this is a difference of *concord*. An example of a morphological difference is *I says* as against *I say*. But it is often difficult in practice to keep these two areas separate. Morphological differences between regional varieties are, however, particularly salient and are often commented upon.

Chapters 4 to 7 originated as pamphlets commissioned by the Economic and Social Research Council (ESRC) as part of a research initiative on regional syntax. These pamphlets differed quite markedly from each other in scope and detail, according to the amount and kind of published material available on the relevant regions. We have retained to a great extent the original forms of these pamphlets, including such matters as appendices and additional suggested reading provided by the authors. Part II concludes with a glossary, the bulk of which was prepared by Jim Miller as an adjunct to Chapter 4. As his definitions have been found to be generally helpful, the glossary is now placed at the end of Part II. There are a few additions to it, and this should make it sufficient for most readers' needs. A more comprehensive treatment of technical terms may be found in David Crystal's *A Dictionary of Linguistics and Phonetics* (3rd edition, Blackwell, 1991). Part III of this book is a directory of dialect resources for the counties of England. Here the reader will find references to books and tape-recordings which can be used to investigate dialect variation further. We hope that this directory will be of particular value to teachers who need to supervise school projects on English language.

Amongst the general public – and even amongst professional

linguists – there is a tendency to underestimate the extent of variation in grammar that exists in the British Isles, and – more particularly – there is a lack of appreciation of the consequences of this variability in such matters as language testing and assessment. As many children in large urban areas use spoken syntax that is to a degree non-standard, it might seem important that teachers, speech therapists and others involved in education should have explicit knowledge of some localized non-standard variety or varieties. We make a distinction here between implicit and explicit knowledge: many people will have some kind of knowledge of a non-standard variety, but they may not always be able to express this knowledge explicitly and accurately, or appreciate the consequences of language differences when they are dealing with pupils or patients.

Unfortunately, some people believe that 'dialects' of English are dying out and that it may not be worthwhile studying and describing them. Some commentators have even claimed that in forty or fifty years from now everyone will be speaking standard English. Presumably, such people believe that problems arising in the educational system as a result of non-standard usage will then disappear and everyone will have equal access to literacy in standard English. We believe that such views are profoundly mistaken, and, if expressed by 'authorities', quite irresponsible. It is worth recalling Samuel Johnson's remark in the Preface to his *Dictionary* (1755) that 'dialects . . . will always be observed to grow fewer and less different, as books are multiplied'. While there is some truth in this remark, there is still a great deal of dialect divergence more than two centuries later and little sign that spoken English is becoming completely uniform.

It is true, of course, that extreme rural dialects are gradually dying out, but this is not due to some magical power inherent in the influence of Standard English. It is more directly due to the repercussions of population growth and urbanization during the nineteenth and twentieth centuries. Most of the urban population speak varieties of English that deviate quite markedly from traditional rural dialects, but they also deviate – just as markedly – from standardized norms. Furthermore, it is these urban varieties – and not 'standard' English – that show the greatest capacity to spread to surrounding rural areas. Thus, they have great vitality and are spoken by millions of people. It is important that educators and others, whatever they may think of these varieties, should know as much about them as possible.

It is also true that many people believe that there is only one form of 'correct' English, and that deviations from this are a result of ignorance or carelessness. In this view 'grammar' is equated with 'acceptability in standard English', and anything which is non-standard is believed to be ungrammatical. This is not how we use the term 'grammar' in this book: all varieties of all languages have their own 'grammars', even if these grammars sometimes differ from standardized grammars. But the contributors to this book certainly recognize that one of the main functions of an educational system is to provide access to a high level of literacy for all citizens, and that literacy involves the use – in writing – of a standardized form of the language. However, the differences between standard and non-standard forms are historically deep-rooted, and it is the standard that has been built on what was originally a regional dialect, rather than vice-versa. The regional dialects are not careless deviations from a standardized norm: they have their own complex histories. There is a close relationship, however, between written English and what we have come to regard as standard English. As a consequence of this, some commentators have believed that non-standard speakers will require more help in achieving literacy than standard speakers will.

In describing English, the categories 'standard' and 'non-standard' are not as well defined as these remarks may suggest. Although some constructions may be characterized as clearly belonging to one category or the other, many more which crop up in (for example) the colloquial English of educated speakers cannot be clearly assigned to either. Similarly, a clear distinction cannot always be drawn between localized non-standard constructions and those that have a wide regional distribution. While some constructions are unique to, say, Tyneside or to the south of England, others (such as *I done it* for *I did it*) are common to most varieties. We can understand these points more fully if we appreciate the nature of language standardization. Accordingly, we proceed in Chapter 1 to consider the place of standard English in our society. We also discuss the process of language standardization and the relation of this to literacy.

Chapters 2 and 3 were previously published, though in different forms, as follows:

CHESHIRE, J., EDWARDS, V. and WHITTLE, P. (1989) Urban British dialect grammar: the question of dialect levelling. *English World Wide* **10** (2): 185–225

CHESHIRE, J. and EDWARDS, V. (1991) Schoolchildren as socio-linguistic researchers. *Linguistics and Education* **3** (3): 225–50.

The three ESRC-funded projects on which these and other chapters in the book are based are as follows:

(1) 'The Survey of British Dialect Grammar' (Research Grant Award C00 232264, held by J. Cheshire and V. Edwards),

(2) A set of specially commissioned pamphlets on the syntax of four regional dialects, along with an editors' introduction ('Regional Variation in British English Syntax, edited by J. and L. Milroy, published by ESRC in 1988), and

(3) A specially commissioned 'Directory of English Dialect Resources' (counties in England only), edited by V. Edwards and published by ESRC in 1990.

We gratefully acknowledge the permission to use this previously published material, and particularly wish to thank ESRC for their financial support.

We are greatly indebted, not only to the contributors for their industry and patience, but to many other people for their interest and help while we were preparing this book. We would particularly like to mention Martin Harris for organizing in Salford in 1984 the seminar out of which the ESRC project on regional syntax emerged; David Crystal for essential advice on the organization and presentation of this volume; and Euan Reid for his careful and helpful editorial assistance.

Acknowledgements

The publishers are grateful to the following for permission to reproduce copyright material:

Ablex Publishing Corporation (New Jersey) for article in Linguistics and Education 3 (1991), pp. 225–249, which forms the basis of Chapter 2; Economic and Social Research Council (1988) *Regional variation in British English Syntax,* (eds J. and L. Milroy); Economic and Social Research Council (1990) Directory of English Dialect Resources (ed. Viv Edwards); John Benjamins 'Urban British dialect grammar: the question of dialect levelling'. *English World Wide,* (10) 2; Abson Books, Bristol (1982) *Krek Waiter's Peakd Bristle,* edited by Dirk Robson and illustrated by Vic Wiltshire.

They are also grateful to Brian Clare, Ethel Fisher, Kate Fletcher and Keith Morgan, for allowing their work to be reproduced in Chapter 8.

Viv Edwards acknowledges with gratitude all those who helped her compile the resource material in Chapter 8, particularly the following officers of dialect societies, librarians and archivists throughout the country who gave unstintingly of their time:

M.E. Arnold, Local History Librarian, Northampton; Amanda Arrowsmith, Suffolk County Archivist; Stephen Best, Local Studies Librarian, Nottingham; David Bromwich, Local History Librarian, Somerset; Janice Brooker, Local Studies Librarian, Hertfordshire; A.M. Carr, Local Studies Librarian, Shrewsbury; Rodney Cousins, Keeper of Social History, Museum of Lincolnshire Life; J.S. Dansie, Local Studies Librarian, Colchester Central Library; L.N. Emery, Divisional Librarian, Stoke-on-Trent; L.J. Feiweles, Chief Librarian, Wakefield; S. Gates, Reference Librarian, Lincoln; S.V. Gill, Local

Studies Librarian, Nottingham; John Goodchild, Principal Local Studies Officer and Archivist, Wakefield; Irving Graham, Lakeland Dialect Society; T. Graham, Head of Cultural and Leisure Activities, Borough of South Tyneside; David Guy, Director of Library and Museum Services, Walsall; Bernard Haigh, Central Librarian, Derby; G.G. Hand, Assistant County Librarian, North Yorks; Robert Harrison, Local Studies Librarian, County Library Headquarters, Bristol; Deidre Heywood, Head of Cultural and Information Services, Oldham; J.M. Hodge, Huddersfield Librarian; H.W. Hodgson, Group Librarian, Carlisle Library; G.R. Hiatt, Divisional Librarian, Gloucester; Brian Hughes, Director of Arts and Education, Bolton Metropolitan Borough; Carolyn Jacob, Reference Team Librarian, Brighton; J. Main, Divisional Librarian, Durham; J.S. Mallam, Divisional Librarian, Darlington; F.W. Manders, Local Studies Librarian, Newcastle upon Tyne; Michael Messenger, Hereford and Worcester County Librarian; J.M. Olive, Local Studies Librarian, Sheffield; P.E. Parker, Local Studies Librarian, Poole; G.S. Payne, County Librarian, Northumberland; R.L. Pybus, Director of Library and Museum Service, Wiltshire; T.D.W. Reid, Senior Reference Librarian, Stockport; D. Saunders, Local History Librarian, Maidstone; Alison Shute, County Librarian, Devon; E. Ken Smith, Yorkshire Dialect Society; Aubrey Stephenson, Leicestershire Studies Librarian; B. Stephenson, Special Collections Librarian, Bedfordshire; Pauline Taylor, Assistant Local Studies Librarian, Suffolk County Council; C.E. Vickers, Barnsley Central Library; J.R.A. Walker, Assistant City Librarian, Birmingham; Jennifer Ward, Local Studies Librarian, Dorchester; Alan Welton, Assistant County Librarian, North Cumbria; C. West, Reference Librarian, Wolverhampton; L. White, County Librarian, Oxfordshire; J.D.A. Widdowson, Director, The Centre for English Cultural Tradition and Language, University of Sheffield; C. Wilkins-Jones, Local Studies Librarian, Norfolk; Stephen Willis, Language and Literature Librarian, Manchester; Diana Winterbotham, Local Studies Librarian, Preston; Dorothy Wood, Chief Librarian, Halifax Central Library; Vincent Wood, Oral Archive Project, Middlesbrough.

The questionnaire reprinted in Chapter 3 is illustrated by Dafydd Morriss.

Part I

Dialect in Education

1 Syntactic variation in non-standard dialects: background issues

Jenny Cheshire and Jim Milroy

1.1 The process of language standardization

In order to understand some of the differences between standard and non-standard forms of language, it's convenient to begin by looking at the process of standardization. We must emphasize that this is indeed a *process* and that it is permanently in progress in any language that undergoes it. That is to say that it didn't terminate at some time in the past – the English language was not finally standardized once and for all in, say, the eighteenth century, and then stabilized in that final form. Standardization is a process that is never complete, but it aims at uniformity and values this above all things.

The term *standardization* can be used of phenomena outside language and means the imposition of uniformity upon a class of objects. Thus, we may describe a set of motor-car components, or electric plugs, or a coinage system, as being 'standardized'. When such objects are described as 'sub-standard', the implication is that they are not of the quality required to perform their function in the most reliable way. When we speak of language as sub-standard, we are, therefore, implying an analogy with factory rejects and suggesting some form of functional inadequacy. When, on the other hand, we speak of items as *non-standard*, there is no such value-judgement. The best analogy here is with hand-made, as against factory-made, tools. Whereas factories produce large numbers of items (e.g. spades) that are all identical, those made by traditional craftsmen are all slightly different. But a factory-made ('standardized') tool is not necessarily in any given instance better or more functional than a hand-made one; indeed it is sometimes the hand-made item that is more highly valued. A *sub-standard* item, however, is defective and will command a low price.

Although such analogies help us to understand the nature of language standardization, language is obviously different in many ways from objects like spades and electric plugs. First, it is incomparably more complex than these other phenomena; secondly, it is a medium of communication and exchange. As a coinage system is also a medium of communication and exchange, we now briefly consider the analogy between language and coinage.

The purpose of standardizing a coinage is to ensure fixed values for the counters in the system: coins of particular denominations must all be of the same size and weight. When a coinage is not standardized, people cannot automatically rely on the value of a coin. With language also, many people seem to feel that variability is inconvenient and uniformity desirable. In practice, however, it is those who wield the most power who have most influence in determining the 'correct' forms of standard languages. They are socio-political, as well as linguistic, entities.

As for its effect on linguistic form, standardization of language necessarily involves the *suppression of variability*. This happens at all levels of language: spelling, grammar, vocabulary and pronunciation. It is never fully successful at all these levels: it has clearly been most successful in spelling (where very little variation is tolerated) and least successful in pronunciation (as many widely divergent accents of English enjoy a flourishing life). The standardization of English grammar has certainly deeply influenced popular attitudes: many people feel a compulsion to accept only one out of two or more variants as the 'correct' form (e.g. *different from* as against *different to*), even when there is no difference in meaning between the forms, and they will often write to the newspapers complaining about alleged misuses. It's assumed by these people that only one of any two variants can be correct – the other must be wrong. Thus, uniformity is desired and variation not tolerated. In vocabulary also, there is a tendency to believe that there is only one 'correct' meaning for a particular word and that some usages of it are 'incorrect' (for example, *aggravating* in the sense 'irritating' is often held to be incorrect). This has not always been the case: in earlier centuries the English language seems to have been more tolerant of variability, and the rather rigid attitudes that we observe nowadays seem to be a consequence of a process of increasing standardization that has taken place gradually over the centuries. We now look briefly at this process.

The process of language standardization characteristically consists of several stages, which may overlap in time. First of all, a particular variety must be *selected* from a pool of competing varieties. If the process is to be successful, the variety chosen must be one that will gain *acceptance* by a group of users who are capable of influencing other groups. The variety must then be *diffused* socially and geographically by various means – often with very far-reaching effects upon speakers of other varieties (which are now becoming 'non-standard'). The diffusion process typically takes place through the writing system, the educational system, and through discrimination of various direct and indirect kinds against speakers of non-standard varieties. The standard language must also be *maintained*, and the process of maintenance is clearly linked to that of diffusion, being promoted through much the same channels – education, literacy and so on. Other stages of standardization that are particularly relevant to educators are: *elaboration of function, codification* and *prescription*. We shall now consider some of these stages, emphasizing their socio-political aspects.

First, we must note that the *selection* and *acceptance* of a given variety depend on social, and not linguistic, factors. The variety selected is not necessarily more logical, more expressive or more elegant than other varieties. What is of most importance is its acceptability amongst the most powerful and influential sectors of society. In the case of English, the London area had become dominant by the late Middle Ages, and it was the language of this area that fifteenth-century printers selected as the language of printed books. As a result of the selection and acceptance of this variety by influential groups, all literate people today use its modern form in writing, whatever their regional origin may be, and they may well be influenced by it in their speech also. But notice also that a consequence of the selection of one variety for standardization is the automatic devaluation of other varieties.

As the standard language is diffused socially and geographically, it also tends to be diffused into a wider variety of functions: it undergoes *elaboration of function*. As the 'official' language, it is used in administrative functions, but also in science, philosophy and literature. As a result, the users of the language usually feel the need for a wider vocabulary for use in these administrative and learned domains. In English, elaboration of vocabulary came about (c.1550–1800) mainly through massive borrowing of words from Latin and Greek.

A relatively late stage in the historical process is *codification*. The standard variety is codified so that interested persons can learn and use the 'correct' forms that they believe will give them social advancement. In English, the great century of codification was the eighteenth century, during which Dr Johnson's *Dictionary* and many grammar books appeared. At this point the codified forms become available for *prescription*; these are now regarded as the 'lawful' or legitimate forms, whereas those forms not admitted to the grammar books and dictionaries become, as it were, illegitimate. In other words, standard norms are subject to legislation, sometimes by lawfully constituted bodies (as in France), but sometimes by influential private persons (as in Britain). Typically, these authorities are now consulted by speakers and writers as the arbiters of correct usage (even though they may sometimes be inaccurate or eccentric). An important mechanism for spreading knowledge of prescriptive norms is the educational system.

It is important to understand that, although the standard variety has achieved social prestige and importance, its *linguistic* forms are not necessarily better or more discriminating than those of other dialects. Some dialects, for example, make grammatical distinctions that are not present in the standard, and these distinctions might be thought useful. The *this/that/yon* distinction found in Northern and Scottish use is a grammatical resource that enables the speaker to distinguish three degrees of distance, whereas standard English distinguishes only two. The chief differences between standard and non-standard varieties are not in their 'superior' or 'inferior' linguistic structures, but in the different levels of social acceptability accorded to them and in the fact that non-standard varieties are not extensively codified or officially prescribed.

1.2 Written standard English and literacy

It is the grammar of written English rather than that of spoken English that has been most extensively codified. The grammar of speech, however, differs very greatly from that of written language. Compare the following pairs of sentences:

(1a) These cats – they're hungry.
(1b) These cats are hungry.

(2a) In the morning will suit me better.
(2b) It will suit me better in the morning.

(3a) I looked up and saw this man.
(3b) I looked up and saw a man.

The first item in each pair exemplifies a structural type commonly found in informal spoken English, but – as far as we can determine – not associated with any particular regional syntax. The interaction between what might be called 'informal spoken standard English' (as exemplified in 1a–3a) and non-standard English is complicated, and the borderline between them not at all clear (for an elaboration of this point, see also the comments on Scots English in Chapter 4).

Conversely, written English makes heavy use of structures that are rare in speech. These include: a relatively high proportion of complex sentences with heavy subordinate clause structures; the use of many subordinating conjunctions and adverbials to mark relations between clauses and sentences (*when, while, moreover, however, firstly, in conclusion*, etc.); heavily pre-modified noun phrases, often in subject position (e.g. *A great many quite definite conclusions* may be drawn . . .); relatively frequent use of passive constructions. Whereas spoken language often uses clauses strung together without marking the relations between them (as in *I'm tired – I had to walk all the way*), written language is likely to insert the subordinator – in this case *because*. Similarly, large numbers of pre-modifying adjectives are avoided in speech, and some of the items are strung out *after* the noun, as in the following: *It was a big dog – very dirty and mangy – a sort of brown colour.*

The eighteenth-century codification of English was carried out on the written language and not the spoken. It seems to be because of this that some people believe spoken language to be simply 'ungrammatical': they notice that it often does not conform to the codified structures described in books of grammar and rhetoric. The truth is, however, that the grammar of spoken English simply has not been fully described. Obviously, it is more difficult to describe spoken language than to describe written language: the former is ephemeral and is not captured on the page for analysis at leisure. Eighteenth-century scholars were at a massive disadvantage in describing speech and had to rely mainly on writing for their data: it is only in the last few decades that the easy availability of tape-recorders has made it possible to collect extensive samples of speech and analyse some of its rules and regularities. All the contributors to this volume have based their work on extensive tape-recordings of spoken English. We now consider an example of the grammar of speech.

In spoken language many so-called 'dislocated' sentences occur, such as in (1a) above or:

(4)   This house – Jack built it.
(5)   Jack – he built this house.

These sentences use 'resumptive' or 'shadow' pronouns: *it, he,* which refer back to the topic of each sentence: *this house, Jack.* Such sentences are extremely common in all spoken English, but they are avoided in written prose. Our point here is that, despite their unacceptability in written English, such sentences are not ungrammatical – we can demonstrate that they are constructed by regular rules. For example, the resumptive pronoun must agree in person, number and gender with the topic noun phrase: we would not say:

(6)   *This house – Jack built them.

These sentences also obey strict rules of word-order. We would not say:

(7)   *Jack – built this house he.
(8)   *Jack this – he built house.

Although we may well have the impression that speech is less tightly organized than written language, it nevertheless has its own grammar. Similarly, although we are all expert users of spoken grammar, we are less explicitly aware of the grammatical conventions of speech than we are of written grammar, and we may therefore tend to believe that speech is, simply, 'ungrammatical'. This seems to be a consequence of the fact that speech has not yet been extensively observed and codified. As spoken English is very variable, both regionally and socially, it follows that attempts to describe speech must also take into account the existence of a great many different varieties. Our tendency to assume that there is only one correct form of English, and that this is modelled on a relatively invariant written form, is a result of the fact that our society is literate. It can also be partly understood by considering the history of standardization of the English language – to which we briefly return in the next section.

1.3   The historical development of standard English

As we have already seen, the history of English has been one of progressive standardization, in which we have been able to distinguish a number of stages. The situation has not always been as it is today; indeed, the contrast in degree of standardization between medieval times and the present day is enormous. We may consider these differences under three headings: functional differences, regional variation in written English, and variability within written texts.

In earlier times, the English language did not possess the range of *functions* that it possesses today. In the period 1100–1300, the language used for administrative and legislative purposes was, largely, French, and there was a thriving Anglo-Norman (French) literary culture. The language used in scholarship was Latin, and Latin remained prominent in this sphere until the seventeenth century. Thus, although spoken English flourished throughout these centuries (hence its ultimate survival), it did not have the status that it now possesses for use in the more public and formal domains.

Until the fifteenth century, written forms of English appeared in a variety of different regional dialects. The consciousness that written usage should conform to the norms of only one particular dialect – that of London and the South-east Midlands – was not well established until after 1500, and then only amongst the best educated and most powerful people. Informal documents (e.g. letters) by less well-educated people continued to be written in regionally varied forms. The dialect selected for literary English was, as we have seen, that of the London area (except that the developing Scottish standard of the period was that of Edinburgh and the Lothians), and this selection depended on commercial and political factors. In the late sixteenth century, there are signs that the London dialect was becoming more highly valued (in England) in its spoken form also. However, the establishment of 'Received Pronunciation' as a desired standard for people to aim at does not seem to have come about until the rise in importance of the public schools in the nineteenth century.

Most important, medieval English – and to a lesser extent Early Modern English (1500–1700) – were much more tolerant of variability within written texts than is present-day English. Some medieval texts spell commonly recurring words in up to six different ways and even accommodate grammatical variants (as if a modern writer were sometimes to write *we were* and sometimes *we was*). Elizabethan printers varied spelling in order to justify the lines of print: thus, if there was room at the end of a line, a consonant letter might be doubled or *e* added (or both); for example, the word *pity* might appear as *pitye*, *pyttye*, and in other variants. The idea that spelling and grammatical forms must be uniform and invariant even within texts and discourses in the same dialect is a characteristic of maximum standardization – a stage which was not achieved in English until the eighteenth century, and then mainly in public, not private, documents.

As a result of this process, we now subscribe to an ideology of language which values uniformity above all things. As one regional variety has been promoted to the status of a standard, other varieties (regional and social) have tended to become devalued. Yet, the majority of people speak varieties that are regional in their basis; it is surely important that we should pay more attention to these varieties. In the next section, we look at some details of social and regional variation.

1.4 Social and regional variation in British English today

People who spend much of their lives reading and writing are obviously far more influenced by the norms governing written language than people for whom these literate activities are less important. As a result they tend to use in their spoken English as well as in their written English the morphological and syntactic features that have been codified as standard: they may use the past tense forms *broke* and *knew*, for example, where other people say *breaked* and *knowed*. Verb forms such as *breaked* and *blowed* have been part of the English language for centuries, but since they were not chosen as the past tense forms for the standard variety of English, they are no longer used in writing or in 'educated' speech. A similar example, this time from syntax, is multiple negation, as in *she never said nothing*. Prescriptive grammarians have been successful in outlawing this pattern of negation from standard English, but it was common in Chaucer's time, used by Shakespeare, and continues to be used by large numbers of native speakers of English today.

Other features that are now considered to be non-standard have evolved through natural processes of language change. The earlier forms are the ones that grammarians have chosen to 'freeze' as standard English, and as a result later developments are now thought of as non-standard. A good example of this is *ain't*, which has evolved through natural phonetic and analogical changes from *have not*, *has not*, *is not* and *are not* (the development of *ain't* is discussed in Cheshire 1982a). The earlier, fuller forms have been 'frozen' as standard English, as well as the partly contracted forms *haven't*, *hasn't*, *isn't* and *aren't*. *Ain't* simply represents a further phonetic contraction, which nowadays is not used by people whose speech has been heavily influenced by written norms.

Non-standard forms often show a great deal of variation, so that the same speaker may say, on different occasions, both *I broke it* and *I breaked it*, or both *I ain't done it* and *I haven't done it*. Variation of this kind was very common in all sections of society before English was standardized. In the writings of Queen Elizabeth I, for instance, present tense forms with third person plural subjects are sometimes written with a *-th* ending (as in *they trusteth*), sometimes written with an *-s* ending (as in *the hunters rates their hounds*) and sometimes with no suffix at all, as in present-day standard English. This was not because Queen Elizabeth was uneducated or knew no better – she was, in fact, extremely well-educated – but simply because at that time it was not considered necessary to be consistent either in spelling or in grammar.

Grammarians and others who wanted to eliminate variation are responsible for the disappearance of much of this type of syntactic variation in standard English. Since the people who use uniform, standard grammar are typically found amongst the more literate sections of society, using standard English morphology and syntax is a mark of belonging to these 'educated' classes. There are a few regional differences in educated spoken English: one such difference is the type of contraction in the negative verb forms *it isn't* and *it's not*, where the former appears to be more frequent in southern England (see Hughes and Trudgill 1987). On the whole, however, it is usually their pronunciation that reveals the regional origins of educated speakers of English, rather than their syntax – though if they speak with Received Pronunciation, or 'BBC English', their pronunciation gives no indication at all of their regional background.

The role that literacy plays in people's lives, of course, depends on several kinds of social factors, which may include socio-economic class. Several surveys have shown that there is often a close relationship between the frequency with which people use a particular non-standard form, and the socio-economic class to which they can be assigned. In a survey carried out in Norwich, for example, a random sample of people was recorded during interviews with the researcher (see Trudgill 1974). In Norwich and other parts of East Anglia, third person singular present tense verb forms sometimes occur without the -s suffix, as in *she go, he say* or *it smell*. The frequency with which the interviewees used non-standard present tense forms such as these showed a regular correlation with their socio-economic class. As Figure 1.1 shows, the local non-standard forms were never used by the higher socio-economic classes, whilst the standard forms, in contrast, were rarely used by the lowest socio-economic class. The intermediate classes used a mixture of standard and non-standard forms, with the proportions patterning neatly with people's position on the socio-economic hierarchy. In cases such as this, then, the non-standard syntactic forms have both a social distribution,

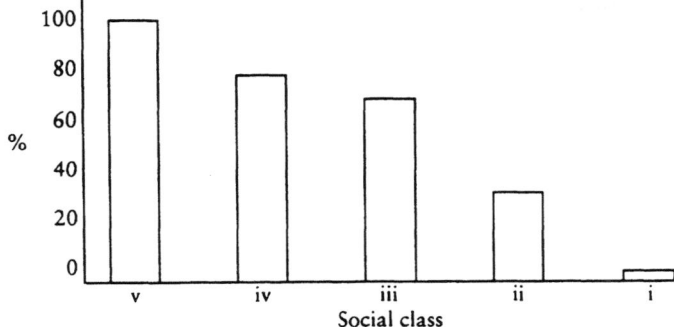

Figure 1.1:   Percentage of nonstandard forms by social class (e.g. *he go* for 'he goes'). After Trudgill, P. 1974, *The Social Differentiation of English in Norwich*. Cambridge: Cambridge University Press.

correlating with socio-economic class, and a regional distribution, localized within a specific part of Britain.⁻

There are other non-standard syntactic forms that occur throughout the British Isles, rather than being restricted to specific regions. Multiple negation is thought to be one such feature; another is the negative form *never*, in constructions such as *she went out last night but I never*. These features are typically not heard in the speech of members of the higher socio-economic classes, nor are they used in formal written English. Chapter 3 of this volume discusses other morphological and syntactic features which, like these, seem to occur in the non-standard English spoken throughout the urban centres of Britain.

It is impossible to divide the British Isles into clear-cut dialect areas and then to describe the distinctive regional syntax that can be heard in each area. This is partly because the different non-standard syntactic forms often overlap in their geographical distribution, rather than co-occurring within neat regional areas; and partly because as yet we simply do not know enough about the nature of regional syntax as it occurs throughout the British Isles. In this volume, however, we have singled out Scotland and Ireland as distinctive linguistic areas for our purposes, partly because we can draw on a considerable body of research into syntactic variation in Scotland and Ireland, and partly because the partial political independence of these countries has allowed some social status to be given to the patterns of syntax that are used there. Scotland was politically independent until as late as 1707, and a variety of Scots English had been well on the way towards becoming a standard variety by that date. In Ireland, too, there is a long history of political power stemming from centres other than London.

Far less is known about regional syntactic variation in the English that is spoken in England and Wales – partly because historians of the English language have tended to focus only on the standard variety of English after about the sixteenth century, ignoring the history of regional syntactic forms. In Wales, English began to displace the Welsh language from very early on (English rule was established in 1284), though now, of course, Welsh is being vigorously promoted. There have been influxes of non-Welsh speaking immigrants into Wales at various periods of history, particularly during the industrialization of the mines in South Wales, with the result that the English spoken in Wales shares at least some of the regional features that occur in England. In particular, it seems that the English spoken in South Wales shares some syntactic features with South-west England, and the English of North Wales with the North-western counties of England. Coupland (1988) describes some of the syntactic features that occur in Cardiff.

1.5   Attitudes towards regional varieties of English

Because standard English morphological and syntactic forms are typically used in written English and in the spoken English of the more powerful and influential people in society, their use has come to be seen as an indication of being educated and 'cultured'. It is hardly surprising, therefore, that these are the forms that are now considered as 'correct' and 'proper' English. This attitude is reinforced by the fact that these are the forms of English that are taught to non-native learners, and that histories and grammars of the language usually describe not 'standard English' but simply 'English', as if no other varieties of the language had a right to the name. Unfortunately, almost all native speakers of English seem to have internalized this view, whether they themselves use mostly standard forms or not. To some extent this is an inevitable consequence of language standardization, as we saw in section 1.1, above. Standard languages typically act as powerful symbols of national culture and national identity, and are perceived not as varieties of a language but as autonomous, separate entities with their own histories and a special aesthetic, 'pure' value (see Downes: 1984).

The other side of the coin, however, is that whilst standard English is valued and considered to be 'the' English language, the syntactic forms that occur in non-standard varieties, such as *we was* or *I breaked it*, are devalued and considered to be 'bad English', 'ungrammatical' or simply 'careless'. Curiously, non-standard vocabulary does not provoke views of this kind. A word such as *tup*, which in some parts of Britain refers to a young ram, or *bait*, referring to a mid-morning snack in some parts of the country, tends to be seen for what it is – in other words, as a regional variant that is no better or worse than the standard English equivalent. Regional forms of morphology and syntax, on the other hand, are not always recognized as regional variants, but instead are seen as corruptions of grammar. Those non-standard forms that are widespread throughout the British Isles and that cannot therefore be associated with a specific region (such as those described in Chapter 3 of this volume) are especially likely to be considered ungrammatical, or just plain 'wrong'.

These attitudes have to be seen partly as a reaction not to the linguistic features themselves but as a reaction to the social groups with which they are associated. However, the problem also seems to lie in the confusion of *standard* with the sense of 'uniform' (see the earlier discussion in this chapter) and *standard* with the sense of 'something to aspire to', as in the idea of setting high standards (Cameron and Bourne 1988: 155). Some people confuse the concept of 'standard English' with the concept of 'standards of English', so that a non-standard feature such as *I don't want none* appears to them to be symptomatic of corruption and decay in the English language. Linguists who have tried to show that non-standard features are not ungrammatical or corrupt in any linguistic sense have been misunderstood or misrepresented in many quarters, including the media and political circles. There is a political dimension to the issue: as Graddol and Swann (1988) point out, linguists are trapped in that their work is often misrepresented by people with right-wing political views; if they protest, they give rise to the impression amongst politicians and the general public that they represent the radical left, and their work may then be further misrepresented and distorted. Discussions about standard and non-standard English can quickly become a highly charged emotional issue.

Fortunately, there seems to be a growing recognition amongst teachers, if not amongst politicians or the general public, that non-standard syntactic forms conform to the grammatical rules of a social and regional variety of English in just the same way that standard English forms conform to the grammatical rules of the standard English variety: the difference is simply that the rules for the standard English forms have been set down in grammar books and taught as 'English', whereas the rules for the dialect have not. Standard English, in other words, has been codified; non-standard English has not.

Because non-standard varieties of English have not been codified, they have sometimes been affected by processes of language change that have not influenced the development of standard English. In some cases, this means that the rules for the non-standard feature are more regular than the rules for standard English. Compare, for example, the regional present tense verb forms in some parts of South-west England, in East Anglia and in standard English (Table 1.1).

Table 1.1:   Varying forms of the present tense

South-west England	East Anglia	Standard English
I loves	I love	I love
you loves	you love	you love
he, she, it loves	he, she, it love	he, she, it loves
we loves	we love	we love
they loves	they love	they love

The non-standard verbal paradigms are simpler and more regular than the standard English paradigm, with its third person singular - *s* suffix. Some further examples of non-standard regional forms that are more regular than the corresponding standard English forms will be found in Chapters 4–7 of this volume.

Current educational thinking, as we will see in section 1.11, is that children should 'extend their linguistic repertoires' while they are at school, so that they are able to use standard English forms in addition to the local non-standard forms. The Cox Report (DES 1989: 4.36), for example, points out that unless children are given the opportunity to become proficient in the standard variety of their language, they will be at a disadvantage in all those situations where the standard is customarily used, and will find many areas of importance in our society closed to them. The Cox Report includes under this heading cultural activities, further and higher education, and important areas of industry, commerce and the professions. It would be naïve in the extreme, however, to think that it is language alone which stands in the way of all our citizens having an equal opportunity to participate in these areas of social life. Far-reaching social changes would be necessary before all children had the same opportunities of participating in areas such as these. Furthermore, it is instructive to compare the situation in Britain with that in other countries. In German-speaking countries, for example, many of these activities would not necessarily be transacted in the standard variety, so that speakers of a non-standard variety would not necessarily be excluded from these areas of life.

The fact remains, however, that as things stand currently, proficiency in standard English conveys distinct social and economic advantages, not only nationally but also in an international context, where English is an important language of international communication. Children should certainly be encouraged to develop the ability to use standard English in conventional ways when they judge it necessary to do so (though this ability is not necessarily easy to acquire, as we point out in section 1.12) but at the same time they should be encouraged to appreciate the historical and political underpinnings to the idea of appropriateness in language (see Fairclough 1992).

1.6   The social significance of regional syntactic forms

It may seem odd that non-standard English morphology and syntax remains so widely used, when there are obvious social and economic advantages to using the standard forms. Although it is often thought that non-standard dialects are dying out, there are no indications that non-standard syntactic forms are declining in use, although their nature and their geographical distribution may be changing, as we see in Chapter 3. The reason for their survival seems to be that just as standard English forms have become associated with education, with the dominant, institutionalized culture and with a relatively high social status, so non-standard forms have become associated with the home, the neighbourhood, and with family and friends. The more closely integrated people are into their local community, the more likely they are to use localized pronunciation (see L. Milroy 1987; J. Milroy 1992); and this applies also to localized forms of syntax.

Hudson (1980) has likened using regional dialect forms to 'wearing a badge', showing where you are from and where you feel you belong. The way that we speak, in other words, is very closely bound up with our social identity and our personal identity. This has important implications for the teaching of standard English in school, for it is hopelessly unrealistic to imagine that children could be taught to simply 'change their badge' from time to time, just because we might think it would be in their best interests that they should learn do this. Ideas about extending the linguistic repertoires of schoolchildren tend to neglect this fundamental social function of language.

The social significance of non-standard English is illustrated in Chapter 2 of this volume.

1.7   The rule-governed nature of variation

As we have mentioned before, speakers of non-standard English normally use both non-standard features and the corresponding standard English forms, although listeners may not notice the variation that occurs. Speakers themselves are usually equally unaware of the variation in their speech. Variation is normal in language, occurring in standard varieties as well as non-standard varieties, although the drive towards uniformity often eliminates a great many alternating forms from the standard.

In standard English relative pronouns still have a number of different forms, and these can serve as a useful illustration of the rule-governed nature of variation. *Whom, who, that* and zero (that is, no pronoun) are all used when the pronoun is the direct object of the following verb and when the noun that the pronoun refers to is animate, as in:

a girl whom I know
a girl who I know
a girl that I know
a girl I know

Many people consider that the first form (*whom*) is the 'correct' form, since this is the form that is very often preferred in formal written English. Nevertheless, most educated English speakers use all four forms on different occasions (if we count the zero form as a form, that is), although they are unlikely to be fully conscious of having chosen one form rather than another. We are more likely to reflect on the pronoun that we use when we write, when there is time to consider our language – and it is no coincidence that it is in written English that the older, inflected form (*whom*) occurs most frequently.

In exactly the same way, variation between non-standard forms and the corresponding standard forms is not usually within people's conscious awareness (variation, that is, between forms such as *we was* and *we were*, or between *we've seen her* or *we've saw her*). The difference is simply that there are fewer variable forms of this type in standard English, since the process of standardization 'irons out' natural variation in language.

Variation between alternative forms, whether they are standard English forms or non-standard forms, may be unconscious but it is not random. The factors governing variation are rarely appreciated in our everyday use of language, but they can be identified by recording people as they speak and by then analysing the frequency with which speakers use the different forms of a single grammatical feature, in different contexts and on different occasions. In this way the different relative pronouns used by educated speakers of English have been found to depend on the length of the relative clause: the zero form occurs more frequently with short clauses, and *who* occurs more often with longer clauses. Relative pronouns are also affected by whether or not they occur immediately after the noun that they refer to, as well as by a number of other linguistic factors (see Quirk 1957).

A further example of non-random variation occurs between the non-standard form of present tense verbs in some parts of Central and South-western England, and the corresponding standard English present tense form. Research carried out in the town of Reading, in Berkshire, found that the use of the suffixed regional form (such as *we wants*) or the standard form (such as *we want*) depended in part on the type of linguistic construction that followed the verb. The non-standard form never occurred in sentences such as *I know where she's going*, where the present tense verb is followed by a complement containing a subject and a tensed verb (*where she's going*). It did, on the other hand, occur with the same verbs in other types of construction, so that it may occur in a sentence such as *I knows her name* (Cheshire 1982a).

1.8 Peer group pressures on language

Peer group pressures may also affect variation in the use of non-standard morphology and syntax. It is, of course, common for children of all ages to form friendship groups and for the members of these groups to share each other's interests and ideas. In adolescence, these peer group pressures often reach a peak: this is the time when many young people care passionately about the way they present themselves to the world, and when they may adopt the clothes and hairstyles favoured by their peer group. It is thought that this is one way of expressing a separate identity and their independence from their parents.

Not surprisingly, the desire to conform to peer group norms of behaviour extends to language. Children, especially young adolescents, use regional forms of syntax – and pronunciation – to show 'who they are', just as they may wear their hair in the style favoured by their friends, and may share their tastes in music and clothes. Quantitative research of the type mentioned earlier has found that the proportion of non-standard forms used in speech increases dramatically in early adolescence. The more closely integrated young people are into a peer group that tries to display its independence from adult values and tastes, the more frequently they use non-standard regional forms of syntax (see Cheshire 1987 for discussion).

Adolescents who are closely involved with this type of peer group may have very strong feelings against using standard English. Some young British speakers have been heard to say that they 'don't want to speak like those snotty kids at the private school'. Even if they are less closely involved in a peer group, they may still want to 'talk like the other kids', so that they do not get teased by their schoolmates for 'talking posh' (this is discussed further in Chapter 2 of this volume). Very often children are keenly aware of competing pressures on their language: this can be seen clearly in the words of a child who took part in research conducted by Cullum in Birmingham (see, for discussion, Romaine 1984):

> You always try to be the same as everyone else. You don't sort of want to be made fun of . . . – sort of posher than everyone else. Then you get sort of picked on. But then if you use a lot of slang and that, people don't think much of you.

Because of the pressures to 'be like everyone else', children from families where only standard English is used may begin to use non-standard forms, if their friends or classmates use them. Parents may be upset by this, not realizing that it is likely to be a temporary phase of behaviour, like the teenage fashions that their offspring like to wear, or their current tastes in music. Rock music, in fact, makes considerable use of non-standard syntax: two well-known lines, for example, are *I can't get no satisfaction*, from the Rolling Stones and *you ain't nothing but a hound-dog*, from Elvis Presley.

1.9   Language development in older children

The comments that children make about 'talking posh' and 'talking like the others' need to be seen in the context of their developing linguistic awareness. As children grow older, they learn an increasing number of different ways of 'saying the same thing' – such as asking for what they want in different ways, so that they can make requests indirectly as well as directly (instead of in their babyhood way of *I want . . .*). When they go to school, they learn to cope with the specific language demands that they encounter there, perhaps remembering to answer a question in 'a complete sentence'. They may also be expected not to answer a question with a response that is framed as a question: for example, it seems that some teachers would prefer the answer *it's Paris* to the question *what is the capital of France?* and would discourage an answer in the form *is it Paris?* (some examples, from a French perspective, are given in Dannequin 1987). Schoolchildren also learn to interpret teachers' utterances as potential directives requiring action, so that if their teacher says *I can hear someone talking* they understand that they should now be quiet (see Holmes 1983).

As children grow older they also begin to adjust their speech to match the speech of others and to suit the occasion. With luck, they will stop embarrassing their parents by loudly asking questions about other people who are present. They may swear when they are with their friends, as a kind of linguistic bravado, but be careful not to swear in front of their grandparents if they think they would be offended or upset (equally, of course, they may choose to swear precisely in order to offend or upset people).

This developing sociolinguistic awareness extends to the way in which children use localized pronunciation and syntax. We saw in the previous section that speakers of non-standard varieties of English alternate in their use of non-standard and standard morphological and syntactic forms. The relative proportions of standard and non-standard forms vary according to the social context: Cheshire (1982b), for example, found that children aged between 11 and 14 used a higher proportion of non-standard forms when they were chatting to their friends outside school than when they were talking to their teachers. As mentioned before, this kind of linguistic adjustment is likely to pass unnoticed unless a quantitative analysis is made of the recorded speech of the same individual talking on different occasions, since the differences are differences of degree, rather than clear-cut either/or differences.

Speakers of non-standard English can exploit this variation in order to symbolically assert their loyalties to the peer group or to their neighbourhood. This type of style-shifting behaviour was found in the research described in Cheshire (1982b): young adolescent boys increased their use of standard English features when they were talking to a teacher whom they liked and respected, but increased their use of non-standard features when they were talking to a teacher with whom they had little rapport or respect.

1.10   Writing

A further aspect of children's language development which occurs during the school years is, of course, that they learn to read and write. When children are very young, their written syntax tends to resemble their spoken syntax. It tends, for example, to consist of short clauses, joined by *and* or *but*. As children grow older, they begin to use a more diverse range of syntactic constructions, many of which occur in their written language but not in their speech. Non-finite adverbial clauses are one example, as in *Having done that I was soon able to iron out my fault* (Handscombe 1976, cited by Perera 1986: 515). They learn to use vocabulary that is more typical of formal writing than of speech – words of Latin or Greek origin, for instance, such as *inhabit* as well as *live*, or *observe* as well as *see*. As their writing becomes more distinct from their speech, children begin to use fewer features of non-standard English in their writing, and those features that they do use tend to occur with a lower frequency than in their speech. Table 1.2 shows the differences Cheshire (1982b) found in the use of four regional syntactic features in the speech and writing of a group of four children (their speech was recorded in the playground, with their friends; their writing was the written work that they had done in school).

Table 1.2:   Children's regional features in speech and writing

	Speech	Writing
present tense verb forms (e.g. *I goes out*)	64%	0%
past tense of BE (e.g. *we was going out*)	88%	60%
multiple negation (e.g. *I don't want nothing*)	93%	40%
relative pronoun *what* (e.g. *a book what I read*)	80%	0%

It can be seen that all four features occur less often in the children's writing, and two of the features are not used at all.

The four children who took part in this study were aged between 11 and 14. By this age, children have usually gained a good idea of many of the ways in which written English differs from spoken English, sometimes without any explicit instruction. Research such as that reported above suggests that children such as these are beginning to realize – probably quite unconsciously – that it is standard English features that are expected in school written work, rather than the non-standard equivalents. This does not mean, of course, that all children will be able to replace all non-standard features by the corresponding standard English features without any guidance from their teacher. It simply shows that the propensity to do so is there by this age, probably at an unconscious level.

1.11   Linguistic assessment

Teachers, speech therapists and others who need to assess children's language abilities face considerable difficulties when they are dealing with children whose English contains features of regional syntax. Consider, for example, the following two sentences:

> I'll not can do it.
> I come home really late last night.

Both sentences would be perfectly well-formed in some non-standard varieties of English. The first is more likely to occur in some parts of the North of England, and also occurs in Scottish English (see Chapters 4 and 6); the second could be more widespread, since the past tense form *come* occurs throughout most of the British Isles. On the other hand, the first sentence might suggest to a speech therapist that a patient has problems with the construction of verb phrases; and the second sentence could indicate that a patient has problems with the distinction between past and present tense forms. Teachers similarly need to be able to distinguish between dialect usage and genuine mistakes, as we will see in the following section.

When constructing or using tests to assess general language abilities, then, it is important to ensure that the tests do not merely test competence in standard English. Some tests, such as those that require verbs to be put into the past tense or that require nouns to be put into a plural form, may unintentionally discriminate against speakers of non-standard varieties of English. On some occasions, of course, teachers or other assessors may decide that they want to test a person's proficiency in the use of standard English syntax – the important point is that tests should do what they are intended to do, and nothing more or less (on the question of language testing, see Milroy and Milroy 1985, chs. 7 and 8).

1.12 Education

Recent educational thinking in England and Wales stresses the importance of teaching standard English in schools. One paragraph from the Cox Report (DES 1989: 4.38) is worth quoting in full:

> Schools should develop their own coherent policies, which are sensitive to their local circumstances, on exactly how and when Standard English should be taught. In general terms, we advocate that there should be explicit teaching about the nature and functions of Standard English in the top years of the primary school; that there should be the beginnings of the expectation of Standard English in written work when appropriate by the age of 11; that there should be the provision of opportunities for oral work where spoken Standard English would be a realistic expectation in the secondary school; and that all pupils should be in a position to choose to use standard English in speech when appropriate by the age of 16.

The place accorded to standard and non-standard English in the National Curriculum has been debated and commented on in several publications (see, for example, Cameron and Bourne 1988; Stubbs 1989; Winch 1989), and a critique of models of language variation that are based on appropriateness has been made by Fairclough (1992). Here we will simply comment on some of the implications that the points made in this chapter seem to have for the teaching of standard English in schools.

First, it is clearly important to beware of the simplistic idea that the most straightforward approach to enabling all children to add standard English to their linguistic repertoire is to teach schoolchildren the differences between localized syntactic forms and the corresponding standard English forms, so that they will be able to use the standard English forms when they decide that it is appropriate to do so. This option may seem possible to some, given that the use of many non-standard features is variable: those speakers of English who use the non-standard form *we was*, for example, will almost certainly also use the corresponding standard form *we were*, although the relative frequency with which they use the two forms will vary from person to person and from occasion to occasion. It might seem, therefore, to be a relatively simple matter to stop using one form (*we was*) and to replace it with the other form (*we were*).

One reason why an approach of this kind would not work is that variation in language is part of a well-organized and structured language system, occurring in specific linguistic contexts, as we saw in section 1.7. Since structured variation of this kind is unconscious it is likely to be beyond our conscious control, and therefore it is naïve in the extreme to suppose that children could be taught to readily substitute one form for another. The systematic nature of linguistic variation is not always appreciated, but it is clearly extremely important to take it into consideration when formulating and implementing language policies.

Secondly, it is important to remember the social function of non-standard syntactic forms, and the way in which people alter the frequency with which they use non-standard forms as a way of demonstrating their attitude towards the person to whom they are talking (as we saw in section 1.6). This means that attempts to correct regional forms in children's spoken English or to encourage the use of standard English forms could at best be met with a lack of understanding and at worst alienate any children who are already, for whatever reason, not particularly receptive to the expectations of the school.

Thirdly, it is by no means certain that children could, in fact, be taught to choose to use standard English syntactic forms in their speech on certain occasions. It is instructive to imagine how we ourselves would feel (assuming that you, as we are, are someone who uses mostly standard English syntactic forms) if we were told that it would be a good idea to sometimes stop saying *we were* or *I did it*, and to start saying, on certain occasions that are deemed appropriate, *we was* or *I done it*. In this case our understandable indignation would have the backing of books on English grammar and the usage of respected members of society, so that we could insist that our way was the 'right' way. Nevertheless, if we stop and think about it, we can gain some understanding of how children might react to the idea that the way that they speak needs to be changed in certain situations, especially if the forms that are to be changed are the forms that they habitually use with their family and friends. We may also, in this way, gain some understanding of how difficult it would be to remember to use the 'right' form *all* the time.

Finally, it is relevant to consider the competing linguistic pressures on children that were mentioned in section 1.8. It is easy to imagine situations in oral work where children might feel forced to make a choice between fitting in with the linguistic norms of their peer group or fitting in with the expectations of the school.

Most teachers will be aware of many of these factors and will treat the topic of standard and non-standard English with the necessary tact and sensitivity. Nevertheless we think that it is worth drawing explicit attention to these important aspects of linguistic variation. Equally, it is worth drawing attention to the research that has been carried out on the use of non-standard syntactic features in children's written work. We saw in section 1.10 that even without their teacher's guidance, some children were already beginning to replace regional features of syntax with standard English forms in their school written work. Research has also suggested, however, that despite this ability children can become extremely confused about the precise way in which they should adjust their language when they are writing. The non-standard present tense verb form ending in -*s* (as in *we goes*), was not used at all in their school written work by the four children who took part in the research mentioned in section 1.10, even though all four of them used this form in their spoken English. However, these four children not only dropped the -*s* from verb forms that do not have the suffix in standard English (for example, they used the standard form *we go* in their written work), but they also dropped the -*s* from verb forms that *do* have the suffix in both their non-standard variety and standard English: third person singular forms such as *it go* and *he live* occurred frequently in the children's work, as did plural nouns without the -*s* suffix. All children make some mistakes of this kind when they are writing. However, children who have to change their habitual use of the -*s* suffix in their school writing seem to be more likely to make this type of mistake than other children.

Similar problems occur with other syntactic features. For example, pupils often use past tense verb forms in their school writing that are different from those that they use in speech, but that are not the forms that are used in standard English. One example of an exercise where mistakes of this kind were found to occur is the one in Table 1.3, in which pupils were instructed to supply the past tense form for the verbs listed in the left-hand column. The forms supplied in the right-hand column are those that were given by one of the 14 year-old boys in the class, and include his own crossings-out and corrections,

Table 1.3:   Past tense forms supplied
              by a school-child

Word	Past tense	
hurry	hurried	
horrify	horrified	
throw	~~throwed~~	thron
take	take	
bring	~~bringed~~	brong
laugh	laughed	
tell	told	
go	~~gond~~	gone
write	~~writed~~	wrote

Many teachers would not set this type of exercise, recognizing the difficulty of supplying a past tense form out of context. The boy's responses here, though, are interesting, since they give an indication of the way in which his mind seems to have been working. His first impulse seems to have been to add the -ed suffix to nearly all the verbs, as in *throwed*; this is, after all, the most common way of forming a past tense in English, both in the standard variety and in non-standard varieties (and in children's immature speech). The problem is that the verbs that form their past tense in this way often differ in the standard and the regional varieties (see Cheshire: 1991 for a discussion of past tense verb forms). In this case, *writed* is a past tense form in the regional variety that the boy speaks; his other deviations from standard English, however, are not. After his initial reaction the boy appears to have reconsidered, and to have remembered that he is expected to give some verbs irregular past tense forms that he himself does not always use. He selects the right verbs as the irregular ones, but although the past tense forms that he gives are indeed forms that he does not use himself, they are not always the standard English forms that would have been expected.

Williams (1989) gives some further examples of the underlying uncertainty that seems to be felt by some children who speak non-standard English, when faced with the need to write standard English forms. The following sentences occurred in the work of one 10 year-old child over the course of two terms:

> We down the housework.
> We don don done are homework
>   *did*
> My brother ~~dond~~[1] ~~done~~[2] a jigsaw
> We ~~done~~[1] did a bit more dancing
> When we had ~~done~~[1] did some housework

The superscript 1 indicates a correction made by the child; the superscript 2 indicates a correction made by the child's teacher.

One of the problems that arises when teaching children to use standard forms rather than non-standard syntactic forms in their school writing is that teachers are not always sure what the local syntactic features are. This was found to be the case in the research reported by Cheshire (1982b) and by Williams (1989). The schools who took part in these two studies did not have a consistent policy for dealing with the non-standard syntactic forms that occurred in the children's work, and the teachers' correcting strategies appeared to be rather a hit or miss affair, with the same mistakes in a single piece of work sometimes corrected and sometimes not. It is understandable that teachers may not want to discourage their pupils by correcting every single slip and error, and covering their work with red ink; but if they are to avoid children's confusion about the forms that they should use in their school writing, it would seem important to develop a coherent policy concerning the correction of non-standard syntactic forms.

Those people who come into contact with social and regional variation in English during the course of their work will, of course, decide for themselves how best to deal with the various issues that have been raised in this chapter. It is likely that most will agree, however, that it is important to be able to distinguish between the syntactic forms that occur in non-standard varieties of English and the syntactic forms that are characteristic of standard English. It may also be important to distinguish between features of regional syntax and other kinds of linguistic features that purists sometimes object to: features of colloquial English (such as frequently occurring words e.g. *get, nice*); contractions (e.g. *gonna, wanna*); slang (e.g. *grotty, kids, telly*); stylistic niceties (split infinitives or 'dangling' prepositions such as the *to* in our phrase *purists sometimes object to,* above); and even personal dislikes (perhaps the use of the sentence adverbial *hopefully* as in *hopefully, it won't rain today*). Presumably, for written English the list would also have to include spelling mistakes. It is sometimes difficult to make a clear distinction between colloquial syntax and non-standard syntax, as we saw in section 1.2. But unless features of non-standard syntax can be distinguished from errors, it is difficult to know what kind of help can be given to individual pupils or patients, and it is even possible, as we have seen, that patients may be wrongly classified as suffering from a linguistic disorder, or that teachers and others will form mistaken impressions about children's language abilities.

It is all the more unfortunate, then, that our knowledge of the regional syntax of the British Isles is still very limited. The chapters in Part II of this volume provide information about some areas of the British Isles where sufficient research has been carried out for us to have a good idea of the syntactic forms that are used in those areas. In other parts of the country, however, the only option may be for people to become their own researchers, listening to the English that is used in the local community and noting for future reference those forms that occur over and over again in the conversations overheard in shops, in public houses, in buses, in children's playgrounds and elsewhere. Listening for recurrent local features will at least ensure that it is local forms that are used as the basis for any linguistic judgements that people may be forced to make in the course of their professional work, rather than the idealized norms of standard English.

Teachers may choose to investigate the regional syntax of the local variety of English in a more structured way, by setting up a class project on the local dialect, after a period of language awareness work. Chapter 2 in this volume discusses the results of some small-scale projects that were carried out as part of language awareness work in schools in different parts of England. Chapter 3 sets out the results of a large-scale research project that was carried out with the help of teachers and their pupils in schools throughout Britain, in order to determine those features of regional syntax that were used in the local community. The project could be replicated in individual schools as a way both of determining features of regional syntax and of involving schoolchildren in constructive discussion of the differences between standard and non-standard English syntax.

1.13 Concluding remarks

A standardized variety of English has existed in our society (with some historical changes) for some centuries now. The standardization of English has been advantageous in some very obvious ways: for example, mass printing has become simpler, and many processes of change in written English have slowed down. One of the results is that the literature of previous generations is accessible to more people than would otherwise have been the case; and without dictionaries and grammars of standard English it would hardly be possible to teach English as a foreign language. But, at the same time, a variety of English has been shaped that is based on the English of an élite section of society and that continues to be used mainly by the more privileged and influential sections of society. The majority of English speakers use at least some non-standard features in their speech, and for these people the advantages arising from the existence of standard English may be far outweighed by the social costs of speaking a variety of English that has been accorded low prestige, through no wish or fault of their own, and that they are invited to 'supplement' with another variety that they may not know well and that they may not even want to know.

Ignorance, prejudice and lack of understanding of the nature of standard and non-standard varieties have tended to compound the problems of linguistic and social inequality in the British Isles. A proper resolution of these problems could only come from their inclusion on the political agenda (see Edwards 1989 for discussion) and there is little hope of this in the foreseeable future. Nevertheless the dissemination of information about the linguistic differences between standard and non-standard English is an important step in combatting ignorance and lack of understanding, and it is for this reason that we present in this volume some detailed information on some of the better-researched varieties of non-standard English that exist within the British Isles.

References

BROWN, G. (1982) The spoken language. In Carter, R. (ed.) *Linguistics and the Teacher*. London: Routledge, pp. 75–87

CAMERON, D. and BOURNE, J. (1988) No common ground: Kingman, grammar and the nation. *Language and Education* 2: 147–60

CHESHIRE, J. (1982a) *Variation in an English Dialect*. Cambridge: Cambridge University Press

CHESHIRE, J. (1982b) Dialect features and linguistic conflict in school. *Educational Review* 34: 53–67

CHESHIRE, J. (1987) Age and generation-specific use of language. In Ammon, U., Dittmar, N. and Mattheier, K.J. (eds) *Sociolinguistics: An International Handbook of the Science of Language and Society*. Berlin: de Gruyter, pp. 760–7

CHESHIRE, J. (1991) 'As the ancient writer would have wrote': past tense verb forms in nonstandard English. In Blank, C. (ed.) *Language and Civilisation*. Frankfurt: Lang, pp. 11–24.

COUPLAND, N. (1988) *Dialect in Use*. Cardiff: University of Wales Press

DANNEQUIN, C. (1987) Les enfants baillonnés (gagged children). *Language and Education* 1: 33–57

DES (Department of Education and Science) (1989) *English for Ages 5–16* (The Cox Report). London: DES and Welsh Office

DOWNES, W. (1984) *Language and Society*. London: Fontana

EDWARDS, V. (1989) A postscript. In Cheshire, J., Edwards, V., Münstermann, H. and Weltens, B. (eds) *Dialect and Education*. Clevedon: Multilingual Matters, pp. 317–23

FAIRCLOUGH, N. (1992) The appropriacy of 'appropriateness'. In Fairclough, N. (ed.) *Critical Language Awareness*. Harlow: Longman, pp. 33–56

GILES, H. and SMITH, P. (1979) Accommodation theory: optimal levels of convergence. In Giles, H. and St. Clair, R.N. (eds) *Language and Social Psychology*. Oxford: Blackwell

GRADDOL, D. and SWANN, J. (1988) Trapping linguists: an analysis of linguists' responses to John Honey's pamphlet 'The Language trap'. *Language and Education* 2: 95–111

HANDSCOMBE, R.J. (1967) *The Written Language of Eleven- and Twelve-year-old Children* Nuffield Foreign Languages Teaching

Materials Project, Reports and Occasional Papers, no. 25. London: The Nuffield Foundation

HOLMES, J. (1983) The structure of teachers' directives. In Richard, J. and Schmidt, R. (eds) *Language and Communication*. London: Longman, pp. 89–115

HUDSON, R.A. (1980) *Sociolinguistics*. Cambridge: Cambridge University Press

HUGHES, G.A. and TRUDGILL, P. (1987) *English Accents and Dialects: an Introduction to Social and Regional Varieties of English*. London: Edward Arnold

LEITH, D. (1983) *A Social History of English*. London: Routledge

MILROY, J. and MILROY, L. (1985) *Authority in Language*. London: Routledge

MILROY, L. (1987) *Language and Social Networks*. Oxford: Blackwell. 2nd edition

MILROY, J. (1992) *Linguistic Variation and Change*. Oxford: Blackwell

QUIRK, R. (1957) Relative clauses in educated spoken English. *English Studies* 38: 97–109. Also in Quirk, R. (1968) *Essays on the English Language Medieval and Modern*. London: Longman, pp. 94–108

PERERA, K. (1986) Language acquisition and writing. In Fletcher, P. and Garman, M. (eds) *Language Acquisition*, 2nd edn. Cambridge: Cambridge University Press, pp. 494–518

ROMAINE, S. (1984) *The Language of Children and Adolescents*. Oxford: Blackwell

STUBBS, M. (1980) *Language and Literacy: the Sociolinguistics of Reading and Writing*. London: Routledge

STUBBS, M. (1989) The state of English in the English state: reflections on the Cox Report. *Language and Education* 3: 235–50

TRUDGILL, P. (1974) *The Social Differentiation of English in Norwich*. Cambridge: Cambridge University Press

WILLIAMS, A. (1989) Dialect in school written work. In Cheshire, J., Edwards, V., Münstermann, H. and Weltens, B. (eds) *Dialect and Education*. Clevedon: Multilingual Matters, pp. 182–9

WINCH, C. (1989) Standard English, normativity and the Cox Report. *Language and Education* 3: 275–90

2 Sociolinguistics in the classroom: exploring linguistic diversity

Jenny Cheshire and Viv Edwards

2.1 Introduction

Many of the findings of sociolinguistic research are directly relevant to the formulation of educational policy and practice. For example, teachers, policy makers and educationists need to take account of differences in the form and function of spoken and written language, of the way in which pupils' gender, social class and ethnic group may affect the way they speak, of the relationship between standard and non-standard varieties of English, and of social attitudes towards linguistic diversity. The changes in education that are currently taking place in the UK have made the sociolinguistic dimension to language use increasingly relevant. The National Curriculum, which is being implemented at breakneck speed in British schools, stresses the importance of oral work in all subjects in the school curriculum, and insists on the assessment of both oral and written English. Sociolinguists may be pleased that the importance of oral work has been officially recognized, but at the same time they have become painfully aware that we still know far too little about many vitally important features of spoken language. Teachers are being asked to draw up assessment procedures for aspects of language which specialists in the field have not satisfactorily described.

2.2 The survey of British dialect grammar

Between 1986 and 1989 we carried out a survey of British dialect grammar, which was designed to contribute to our understanding of just one of the educationally relevant aspects of language: the relationship between standard and non-standard English syntax. Our aim was to obtain information on dialect syntax and, eventually, to present this in a way that would be helpful and accessible to school teachers. We planned the dialect survey before the introduction of the National Curriculum, already seeing that this type of information was urgently needed. Research in Britain had shown the problems that could be caused by an incomplete understanding of the differences between the linguistic forms of standard English and those of non-standard varieties: Edwards (1983), for example, discusses some of the inappropriate teaching strategies that teachers may use when teaching reading skills; and Edwards (1979) and Cheshire (1982a) give examples of hypercorrect forms produced by schoolchildren in their written work.

We did not set out to address the grammatical differences between spoken and written standard English, which continue to elude linguists who have been working on spoken English for many years (see, for discussion, Crystal 1980). Instead, we aimed simply to increase the amount of information on dialect syntax that is available for teachers to consult, and to involve school children and their teachers in gathering that information. In Britain dialectologists and sociolinguists know less about dialect grammar (by which we mean morphology and syntax) than about dialect vocabulary or phonology (see Edwards, Trudgill and Weltens 1984). Teachers can consult various general accounts of differences in dialect grammar (for example, Edwards 1983; Milroy and Milroy 1985), but more detailed information is available on just four areas of the British Isles (Scotland, Northern Ireland, Southern England and Newcastle upon Tyne – as in this volume). For the most part, teachers have had to try to establish the differences between standard and non-standard dialects of English without the help of linguists. There has been widespread public confusion of dialect grammar with 'sloppy' or 'incorrect' English (see Chapter 1), and in the absence of any proper linguistic or sociolinguistic training for teachers there seems little reason to expect this group to be any less confused than the rest of the general public.

The importance of 'knowledge about language' (cf. DES 1988) achieved fresh prominence in 1989 with the introduction of the National Curriculum in English and Welsh schools. Oral work in all subjects has become important, and both oral and written English are now assessed. The Recommendations of the Cox Committee to the Secretary of State for Education (DES 1989) are uncompromising in their insistence on the place of standard English in the English curriculum:

> The development of pupils' ability to understand written and spoken standard English and to produce written standard English is unquestionably a responsibility of the English curriculum (DES 1989: 4.34).

They are equally uncompromising in deciding who will carry the burden of dealing with the linguistic differences between standard and non-standard varieties of English, assuming that teachers 'themselves have an accurate understanding of the differences between written standard English, spoken standard English and spoken local varieties of English' (DES 1989: 4.40). Such an assumption would appear, at the very least, to be optimistic. A study of the level of linguistic knowledge and awareness among student teachers training to be primary teachers (Chandler et al. 1988) indicates considerable gaps in their understanding of linguistic matters. There have also been widespread criticisms of the ideological underpinnings of the National Curriculum approach to linguistic diversity (see, for example, Cameron and Bourne 1988; Stubbs 1989; Winch 1989; Fairclough 1992).

The time was ripe for an initiative such as the Survey of British Dialect Grammar, not only because of the fresh emphasis on standard English in the National Curriculum but also because of the marked increase of 'language awareness programmes' at both primary and secondary levels of schooling. A central tenet of such programmes is that children themselves are the experts: they are all competent users of at least one language – which is a considerable achievement in itself – and this knowledge can be used in understanding and explaining a wide range of social and political issues (Clark et al. 1990; 1991).

We established a nationwide network of teachers who were willing to take part in collaborative teacher–pupil projects on language use in the local community (see Chapter 3, for details). The collaboration between schools and linguists is an important development. On the one hand, teachers are interpreting for their pupils the accumulated knowledge of linguists and, in particular, of sociolinguists. On the other hand, the rapidly developing awareness of language in teachers and children opens up many new possibilities for linguists. There had, of course, been notable previous initiatives in this area, including the survey of languages and dialects of London schoolchildren (Rosen and Burgess 1980) and the much larger Linguistic Minorities Project (1985). However, to our knowledge our own survey is the first attempt to involve schools in directly gathering detailed linguistic data rather than general information about language use.

For reasons of economy, the Survey had to take the form of a questionnaire, which we sent to all the participating schools. The questionnaire consisted of 196 linguistic features, drawn from the main areas of dialect grammar described in Edwards et al. 1984 (see Appendix 3.1 in Chapter 3). As we discuss in Chapter 3, we felt it essential that a period of language awareness work (see Hawkins 1984; Jones 1989) should precede the administration of the questionnaire, in order to ensure that children provided reliable information, rather than simply the answers that they assumed their teachers wanted. In order to reinforce this point, we developed a series of lesson outlines and materials, tried these out during the pilot stage of the research, and sent the modified version to all teachers who participated in the Survey. The lesson outlines covered topics such as multilingual Britain, language variation, language change, standard English, and 'talking proper'. The questionnaire on local dialect usage was presented as the end point of the work on language awareness, with the intention of consulting pupils as the experts on their local variety of English, and asking them to tell us whether the forms listed on the questionnaire were used locally.

The results of the Survey provided the information that we had hoped for, giving us a general picture of the regional distribution of those features of dialect grammar that had been included on the questionnaire (see Chapter 3 for discussion of this aspect of the Survey, and Cheshire et al. 1989). In addition, we obtained some sociolinguistic information of a more general kind, as a by-product of the lesson suggestions that were sent to the teachers participating in the Survey.

Teachers who returned the questionnaires were invited to comment on the usefulness of working on dialect issues in the ways that we suggested in the lesson outlines, and on practicalities surrounding the completion of the questionnaire. Their responses were, without exception, favourable; the general feeling was that the topics used as the basis for classwork were very successful, generating a great deal of constructive discussion and, in many cases, written work (Edwards and Cheshire 1989). Some teachers offered us extensive examples of the written work that their pupils had produced as part of their exploration of dialect. The examples were of interest to us as sociolinguists, in some cases providing a qualitative counterbalance to experimental research on attitudes to regional variation in English, in other cases giving us direct evidence of children's reactions to linguistic diversity and of their interest in exploring the everyday realities of language use in their local community. The work that we received convinced us of the value of incorporating language work in the classroom which will allow children the opportunity to explore their personal reactions to linguistic variation and to develop their skills as sociolinguistic researchers in the local community. In the following sections we give some examples of the work that we found the most interesting.

2.3   Reactions to linguistic diversity

The work that we received covered a range of topics. We were particularly interested in the topic of correction, both because we wanted to see which linguistic variables are salient to the teachers, parents and other adults who feel the need to monitor children's language and because we were curious about the children's reactions to being corrected. We were also interested in some written work that illustrated the way in which language functions as a symbol of individual and social identity, and in work which described children's attitudes to regional variation. Here we shall first consider correction.

2.3.1 Correction

Part of the lesson outline on the topic of 'talking proper' invited children to reflect on whether teachers or other people ever corrected the way they spoke or wrote, to consider the kinds of things that these people said, and to explore their feelings about being corrected. Two teachers sent us the written work that their classes of 14 year-old pupils had prepared on this topic. This work was of interest for a number of reasons. First, we were interested in the identity of the forms that pupils said were corrected, since there is little precise information available on stigmatized forms in the research literature, and few hypotheses offered to explain why some variables are more salient to speakers than others. Condemnation of 'h' dropping, for example, is very widespread in Britain, but people do not seem to be concerned about vowel alternations (such as regional variation in the pronunciation of a word such as *bus*, which may be [bʌs] or [bʊs]).

Trudgill (1986: 11) suggests that overt stigmatization occurs when there is a high status variant of the stigmatized form which tallies with the orthography, while the stigmatized form does not. Many of the corrections concerning pronunciation that schoolchildren wrote about gave support to this view. Sometimes (as in examples 1 and 2) corrections were expressed in terms of 'dropped letters' or additional 'letters':

(1) Mum corrects my speech when I drop letters especially 'h' and it annoys me but I suppose she's right.
(2) Yes they moan at me when I start to speak like a Scouser. I say *married* as if there's about seven rs in it – *marrrrrrried*.
(3) Yes like when I say *ye* they always correct me and say *yes*.

Predictably, other corrections concerned features of non-standard English grammar, which were denied existence (example 4) or said to be 'not English' (example 5):

(4) Yes because I use words like *worser* and other things like that when there's no such word.
(5) Yes they correct me when I am saying something and say that's not English. If I say *what* they say *that*. If I say *can I borrow this* they say it's not *borrow* it's *lend*.

A second reason for our interest was the information that we received, indirectly, on whether correcting children's language is a worthwhile exercise. Teachers in England and Wales are sometimes advised on the kinds of corrections that they should make. For example, the Cox Report (DES 1989: 4.46) rightly points out the dangers of indiscriminate correction, but suggests that teachers should correct non-standard forms and highly stigmatized forms (such as the past tense forms of *see*) that occur frequently. The work which we received, however, did not lead us to share the view that correction is worthwhile. Several children reported 'corrected' versions of their speech that we are confident were not made in that form:

(6)   Teachers normally correct me when I say *can I lend a pen* but you should say *can you please borrow me a pen*.

(7)   Yes. When I say *I saw something* they (teachers) say to say *seen* but my parents say it the opposite. This confuses me.

(8)   When you ask to lend something they always say *borrow* is the right word then your next lesson you ask to borrow something and they say *lend* is the right word.

Examples such as these indicate to us that correcting pupils' speech is ineffectual. Explanations appear to be only half understood and may well lead to confusion about the linguistic relationship between features of standard and non-standard English.

Sociolinguists stress that language is closely bound up with individual and social identity. It is certainly not difficult to envisage a scenario in which persistent corrections of a child's language can lead to a reticence in oral work and even, in extreme cases, to alienation from the school. We were interested, therefore, in the reactions that children expressed to being corrected. Examples 9–12 illustrate a broad range of professed reactions:

(9)   I feel very angry because I know what I am saying and so does the teacher.

(10)   I am not really bothered: I know what I mean and so do they.

(11)   My mum corrects me and it annoys me but I suppose she's right.

(12) It doesn't bother me because they [teachers] know how to speak better than I do.

With the possible exception of the sanguine response in example 10, this range of reactions confirms our view that it is not a good idea to correct children's speech. In this respect, the repeated complaints of older dialect speakers also consulted during the course of the survey presents a point of comparison. One Northern octogenarian commented:

> Any child using dialect speech would be severely reprimanded or ignored, depending on which teacher was in charge. Some teachers would endeavour kindly to explain that this was not on; others, less sympathetic, would perhaps resort to sarcasm or pretend to deliberately misunderstand.

Although tolerance of variation in the spoken word has certainly increased in recent years, it is extremely doubtful whether the attempts of present-day teachers to change dialect speech or writing will be any more effective than those of the past. As one fourth year pupil in Rotherham reflected:

> Teachers always correct the way I write. They correct the way I write more than anything. When I write a story and include talking I write it how I would speak. But sometimes teachers cross it out and put in how they would talk. I don't think they should do that. They should leave it as is.

Though we remain sceptical about the usefulness of correcting non-standard forms, we are convinced of the value of including discussion of this aspect of 'talking proper' in the school curriculum. We agree with the Cox Committee's view that every child is entitled to learn not only the functions but also the forms of standard English (DES 1989: 4.7) However, it is by no means clear how this should be achieved, nor how teachers could achieve the Cox Report's recommendations that children should be taught the grammatical differences between the speech of their local area and spoken standard English (DES 1989: 15.37ii). Even if teachers decide against correcting children's spoken language, parents and other concerned adults are likely to feel a need to monitor their children's language, and the opportunity to air personal reactions to corrections and to see the range of reactions amongst classmates seems a necessary prerequisite for constructive teaching of the linguistic differences between standard and non-standard English.

2.3.2   Attitudes to regional variation

The research literature in sociolinguistics and social psychology is unanimous about the nature of attitudes towards regional varieties of English. A series of matched guise experiments has shown that accents associated with rural areas of Britain tend to be perceived by British speakers of English as more attractive than accents spoken in heavily urbanized areas (see Trudgill 1983), and further experiments have repeatedly shown that speakers with Received Pronunciation (sometimes called 'the Queen's English') are considered to be more intelligent and more competent than speakers who have a regional accent. This perception has been found to be shared by speakers of standard and non-standard English alike, although speakers of non-standard English may have strong feelings about the value of their own speech, associating it with friends, family and neighbourhood, with social attractiveness and with integrity (Giles and Powesland 1975; Ryan and Giles 1982).

The lesson suggestions which we sent to teachers participating in the Survey of British Dialect Grammar invited children to consider which types of accents they liked best, and which they liked least, and to give reasons. One teacher in a school in the urban centre of Widnes, Lancashire (in North-west England) sent us some written work that her class had prepared on this topic. This work did not give us any insights into attitudes towards Received Pronunciation, but it did show us that 'talking posh' was often associated with the South of England, particularly London:

(13) I dislike London accent. It sounds really posh.
(14) I dislike London accent because they are stuck up snobs.

As for other accents, the most striking feature of the children's comments was the complete lack of unanimity in their likes and dislikes, and the very wide range of reasons that were given in support of these opinions. Many of the attitudes that were expressed within a single class of pupils directly conflicted with each other. Compare, for example, 15 with 16, 17 and 18; 19 with 20; and 21 and 22 with 23 and 24:

(15) I like Cockney because it gives you a laugh. I also like American because it's dead cool. Geordie (i.e. Tyneside) is OK as well.

(16) I dislike Geordie accent because of the way they say it, it just gets right up my nose.

(17) I detest American accents because there is too much of it going on TV.

(18) I don't like Cockney accents because it sounds like they're talking out of their nose.

(19) I like the Welsh, Manchester, and Australian accents because they're good.

(20) I dislike Manchester accent because I don't like Manchester and everything's slower.

(21) I like Scottish because of the way they say it and when they say it fast it sounds dead cool.

(22) Scottish is the best because it sounds so easy going.

(23) I dislike Scottish because I can't understand what they are saying.

(24) I dislike Scottish accent because they speak so quick I can't understand it.

The comments that pupils made about different regional accents revealed a very interesting selection of idiosyncratic likes and dislikes, which they justified in equally idiosyncratic ways:

(25) Norfolk accent is the best. The people sound like farmers.

(26) I like the Australians and the French because they're different and good.

(27) Scousers (i.e. Liverpool people) speak terrible. Apart from that I don't really mind the rest of them except the people from Devon, they're really stuck up.

(28) I hate the Birmingham accent because it makes them sound thick.

(29) I dislike Newcastle. They talk really slow and drawn out.

(30) I like Welsh: it's got a nice sound to it.

This diversity of attitudes within a single class of schoolchildren is in stark contrast to the unanimity that has been found amongst participants in matched guise experiments. Perhaps this is because experiments direct participants to choose from a pre-selected closed set of characteristics (usually, of course, characteristics which have been elicited previously by open questioning); in a less structured situation, when people are invited simply to express their personal likes and dislikes, it is easier to see the very wide range of opinions that individuals hold and to appreciate the very personal and idiosyncratic nature of attitudes towards linguistic variation. Airing these personal views in the context of a class discussion is a valuable educational experience, showing those individuals who have very strong linguistic prejudices that others may have equally strong, but different, prejudices. Teachers who have studied sociolinguistics may be able to tell their pupils about linguistic prejudice, and about the systematic results of matched guise investigations of the social evaluation of regional accents. Relaying information, however, cannot take the place of exploring personal motivations for individual's own linguistic likes and dislikes. Incorporating language awareness work of this type into the English curriculum may allow schoolchildren to develop into adults who will be more linguistically tolerant than their predecessors.

2.3.3   Linguistic variation as an expression of individual and social identity

Another aspect of the lesson outline on 'talking proper' invited pupils to consider what they liked and what they disliked about speaking the way they did. The statements about what they liked confirmed the function of language as an expression of personal identity:

(31) I enjoy speaking the way I do as I think it's me.
(32) I feel comfortable speaking the way I do and I think it's good.

Similarly, there was confirmation of the role of language as a symbol of loyalty to the neighbourhood (examples 33 and 34) and to the peer group (examples 35 and 36):

(33) I like the way I speak because it sounds normal in this town.

(34) I like Widnes accent best because it goes with the town and it's different from all the others.

(35) I like it because you don't feel stupid, because all your mates speak it.

(36) I like the way I speak because my friends all speak the same way and I can understand them.

The territoriality of language was mentioned by one cautious pupil:

(37) If you go to Liverpool you might change the way you talk because you might get beat up.

There were few comments, however, about aspects of their speech that children disliked. We were surprised by this, since research carried out in Britain has sometimes shown that individuals who speak with an accent typical of a heavily urbanized part of the country experience linguistic insecurity about their speech. Macaulay (1977), for example, notes the comments made by one Glaswegian about his own speech:

> I mean I'm not a speaker as you can see. I don't ... I'm just a common sort of, you know I'm not ... I've often wished I'd gone to some sort of elocution lessons because I meet so many people in my job and I feel as if I'm lower when it comes to speaking, you know.

Trudgill (1983: 209) similarly notes that linguistic insecurity may cause individual speakers who have stigmatized accents to become inarticulate and reluctant to express themselves, in certain circumstances. Some of the comments that we received showed that pupils were aware of the social prestige associated with certain kinds of speech:

(38) When I am talking to posh people I feel terribly common.

But other comments, such as 39 and 40, revealed an antipathy to 'talking posh', and we were interested, and encouraged, to note that most children commented as in example 41:

(39) What I like is that I speak just like anyone else and not like a Yuppie (posh person).

(40) I like it because it doesn't sound posh.

(41) I don't really dislike anything about the way I speak.

Thus we found little evidence of the linguistic insecurity that has been reported as typical of children who speak with a regional accent. Perhaps insecurity develops later, if individuals mix with people from outside their region after they have left school; or perhaps times are changing, and attitudes to regional accents are becoming more tolerant. We would like to believe in the latter explanation; after all, some newsreaders and programme presenters on the BBC now have (slight) regional accents, especially on local BBC stations, and accents other than Received Pronunciation are increasingly heard in public life. One recent study, however, suggests that this interpretation is overly optimistic: Collins (1988) found that the prestige of Received Pronunciation is still firmly entrenched, at least in London schools. Even those school teachers who had been teaching in an Equal Opportunities school for fifteen years and who professed to have liberal attitudes towards regional accents nevertheless gave the highest ratings in a matched guise experiment to the Received Pronunciation guise. Trainee teachers who participated in this study also gave the highest ratings to Received Pronunciation.

2.4   Resources for diversity

Classroom discussions of dialect are useful not only for raising children's social and linguistic awareness, but also for their development as writers. The work which teachers shared with us demonstrated not only that children write with interest and enthusiasm *about* dialect but also that they write very competently *in* dialect. Teachers who participated in the project used a wide range of stimulus material − texts about dialect, short stories and poems in dialect, records, tapes and television programmes. Children have recorded an equally wide range of responses. They have improvised plays which they have later transcribed. They have written plays in dialect which they have then performed. They have also composed poems and stories in dialect. Yasmin, a 12 year-old Pakistani girl from Blackburn, wrote a series of ten poems in Lancashire dialect, including this memorable one about her grandmother's wish to visit a disco:

T'disco

I wer the best looking un there
Wi mi jumper an mi mini skart.
Mi dad wer reet proud of mi.
O'boys ran far mi.
I loked like on' of them Miss World
Wi mi hair done and mi face.
I've been t'disco 'ut none like this.
Mi granny ses she wana go, er.
An ah ses, 'Yer t'old granni, love!'
An she ses she's 'oing there today,
So ah as sum sharp words ready.
Wah! Mi old granny going t'disco!

Work on the project made it clear that dialect continues to be a source of fascination for a wide range of people – for academics who believe that the description of dialect is as important to linguistic theory as standard English; for teachers who feel that education should acknowledge and build on children's speech, rather than criticizing and rejecting it; for writers and performers who find dialect a versatile vehicle for their work; and for the large body of lay people who identify with regional speech and want to find out more. It also became clear that there was a very great need for a central source of information on dialect resources. For this reason we decided to compile a Directory of English Dialect Resources, which attempted to bring together as comprehensive as possible a range of books and commercially available sound recordings, together with information on dialect societies, resource centres and sound collections. This appears as Chapter 8 of this book.

2.5 Research in the local community

The children taking part in the dialect survey carried out two kinds of research in the community. One was systematic research into the distribution of the specific features listed on the questionnaire, which was carried out as collaborative classroom projects and analysed by us (this is discussed in Chapter 3). The other type of research consisted of mini-projects on various aspects of linguistic variation, which were carried out as individual research projects by the children, and written up as part of their school work.

2.5.1   Small-scale projects

The lesson outline on language variation that we sent to teachers invited schoolchildren to write down in a notebook the different phrases that they heard used during the course of a single day for greeting, thanking or taking leave of people. This activity produced a great deal of written work, with some children carrying out detailed analyses of the phrases used by people of different ages and different sexes. The value of this kind of work can perhaps be seen most clearly from the comments of one 16 year old, who recorded seven ways of thanking people (*ta, thanks, thanks a lot, cheers, good on yer, proper job, many thanks*) and five ways of taking leave of them (*see you, tara, bye then, cheerio, cheers then*) and wrote that she was amazed to find that she had not recorded a single occurrence of *thank you* or *goodbye*. Carrying out mini-research projects of this kind, then, can clear preconceived ideas about language out of the way and help pupils to develop linguistic sensitivity.

Another mini-project which resulted in written work was research into dialect vocabulary, with pupils noting down some words which were used locally and which they thought might not be understood by people from outside the locality. Thus we learned that a 60-year old man from Lydford, Devon used *gaiky* ('ugly'), *emmett* ('tourist' or 'visitor') and *dashels* ('thistles'); that in Leicester people said *cob* ('bap'), *me duck* (term of address from a man to a woman) and *mashing tea* ('brewing tea'). Another pupil in Devon recorded different ways of giving emphasis to what people were saying, mentioning intonation, swearing and the use of *you* (as in *he was a big man you*). All these projects seem to us to be invaluable ways of extending the linguistic awareness of schoolchildren. They also provided us with some useful information that we did not have before (for example, the use of *you* for emphasis has not, as far as we know, been reported before).

2.5.2 The questionnaire on local dialect grammar

The most useful information on linguistic variation, however, was perhaps contained in the questionnaires that were returned. As mentioned at the beginning of this chapter, the end point of the lessons on language awareness was designed to be the completion of a collaborative teacher–pupil project on dialect grammar. We suggested to teachers that classes working collaboratively should divide into three groups, each dealing with one page of the questionnaire, and that each group should report on the forms of dialect grammar listed on their page, that were used in their local community. If more funds and research staff had been available it would, of course, have been preferable for our purposes to have based this part of the survey on audio recordings of a sample of speakers in different parts of Britain. However, teachers reported that the questionnaire provided a useful end point for the series of lessons on language awareness, with pupils seeing themselves as experts on local speech; the questionnaire, therefore, served as a further way of developing pupils' linguistic sensitivity. And since the questionnaire responses had been systematically collected, they could be used in the way that we had intended – as a first step in investigating whether dialects in Britain are gradually levelling to a uniform variety of non-standard English. We discuss this aspect of the research in Chapter 3.

2.6 Conclusion

The Survey of British Dialect Grammar was an attempt to incorporate sociolinguistics directly into the classroom, with the short-term aim of enlisting teachers and their pupils as researchers, asking them to help us in the systematic collection of data on local dialect grammar. We have used these data to formulate hypotheses on dialect levelling, which now await empirical testing (see Cheshire et al. 1989; and Chapter 3). They might also usefully serve as the basis of classroom materials on standard and non-standard English (or, perhaps, between features of formal written English and features of spoken English). Materials of this kind would certainly be of some help to teachers in their difficult task of implementing the National Curriculum.

We also found that schoolchildren were interested in acting on their own account as sociolinguistic researchers, exploring their personal reactions to linguistic diversity as well as investigating the linguistic variation that exists in their local community. These personal explorations seem to us to be an essential first step towards achieving the aims of the National Curriculum, paving the way for a dispassionate explanation of the differences between written and spoken English which can be linked to discussion of standard and non-standard English and, perhaps, towards the addition of standard English to the repertoire of those children for whom standard English is not their native dialect (see DES 1989: 4.43). These explorations, however, are also a valuable educational experience in their own right, allowing children the opportunity to share their experiences of linguistic diversity with their peers and their teacher, and empowering them to face the adult world (see Clark et al. 1990; 1991 for further discussion).

Activities of this kind also offer interesting challenges for teachers. Children are allowed to assume the role of expert and, in most cases, will be able to speak with greater authority on the local dialect than their teachers. Children's views on non-standard speech may, on some occasions, cause teachers to reappraise their own classroom practice, particularly in relation to the 'correction' of non-standard forms.

The scope of work on standard and non-standard language is impressive. Children can be encouraged to explore the use of standard and non-standard English in role play and drama. They can express their views on standard and non-standard English through their writing. They can be presented with examples of dialect literature and invited to discuss the particular effects which dialect can create as a prelude to their own compositions. Small-scale research projects on language provide experience of questionnaire design, data collection and analysis. It seems to us that this approach to language study offers ample opportunities for a wide range of educationally valuable activities which can be actively promoted within the framework of the English curriculum.

References

CAMERON, D and BOURNE, J. (1988) No common ground: Kingman, grammar and the nation. *Language and Education* 2: 147–60

CHANDLER, P., ROBINSON, W.P. and NOYES, P. (1988) The level of linguistic knowledge and awareness among students training to be primary teachers. *Language and Education* 2: 161–73

CHESHIRE, J. (1982) Dialect features and linguistic conflict in schools. *Educational Review* 34: 53–67

CHESHIRE, J., EDWARDS, V. and WHITTLE, P. (1989) Urban British Dialect Grammar: the question of dialect levelling. *English Worldwide* 10: 185–226

CLARK, R., FAIRCLOUGH, N., IVANIC, R. and MARTIN-JONES, M. (1990) Critical language awareness, Part 1: A critical review of three current approaches to language awareness *Language and Education* 4: 249–260

CLARK, R., FAIRCLOUGH, N., IVANIC, R. and MARTIN-JONES, M. (1991) Critical language awareness, Part 2: Towards critical alternatives. *Language and Education* 5: 41–54

COLLINS, P., (1988) Teachers' Evaluations of Accent in a GCSE Simulation. Unpublished MA dissertation, Department of Applied Linguistics, Birkbeck College, University of London

CRYSTAL, D. (1980) Some neglected grammatical factors in conversational English. In Greenbaum, S., Leech, G. and Svartvik, J. (eds), *Studies in English Linguistics* Harlow: Longman, pp. 134–52

DES (1988) *Report of the Committee of Inquiry into the Teaching of English* (The Kingman Report). London: DES

DES (1989) *English for Ages 5–16* (The Cox Report). London: DES and Welsh Office

EDWARDS, V. (1979) *The West Indian Issue in British Schools*. London: Routledge

EDWARDS, V. (1983) *Language in Multicultural Classrooms*. London: Batsford

EDWARDS, V. AND CHESHIRE, J. (1989) The survey of British Dialect Grammar. In Cheshire, J., Edwards, V., Münstermann, H., and Weltens, B. (eds) *Dialect and Education: Some European Perspectives*. Clevedon: Multilingual Matters, pp. 200–15

EDWARDS, V., TRUDGILL, P. and WELTENS, B. (1984) *The Grammar of English Dialect*. London: Economic and Social Research Council

FAIRCLOUGH, Norman (1992) The appropriacy of 'appropriateness'. In Fairclough, N. (ed.) *Critical Language Awareness*. London: Longman, pp. 33–56

GILES, H. and POWESLAND, P. (1975) *Speech Style and Social Evaluation*. London: Academic Press

HAWKINS, E. (1984) *Awareness of language: an Introduction*. Cambridge: Cambridge University Press

JONES, A.P. (1989) Language awareness programmes in British schools.

In Cheshire, J., Edwards, V., Münstermann, H., and Weltens, B. (eds) *Dialect and Education: Some European Perspectives.* Clevedon: Multilingual Matters, pp. 269–81

LINGUISTIC MINORITIES PROJECT (1985) *The Other Languages of England.* London: Routledge

MACAULAY, R.K.S. (1977) *Language, Social Class and Education: a Glasgow Study.* Edinburgh: Edinburgh University Press

MILROY, J. and MILROY, L. (1985) *Authority in Language.* London: Routledge

ORTON, H. (1969) *Survey of English Dialects. (A): Introduction.* Leeds: E. J. Arnold for University of Leeds

ROSEN, H. and BURGESS, T. (1980) *The Languages and Dialects of London Schoolchildren.* London: Ward Lock Educational

RYAN, E.B. and GILES, H. (1982) *Attitudes Towards Language Variation.* London: Edward Arnold

STUBBS, M. (1989) The state of English in the English state: reflections on the Cox Report. *Language and Education* 3: 235–50

TRUDGILL, P. (1979) Standard and non-standard accents and dialects of English in the United Kingdom. *International Journal of the Sociology of Language* 21: 9–24

TRUDGILL, P. (1983) *On Dialect.* Oxford: Blackwell

TRUDGILL, P. (1986) *Dialects in Contact.* Oxford: Blackwell

WINCH, C. (1989) Standards in English, normativity and the Cox Report. *Language and Education* 3: 275–90

3 Non-standard English and dialect levelling

Jenny Cheshire, Viv Edwards and Pamela Whittle

3.1 Introduction

This chapter identifies some grammatical features that appear to be shared by the urban dialects of the major centres of Britain. Urban dialectologists seem to agree that the growth of cities has been accompanied by very rapid mixing of a number of different dialects from surrounding areas (see Milroy 1984:214), as former rural populations become increasingly urbanized. Some writers have suggested that as a result dialect diversity in Britain is reducing and being replaced not by the grammatical forms of standard English but by a development towards a levelled non-standard dialect (see Edwards and Weltens 1984: 121–2). Some empirical analyses of the phonological consequences of urbanization have been carried out: Harris (1985) and Milroy (1982), for example, showed that one effect in Belfast was the rapid reduction of allophones. So far, however, there have been no comparable studies that focus on morphology and syntax, and the question of whether there has been a reduction of grammatical variation as a result of urbanization has yet to be addressed. Although this is a question that can only be properly addressed by empirical investigations of actual usage, we were able to make some preliminary statements about the dialect features that are shared by the urban centres of Britain, within the context of a Survey of British Dialect Grammar.

3.2 The Survey of British Dialect Grammar

This survey[1] was carried out between 1986 and 1989, and had two main aims. The first was to increase our knowledge of the morphology and syntax of British English dialects, which at present lags far behind our knowledge of their phonology. This was made clear, for instance, in *The Grammar of English Dialect: A Survey of Research* (Edwards et al. 1984), which overviewed more than 200 studies of English dialects from the beginning of this century until 1982, and abstracted any information about grammar that was presented in them (see also Edwards and Weltens 1984). By far the greatest part of that information had to be derived indirectly, from discussions of phonology or vocabulary in which grammar played only a peripheral role. The Survey of British Dialect Grammar therefore focused primarily on morphology (patterns of word formation) and on syntax (patterns of clause formation), although in some cases, of course, it was difficult to draw a clear dividing line between vocabulary and 'grammar' in the sense in which we defined it (i.e. morphology and syntax) and between phonology and 'grammar'. The survey attempted to determine those morphological and syntactic features of British English dialects that are widespread throughout Britain, to establish the regional distribution of features that are less widespread, and to provide some informed preliminary hypotheses about the nature of grammatical variation and change in contemporary British English dialects.

The second aim of the survey was concerned with the educational implications that arise from the co-existence of standard English and non-standard English grammar. The British education system rests on the assumption that teachers and pupils will use the grammar of standard English. However, the majority of British children are speakers not of standard English but of a non-standard variety of English (a dialect), and this has been recognized as posing several extremely important problems concerning language in education. For example, teachers sometimes evaluate dialect-speaking children more negatively than their standard English speaking peers (see J. Edwards, 1979; V. Edwards, 1979), as a direct result, it seems, of translating negative attitudes towards non-standard speech into negative attitudes towards the speakers themselves; in addition, a wide range of bad pedagogic practices are likely to result from inadequate information about the nature of dialect differences (see, for discussion, V. Edwards 1983; Cheshire 1984; 1989). The burden of coping with these problems is usually assigned to schoolteachers, but initial teacher education rarely includes courses on dialectology or sociolinguistics; furthermore, very little information about dialect grammar is available, as yet, for teachers to consult. The second aim of the survey, therefore, was to investigate the possibility of producing material on dialect diversity that would be useful in teacher education and as a classroom resource, as well as to increase the amount of information on dialect grammar that is currently available to teachers.

It was with these twin aims in mind, then, that the Survey of British Dialect Grammar was conceived. The acute shortage of funds for research at all levels in the United Kingdom at that time, however, meant that the prospect of properly extending our knowledge of non-standard dialect grammar was bleak. A full-scale research project would have needed to draw on the expertise of a number of linguists and would have required a team of fieldworkers to make many tape-recordings of a representative range of speakers throughout the country. A project of this magnitude was simply not achievable in the current economic climate. However, there has been a surge of interest in language in British schools, at both primary and secondary levels, and we thought it possible, therefore, that schools could become a starting place for the collection of data on non-standard English grammar. The interest stems in part from a host of government reports and other influential publications which have acknowledged some of the educational problems arising from the co-existence of standard and non-standard varieties of English, and which have acknowledged the importance of valuing the language and culture of the child's home (see, for instance, Bullock 1975; DES 1984; Swann 1985). This theme has been mirrored in the mushrooming of language awareness programmes both in primary schools and as part of the modern languages or English curricula in secondary schools (see Hawkins 1984; Jones 1989). A central tenet of these programmes is that the children themselves are the experts and that their knowledge of their own language can be used in understanding and explaining a range of important social issues. We decided to enlist the co-operation of teachers and children who were involved in language awareness programmes, by asking them to help us to discover the regional features of British syntax.

Working with teachers and their pupils is not, of course, a straightforward process. Because non-standard English has low status and has traditionally been the subject of a great deal of corrective pressure from teachers, it would be very optimistic to imagine that data on dialect grammar collected from unprepared pupils would be reliable for our purposes. For this reason, our survey was designed to be the end point of an extended period of work on language, which could be viewed as a collaborative effort between teachers and pupils. This approach to learning departs significantly from the traditional model, but is by no means novel or unique, and collaborative learning techniques have attracted a considerable following in the United Kingdom in recent years.

Full details of the pilot study and the organization of the Survey were given in Edwards and Cheshire (1989). The procedure, in brief, was to provide those teachers who agreed to take part in the survey with a set of lesson suggestions, designed to form part of a course on Language Awareness (see Hawkins 1984; Jones 1989). At the end of the course, pupils completed a questionnaire on local dialect, as a collaborative classroom project. The questionnaire is briefly discussed in section 3, and is reproduced at the end of this chapter as Appendix 3.1. Pupils were asked to work in groups, with each group completing one page of the questionnaire, recording those forms that they had heard regularly in the local community. By treating the children as experts on local dialect, we hoped to raise the status of dialect in the classroom and to ensure that the topic was treated with the necessary tact and sensitivity. By using collaborative techniques, we hoped that the dialect features on the questionnaire would be discussed by groups of pupils and their teacher, and that the class as a whole would report on community usage, rather than on the usage of individual pupils. The survey thus aimed to provide both a focus for work on language awareness and a way of collecting systematic information on the regional distribution of features of regional morphology and syntax.

3.3   The questionnaire

The questionnaire that was used for the collaborative class projects contained 196 features, most of which were morphological and syntactic features reported by Edwards and Weltens (1984) as occurring in British English dialects. As mentioned above, the questionnaire is reproduced as Appendix 3.1. We included two items as a check on the reliability of the responses, expecting them to be reported by virtually all the schools taking part in the Survey: these were epistemic *must* (item 65: *he's out of tune, he must be stone deaf*) and deontic *must* (item 62: *you must be at your music class by 9 a.m.*). The two schools in Glasgow might have been exceptions, since one study (Macafee 1980) has reported that *must* is reserved for epistemic necessity. In fact, all schools reported these items as occurring in their area, including the two schools in Glasgow. The other features on the questionnaire covered a wide range of linguistic phenomena, including the expression of negation (items 1–11), the use of clefting and extraposition (items 21–25), imperative forms (items 69–72), modal constructions (items 59–61), invariant tag questions (items 30 and 31), present and past tense verb forms (items 12–19, 28, 33–41), and prepositions (items 99, 102, 105, 107–109). We included most of the grammatical features whose distribution had been analysed by the Survey of English Dialects (Orton et al., 1962–71), so that it would be possible, at a later stage, to trace the extent to which the current distribution of these features reflects earlier boundaries. The grammatical features included both in the Survey of English Dialects (the SED) and the Survey of British Dialect Grammar were a range of pronoun forms, certain prepositions and conjunctions, certain auxiliary verbs (including deontic *must*) and forms of the verbs DO, HAVE, BE. The questionnaire also included a small number of additional features in which we were particularly interested, such as *should of* (item 196) and the intensifier *in arf* (item 20), as well as a few features which we thought were used in informal speech by speakers throughout Britain, such as *there's* and *there was* with a plural 'pseudo' subject (items 29 and 58; see, for discussion, section 3.4.1). Inevitably, perhaps, some features of interest had to be left out of the questionnaire, in order to keep it to a manageable length; we did not include, for example, some of the features that are thought to have a different regional distribution in educated speech, such as the use of participle forms after NEED or WANT, as in *this shirt needs washed/ this shirt needs washing* (see Hughes and Trudgill, 1987) – though we did include one such feature: constructions with direct and indirect pronouns and GIVE, as in *give it me* and *give me it* (Hughes and Trudgill, 1987).

We tried to arrange the 196 items on the questionnaire in as clear and graphically acceptable a manner as possible, bearing in mind that the questionnaires would be completed by pupils of a wide range of ages and abilities. The questionnaire was three pages long and risked placing an unreasonable strain on the concentration of younger and less able pupils. We suggested to teachers that classes working collaboratively should divide into at least three separate groups, each dealing with one page of the questionnaire.

The survey had to take the form of a questionnaire, partly because this provided the most economical method of collecting data and partly because this made it possible to integrate the educational aims of the survey with the linguistic aims. However, we were very conscious of the limitations of data collection using questionnaires, and we tried to guard against these limitations as far as possible. Each completed questionnaire was examined on return to see if schools had reported examples of dialect usage which, on the basis of existing knowledge, was unexpected for their area. Although such examples were infrequent, they did sometimes occur. Our procedure in those cases was to write to the teacher concerned in order to query the feature, or features, and to ask for further examples of sentences containing the feature(s). This allowed us to judge for ourselves whether misreporting had taken place.

Some items on the questionnaire proved to be problematic, although they had not emerged as such during the pilot study. For example, some items that were distinct in speech were clearly not seen as distinct when presented to teachers and pupils in writing: this applied to items 63 and 64 (*You mun be at our music class by 9 a.m.*; and *You maun be at your music class by 9 a.m.*); and to items 173 and 174 (*This is wer car*; and *This is wir car*). Item 52 (*we wan singing*) was interpreted by some pupils as *we weren't singing*. The *was/were* forms of BE generally were perhaps less suitable for presentation in written form than some other features, since in speech the weak forms of *was* and *were* may both be realized as [wə] (see, for example, Petyt 1985: 194). Some of the questionnaire items were intended to investigate the use of perfective aspect, such as item 83 (*Did you have your dinner yet?*), 92 (*I did eat chicken every day when I lived there*) and 93 (*And I did eat chicken yesterday too*); it was clear from the answers to our queries on usage, however, that the *did* constructions were frequently interpreted as conveying emphasis rather than aspect: our use of bold type, which we had thought would direct pupils' attention to the verb form, seemed to have been interpreted by some of them as indicating that extra stress was to be placed on the verb form. A further problem arose with item 89 (*I d'eat chicken every day*), which was frequently misread as *I'd eat chicken every day*.

The majority of items on the questionnaire, however, did not seem to be problematic, and the majority of responses were uncontroversial. We found that one advantage of a questionnaire survey, compared to the methodology used for the Survey of English Dialects (which relied on a fieldworker noting individual speakers' responses), was that we were able to investigate variation. For example, pupils in some parts of the country reported both *give me it* and *give it me*, whereas the SED had been able to elicit only one form or the other. Nevertheless, we do not wish to claim that the results of the Survey of British Dialect Grammar offer a definitive account of present-day grammatical variation in Britain. The primary purpose of analysing the data was to raise linguistically interesting and informed questions and to suggest hypotheses which merit further in-depth analysis using more reliable techniques of data collection. We mentioned earlier that the survey responses allowed us to make some preliminary statements about shared dialect features in the major urban centres of Britain. As we will see, they also suggested that for some features, variable grammatical forms are being reduced in some of the major urban centres of the country, and being replaced by a single non-standard form.

3.4 Regions included in the survey

Our original intention was to draw on schools throughout the British Isles, and to include schools in rural areas as well as in the towns and cities of Britain. Unfortunately, however, the period of the survey coincided with a period of industrial action by schoolteachers and with the introduction of new GCSE public examinations for 16 year-old pupils, which were held for the first time in 1988. The industrial action involved one-day strikes and withdrawal from all non-essential activities; the new examinations involved teachers in a great deal of planning and preparation for new syllabi and new methods of teaching and assessment. The net result was that the school-based method of data collection was a great deal less successful than had been anticipated, and the total of 87 schools that eventually participated in the survey was much lower than we had counted on.

Some of the analyses that we had hoped to undertake, such as a preliminary investigation of rural-urban interaction, were therefore out of the question. However, the data that we obtained give extremely good coverage of the more heavily populated urban regions of the country, as we describe below. Although it was not our original intention to restrict the survey to the major urban areas of the country, this, in the event, is what happened. The Survey of British Dialect Grammar therefore contrasts sharply with the only other survey of English dialects (the SED) both in its focus on morphology and syntax rather than on phonology, and in its emphasis on urban areas rather than on rural areas. Because of its focus on urban areas we are able to give a preliminary assessment of the extent to which dialect levelling has occurred in the British Isles; as mentioned earlier, the decline of linguistic diversity in the British Isles has been assumed to be the result of a general population movement away from rural areas into the towns. It is in the towns, in other words, that speakers of different dialects are most likely to have come into contact with each other.

We classified the locations of the schools taking part in the survey in terms of the CURDS (Centre for Urban and Regional Development Studies, University of Newcastle) Functional Regions system. The CURDS system is widely used by human geographers and regional scientists working on patterns of social and economic change in the cities, towns and rural areas of Great Britain. It divides the country into a consistently defined set of urban centres on the basis of statistical information concerning employment and retailing, depicting the size and the characteristics of the population that looks to these urban centres for a range of everyday activities including, crucially, employment. The cores of these urban centres are described as the 'pivotal nodes of economic activity and social life' (Champion and Coombes, 1983); the areas that are linked to these cores are then defined in terms of commuting patterns (in other words, in terms of the degree to which their residents depend on the cores for their jobs), as 'rings', 'outer areas' or 'rural areas'. Table 3.1 shows that 68 of the 87 schools who took part in the survey were located in core regions: in other words, 78% of the responses reported on dialect usage in the 'pivotal nodes of economic activity and social life'.

Table 3.1:   Location of schools participating in the survey

Core	Ring	Outer area	Rural	Total
68	12	5	2	87

More importantly, perhaps, 65 of the survey responses (74.7%) were from schools located in metropolitan regions. The CURDS framework identifies 20 of these metropolitan regions, which are the more heavily populated urban regions of the British Isles. Whereas freestanding urban areas, as their name suggests, constitute relatively independent areas, each with their own core, ring, outer areas and rural areas, the urban areas within the metropolitan regions are highly interdependent, linked by strong commuting ties. Seventeen of the 20 metropolitan regions of Britain were represented in the survey, including one of the two metropolitan regions in Scotland (Glasgow) and two of the three metropolitan regions in Wales (Cardiff and Swansea). Only Edinburgh (Scotland), Newport (Wales) and Portsmouth (England) were unrepresented. Figure 3.1 shows the functional regions and the metropolitan regions of the British Isles. Appendix 3.2 lists the regions that are represented in the survey. Fuller details of the CURDS framework and of the geographical locations of the schools participating in the survey (and, that is, of the local areas whose dialect usage is reported on) are given in Cheshire et al. (1989).

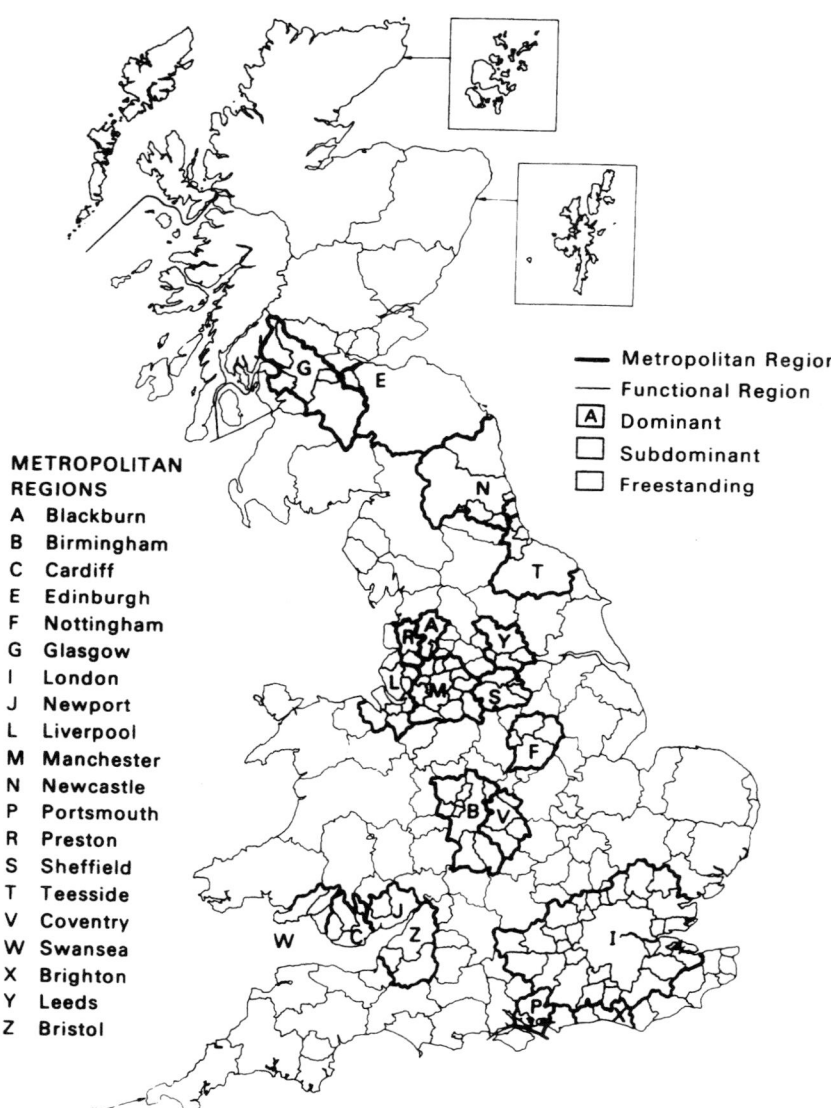

METROPOLITAN REGIONS

A   Blackburn
B   Birmingham
C   Cardiff
E   Edinburgh
F   Nottingham
G   Glasgow
I   London
J   Newport
L   Liverpool
M   Manchester
N   Newcastle
P   Portsmouth
R   Preston
S   Sheffield
T   Teesside
V   Coventry
W   Swansea
X   Brighton
Y   Leeds
Z   Bristol

Metropolitan Region
Functional Region
Dominant
Subdominant
Freestanding

Figure 3.1:   Functional Regions and Metropolitan Regions

The CURDS system is potentially of great value for research into patterns of linguistic variation and change in the British Isles, since it identifies important patterns of social communication between people from different geographical areas, on the basis of their economic activity. Secondary sources are readily available, including employment statistics and the full range of information gathered in the 1971 and 1991 censuses. Unfortunately, we were unable to draw on the explanatory potential of the CURDS system because of our small data base. We therefore used the framework simply to ascertain that the questionnaire responses were mainly from core urban regions, where dialect levelling, if it exists at all, would be most likely to have occurred and, in particular, that the responses were from the major metropolitan regions of the British Isles, where we assume that there has been the greatest amount of interaction between people from different linguistic backgrounds.

3.5 Shared morphological and syntactic features of British urban dialects

Some writers have identified the non-standard grammatical features that they believe to be common to most urban varieties of English. Hughes and Trudgill (1987), for example, list 13 types of difference between standard English and non-standard urban varieties of British English. These are: multiple negation, *ain't* and 'other aspects of negation', past tense forms of irregular verbs, *never* as past tense negative, present tense verb forms, relative pronouns, reflexive pronouns, comparatives and superlatives, demonstratives, 'adjectival' forms with adverbial function (including adverbs such as *quick*, without the *-ly* suffix), unmarked plurality (on some quantified nouns after numerals, as in *twenty mile*) and prepositions of place. Coupland (1988: 35) suggests that seven of these features are so widespread that they are better seen as characteristic of British social dialects, marking the socio-economic class of speakers rather than their regional provenance. These seven features are: multiple negation, *never* as past tense negative, *them* as a demonstrative adjective, unmarked plurality, 'adjectival' forms with adverbial function, reduction of complex prepositions such as *up to* (as in *I'm going up London*), and regularizing of the reflexive pronoun paradigm (as in *hisself* and *theirselves*).

Given the paucity of empirical research on morphological and syntactic variation in British English, these assumptions have inevitably been unsupported by factual evidence. The questionnaire responses obtained by the survey therefore provide some useful systematic information on those features of dialect grammar that are reported as occurring in most of the urban centres of the British Isles.

With the exception, as mentioned earlier, of items 62 and 65, we calculated the percentage frequency with which each of the features on the questionnaire was reported by schools in the core and ring zones participating in the survey (that is, in the more heavily populated urban areas of Britain). Several features were reported infrequently (61 of the 196 features on the questionnaire − 31% − were reported by fewer than 5% of the schools). One feature, on the other hand, was reported by more than 90% of the schools in the core and ring zones, and a further twelve by more than 80% of these schools. These thirteen features were also reported by the two schools located in rural zones and by virtually all the schools in the outer zones.[2] We list these 13 features below, together with the percentage frequency with which they were reported by schools in the core and ring zones, and with the questionnaire item that was used to ask about them. Note that we attach no importance to the actual percentage frequencies; these were calculated simply as a way of identifying those features that were reported more frequently than others. The list is followed by a brief discussion of these widespread features, which are identified here by their questionnaire item numbers.

---

them as demonstrative adjective (item 125: Look at them big spiders)   97.5%

should of (item 196: You should of left half an hour ago!) 91.3%

absence of plural marking (item 95: To make a big cake you need two pound of flour)   87.5%

what as subject relative pronoun (item 115: The film what was on last night was good)   86.3%

never as past tense negator (item 7: No, I never broke that) 85.0%

there was with plural 'notional' subject (item 58: There was some singers here a minute ago)   85.0%

there's with plural 'notional' subject (item 29: There's cars outside the church)   82.5%

perfect participle *sat* following BE auxiliary (item 46:

She was sat over there looking at her car)	82.5%
adverbial *quick* (item 86: I like pasta. It cooks really quick)	82.8%
ain't/in't (items 9 and 10: That ain't working/that in't working)	82.5%
give me it (item 149: Give me it, please)	82.5%
perfect participle *stood* following BE auxiliary (item 47: And he was stood in the corner looking at it)	82.5%
non-standard *was* (item 51: We was singing)	80.0%

3.5.1 Discussion

Demonstrative *them*

It came as no surprise to find that demonstrative *them* (item 125) was the most widely reported feature. Edwards and Weltens (1984: 117) found that this appeared to be a common feature of British dialects, and this conforms with the views of Hughes and Trudgill (1987) and Coupland (1988). The only schools that did not report demonstrative *them* were the two schools in Glasgow. One of these Glasgow schools reported both singular and plural *thon* (questionnaire items 130 and 126, respectively) as well as *thae* and *yon*, which suggests that the demonstrative system is different in Glasgow (and probably in Edinburgh and much of the rest of Scotland) compared to urban centres in the rest of Britain (see page 108, below).[3] This is further suggested by the fact that *this here* and *that there* were not reported by the schools in Glasgow – nor by schools in the North of England, except for one school in Newcastle upon Tyne, which reported them as used by older speakers – though they were widely reported elsewhere. *Thae* and *yon* were also reported in Woodbridge, Suffolk (a rural zone in the Ipswich region), and *thae* was reported by three schools in South-west England (two in freestanding regions – Salisbury and Swindon – and one in Wanswell, Gloucestershire, the outer region in the Bristol metropolitan area). The survey suggests, then, that with the probable exception of Scotland (note that our data are from Glasgow only), *them* is the preferred demonstrative form in the urban centres of England; it further suggests that other historical forms of the demonstrative adjective may now survive only in regions that are relatively independent of the urban centres, such as freestanding regions or the outer or rural zones of metropolitan regions.

Should of

This feature was not reported by the studies reviewed in Edwards and Weltens (1984), but we included it in the survey because we knew that it occurred in children's writing in schools in southern England, to the consternation of schoolteachers, and we wanted to discover whether its occurrence was widespread throughout Britain. There is no mention of this feature in early works on dialect nor, as far as we know, in prescriptive handbooks on English usage, and it may well be of relatively recent origin. *Should of* was reported by 73 of the 80 schools in the core and ring zones of the functional regions.[4] *Should of* appears, then, to be widespread throughout Britain.

Our questionnaire item gave *should of* in a full verbal phrase (*you should of left half an hour ago*), but it also occurs in speech in an apparently ellipted form, such as *you should of* [əv] or *you'd better of* [əv]. It seems likely that *should of* (and parallel forms such as *must of, could of* and *better of*) derives from the phonetic reduction in informal spoken English of unstressed *have* to /əv/, which is phonetically identical to unstressed *of* (in, for example, *some of that* [sʌməvðæt]). The full form in both cases is then produced as [ɒv], with the original syntactic derivation of the verbal construction apparently forgotten. It is probable that *should of* and related forms appeared first in written English, as an attempt to spell the full form of verb forms which in spoken English are usually contracted.

Two pound of flour

Edwards and Weltens (1984: 114) found that in British dialects it is 'almost a universal rule that, after numerals, nouns of measurement and quantity retain their singular form'. Examples such as *twenty foot, two pound of flour* abound in the literature. Coupland (1988) and Hughes and Trudgill (1987) agree that the absence of plural marking on nouns of measurement is very widespread. Hughes and Trudgill, however, note that *three inch* 'does not seem to occur'; Edwards and Weltens (1984: 115) found no reports of *inch* as an unmarked ‘plural form and conclude that Hughes and Trudgill ‘might be right’.

The survey questionnaire included *three inch* (96) and *twenty mile* (94), in addition to *two pound*. *Twenty mile* was reported less frequently than *two pound* (by 75.9% of the schools); and *three inch* still less frequently (by 43.7% of the schools). *Three inch* does seem to occur in urban varieties of English, then, though it is less widely reported than the other nouns of measurement that we investigated. The schools that reported its occurrence were located throughout Britain, including the two in Glasgow and the two in Wales. We conclude that absence of plural marking is indeed very widespread in urban varieties of English, but that some nouns of measurement seem more likely to be unmarked for the plural than others.

Never as past tense negator

We were not surprised to find that *never* as a past tense negator was amongst the most widely reported features in the Survey: as Cheshire (1985) points out, this feature is commonly considered to be non-standard (by, for example, Hughes and Trudgill 1987; Labov 1973; Cheshire 1982; Coupland 1988), yet it is very frequent in all varieties of English, including formal written English and spoken ‘educated’ English. There are two major ways of forming a negative sentence in English: the first involves using *not* and the auxiliary verb DO (compare, for example, *I broke the window* and *I didn't break the window*) whilst the second involves using simply *never* (compare here *I broke the window* and *I never broke the window*). *Never* invokes the concept of universal temporal negation, and this has been a favoured strategy of negation throughout the history of English (*not*, for instance, derives from *ne a wiht*, ‘not ever anything’). *Never* as a negator does not occur only with reference to past time. The following examples illustrate the use of *never* in sentences which refer to present time and to future time, respectively: *Jane never eats fish, Josephine will never get to Paris*. However, it is only its use with past tense verbs that has been proscribed by prescriptive grammarians, and presumably this prescriptive legacy accounts for the conventional view that *never* as a past tense negator is a feature of non-standard English.

I never (item 6) was reported less frequently (by 74.7% of the schools). Interestingly, all except three of the schools who reported the use of item 6 also reported item 7 (*No, I never broke that*). This suggests to us that constructions such as *I never* may derive from fuller constructions such as *I never did (it)*. Like *should of* (see above), this is a syntactically anomalous form of spoken English, which clearly does not fit easily into the analytic frameworks that are conventionally used for describing the syntactic structure of English.

Relative *what*

Relative clauses can be parenthetic (often termed non-restrictive) or restrictive. Parenthetic clauses give additional, non-essential information about the noun that they modify: for example, *the play, which I saw last night by the way, is very good*, contains a parenthetic clause *which I saw last night*. Restrictive relative clauses, on the other hand, give essential information which identify the noun that they modify: in *the play which I saw last night is very good*, the relative clause specifies the particular play that is considered to be good (see further Chapter 5, section 5.2.7). Most of the relative clauses that occur in spontaneous spoken English are restrictive, and we therefore included only restrictive relative clauses on the Survey questionnaire.

Items 110–13 (*the films what/as/at I like best are horror films*) asked about relative pronouns as object pronouns, items 115–17 asked about subject pronouns and items 118–22 asked about possessive (genitive) relative pronouns. Although Hughes and Trudgill (1987) say that the relative pronoun *what* is particularly common in urban varieties of English, Edwards and Weltens' review of research (1984: 116) found that *what* appeared to be used less frequently than other non-standard relative pronouns such as *as*, and that it did not seem to occur at all in the North of England. We were interested to find, therefore, that the schools taking part in the survey reported *what* far more frequently than any of the other non-standard relative pronoun forms, and that relative *what* was reported just as frequently in Glasgow and the North of England as in the South. *As* and *at* as relatives were reported very infrequently. *What*, then, appears to be the preferred relative pronoun in the urban centres of Britain today.

It is usually thought that in 'educated' spoken English the relative pronouns in restrictive clauses are more likely to be *that* or zero than a *wh*-form, so that speakers would prefer *the play that I saw* or *the play I saw* to *the play which I saw* (see Quirk 1968; Milroy, 1984: 23; and see later chapters, especially Chapter 4). The fact that *what* is reported very frequently in the restrictive clauses of the survey questionnaire indicates a striking difference, then, between non-standard spoken English and standard spoken English, for *wh*-forms appear to be common in the former. The *wh*-forms in question are, of course, different: in spoken standard English *who* is the subject pronoun, *whom* or *which* is the object pronoun (depending on whether the referent is animate or inanimate) and *whose* is the possessive pronoun, whereas in non-standard English the relative pronoun would be *what* as both subject and object and *what's* as possessive. Perhaps the greater simplicity of the non-standard system accounts for the fact that the *wh*-form appears to be so widespread in non-standard English.

What as subject pronoun was reported more frequently than *what* as object pronoun (item 110) or *what* as genitive pronoun (item 118). The percentage frequencies were 86.3%, 78% and 24.1% respectively. Interestingly, there was an implicational relationship between the responses, such that all schools reporting the occurrence of *what* as a genitive pronoun also reported *what* as object pronoun, and all schools reporting *what* as object pronoun also reported *what* as subject pronoun. If we accept that the survey results indicate that *what* as relative pronoun has now replaced other non-standard forms such as *as* or *at* in urban varieties of English, then this implicational relationship suggests that the introduction of the *what* forms in non-standard English has taken place in precisely the reverse order to the introduction of the *wh*-forms in standard English. Keenan and Comrie (1977) have set up an accessibility hierarchy for relative clauses, with the lower positions on the hierarchy corresponding to relative clauses that are syntactically more complex, and the higher positions corresponding to the relative clauses that are syntactically simpler. In standard English the first appearances of the *wh*-relatives were at the lower end of the accessibility hierarchy, in oblique object or genitive positions (in constructions such as *to which* or *of which*) and only in very formal styles; the subject pronoun *who* was the last to appear (see Romaine 1984). As Lass (1987: 191) points out, the presumed syntactic complexity of the lower positions on the hierarchy correlates with complexity in a stylistic sense, in that historical records show the new *wh*-forms as appearing first in the more formal, elaborate styles of written English. The non-standard relative pronoun *what*, on the contrary, which is a feature of informal, spontaneous spoken English, appears to have been introduced at the top of the accessibility hierarchy, where relativization is a less complex syntactic process, and to have been introduced subsequently at successively lower positions on the accessibility hierarchy. The questionnaire results, then, have given rise to an interesting hypothesis concerning the history of relative pronoun forms; but, of course, this hypothesis needs to be tested against recordings of real speech.

There was and *there's* with plural subject

Items 29 and 58 on the questionnaire contained *there's* and *there was* respectively, with what Quirk et al. (1985) term a plural 'pseudo-subject'. This feature illustrates clearly the difficulty of drawing a clear distinction between non-standard English and informal colloquial English: some writers consider *there was* or *there is* with a plural subject as a feature of non-standard English (see, for example, Petyt, 1985: 237; Eisikovits, 1991), yet they are attested in informal 'educated' English (Quirk et al., 1985). We included these items in the questionnaire in order to gain some idea of how widespread they were. Since they appear to be very widespread indeed, we conclude that they are best seen as a stylistic feature of English, characteristic of colloquial, informal speech, rather than as a non-standard feature. They can be considered, perhaps, as an oral strategy, similar to French *il y a* and German *es gibt*, used to signal to the addressee that new information is being introduced in the thematic position in a sentence (see further Chapter 4; and Quirk et al. 1985).

Sat and *stood* following BE auxiliary

The use of *sat* and *stood* where standard English has *sitting* and *standing*, although known and commented on, has not been considered previously to be a widespread feature of regional syntax. Hughes and Trudgill (1987) say that these forms are 'widely used in parts of the north and west of England', but

Edwards and Weltens (1984: 109) found them reported in only five areas of Britain (Manchester, North Lancashire, West Wirral, Herefordshire and Reading).

Perhaps we should have been alerted to the fact that these features are more widespread than this by the fact that they have been noticed by prescriptivists. Burchfield (1981: 55), for example, in his guide for the BBC, considers *he was sat there* as 'unacceptable in any circumstances'. As so often happens, we have become more aware of these forms since analysing their occurrence in the survey responses, and we could now give many examples of their use in educated spoken English and in written, semi-formal English. We give one example below, from the Reading local newspaper:

> The Broad Street Mall shopping complex came to a standstill on Monday when a young woman threatened to jump from the top of the multi-storey car park. The woman was *sat*, perched on the edge of the car park's surrounding wall, when she was seen by off-duty policeman. . . . (*Reading Chronicle*, 24.2.89).

Although these two features were reported by the majority of the schools taking part in the survey, there were some regional preferences. All the schools in the North of England reported their occurrence, but the two schools in Glasgow did not; and there were some schools in the South and in the Midlands that did not report them. Their occurrence was reported in 81% (N = 26) of schools in the South and 67% (N = 21) of schools in the East and West Midlands. Perhaps this distribution points to a recent diffusion of these features from the North and the West of England, so that although they once had a regional distribution, they are now becoming characteristic of a general non-standard or semi-standard variety of English. Their occurrence in written English points once again to the difficulty of identifying clearly the features that are characteristic of non-standard English rather than standard English.

We was

Was as a generalized past tense form of BE is said to be very common by Edwards and Weltens (1984: 110). As expected, the survey responses reported the occurrence of non-standard *was* throughout the urban centres of the country, but they suggested that the form is less widespread in Glasgow and in the urban centres of the North of England than it is elsewhere. Interestingly, non-standard *were* was also reported frequently, in conjunction with non-standard *was*, by schools in the North-west, Yorkshire and Humberside, and in the East and West Midlands; though Birmingham was an interesting exception (see section 3.5). Non-standard *were* was also reported as co-occurring with non-standard *was* by schools in the South (though less frequently than non-standard *was*). The negative form *Mary weren't* (item 57) was reported very frequently except, again, in Glasgow and the North of England. Ten schools (scattered throughout the country) reported the use of *Mary weren't*, but not the use of *I were* (item 55) or *so were John* (item 56). This suggests that in these varieties *were* is reserved mainly for the negative past tense form of BE, as is the case in Reading, Berkshire (see Cheshire 1982). Again, empirical studies would be needed to confirm this hypothesis. We had expected *you was* to be reported more frequently than *we was.* The form *you was*, addressed to a single individual, is said to have been common during the sixteenth to eighteenth centuries (see Petyt 1985: 237), and it seems reasonable, therefore, to assume that *we was* and *they was* are later forms, produced by analogy with *you was*. *You was* is thought to have been used to restore the distinction of number in second person verb forms, which was lost when the *thou/you* contrast disappeared. Some urban varieties of English preserve this distinction by using the plural pronoun *youse* (item 159) or by retaining *thou* forms (items 156, 157 and 158). Although we can only speculate on the origins of non-standard *was*, it is noteworthy that *youse* is more frequently reported by schools in Glasgow and the North of England, where non-standard *was* is *least* frequently reported (and where *you was* is less frequently reported than the other non-standard *was* forms). This is certainly in line with the possibility that non-standard forms of BE have developed, at least in part, as a result of the loss of the number distinction in pronouns.

Adverbial *quick*

The widespread reporting of adverbial *quick* was not unexpected. 'Adjectives with adverbial function' are included in Coupland's suggested list of seven features that are features of social dialect rather than of regional dialect; and Hughes and Trudgill (1987) claim that adverbial *quick* occurs in colloquial educated English, 'although some speakers might not accept this as standard English'. Again, then, it is impossible to distinguish between non-standard English and spoken colloquial English. It is possible that forms without the *-ly* suffix express intensity or emphasis; in American English, for example, some adverbial forms without *-ly* are used as intensifiers, as in *that's real good, it's sure fine*.

Ain't/in't

It is well known that both *ain't* and *in't* occur as negative forms of BE and HAVE, with singular and plural verb forms and with first, second and third person subjects. Edwards and Weltens (1984: 107), however, found only *in't* reported for Scots (and only in tag questions). We decided that it was unrealistic to investigate all possibilities, and included in the questionnaire only *ain't* and *in't* as third person singular forms of auxiliary BE (items 9 and 10). As expected, neither *ain't* nor *in't* was reported in Glasgow; and these forms were mentioned only rarely by schools in the North of England. Elsewhere, however, they were reported very frequently, with a preference for the *ain't* form in most places, except for the East and West Midlands.

The sentences used on the questionnaire were declarative in form (*that ain't working* and *that in't working*). Cheshire (1981) found evidence of a functional distinction between *ain't* and *in't* in Reading, Berkshire, with *in't* the preferred form in tag questions, particularly in 'aggressive' tags where the speaker was conveying hostility towards the addressee, and *ain't* the preferred form in declarative sentences. It is possible that this distinction exists in other parts of Britain, and that this accounts for the preference for the *ain't* form in the declarative sentence used on the questionnaire. However, pragmatic meanings of this kind cannot be investigated using a questionnaire; empirical investigation would be needed to test this hypothesis.

Give me it

We wanted to determine whether there was a regional distribution to the reporting of items 148 (*give it me*) and 149 (*give me it*).

Give me it is a more recent construction than *give it me*, which in turn is a more recent construction than *give it to me*, where the prepositional group *to me* reflects the function of the Old English dative case. As far as we are aware, the relative positions of direct and indirect object pronouns have never been discussed in terms of standard English and non-standard English, although Hughes and Trudgill (1987) point out that most grammatical descriptions of (standard) English state that the indirect object precedes the direct object – in other words, that the more recent *give me it* order is more usual. Hughes and Trudgill (1987) also mention that the reverse order is very common in the speech of educated people from the North of England, and is 'quite acceptable to many southern speakers'. Although irrelevant, then, to a discussion of non-standard English, the distribution of these two constructions is very relevant to the question of syntactic levelling. Data from the Survey of English Dialects, for example, are interpreted by Kirk (1985: 133–5) as representing a historical pattern of syntactic evolution, with the oldest *give it to me* forms 'taking to the hills or the coast' (ibid.: 134), the later *give it me* forms occurring in transitional areas in the West Midlands and the South, and the newer *give me it* responses intruding into the historical and transitional areas 'quite forcefully'.

We wanted to see, therefore, whether one of these constructions was reported more frequently than the other by the schools participating in the survey, since this would suggest that syntactic levelling had occurred in the urban centres of Britain. The survey responses do, in fact, suggest that the more recent *give me it* construction is now well established in urban centres throughout the country, particularly in the North and the South of England. However, there was no evidence of syntactic levelling: most schools taking part in the survey reported the use of both constructions. Five schools (scattered throughout England) reported only the older *give it me* construction (one of the four Manchester schools, one of the Nottingham schools, and the schools in Southend-on-sea, Gloucester, and Heanor and Ripley). On the other hand, nine schools reported only the newer *give me it* construction, seven of them in South-east England: four of the London schools, and the schools in Braintree, Chatham (Kent) and Crawley. The remaining two schools were in Sheffield and in Bridgend (South Wales). All these areas are identified by Kirk (1985) as transition zones, indicating, perhaps, that the newer form has now replaced the older forms in these areas. The responses obtained in the Survey of British Dialect Grammar cannot, however, be directly compared with those obtained from the SED; the questionnaire used in our survey allowed respondents to report the occurrence of both forms, whereas the Survey of English Dialects recorded only one form for each participant. We simply note, therefore, that in some urban areas, though by no means all, the newer construction appears to have ousted the older construction, but that there is no clear-cut regional distribution to the two forms; and that the newer *give me it* construction appears to be firmly established in urban centres throughout the country.

In summary, the survey responses suggest to us that this group of widespread features can be considered as characteristic of the English that is spoken in the major urban centres of Britain. Some of these features are conventionally considered to be widespread features of urban dialects of English, and the survey has been able to confirm that this is indeed the case, these are: *them* as demonstrative, absence of plural marking on nouns of measurement, *what* as relative pronoun, non-standard *was*, adverbials without the *-ly* suffix (note, however, that the questionnaire included only one such form), and *ain't/in't*.

3.5.2 Responses with a regional distribution

On the other hand, there were some features which are conventionally assumed to be widespread in urban varieties of English, but which were not reported as frequently as we had expected. These include: multiple negation; the use of simple prepositions such as *up*, *round* and *over* where standard English has complex prepositions such as *up to*, *round to* or *over at*; the regularized reflexive pronoun forms *hisself* and *theirselves*; and the past tense form *done* for full verb DO. In this section we briefly discuss the survey responses for these features.

Multiple negation

Multiple negation is typically considered to be common in most English dialects (see, for example, Edwards and Weltens, 1984: 107), including urban varieties (see Coupland 1988; Hughes and

Trudgill 1987). However, only 58 of the 80 schools participating in the survey (72.5%) reported hearing sentences such as item 2 (*count on me, I won't do nothing silly*). Table 3.2 shows the number and the percentages of urban schools that reported multiple negation.

Table 3.2:   Reports of multiple negation (questionnaire item no. 6)

	Metropolitan region	Freestanding region	Total
North	67% (N=30)	70% (N=10)	67.5% (N=40)
Midlands	55% (N=11)	100% (N=8)	73.7% (N=19)
South	93% (N=15)	80% (N=10)	88% (N=25)

It can be seen that multiple negation was reported less frequently in the North of Britain than in the Midlands, and most frequently in the South. Furthermore, although it was reported in all the freestanding regions in the Midlands, only about half of the schools in the metropolitan regions of the Midlands reported it as occurring in their locality. These schools include all four in Nottingham. Multiple negation was not reported in any of the three responses from Newcastle upon Tyne, nor by two of the three schools in the Sheffield metropolitan region.

Many different interpretations of these results could be offered. The questionnaire item may have been unsuitable in some way; or multiple negation may be less amenable than other aspects of language to investigation by questionnaire. In support of this possibility it can be pointed out that although multiple negation was not reported by the three schools in Newcastle upon Tyne, there are authoritative reports based on empirical observation which claim that it does in fact occur there (see Chapter 6). Alternatively, multiple negation may be so heavily stigmatized that despite our best efforts to raise the status of dialect in the classroom, pupils simply failed to report it. Finally, it is conceivable, of course, that multiple negation is recessive in some of the urban centres of Britain. Once more, we have to conclude that empirical research is needed in order to determine what really is happening to syntactic variation in urban varieties of English.

Prepositions

Edwards and Weltens (1984: 114) and Hughes and Trudgill (1987) note that there is a wide range of variation where prepositional usage is concerned, so that Coupland (1988) is perhaps over-generalizing when he attempts to restrict this variation to one overall tendency, that of the reduction of complex prepositions. The survey questionnaire included both the use of simple pre-positions where standard English has complex prepositions (items 106, 107 and 108: *I'm going up/down/over my friend's house later*) and the use of a complex preposition where standard English has a simple preposition (item 99: *he knocks his hat off of his head*). In both cases there was a regional distribution to the responses, with non-standard forms reported more frequently in the South of the country than in the Midlands or the North. *Off of*, in particular, was never reported in the North of England, and was reported only rarely in the North-west.

Regularization of reflexive pronouns

Edwards and Weltens (1984: 116) note that virtually all British dialects regularize the reflexive pronoun system, with the use of *hisself* and *theirselves* (176, 177) in place of the anomalous standard English forms *himself* and *themselves*. Coupland (1988) includes this as one of his seven 'social dialect features', on the grounds that it is extremely widespread in all urban dialects. Although the regularized reflexive pronoun forms were not reported as frequently as other items on the questionnaire, they were nevertheless reported relatively often. *Theirselves* was reported more often than *hisself* (by 77% and 63.2% of the urban schools, respectively). There was no regional pattern to the distribution of responses.

Past tense done

This form is usually considered to be very widespread in urban varieties of English (see, for example, Hughes and Trudgill 1987). It is thought to be used only for the lexical verb DO, which means that a formal distinction is made in the past tense between the full verb DO and the auxiliary verb, which has the past tense form *did*, as in *he done the shopping this morning, didn't he?*

Table 3.3:   Reporting of *do*, *does* and *done*

Feature	% frequency in the North (N=38)	% frequency in the Midlands (N=21)	% frequency in the South (N=26)	Total (N=85)
past tense *done*	60.5	67	92	72
aux. 3rd sing *do*	8	1	46	20
full verb *does*	16	14	50	25

Table 3.3 shows the frequency with which past tense full verb *done* (item 26), present tense full verb *does* and present tense auxiliary *do* were reported by the urban schools in our sample.

It can be seen that the past tense form *done* is reported by virtually all the schools in the South of the country, but that it is less widespread elsewhere. We found this interesting, since a tendency for the past tense form *done* to be more widespread in the South of Britain than elsewhere has not previously been recognized. Table 3.3 shows that the non-standard present tense forms *does* (full verb) and *do* (auxiliary) are also reported more frequently in the South. This is unsurprising in itself (see, for example, Edwards and Weltens 1984: 109), but it is noteworthy that there was an implicational relationship between the reporting of the past tense form *done*, the present tense full verb form *does* (item 45) and the present tense auxiliary form *do* (item 42). With only two exceptions (the schools in Manchester and Wakefield), those schools that reported item 42 (non-standard present tense auxiliary *do*) also reported item 45 (non-standard present tense full verb *does*), and those schools that reported item 45 also reported item 26 (past tense full verb *done*). In other words, these responses suggest that the functional distinction between auxiliary and full verb DO is formally marked in the present tense only in those areas where a distinction is also marked in the past tense.

The fact that the formal distinction is more widespread in the past tense forms of DO than in the present tense is, we suggest, because the past tense form *done* is a 'preferred' past tense form. Bybee and Moder (1983) provide evidence that the /ʌ/ plus nasal or velar consonant phonetic shape is a preferred schema for past tense forms in English, reflecting the way in which they are stored and accessed in the mental lexicon as well as the way in which they have developed historically; Cheshire (1991) lists a number of non-standard past tense forms that conform to this schema. The relatively widespread use of *done* as a past tense form throughout the country may be due, at least in part, to the fact that *done* conforms to a preferred psycholinguistic schema; this would then be one reason why speakers of (non-standard) English have maintained a formal distinction between the past tense form of auxiliary DO and the past tense form of the full verb DO.

The survey responses also reveal a correlation between the use of the non-standard suffixed form for lexical, or full, verbs (such as item 14: *we likes toffees*) and the existence of a formal distinction between the present tense forms of auxiliary and full verb DO: in every case, schools that reported the occurrence of the non-standard auxiliary *do* form and the non-standard full verb *does* form also reported the occurrence of the non-standard suffixed form of lexical verbs. This, then, may be a factor influencing the distinction made in some parts of Britain between the present tense forms of auxiliary DO and full verb DO: where lexical verbs have non-standard inflected present tense forms, this will include the lexical or full verb DO (but not the auxiliary verb DO); this in turn enables the functional distinction to be formally marked between present tense forms of the full verb DO and present tense forms of auxiliary DO.

3.5.3 Reduction of variation

As mentioned in section 4, the CURDS Functional Regions system is potentially very useful for dialectologists wishing to investigate patterns of linguistic variation and change in the British Isles. Although there were too few survey responses for us to make proper use of the CURDS system, we found indications that some of the dialect features that are more widespread throughout Britain are being adopted in the central zones of some of the larger urban regions, at the expense of less widespread forms. Tables 3.4 and 3.5 give an example of this. Table 3.4 shows the number of non-standard *were* forms reported in the central zone of the Birmingham metropolitan region, compared to the number of non-standard *were* forms reported by other schools in the rest of the West Midlands and in the East Midlands.

Table 3.4:   Non-standard *were* forms

Questionnare item:	55: I were singing	56: so were John	57: Mary weren't singing	Total
Birmingham	0/4	0/4	2/4	2/12
Rest of West Midlands	3/3	1/3	3/3	7/9
East Midlands	9/11	6/11	7/11	20/33

It can be seen from Table 3.4 that non-standard *were* is reported only in the negative construction (item 57) by all four schools in the central Birmingham zone, whereas other schools in the West Midlands and the East Midlands report the use of non-standard *were* in other types of construction also. As mentioned above (section 3.4.2), there were indications that *weren't* is reserved for use in negative constructions in many urban centres throughout Britain, so that in this case Birmingham would be following a tendency that is common to urban varieties of English.

Table 3.5 shows that non-standard *was*, on the other hand, is reported by schools in the West Midlands and East Midlands, including the four schools in Birmingham.

Table 3.5:   Non-standard *was* forms

Questionnare item:	49: you was singing	51: we was singing	53: they was singing	Total
Birmingham	2/4	4/4	3/4	9/12
Rest of West Midlands	2/3	3/3	2/3	7/9
East Midlands	8/11	10/11	7/11	25/33

The *Survey of English Dialects* (Orton et al. 1963–9), though not directly comparable with our survey (since it could not report variation) is a useful reference point in this instance, since it showed that non-standard *were* and non-standard *was* both occurred in the West and East Midlands. It is possible, then, that variation in the past tense forms of BE persists in the Midlands generally, but that in the core of the metropolitan region of Birmingham this variation has been reduced, resulting in the use of the preferred urban form *was*, with *were* reserved for negative constructions.

A further example of a possible reduction in variation comes from demonstrative adjective forms in the metropolitan region of Manchester. All schools in the Manchester metropolitan region reported the use of demonstrative *them*, as well as schools elsewhere in the North-west. Most of these schools also reported the use of other demonstrative adjectives, particularly *this here* and *that there*. Table 3.6 shows that in the central zone of the Manchester region, however, *this here* was reported by only one school, and that no schools in this zone reported *that there*.

Table 3.6:   Demonstrative adjectives in the north-west

	125: them	136: this here	137: that there
Manchester	4/4	1/4	0/4
Rest of Manchester metropolitan region	9/9	7/9	7/9
Others in North-west	5/5	4/5	4/5
Total	18/18	12/18	11/18

The survey responses did not suggest, however, that reduction of syntactic variation is a general process applying to all features in all urban regions. Some features show the reverse tendency, in that they were reported in the core zones of towns, but not elsewhere in the region. Table 3.7, for example, shows that schools in the core of the Manchester metropolitan region consistently reported the occurrence of the pronoun *youse*, whereas schools elsewhere in the region did not.

Table 3.7:   *Youse* in the north-west

Manchester (core)	4/4
Schools in the rest of the Manchester metropolitan region	1/9
Other schools in the North-west	1/5
Total	6/18

3.6   Conclusion

All the statements made in this chapter need to be confirmed by sociolinguistic research into the speech of the people living in the urban centres of Britain. The Survey of British Dialect Grammar was not intended to take the place of empirical investigations of language as it is used in daily life; it aimed simply to make some principled statements about the nature of dialect levelling in Britain, on a more systematic basis than has previously been possible.

One such statement, then, is that there do indeed seem to be certain grammatical features that are common to the English spoken in the major urban centres of Britain. These include the eleven features discussed in section 3.5.1 of this chapter. If standardization of language involves the suppression of variability, as we saw in Chapter 1, we should perhaps acknowledge the development of a 'standardizing' non-standard variety of English. Variation is not being reduced in every aspect of non-standard morphology and syntax, however, as we saw in section 3.5.3. Furthermore, some grammatical features that previous writers have considered to be widespread throughout Britain and that might therefore have been considered as part of a levelled variety of non-standard English appear from the survey to occur with a restricted regional distribution: as we saw in section 3.5.2, multiple negation, certain types of prepositional usage and the past tense form *done* were all reported more often in southern Britain than elsewhere.

We also identified some syntactic features that are not usually included in descriptions of widespread features of urban varieties of British English but that appear from the survey responses to occur throughout the urban centres of the country: these are *should of*; *there's* and *there was* with plural subjects; and the perfect participles *sat* and *stood* in expressions such as 'She was sat . . .'.

Given their widespread occurrence throughout the urban centres of Britain, some writers have suggested that some of the features discussed in this chapter should be thought of as 'social dialect' features rather than as regional dialect features (see, for example, Coupland 1988). We have been able to confirm that 'regional dialect' is a misnomer for many of the features discussed in this paper, but their social distribution has yet to be determined. As we saw above, the survey has demonstrated that some of our previous assumptions about the regional distribution of widespread features of urban varieties of English appear to be inaccurate; and this should caution us against making unsupported assumptions about the social distribution of such features.

The stylistic distribution of many of these features also needs to be properly investigated. Some of the features discussed in this chapter occur in some styles of written English as well as in spoken English: if they are new forms, resulting from dialect levelling, then they appear to be spreading, and will perhaps soon take their place in grammars that describe standard English: *sat* and *stood* after auxiliary BE are perhaps the most likely candidates.

A point that arose again and again in section 3.5.1 was the difficulty of applying the categories of standard English and non-standard English to specific grammatical features. The distinction became particularly problematic when it involved features that are thought to be used by all sections of society, and when the features had been attested in written English as well as in spoken English. Although from a linguistic point of view the distinction may well be irrelevant, it is a necessary one, unfortunately, for those people who have to teach and assess the use of standard English – and for those people whose language is the object of assessment. Perhaps a more relevant distinction for these purposes would be one between the grammar of present-day spoken English and the grammar of formal written English. All the features discussed in section 3.5.1 are characteristic of present-day English as it is spoken in the urban centres of Britain or 'the pivotal nodes of economic activity and social life' (see section 3.4); we can be certain that whether we consider them to be features of dialect, features of non-standard English, or features of educated colloquial English, they are just as familiar to native speakers of English as are the features that are normally considered to be typical of standard English.

Notes

1. The Survey was financed by the United Kingdom Economic and Social Research Council (Award No. C00 232264). We are very grateful to Mike Coombes (Centre for Urban and Regional Development Studies, University of Newcastle) and Paul Cheshire (Department of Economics, University of Reading) for their advice

on geographical regions; and to Manfred Görlach, Peter Trudgill and Euan Reid for their helpful comments on an earlier version of this chapter. The defects remain our own responsibility.

2. Wanswell, Glos., in the Bristol outer area, did not report item 58 (invariant *there was*); Shaftesbury, Dorset, in the Salisbury outer area, did not report items 51 (*we was*) and 95 (*two pound*); Skelmersdale, Lancs., in the Wigan outer area did not report item 115 (subject relative *what*), item 110 (object relative *what*) or item 51 (*we was*).

3. A number of grammatical features distinguished Glasgow and urban centres in the North of England from the other urban centres in the sample. These were the negative auxiliary form *dinna* (item 1 on the questionnaire), which was reported only in Glasgow, Sunderland and Peterlee, the double modal constructions in *he'll not can stay, he might can do it* and *he won't can't do it* (items 59, 60 and 61), which were reported only in Glasgow and Newcastle upon Tyne, and the non-periphrastic *think you* tag in *would he do such a thing, think you?* (item 150), which was also reported only in Glasgow and Newcastle upon Tyne. Glasgow was also distinguished by the large number of features that were not reported there but that were reported in most of the other urban centres throughout the country (including, for example, *ain't* (item 9), *in't* (item 10), *in arf* (item 20) and the past tense form *give* (item 34)). Apart from the two schools in Glasgow, no other schools in Scotland participated in the survey, and so we cannot say, on the basis of our data, to what extent Glasgow shares these features with other areas of Scotland. Miller's description of Scottish English (which he defines as spoken mainly by urban dwellers) includes *desnae* (cf. St E *does not*) and *didnae* (cf. St E *didn't*), double modal constructions and various tags (see Chapter 4).

4. Those schools that did not report *should of* were scattered throughout the country, in the North-west (Oldham and Warrington), Yorkshire and Humberside (Rotherham and Scunthorpe) the East Midlands (one of the four Nottingham responses, and Heanor and Ripley), and in the South (one of the two Oxford schools).

References

BURCHFIELD, R. (1981) *The Spoken Word* London: BBC

BURCHFIELD, R. (1985) *The English Language* Oxford: Oxford University Press

BYBEE, J. L. and MODER, C. L. (1983) Morphological classes as natural categories. *Language* 59: 251 –70

BULLOCK, SIR A. (1975) *A Language for Life*. London: HMSO

CHAMPION, T. and COOMBES, M. (1983) *Functional Regions: Definitions, Applications, Advantages*. Centre for Urban and Regional Development Studies, University of Newcastle: Factsheet 1.

CHESHIRE, J. (1981) Variation in the use of *ain't* in an urban British dialect. *Language in Society* 10 (3): 365–81

CHESHIRE, J. (1982) *Variation in an English Dialect: a Sociolinguistic Study*. Cambridge: Cambridge University Press

CHESHIRE, J. (1984) 'Indigenous non-standard English varieties and education'. In Trudgill, P. (ed.) *Language in the British Isles*. Cambridge: Cambridge University Press, pp. 546–58

CHESHIRE, J. (1985) English *never* and the problem of where grammars stop. *Polyglot* 6: fiche 1

CHESHIRE, J. (1989) Great Britain. In Ammon, U. and Cheshire, J. (eds) *Dialect and the School. Sociolinguistica: International Yearbook of European Sociolinguistics*, 3: 42–53

CHESHIRE, J. (1989) Addressee-oriented features in spoken discourse. *York Papers in Linguistics: Special Issue in Honour of R.B. LePage*, pp.49–64

CHESHIRE, J. (1991) 'As the ancient author would have wrote': past tense verb forms in non-standard English. In Blank, Claudia (ed.) *Language and Civilisation*, Vol. 2. Frankfurt: Peter Lang. pp. 11–24

CHESHIRE, J., EDWARDS, V. and WHITTLE, P. (1989) Urban British dialect grammar: the question of dialect levelling. *English Worldwide* 10: 185–226

COUPLAND, N. (1988) *Dialect in Use: Sociolinguistic Variation in Cardiff English*. Cardiff: University of Wales Press

DES (Department of Education and Science) (1984) *English from 5–16. Curriculum Matters 1*. London: HMSO

EDWARDS, J. (1979) *Language and Disadvantage*. London: Edward Arnold

EDWARDS, V. (1979) *The West Indian Language Issue in British Schools: Challenges and Responses*. London: Routledge

EDWARDS, V. (1983) *Language in Multicultural Classrooms*. London: Batsford

EDWARDS, V. and CHESHIRE, J. (1989) The Survey of British dialect grammar. In Cheshire, J., Edwards, V., Münstermann, H., and Weltens, B. (eds) *Dialect and Education: Some European Perspectives*. Clevedon: Multilingual Matters, pp. 200–15

EDWARDS, V., TRUDGILL, P. and WELTENS, B. (1984) *The Grammar of English Dialect: a Survey of Research*. London: Economic and Social Research Council

EDWARDS, V. and WELTENS, B. (1984) Research on non-standard dialects of British English: Progress and prospects. In Viereck, W. (ed.) *Focus on: England and Wales*. Amsterdam: Benjamins, pp. 97–139

EISIKOVITS, E. (1991) Variation in subject-verb agreement in inner Sydney English. In Cheshire, J. (ed.) *English Around the World: Sociolinguistic Perspectives*. Cambridge: Cambridge University Press, pp. 235–55

HAWKINS, E. (1985) *Awareness of Language*. Cambridge: Cambridge University Press

HARRIS, J. (1985) *Phonological Variation and Change*. Cambridge: Cambridge University Press

HUDSON, R. (1983) *Sociolinguistics*. Cambridge: Cambridge University Press

HUGHES, G.A. and TRUDGILL, P. (1987) *English Accents and Dialects: an Introduction to Social and Regional Varieties of English*. London: Edward Arnold

JONES, A. (1989) Language awareness in British schools. In Cheshire, J., Edwards, V., Münstermann, H., and Weltens, B. (eds) *Dialect and Education: Some European Perspectives*. Clevedon: Multilingual Matters, pp. 269–84

KEENAN, E. and COMRIE, B. (1977) Noun phrase accessibility and universal grammar. *Linguistic Inquiry* 8: 63–99

KIRK, J. (1985) Linguistic atlases and grammar: the investigation and description of regional variation in English syntax. In Kirk, J., Sanderson, S. and Widdowson, J. D. A. (eds) (1985) *Studies in Linguistic Geography*. London: Croom Helm, pp. 130–56

LABOV, W. (1973) Where do grammars stop? In Shuy, R. (ed.) *Sociolinguistics: Current Trends and Prospects*. Washington, DC: Georgetown University Press, pp. 43–88

LASS, R. (1987) *The Shape of English*. London: Dent

MACAFEE, C. (1980) *Characteristics of Non-standard Grammar in Scotland*. Manuscript.

MILROY, J. (1982) Probing under the tip of the iceberg: phonological 'normalization' and the shape of speech communities. In Romaine, S. (ed.) *Sociolinguistic Variation in Speech Communities*. London: Edward Arnold, pp. 35–48

MILROY, J. (1984) The history of English in the British Isles. In Trudgill, P. (ed.) *Language in the British Isles*. Cambridge: Cambridge University Press, pp. 5–31

MILROY, L. (1984) Urban dialects in the British Isles. In Trudgill, P. (ed.) *Language in the British Isles*. Cambridge: Cambridge University Press, pp. 219–18

ORTON, H., BARRY, M.V., HALLIDAY, W.J., TILLING, P.M. and WAKELIN, M.F. (1963–9) *Survey of English Dialects*, 4 vols. Leeds: E. J. Arnold

ORTON, H., SANDERSON, S. and WIDDOWSON J. (eds) (1978) *The Linguistic Atlas of England*. London: Croom Helm

PETYT, K.M. (1985) *Dialect and Accent in Industrial West Yorkshire*. Amsterdam: Benjamins

QUIRK, R. (1968) Relative clauses in educated spoken English. In Quirk, R. *Essays in the English Language Medieval and Modern*. London: Longman, pp. 94–108

QUIRK, R., GREENBAUM, S., LEECH, G. and SVARTVIK, J. (1985) *A Comprehensive Grammar of English*. London: Longman

ROMAINE, S. (1984) Towards a typology of relative clause formation strategies in Germanic. In Fisiak, J. (ed.) *Historical Syntax*. Berlin: Mouton

SWANN, LORD (1985) *Education for All*. London: HMSO

WAKELIN, M. (1984) Rural dialects in English. In Trudgill, P. (ed.) *Language in the British Isles*. Cambridge: Cambridge University Press, pp. 70–93

Appendix 3.1: Questionnaire used in the Survey of British Dialect Grammar

No, no a thousand times no!

1. ☐ **Dinna** run too fast
2. ☐ Count on me, I **won't** do **nothing** silly
3. ☐ You **shouldna** go in there!
4. ☐ You've **no** to go in there!
5. ☐ **Anyone** mustn't go in there
6. ☐ My friend broke that, **I never**
7. ☐ No, I **never** broke that
8. ☐ **Will you not** try to mend it – we need an expert
9. ☐ That **ain't** working
10. ☐ That **in't** working
11. ☐ That **ay** working

Got a sweet tooth?

12. ☐ I **likes** toffees
13. ☐ We **liken** toffees
14. ☐ We **likes** toffees
15. ☐ Thee **likes** toffees
16. ☐ Thee **like** toffees
17. ☐ She **like** toffees

What an idiot!

18. ☐ Billy **be** stupid
19. ☐ Billy **am** stupid
20. ☐ He **in arf** stupid
21. ☐ **He's stupid, him**
22. ☐ **It's stupid he is**
23. ☐ **There's stupid he is**
24. ☐ **He's stupid is Billy**
25. ☐ **It was stupid he was**
26. ☐ He **done** that wrong
27. ☐ You **has** to see it to believe it

Wedding Bells

28. ☐ Mary and John **is** getting married on Saturday.
29. ☐ There's cars outside the Church
30. ☐ The bride's walking into the Church, is it?
31. ☐ I'm going to see them now, isn't it?
32. ☐ I **done bought** them a wedding present.

Happy Birthday!

33. ☐ We always **has** a big cake on our birthday
34. ☐ I **give** her a birthday present yesterday
35. ☐ I **gived** her a birthday present yesterday
36. ☐ What **have** her mother bought her?
37. ☐ We've **gotten** her a present, too – a car!
38. ☐ Is that the car I **see** last night?
39. ☐ Is that the car I **seed** last night?
40. ☐ Is that the car I **sawed** last night?
41. ☐ Is that the car I **seen** last night?
42. ☐ **Do** it go fast?
43. ☐ **Does** we want to go fast?
44. ☐ Fred **do** motor mechanics at college.
45. ☐ But I **does** it at school
46. ☐ She was **sat** over there looking at her car
47. ☐ And he was **stood** in the corner looking at it
48. ☐ I've **a-found** my keys. Let's go!

Music is the food of love

49. ☐ You **was** singing
50. ☐ You **wan** singing
51. ☐ We **was** singing
52. ☐ We **wan** singing
53. ☐ They **was** singing
54. ☐ They **wan** singing
55. ☐ I **were** singing, too.
56. ☐ And so **were** John.
57. ☐ But Mary **weren't** singing
58. ☐ There **was** some singers here a minute ago

59. ☐ One of the singers said he'll **not can** stay
60. ☐ But he **might can** do it tomorrow.
61. ☐ The other one said he **won't can't** do it.
62. ☐ You **must** be at your music class by 9 a.m.
63. ☐ You **mun** be at your music class by 9 a.m.
64. ☐ You **maun** be at your music class by 9 a.m.
65. ☐ He's out of tune, he **must** be tone deaf.
66. ☐ He's out of tune, he **mun** be tone deaf
67. ☐ He's out of tune, he **maun** be tone deaf

Do as I tell you!

68. ☐ You **haven't got to** be late, or you'll be in trouble
69. ☐ **Let you be listening** to me, Joanna.
70. ☐ **Do ee listen** to me
71. ☐ **Don't be talking** like that
72. ☐ **Not do that**, John

Running repairs

73. ☐ I've come **for to** mend the window
74. ☐ And I've come **for** mend the door.
75. ☐ We **managed mend** it ourselves.
76. ☐ We'd like to **looken** at the TV you broke
77. ☐ How the dog **do jumpy**! He'll knock it over.
78. ☐ I **know** that builder all my life.

79. ☐ She's been a walking disaster **since she's here**
80. ☐ **Are you waiting** long for the plumber?
81. ☐ **He's after going.**
82. ☐ He **has it mended** twice already

Food Glorious food

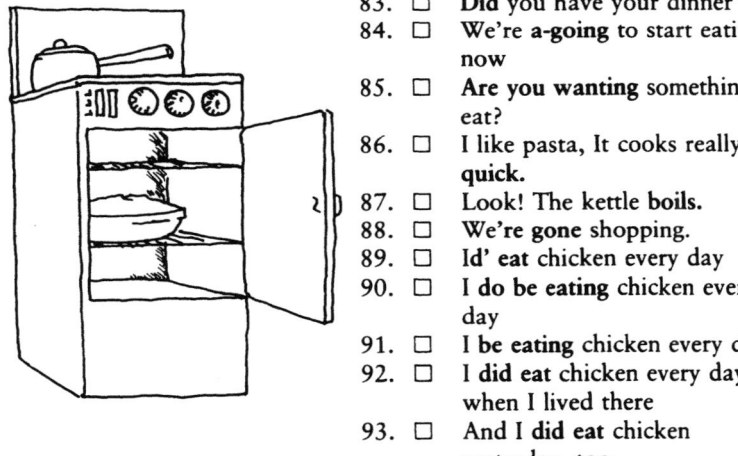

83. ☐ **Did** you have your dinner yet?
84. ☐ We're **a-going** to start eating now
85. ☐ **Are you wanting** something to eat?
86. ☐ I like pasta, It cooks really **quick.**
87. ☐ Look! The kettle **boils.**
88. ☐ We're **gone** shopping.
89. ☐ **Id' eat** chicken every day
90. ☐ **I do be eating** chicken every day
91. ☐ **I be eating** chicken every day
92. ☐ **I did eat** chicken every day when I lived there
93. ☐ And I **did eat** chicken yesterday, too.

Count down

94. ☐ That town is nearly twenty **mile** away
95. ☐ To make a big cake you need two **pound** of flour
96. ☐ This string is three **inch** long
97. ☐ This is a **scissors**

Up and Over

98. ☐ He **ups** and gets at him
99. ☐ He knocks his hat **off of** his head
100. ☐ Stop it! He's my best friend, **like**
101. ☐ Goodbye, I'll **away** now
102. ☐ She goes to church **of** a Sunday
103. ☐ If you **had've** been there you would have seen her
104. ☐ If you **would've** been there, you would have seen her
105. ☐ We live **aside** the cinema.
106. ☐ We're **going** pictures
107. ☐ I'm going **up** my friend's house later
108. ☐ I'm going **down** my friends house later
109. ☐ I'm going **over** my friend's house later

Scared stiff

110. ☐ The films **what** I like best are horror films
111. ☐ The films **as** I like best are horror films
112. ☐ The films **at** I like best are horror films
113. ☐ Let's go to that film that you wanted to see **it**
114. ☐ I've got a friend can watch films all night
115. ☐ The film **what** was on last night was good
116. ☐ The film **at** was on last night was good
117. ☐ The film **as** was on last night was good
118. ☐ That's the girl **what's** mum loves horror films

119. ☐ That's the girl **at's her** mum loves horror films
120. ☐ That's the girl **as her** mum loves horror films
121. ☐ That's the girl **what her** mum loves horror films
122. ☐ That's the girl **that her** mum loves horror films
123. ☐ **Himself** gets scared
124. ☐ Did you see **herself** there?
125. ☐ Look at **them** big spiders
126. ☐ Look at **thon** spiders
127. ☐ Look at **they** big spiders
128. ☐ Look at **this** big spiders
129. ☐ And at **yon** big beetle
130. ☐ And at **thon** worm
131. ☐ Look at **thir** spider.
132. ☐ Look at **thick** spider.
133. ☐ Look at **thicky** spider.
134. ☐ Look at **thuck** spider.
135. ☐ Look at **theasum** spider.
136. ☐ And at **this here** worm
137. ☐ And at **that there** creature.

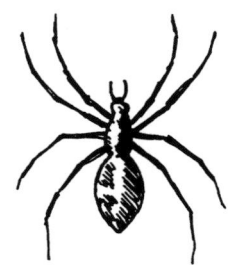

Possession is nine tenths of the law

138. ☐ Look at these coins. I found about **a fifty** of them.
139. ☐ That's the father **on** Mary
140. ☐ Don't break the **cup's handle**
141. ☐ That's the **dogs's** dinner
142. ☐ These are my **father boots**
143. ☐ These are my father **boots laces**
144. ☐ Who is this book **belonging** to?
145. ☐ This is my book. **Whosen** is that?
146. ☐ **It cover's** got a mark on it.
147. ☐ **O'it cover's** got a mark on it.
148. ☐ **Give it me.** That's my book
149. ☐ **Give me it,** please

150. ☐ Would he do such a thing, **think you**?
151. ☐ I asked him **did he know** who had taken it?

Who's who?

152. ☐ **Her's** got a good appetite
153. ☐ **Him's** got a good appetite
154. ☐ **Them's** got a good appetite
155. ☐ **Me's** got a good appetite
156. ☐ Eat up **thee** cake
157. ☐ Eat up **thy** cake
158. ☐ **Thee's** hungry, I expect
159. ☐ Are **youse** hungry, too, you boys over there?
160. ☐ Give **I** a cup of tea!
161. ☐ Give **he** a cup of tea!
162. ☐ Give **she** a cup of tea!
163. ☐ Give **we** a cup of tea!
164. ☐ Give **they** a cup of tea!
165. ☐ This is **me** cup
166. ☐ This is **o'me** cup
167. ☐ This is **mines** cup
168. ☐ This is **he's** cup
169. ☐ That's my car, where's **yourn**?
170. ☐ That's my car, where's **hisn**?
171. ☐ That's my car, where's **hern**?
172. ☐ This is **us** car
173. ☐ This is **wer** car
174. ☐ This is **wir** car
175. ☐ We service it **usselves**
176. ☐ John likes doing that **hisself**, too
177. ☐ Yes, lots of people do it **theirselves**

Property page

178. ☐ This is the **beautifullest** house I've seen
179. ☐ This is the **most beautifullest** house I've seen
180. ☐ I've never seen a **beautifuller** one
181. ☐ I've never seen a **more beautifuller** one
182. ☐ This is a **more better** one
183. ☐ This is a **more betterer** one
184. ☐ John's got a nice house, but yours is **more nice**
185. ☐ But this is the **worstest** one I've seen
186. ☐ But this is the **baddest** one I've seen
187. ☐ I've never seen a **worser** one
188. ☐ I've never seen a **badder** one
189. ☐ We've got **a old** house
190. ☐ We've got **old** house
191. ☐ Your house is **an recent one**
192. ☐ I'd like to buy this house **without** you want it
193. ☐ I'll have **the headache** if I carry on talking
194. ☐ Yes, change the subject, **else** I'll go mad
195. ☐ Look **at time**: you're late for school!
196. ☐ You should **of** left half an hour ago!

Appendix 3.2: Regions represented in the Survey

CURDS ref.	Region	zone	CURDS ref.	Region	zone
ABB1	Blackburn	core	OBD2	Bradford	ring
ABB1	Blackburn	ring	OBH1	Bournemouth & Poole	core
BB11	Birmingham	core	ODE1	Derby	core
BB11	Birmingham	core	OEX2	Exeter	ring
BB11	Birmingham	core	OGL1	Gloucester	core
BB11	Birmingham	core	OGL2	Gloucester	ring
BRD6	Redditch	rural	OGR1	Grimsby	core
CBJ1	Bridgend	core	OHG1	Harrogate	core
FNG1	Nottingham	core	OIP6	Ipswich	rural
FNG1	Nottingham	core	OKE1	Keighley	core
FNG1	Nottingham	core	OKE1	Kings Lynn	core
FNG1	Nottingham	core	OLB1	Loughborough	core
FRP1	Heanor & Ripley	core	OLE1	Leicester	core
GGG1	Glasgow	core	ONN2	Northampton	ring
GGG1	Glasgow	core	ONN1	Northampton	core
IBC1	Braintree	core	OOX2	Oxford	ring
ICY1	Crawley	core	OOX2	Oxford	ring
ILO1	London	core	OSC1	Scunthorpe	core
ILO1	London	core	OSN1	Swindon	core
ILO1	London	core	OSN3	Swindon	outer area
ILO1	London	core	OSO1	Southampton	core
ILO1	London	core	OSP3	Salisbury	outer area
ILO2	London	ring	OSR1	Sunderland	core
IME1	Medway towns	core	OSR1	Sunderland	core
ISS1	Southend on Sea	core	OSR1	Sunderland	core
LW11	Widnes & Runcorn	core	OWK1	Worksop	core
LWN3	Wigan	outer area	OWQ1	Workington	core
MAH1	Ashton & Hyde	core	OWR1	Worcester	core
MBL1	Bolton	core	RPR1	Preston	core
MBU1	Bury	core	SRT1	Rotherham	core
MLG1	Leigh	core	SSH1	Sheffield	core
MMC1	Manchester	core	SSH2	Sheffield	ring
MMC1	Manchester	core	TPQ1	Peterlee	core
MMC1	Manchester	core	TTS1	Stockton on Tees	core
MMC1	Manchester	core	TTS1	Stockton on Tees	core
MMC2	Manchester	ring	VCV2	Coventry	ring
MOL1	Oldham	core	WSA1	Swansea	core
MSK1	Stockport	core	WSA2	Swansea	ring
MWA1	Warrington	core	XBN1	Brighton	core
NNE1	Newcastle upon Tyne	core	XBN3	Brighton	outer area
NNE1	Newcastle upon Tyne	core	YWF1	Wakefield	core
NNE1	Newcastle upon Tyne	core	YWF1	Wakefield	core
OBD1	Bradford	core	ZBS3	Bristol	outer area

Part II

Regional Variation in English Grammar: Case Studies

4 The Grammar of Scottish English

Jim Miller

4.1 Introduction: Scottish English

Specifying Scottish English can seem as tricky as the party game in which, blindfolded, you have to pin a tail on the drawing of a donkey. For example, many words that Scots consider typically Scottish are common to all varieties of Northern English and some occur quite far away, such as *bide* (= 'stay'), which turns up in Hardy's novels. Another example is the use of *though* at the end or in the middle of a clause and used by the speakers to concede that such-and-such is indeed the case in spite of their expectations to the contrary: e.g. *It's cauld the day, though* (= 'It's cold today but who would have expected it'). This construction is very frequent in the speech of Scottish speakers but it occurs outside Scotland and is given in the Longman Dictionary of Contemporary English.

The solution to the problem of shared vocabulary and constructions is not to throw away the concept of Scottish English but to accept that the geographical varieties of non-standard English should be viewed as intersecting sets of constructions. Scottish English may share one construction with Tyneside English, a second with Hiberno-English and a third with the West Midlands, but it may be alone in possessing all three constructions. On a wider scale, we would have to recognize that Scottish English shares constructions with the English of Canada and the southern United States.

The problem of constructions whose status is indeterminate – not clearly Scottish English but not clearly standard written English either – can be handled by adopting the concept of a continuum.

At one end of the continuum is Broad Scots (a term widely used in Scotland) and at the other end is standard written English. Without trying to establish a range of intermediate varieties, we can locate individual constructions in between the two poles. The essential point is that Scottish speakers draw on Broad Scots and standard written English to varying degrees, depending on degree of formality (topic, location of conversation, participants in the conversation) but also on the inclinations of the individual speaker. Some speakers draw on Broad Scots very little, others a great deal; and even within one situation code-switching occurs. (Cf. the comments in Macafee (1983: 18–25).)

This chapter concentrates on the colloquial language, which tends towards the 'Broad Scots' end of the continuum. However, as it is not our purpose here to define and delimit different varieties, we will use the terms 'Scots' 'Broad Scots' and 'Scottish English' fairly freely in reference to our data. Since 1974 spontaneous conversational and narrative data has been collected in Glasgow, Edinburgh and Ayrshire by Macafee (1983), Brown et al. (1980), Romaine (1975), Reid (1976), Brown and Miller (1980), Macaulay (1987, 1991). Macafee draws on language she has herself recorded, together with data from dialogue in plays and novels, cartoon strips, and radio interviews. Romaine and Reid have recorded conversation from schoolchildren; Macaulay has recorded narratives from working- and middle-class Ayrshire adults; Brown and Miller recorded and transcribed on to computer files 250,000 words of conversation, narrative and jokes.

The Scots described here is based on the Brown–Miller data, cross-checked with data from the other sources mentioned above, and supplemented with data collected by various elicitation techniques and from informal observations – that is, data collected on the hoof with notebook and pencil, but not recorded on tape and not publicly observable. Another source of data is the corpus of dialogues collected by Anne Anderson and Simon Garrod in the Department of Psychology, University of Glasgow (we shall refer to these as 'map-task dialogues'). The task involved pairs of people playing a game in which one person has a map with landmarks and a route on it and the other person has a map with landmarks (not necessarily the same) but no route, just a starting point. The first person has to instruct the second person to draw the route. Further examples are from written work by secondary school pupils. (Further cross-checking involved the earlier descriptions by Grant and Main-Dixon (1921) and Wilson (1915).)

In the account that follows, where examples are from conversation, there is a minimum of punctuation to indicate pauses but no capital letters or full stops. Where examples are from written work, the original version is given.

4.1.1 Some historical remarks

Scots is distinguished from other non-standard varieties of English by having been the language of the Scottish court until 1603, when James VI inherited the English throne. It was the language of government and judiciary and the vehicle of a small but first-rate mediaeval literature. After the removal of the Scottish court to London, Scots ceased to be a language of government, but many scholars see the major cause of its decline as the introduction of an English Bible (as opposed to one in Scots).

The language continued to be used for poetry, by a number of minor figures as well as by the major poets, Burns and McDiarmid. This is an important aspect of Scottish English, because many educated speakers learn Scots poetry at school and use Scots words and phrases in certain contexts, including writing. The latest major contribution to Scottish Literature is a Scots New Testament (Lorimer, 1983), the product of many years' work by a former Professor of Greek at the University of St Andrews. Although four hundred years too late, it is used regularly (not necessarily frequently) in some churches: sadly, not all the vocabulary is understood by all members of the congregations.

Mediaeval Scottish literature draws our attention to an important fact: grammar and vocabulary are independent of each other. Mediaeval Scottish poetry displays Scots syntax and morphology combined with Greco-Latinate vocabulary, the combination being handled with great skill. One moral to be drawn is that speakers of non-standard English do not need to abandon their native grammar in order to acquire a large vocabulary and rhetorical skills.

Varieties of 'Broad' Scots are now spoken quite widely by urban dwellers. It is often asserted in letters to newspapers that modern urban Broad Scots is a mere gutter-language, a highly degenerate form of earlier Scots – doubtless the other non-standard varieties of

English are held to be degenerate. This view is quite wrong. In the first place, urban varieties of English are systematic in their own way. This will be demonstrated with respect to Scottish English, and where appropriate attention will be drawn to features of Broad Scots which might be considered idiosyncratic but which are common in other standard languages.

In the second place, the modern urban varieties of English are not new-born mongrels: at least, there is good evidence that urban Broad Scots is not, and there is no reason to suppose that the others are different. The evidence comes from two monographs – Murray (1873) and Wilson (1915). Both are descriptions of rural varieties and both show that many constructions frequent in modern Scottish English, such as relative clause and modal verb structures, were the norm for these rural varieties a hundred years and more ago. This historical pedigree extends to features that might be seen as accidents of conversation, such as the 'shadow pronouns' in relative clauses (cf. section 4.3.3).

Of course, any variety of a language changes over time, and Scots is no exception. Pronunciation has changed in various respects, and a very large number of lexical items have been lost, even by the oldest speakers. In contrast, the basic grammar is much the same. It is worthwhile mentioning again the long history of the non-standard varieties. Political and economic accidents have ensured that certain varieties became non-standard, but that does not nullify their linguistic history or their standing as linguistic systems. Broad Scots is fortunate in having its earlier stages partly recorded in written texts.

4.1.2 Attitudes to Scots

We must take account of two sets of attitudes towards non-standard English: those of teachers, employers and the 'establishment', and those of the speakers of non-standard English, here represented by the majority of the population of Scotland.

One important point is that the outstanding question for many speakers is what counts as 'good' English, written or spoken. It affects most people whose written or spoken words are to be exposed to public scrutiny, and it looms very large in schools, even if a number of teachers are generous as to what they accept from their pupils by way of language. But even for teachers who tolerate non-standard English it is important to know what is a systematic feature of a particular non-standard variety as opposed to the idiosyncratic usage of a particular pupil. If teachers lack this knowledge, pupils may not understand why aspects of their native tongue are stigmatized as errors – a point that has been discussed in Chapter 1 (see section 1.12).

Just as important for success in education and employment are the attitudes of the speakers themselves. Researchers say, on the basis of experiments, that from an early age children who speak non-standard English associate standard English with intelligence and leadership but associate their own variety with friendliness, warmth and trustworthiness. On a BBC television programme broadcast in 1985, dictionary makers claimed that people looked to dictionaries for linguistic guidance and required a standard language for linguistic security. It was also asserted that in fifty years the geographical non-standard varieties would have disappeared, to be replaced by standard English.

Statements like the above are far from being the whole story. They take no account of the fact that every geographical variety of English has an educated version in addition to the 'broadest' version. For instance, a number of prominent Members of Parliament are Scots, with unmistakable Scottish pronunciation, but are taken seriously by studio audiences, other Members of Parliament and the national newspapers. Furthermore, local communities in Britain, far from abandoning their own varieties of English, are usually proud of their language.

Researchers on language-attitudes may well run into two barriers: the tendency of speakers of non-standard varieties to deprecate their language in the presence of outsiders, especially educated outsiders; and the speed with which children learn at primary school what opinions will gain public approval and what ones are best confined to their close friends.

These points are doubtless controversial, but certain facts are clear. Many speakers of non-standard varieties (the bulk of the population) do not actively look for linguistic leadership and do not abandon their own variety of English. This is not to deny that everybody is to some extent affected by social distinctions, but as demonstrated in Milroy and Milroy (1978), the speakers of one social group may change their linguistic habits under the influence of other groups speaking non-standard English. Finally, as shown by the experience of teachers at least in Scotland, immense hostility to school and education is engendered by the inevitable linguistic clashes in the classroom.

4.1.3   Applications to educational testing

At the time of writing, a national curriculum has been developed for schools in England and Wales and a system of national tests is being prepared. In Scotland, because the leaving certificate examinations are prepared and organized centrally, there has in effect been a national curriculum in secondary schools, but national tests too are to be introduced at age 8, 11 and 14. Scotland has for the past six years been introducing what are called Standard Grade examinations to be taken by pupils at the end of their fourth year of secondary schooling. Since 1960 the proportion of pupils at Scottish schools sitting at least one subject at Higher or O-Grade has risen to 80% and the new Standard Grade is to be taken by every pupil. It must be emphasized that the Standard Grade examination is on three levels. Credit level, which is harder than the current O-Grade, will be taken by a small number of very able pupils, and the Credit courses are designed to stretch them. Pupils of average ability will take General level examinations, and the least academically successful pupils will take Foundation level examinations.

One major goal of the Standard Grade examinations is to encourage more pupils to stay on at school and to obtain skills, knowledge and formal qualifications. The achievement of this goal is essential in our society with its demand for skilled workers and the lack of the traditional type of manual jobs. Already, however, language problems have been revealed. For instance, many Foundation level candidates cannot cope with the complex language in which mathematics and examination problems are written. The difficulties extend from an excess of Greco-Latinate vocabulary and concise but complex syntax to simple but destructive differences between standard English and Scottish English. One misunderstanding, which was explicitly dealt with in a document circulated to schools by the Scottish Examination Board, related to a mathematics question at Foundation Level, which asked candidates *how* they had carried out a particular calculation. The purpose of the question was to elicit an account of the steps involved in the calculation, but instead it elicited justifications for the calculation. The reason is simple: in Scottish English *how* is equivalent to standard English *why*, so candidates understood it to be asking *why* they had carried out the calculation.

The first Foundation Level examination indicated that attention would have to be paid to the pupils' command of English. In particular, the language of the mathematics teaching texts and of the examination questions would have to be considered, and thought would have to be given to improving the pupils' knowledge and control of standard English without alienating them. The problems have now been exacerbated, not so much by the National Curriculum as by the national tests.

Let us accept that one major task of the schools is to teach children formal written English – the word *written* is emphasized – since without a knowledge of written English, people are excluded from major activities in society, not least the exercise of political power. The task of learning written English is difficult enough for children who come from homes where there are books, where reading is encouraged and where the parents use standard syntax and vocabulary, or an approximation to them. The task is immeasurably greater for children who come from homes with no or few books, where reading is not a normal activity and where the parents and other relatives speak non-standard English. Indeed, one of the goals of the later sections of this chapter is to demonstrate the large and systematic differences in grammar between Broad Scots, as a representative of non-standard English, and standard English. Children whose native tongue is non-standard English have to scale certain barriers. They have to adjust their pronunciation – not to RP in Scottish schools – but towards some type of educated Scottish pronunciation. They have to adjust their own spoken language and adjust to the spoken language of the teachers and other pupils. And they have to learn formal written English.

It is not clear why it is so important for such children to have reached a certain stage in their mastery of written English by age 8. The fact is that children from homes with books and standard or close-to-standard English will, as always, pass tests with ease, while the children who will feel the strain are the very ones who are to be encouraged to stay on to swell the ranks of the skilled workers.

It is worthwhile noting in passing that language is one subject on which politicians and industrialists are allowed to control policy from a position of profound ignorance. In particular, the latter group do not realize that no comparison with the past is possible. The people who forty years ago would have not thought of going on to higher education of any sort now strive to pass the Leaving Certificate and go on to further study. The clerks and clerkesses of the past correspond to the administrative assistants and computer operators of tomorrow, and the unskilled workers of the past correspond to the clerks and clerkesses of today. The consequence is that schools are trying to teach formal written English to a set of pupils whose counterparts in the past would not have been called on to take formal written tests and to display a public mastery of written English. These pupils are among the heaviest users of non-standard English, and their difficulties are closely implicated in the following description of Broad Scots.

4.2 Morphology

4.2.1 Introduction

Before we start the account of Scots, the reader's attention is drawn to the glossary at the end of Part II. Since the description of language, like the description of flora, fauna, rocks and so forth, requires special concepts and vocabulary, a minimum of technical terms cannot be avoided. The glossary explains the less familiar terms.

Morphology deals with the shapes of words. Here we will concentrate on the past tense forms of verbs, past participles, plural nouns and some pronouns. (The list of words below is merely illustrative.)

With respect to Table 4.1, *seen, done* and *taen* result from a tendency to generalize the past participle form to the past tense. This process has happened in several varieties of non-standard English and is described in other chapters. Had it applied to all irregular verbs, they would have been brought into line with the regular verbs: cf. *She played tennis* and *She has played tennis. Sellt* and *tellt* indicate that irregular verbs can be made regular. *Sellt* is simply *sell + ed, ed* being realized as *t* in Scottish English after *l* and *n* – cf. *killt* (= killed).

With respect to Table 4.2, *broke* and *forgot* occur in earlier stages of standard English. *Went* as a past participle has a long history, occurring in Dunbar's poem 'Celebrations', (end of the fifteenth century). *Gave* and *knew* are 'foreign': the original verbs, still very much alive among older speakers and in rural areas, are *gie*, with past tense *gied* and past participle *gien*, and *ken*, with *kent* as past tense and past participle.

Table 4.1:   Past tense forms of verbs

seen (=saw)	*taen* (=took)	*come* (=came)
done (=did)	*killt* (=killed)	*sellt* (=sold)
tellt (=told)	*brung* (=brought)	*sunk* (=sank)

Table 4.2:   Past participles

broke (=broken)	*gave* (=given)	*took* (=taken)
went (=gone)	*forgot* (=forgotten)	*fell* (=fallen)
saw (=seen)	*knew* (=known)	*feart* (=frightened)
froze (=frozen)	*beat* (=beaten)	*came* (=come)

4.2.2   Plural nouns

Earlier stages of Broad Scots had plural forms not found in standard English, such as *een* (= eyes), *shin* (= shoes) and *treen* (= trees). In modern Scottish English the forms that are frequent and worthy of note are the equivalents of the standard plurals *wives*, etc. The Scottish English forms are *wifes, knifes, lifes, leafs, thiefs, loafs, wolfs.* That is, the relationship between singular and plural is regular, unlike the standard English relationship: *wife* and *wives*, but not *rooves*. (And is it *hoofs* or *hooves?*)

Speakers are generally more aware of the verb forms than the plural nouns. This may be partly because the differences are more noticeable, but the verb forms are a major shibboleth for all with educational or social pretensions. Speakers with higher education (not all, of course) do use the Scottish plurals in speech but avoid the verb forms.

4.2.3   Pronouns

Scots has a second person plural *yous* or *yous yins*, very frequent and assiduously avoided by educated speakers even in informal situations. As in other non-standard varieties, *us* is regularly used instead of *me*, particularly with verbs such as *give, show,* and *lend*: e.g. *Can you lend us a quid?* This usage can be found among educated speakers in informal situations (but see particularly Chapter 6).

The first person singular possessive pronoun is *mines* (not *mine*) when it is the complement of the sentence. *Mines* makes the possessive pronouns uniform in having an *-s* ending: *It's yours/his/hers/ours/theirs/mines.*

The reflexive pronouns have likewise been made regular. Instead of *himself* and *themselves*, there is *hisself* and *theirselves*, which are on the same pattern as *yourself, herself, myself,* and *ourselves*, which consist of a possessive form + *self* or *selves*. The reflexive forms are general in non-standard English.

Note the construction exemplified by *Me and Jimmy are on on Monday our two selves* (= by ourselves). *Two* is inserted between *our* and *selves*, which raises the question as to whether *myself*, etc. should be considered as one word or two.

4.2.4   Demonstrative adjectives

Corresponding to standard English *those*, Scots has *thae* (pronounced like *they*), as in *Thae cakes was awfy dear* (= These cakes were very dear). *Thae* is still very much alive but has a competitor in *them*: *Them cakes was awfy dear.* (*Thae* and *they* derive from different words in Early English.)

4.2.5   Adverbs

Like all Germanic languages (except standard English), Broad Scots does not add *-ly* to adjectives to create adverbs. Instead the same form functions as adjective and adverb: *They got on real good, Drive slow* (on a sign at a roadworks). In this respect, Broad Scots resembles all non-standard varieties of English.

4.3 Syntax

Syntax deals with the ways in which words combine to create phrases and sentences.

4.3.1 Number agreement

Plural subject nouns usually combine with *is* and *was*.

(1) the windies wiz aw broken (= The windows were all broken)
(2) the lambs is oot the field (= The lambs are out of the field)

Wiz turns up with *we*, as in *we wiz aw asleep* (= We were all asleep), but *we were* is frequent. *We is* does not occur.

The above construction is avoided by educated speakers but many educated speakers use *is* and *was* with plural nouns, as in (3) and (4):

(3) there's no bottles
(4) is there any biscuits left?

Macafee (1983:50), describing Glasgow speech, cites *was* combining with *you*: *an they'll look at you as if you was a Dalek or something* (spelling altered for convenience, JM). She points to the use of *goes* (and other third person singular verbs) as a narrative form: '*Naw', I goes, near screaming, you know?*

4.3.2 Measure phrases

In phrases containing a numeral followed by a measure noun such as *mile, foot*, etc., the latter is regularly singular:

(5) five mile long, two foot high, weighs eight stone, two year old

In phrases containing the measure nouns *bit* and *drop* followed by another noun, there is regularly no preposition between the two nouns:

(6) a bit paper, a bit steel, a drop water

These constructions are typically Germanic and correspond to the standard German *zwei Meter lang* (= two metres long), *ein Stück Papier* (= a piece of paper). The construction is restricted in Scottish English compared with German: *eine Tasse Tee* (= a cup of tea) and *ein Glas Bier* (= a glass of beer) are the norm, but Broad Scots does not have *a cup tea* and *a glass beer*.

Finally, *less* and not *few* is normal with plural count nouns, as in *less cars*. To a phrase such as *more cars* is normally added the intensifier *much* and not *many*: *much more cars*.

4.3.3   Relative clauses

As mentioned in the glossary, relative clauses can be introduced by WH words, such as *who* and *which*, or by *that*. The WH system has *who* in relative clauses modifying human nouns, as in (7), *which* in relative clauses modifying inanimate nouns, as in (8), *whose* as a possessive, as in (9), and regularly preposition + WH word at the beginning of a relative clause, as in (10).

(7)   the customer who complained about the book
(8)   the book which was selling well
(9)   the customer whose purse was stolen
(10)   the shop in which her purse was stolen

The WH word can be omitted if it is the direct object of the relative clause, as in *the purse the thief stole belonged to my mother*.

The WH system occurs, though not exclusively, in formal written English and is regarded by many users as the latter's hallmark.

Before we look at the Scots system, two further distinctions must be drawn. The examples in (7)–(8) are called restrictive relative clauses: *who complained about the book* helps the listener to pick out that particular customer from the other customers. That is, it restricts the set of customers to the relevant one. Suppose the example were: *The customer, who complained about the book, was a friend of the manager.* The commas after *customer* and *book* correspond to a pause or break in rhythm in speech. The relative clause here is not used to restrict the set of customers but to provide extra information, an optional addition to the main message.

Let us turn to (11).

(11) my Dad came to an Elton John concert with us which at the
      time we thought was great

The conversation from which (11) is taken makes it clear that the relative clause, *which at the time we thought was great*, relates to the speaker's Dad coming with them to the concert, i.e. to the entire event. *Which* here introduces an 'event relative clause.'

On the basis of the map-task dialogues, the free conversation, further informally collected spoken data, and written work by pupils at Edinburgh secondary schools, the system of relative clause constructions summarized in (a)–(f) below can be postulated. Strictly speaking, it is a system for Broad Scots, but there are good grounds for supposing that a similar system operates in all non-standard varieties of British English and to some extent in informal spoken standard English. (Colleagues who work on other non-standard varieties recognize the constructions, and they can, for instance, be heard in radio discussion programmes.)

(a) Restrictive relative clauses are introduced by *that*, but also by *where* for example: *just about that other place where I started*. Relative clauses modifying time nouns such as *day*, *month*, etc. do not usually contain a WH word: *the day she arrived* or *the day that she arrived*. The first version is the only type attested in the conversations (Macafee (1983:52) notes that restrictive relative clauses in the Broad Scots of Glasgow are occasionally introduced by *what*: *like the other birds what takes Dexedrine*).

(b) Event relative clauses are introduced by *which*, never by *that*.

(c) Instead of *whose*, *that* + possessive pronoun is used: *the girl that her eighteenth birthday was on that day was stoned – couldnae stand up*.

(d) The shadow pronoun is a typical feature of relative clauses, particularly if the relative clause contains a long constituent or another clause: *the spikes that you stick in the ground and throw rings over them, an address which I hadn't stayed there for several years.* (Both examples recorded informally.)

(e) Prepositions occur only at the end of the relative clause: *the shop I bought it in*, but prepositions are frequently omitted: *of course there's a rope that you can pull the seat back up; I haven't been to a party yet that I haven't got home the same night* (informally recorded – radio discussion). With prepositions the examples would be: *of course there's a rope that you can pull the seat back up with*, and *haven't been to a party yet that I haven't got home from the same night*.

(f) *That* (as subject relative pronoun) can be omitted in existential constructions:

> *we had this French girl came to stay*
> *my friend's got a brother used to be in the school*
> *there's only one of us been on a chopper before* (informally recorded)

(g) Non-restrictive relative clauses are notable for their scarcity. In the map-task dialogues and conversations there are no non-restrictive relative clauses with *who*. Of the non-restrictive relatives with *which*, nineteen came from conversations involving university undergraduates or from 17 year olds at an Edinburgh fee-paying school. Only three non-restrictive relative clauses came from other informants – 16–17 year olds at state schools and adults.

Instead of non-restrictive relative clauses, speakers of Scots use co-ordinate clauses: *the boy I was talking to last night – and he actually works in the yard – was saying it's going to be closed down.* With a non-restrictive relative clause the example would have been: *the boy I was talking to last night, who actually works in the yard, . . .*

The construction in (f) is not confined to Scottish English but has been observed in the captions to Giles cartoons and is used by Trollope's racier characters in his political novels.

The constructions in (c) and (d) both involve shadow pronouns: what we are calling the relative clause looks like a main clause, preceded by *that* and containing an ordinary pronoun. Some analysts see this structure as an accident of fast speech, but various facts support the view that the construction deserves more status. One of the examples in Murray (1873) is *the man that his wife's deid* (= dead): i.e. the possessive construction is of long standing. Furthermore, the constructions in (d) have exact counterparts in other *written* languages, such as Hebrew and Modern Written Arabic.

The Scots data suggests that *that* in relative clauses is not a relative pronoun but a conjunction. In earlier stages of the language *that* was a pronoun, but in certain contexts it has become a conjunction: in relative clauses, but also in complement clauses. It seems as though *which* is following the same path. Consider (12), especially the second *which*:

(12)   you can leave at Christmas if your birthday's in December to February which I think is wrong like my birthday's March and I have to stay on to May which when I'm 16 in March I could be looking for a job

The second *which* – *which when I'm 16 in March* – is not a relative pronoun tying a relative clause to a particular noun but functions to signal a connection between the preceding chunk of text and the following one. (Again, some analysts see this an accident of fast speech, but it is of long standing. Mr Wegg in *Our Mutual Friend* uses the construction, and throughout the nineteenth century it was a favourite device of cartoonists in *Punch* who wanted to signal that a character was working class).

Finally in this section, we should note that shadow pronouns occur in another construction that can be heard on radio and television. Consider (13) and (14)

(13)   in New York on Manhattan Island there is a theatre there that . . .
(14)   out of the last eleven points Mrs Lloyd won ten of them

For the purist, the pronouns *there* and *of them* are unnecessary and simply repeat what came at the beginning of the clause. The question is, however, whether the examples are single clauses. An alternative analysis is that the speaker used the initial phrase – *in New York on Manhattan Island, out of the last eleven points* – to announce what was important and what he (in the given cases) wanted to talk about. The phrases can be seen as independent 'flags' which do not belong to the following clause, although the clauses refer back to them. They are devices of spoken – as against written – English generally.

4.3.4   Negation

In Scots, the verb in a sentence is negated by the independent words *no* and *not*, as in (15), or by the dependent forms *nae* and *n't*, which are always attached to other words, as in (16)

(15)(a) She's no leaving.
    (b) She's not leaving.
(16)(a) She isnae leaving.
    (b) She isn't leaving.

In (15a,b) the auxiliary verb *is* has become attached to the preceding pronoun and is reduced. In the conversations corpus *no* is most frequent with BE, and next most frequent with *'ll*, the reduced form of *will* (*she'll no be coming to the party*), and *'ve* and *'s*, the reduced forms of *have* and *has* (*I've no seen him the day, She's no 'phoned yet*). *Nae* is added to all the modal verbs and to DO: *He doesnae help in the house*. Educated speakers prefer *n't* to *nae*, certainly in formal contexts, but forms like *isnae* can be heard in informal circumstances from educated speakers. More frequent in the speech of educated speakers than either *nae* or *n't* is *not*, as in (15b). In negative interrogatives, such as (17), *n't* (which is normal in other varieties of English) is usually avoided and *not* is used.

(17)   Are you not coming with us?

One construction in which *n't* is relatively frequent is the tag question, illustrated in (18a), but even here *not* and *no* occur, as in (18b).

(18)(a) they're few and far between aren't they?
    (b) that's miles away is it no

The form *amn't* is found in tag questions, as in (19)

(19)   I'm coming with you amn't I

It was stated above that *nae* is added to modal verbs. This is true when *nae* applies to the modal verb itself. Thus, *he cannae come to the party* can be paraphrased as *he is unable to come to the party*. However, *no* (and *not*) also occur with modal verbs, but they apply to the piece of the sentence following the modal: thus, *You can no come to the party if you dinnae want tae* has the paraphrase *You are able not to come . . .* or *you are permitted not to come . . .* (see section 4.3.5, below). Note the contrast in the paraphrases between *unable to come* and *able not to come*.

Macafee (1983:47) gives the example (heard in Glasgow) *will you not put too many on there in case they fall in the street please*. Here *not* can only apply to *put too many on there*. *Won't you put too many . . .* would have precisely the opposite force: the speaker would be asking for too many to be put on.

Where there is no auxiliary verb, as in *I got the job*, the sentence is made negative by using DO: *I didn't get the job*. In Broad Scots the normal negative with past tense verbs is *never*, as in (20).

(20(a) . . . I could've got the job . . . but I telt them I couldnae leave till the end of May so I never got it.
  (b) I sat down to that . . . essay at 7 o'clock. I never got it started till nine.

This use of *never* is found in the speech of many educated people: (20b) was uttered by a university undergraduate. It has not made its way into formal writing, although it occurs in essays by some secondary school pupils.

Two final comments on *never*. It is regularly not emphatic, unlike the standard English example *You will never catch the train tonight* (= It is utterly impossible that you will catch the train tonight). And as *never* acquires the meaning and function of *not* (with past tense verbs), what expresses the meaning 'at no time in general'? For many speakers the answer is *never ever*.

A final difference between standard written English and Scottish English has to do with the relationship between *not, n't* etc. and quantifying words such as *all, each* and *every*. Consider (21).

(21) all the hotels take British guests

The negative of this is expressed in standard written English by

None of the hotels take British guests. However, it is possible to negate only the phrase *all the hotels*, to give the meaning 'some do and some do not': this meaning is expressed in standard written English by *Not all the hotels take British guests.* However, in Scottish English this (second) meaning is expressed by (22) (which was observed in conversation and in the context could only have this meaning):

(22)   All the hotels don't take British guests

N't modifies *all* but is attached to *do*. This construction is the norm in many non-standard varieties of English, including American ones. Indeed, we might regard *not all the hotels* as peculiar to formal discussion among academics or in very formal radio and TV discussions. Other examples similar to (22) are given in (23).

(23)(a)   It is not democratic, because every member is not consulted on the decision.
   (b)   We all don't have to be there.

In the context in which (23a) was uttered, the meaning was clearly that some members are consulted but not others, and (23b) was being used as a justification for not attending a meeting: colleagues of the speaker would be there and the speaker could therefore stay away.

4.3.5   Modal verbs

Modal verbs occupy an important place in the grammar of any variety of English, and this is one area in which Scottish English is massively different from standard English. The major differences are these.

(1)   Broad Scots lacks SHALL, MAY and OUGHT.
   The lack of SHALL was mentioned almost seventy years ago by Jespersen as a feature of Scottish, Irish and American English. SHALL is missing both as a marker of future tense (cf. standard *We shall arrive in the morning*) and as the expression of a promise *You shall have the money tomorrow (I promise you)*. MAY is not used to express

permission. This is expressed by CAN, GET TO and GET
+ gerund as in (24).

(24)(a) You can have this afternoon off.
   (b) the pupils get to come inside in rainy weather (= They are
        allowed to . . .)
   (c) they get watching TV till 8 pm
   (d) they got going to the match (= They were allowed to . . .)

The equivalent of standard English OUGHT is SHOULD, but
WANT is often used, as in (25), uttered by a judo instructor.

(25) you want to come out and attack right away

The construction in (25) is avoided by educated speakers, especially
in formal situations.

   (2) MUST is in the Scots system but is restricted in meaning.
        Two major meanings are expressed by MUST in standard
        English. The interpretation of (26a) is 'From the evidence
        I conclude that you are exhausted': this is the conclusion
        meaning. The interpretation of (26b) is 'it is necessary to
        you to be at the airport by nine': this is the obligation
        meaning.

(26)(a) You must be exhausted (judging by your appearance).
   (b) You must be at the airport by nine (or your ticket will be
        given to a standby passenger).

   In Broad Scots MUST expresses only the conclusion meaning,
while the obligation meaning is expressed by HAVE TO and
NEED TO (compare this with the uses of *must* discussed in
Chapter 3).
   In descriptions of English it is often said that MUST relates
to internal or self-compulsion, whereas HAVE TO relates to
external compulsion: you make yourself do something or you
do something because someone else makes you or because of
general circumstances. These distinctions are not relevant to the
use of MUST by Scots. Various tests have shown that even Scottish
university undergraduates (and some English ones too!) have no

clear intuition about the obligation MUST, but do have clear intuitions that HAVE GOT TO relates to external compulsion and that WILL HAVE TO relates to much milder compulsion, which can even be self-compulsion, as in (27).

(27) I'll have to write to Carol because she wrote to us six month ago.

HAVE TO expresses external compulsion, but is less strong than HAVE GOT TO. It can also have the conclusion meaning, as in (28), which is typical of non-standard English in general.

(28) that has to be their worst display ever

(3) NEED behaves like a main verb in Scots.
Instead of *Need you leave immediately?* and *You needn't leave immediately*, which are standard English, Scottish English has *Do you need to leave immediately* and *You don't need to leave immediately*. The auxiliary *do* is used and *need* is followed by *to* + verb. In addition, NEED occurs in the progressive: *They're needing to paint the windows*. NEED expresses only the obligation meaning, and the latter appears to be no less strong than for HAVE TO. The examples in (29) are typical of the answers produced by university undergraduates during a test in which they were given, e.g. *I must be back at midnight because*, and asked to complete the sentence.

(29)(a) I must be back by midnight because I need to switch off my electric blanket.
   (b) I have to go to the library because I need to do my French essay today.

NEED can express external compulsion as in (30), from the conversational corpus.

(30) you'd need to go down there and collect her and drop her

The author's impression as an occasional speaker and regular observer of Broad Scots was that NEED occurred more frequently than HAVE TO, but this was not borne out by the recorded data. It may well be, however, that NEED is more frequent in Broad Scots than in other varieties.

It is often asserted that in standard English the conclusion MUST cannot be negated and has to be replaced by CAN: *This must be the place* but *This can't be the place*. In Broad Scots *mustn't* expresses 'I conclude that not', as in (31). This usage is found in other varieties of English. (See also Chapters 3 and 6.)

(31)(a) this mustn't be the place
     (b) I mustn't have read the question properly
     (c) they mustn't be going to ask me
          [All observed in conversation.]

Obligation can also be expressed by SUPPOSED TO or MEANT TO, as in (32).

(32)(a) you're supposed to leave your coat in the cloakroom
     (b) you're meant to fill in the form first

MEANT TO also occurs with the meaning 'It is said that': *The new player is meant to be real fast*.

(4) For standard English it is claimed that in, e.g. *You may not come to the party, not* can apply to *may* or *come to the party*.
     The former interpretation can be expressed as *You don't have permission . . .*, the latter − as *You have permission not to*. MAY is missing from most Scottish English, and *can't, cannot* and *cannae* all express 'not have permission to'. To express 'have permission not to', speakers of Scottish English use *don't need to, don't have to* and *are allowed not to*.

(5) In standard English only one modal verb can occur in a given clause, but in Broad Scots double modal verbs are frequent as in (33), and compare 6.3.3.

(33)(a) he'll can help us the morn/tomorrow
     (b) They might could be working in the shop.
     (c) She might can get away early.

Will in (33a) can be moved to the front to form an interrogative – *Will he can help us the morn/tomorrow?* – but *might* in (33b,c) cannot: **Might they could be working in the shop?* There are grounds for supposing that *might* (33b,c) is developing into an adverb, syntactically equivalent to *maybe*: note sentences such as *They maybe could be working in the shop*, where *maybe* occupies the same position as *might*.

Might can combine with *should* and *would*, as in (34), though this combination is less frequent.

(34)(a) you might would like to come with us
    (b) you might should claim your expenses

Here again *might* is equivalent in meaning and in position to *maybe*. Note too the parallel between (35a) and (35b).

(35)(a) he might no could do it
    (b) he maybe no could do it

The double-modal sequence *will can* is relatively old, being mentioned by Wilson (1915) and Grant and Main-Dixon (1921). The other sequences appear to be newer, but the general construction, far from being the whim of urban dwellers, dates from at least the last century and is widespread in the southern United States and in northern England. (If, as is sometimes supposed, the construction was taken to the United States by Scotch-Irish immigrants, it is much older).

(6)   In standard English, modal verbs do not occur after the infinitive marker *to*, but they do in Broad Scots, as shown in (36). This too is not a new feature but is mentioned by Grant and Main-Dixon.

(36)(a) you have to can drive a car to get that job
    (b) he's gonna can pass his driving test next week
    (c) I'd like to could do that

According to one informant, a gamekeeper's son born and brought up in Galloway, a graduate in Modern Languages and endowed with a keen linguistic ear, examples such as (37) are common.

(37) ah would uh could uh done it (= I would have been able to
      do it).
      The two instances of *uh* are equivalent to *'ve* or *have*, and
      an unusual feature is *could* preceded by *have*.

4.3.6   Tense

'Tense' is used here as a cover term for phenomena that strictly
speaking should be divided between tense and 'aspect'. For
similarities in tense/aspect usage between Scots and Irish English,
see also Chapter 5.

Progressive

The progressive construction in English consists of BE + a verb
in *-ing*, as in *I am writing*. In descriptions of standard English it
is usually said that certain verbs, such as KNOW and LIKE, do
not occur in the progressive, and that other verbs, such as SEE
and HEAR, occur rarely in the progressive. Utterances have been
observed with such 'stative' verbs in the progressive, as in (38):

(38)(a) I wasnae liking it and the lassie I was going wi wasnae
         liking it
   (b)   we werenae really wanting to go last year but they sent us
         a lot of letters to come
   (c)   he's not understanding a single thing you say
   (d)   they're not intending opening the bottle tonight surely

(Note that (38d) is an instance of the 'double-*ing*' construction
– two words ending in *-ing* and one following the other. The
construction is infrequent but not avoided altogether as has been
alleged.)
   It may be that examples such as (38) are current in other
non-standard varieties of English and that it is the standard
written language that banishes these verbs from the progressive.
The examples in (39) are interesting, because they are from written
work by Scottish undergraduates and contain the progressive in
contexts where the simple form is required by the strict standard
canon. The relevant verbs are DENOTE in (39a), OCCUR in (39b)
and CONFORM in (39c).

(39)(a) Thus the nominal construction is denoting a process – typically a function connected with verbs

(b) . . . although 'coffee' and 'black' are occurring together as a unit, it is not grammatical

(c) It seems that Extraposition is conforming to two conditions

Various native speakers, Scots and non-Scots, have expressed unhappiness with the above examples. The difficulty is that in formal writing the progressive is confined to verbs denoting actions (with some exceptions such as STAND, LIE, SLEEP), and to sentences in which the speaker presents an action as on-going, as in *The scientists are developing a new filter*. The verbs in (39) do not denote actions and the subject nouns are inanimate.

In contrast, the examples in (40) do not sound odd – precisely because they are the type of example where a simple form is expected in formal writing such as academic papers and books.

(40)(a) Prepositional phrases, again, occur after the noun they are modifying

(b) Here the subordinate clause 'who were good' replaces the adjective 'good'

The problem may be one of stylistic preference, or it may arise from the larger number of verbs for which the progressive is natural in Scottish English. Whatever the reason, it is a barrier to be cleared by many pupils and students aiming at good formal style.

Past and Perfect tense

It is usually claimed that in standard English the Perfect tense does not occur with time adverbs denoting a definite reference time: thus *We have seen the exhibition this morning* and *We have been to New York last year*. While it is true that the Perfect Tense does not frequently occur with definite time adverbs, such examples do occur. Since they do not have pauses or breaks in intonation between the Perfect Tense and the adverb, it is difficult to treat the adverb as an afterthought. Two examples are given in (41).

(41)(a) I've seen him last year.
   (b) I've been to the exhibition last year.

The Perfect Tense, especially in the Progressive, can refer to recent past time. Examples such as *Kirsty has been working with the Royal Bank* are appropriate either if Kirsty is still working with the bank when the speaker makes the statement or if Kirsty had been working with the bank until quite recently. Reference to an event that took place recently but is now finished is achieved in Broad Scots by the past progressive + *there*, as in (42).

(42)(a) I was speaking to John there.
   (b) I was speaking to John last Friday there.

Note that *there* does not point to a place. The standard English sentence *The electrician has just phoned* is used to talk about an event that has happened in the immediate past. It contains the Perfect Tense, *has phoned*, and the adverb *just*. In Scottish English the same effect is conveyed by *The electrician just phoned*, with a simple verb form and *just*. This is also an American construction.

Pluperfect tense

Examples of the pluperfect tense are *had written* and *had gone*. It occurs in main clauses in Scottish English, though not frequently, but is not used in certain subordinate clauses where it is required by formal written English. The examples in (43) have been declared acceptable by linguists presented with them out of context, but from comments by teachers on the children's written work in secondary schools it is clear that official arbiters of language want the pluperfect.

(43)(a) He said his mum had brought him the fireworks but she
          really didn't [hadn't]
    (b) . . . he . . . was angry I didn't stay in the cafe [= hadn't
          stayed]
    (c) I noticed the van I came in was not really a painter's van
          [= had come in]

Tense in conditional clauses

The conditional clause in (44a) describes an event that has not happened but could happen. The conditional clause in (44b) describes an event that can no longer happen.

(44)(a) If she came to see things for herself, she would understand.
    (b) If she had come to see things for herself, she would have understood.

Broad Scots frequently replaces the past tense verb with *would* + verb, and the pluperfect is replaced by *would* + *have* + participle.

(45)(a)(= 44a) If she would come to see things for herself . . .
    (b)(= 44b) If she would have come to see things for herself . . .

The above constructions occur in the speech of educated Scots, are not confined to Broad Scots and may find their way into standard written English, as is shown by (46), taken from *The Times*.

(46) Suppose further that all Conservative and Labour voters in England *would have given* the Alliance as their second choice and that Alliance voters *would have divided* equally between Conservative and Labour. [our italics]

The standard canon requires *had given* and *had divided*.
Conditional clauses expressing events that can no longer happen also occur with the pluperfect replaced by *had* = *have*, the latter typically in its reduced form *'ve*. The same construction is also found in clauses introduced by *wish*, which likewise present an event as no longer possible. (Cf. (47).)

(47)(a) I reckon I wouldnae have been able to dae it if I hadnae've been able to read music [= hadn't been able]
    (b) you wouldn't have got Mark's place if you'd've come up last year [= had come up]
    (c) I wish he'd've complimented me, Roger [= had complimented]

4.3.7   Interrogatives: direct questions

Broad Scots and standard English share the same basic yes-no and WH interrogatives, but they differ in various features and Broad Scots has its own tag question. The differences with respect to the basic constructions are these:

(1)   Broad Scots regularly uses *how* where standard English uses *why*. (Cf. (48) and the comments in section 4.1 on the misunderstood examination question.)

(48)(a)   A: Susan, how's your ankle?
        B: I can walk on it I think. How? [= why?]
   (b)   how did you not apply? [in the context = why did you not apply?]

(2)   *Whereabouts* is used instead of *where* and is regularly split into *where* and *about*. *Where* + *about* express approximate location but *how* + *about* express approximate quantity. (Cf. (49).)

(49)(a)   *Whereabouts* did you see him?
   (b)   *Where* does she stay *about*?
   (c)   *How* old was he *about*?

(3)   *What time . . . at?* frequently replaces *when?*, as in *What time does it finish at?*
(4)   In standard English, *which book?*, e.g. invites the addressee to specify one of a set of known books; *what book?* asks the addressee to specify one out of the set of all books. In Scots English *what* fulfils both functions, as in (50).

(50)(a)   What book have you been buying? [Appropriate when meeting a friend carrying a paper bag obviously containing a book.]
   (b)   What book on the reading list have you read? [Appropriate when someone mentions having read a book on the list.]

All the above usages are common, even in the speech of educated speakers, although they do not appear, for example, in the formal written language of university undergraduates.

4.3.8   Interrogatives: indirect questions

Indirect questions differ, but the Scots construction is widespread throughout spoken English, occurs in the speech of educated people, and is finding its way into written texts such as letters to newspapers. The standard English construction is exemplified in (51).

(51)(a)   the teacher asked who had not read the book.
　　　　　[Cf. Who has not read the book?]
　　(b)   The teacher asked what book they had read.
　　　　　[Cf. What book have you read?]
　　(c)   The teacher asked where they were going.
　　　　　[Cf. Where are you going?]

The indirect questions (51b,c) have the order WH word + subject pronoun + auxiliary verb: the direct questions have the order WH word + auxiliary verb + subject pronoun. Where the WH word is the subject, the direct and indirect questions have the same order. In Scots indirect questions are the same as the direct questions. Note that the examples in (52) involved no hesitations or changes in intonation but were uttered as one chunk.

(52)(a)   I can't remember now what was the reason for it.
　　(b)   If they got an eight they had to decide where was the best
　　　　　place to put it.
　　(c)   You sort of wonder is it better to be blind or deaf.
　　(d)   I asked her what's wrong but I received no answer.

4.3.9   Interrogatives: tag questions

Scottish English possesses a different tag-question construction from standard English. The latter's tag-question is illustrated in (53).

(53)(a)   John has left, hasn't he
　　(b)   John hasn't left, has he?

Speakers make statements by means of a declarative clause – *John has left* – and tag on an interrogative piece – *hasn't he* – asking the addressee to confirm their expectations. If the declarative clause is positive, the tag is negative, as in (53a), and vice-versa in (53b). The typical Scots tag is *e* – pronounced like the name of the first letter of the alphabet. *E* is added to positive and negative declarative clauses, as in (54a,b) but there is a tag *e no* that is added to positive clauses, as in (54c).

(54)(a) ... we know him quite well by now *e*? [= don't we]
    (b) it's no too dear *e*? [= It's not too dear, is it?]
    (c) you're taking her to the pictures *e no*? [= aren't you]

We should note that the same tag occurs in imperative sentences that are not commands but requests, even coaxing requests. In questions the tag asks the addressee to agree with the speaker's statement; analogously, in imperatives the tag asks the addressee to agree with (and act upon) the speaker's command. (Cf. (55).)

(55)(a) let me tie my lace *e*
    (b) put it down there *e*
    (c) be good to her *e*

In standard English the above imperatives could have the tag *won't you*. However, such a tag, with suitable tone of voice, can increase the sharpness of a request, but the *e* of Scots always reduces the sharpness.

Many Scots, including educated people, use the *e* tag in informal speech, but not in formal speech and not in writing.

Scots (speakers) also have a tag question resembling the standard English one, but two points must be mentioned.

(1) The negative tag usually contains *no* or *not* rather than *n't*.

(2) A regular construction has a positive clause followed by a positive tag, as in (56). The force of the tag seems to be that speakers expect a positive answer to their question.

(56)(a) A: aye that's cos I didnae use to go?
       B: did you start skiving did you?
    (b) are you still working at Woolie's are you?
    (c) have you just had your weekend have you?
    (d) is BS still here is she?

Other tags available in Scots - and in other non-standard varieties – are illustrated in (57).

(57)(a)   you don't go for that sort, no?
   (b)   you've mentioned this to him, yes?
   (c)   they're not intending opening the bottle tonight surely?
   (d)   he's not trying to make all of it, not really?
   (e)   he's coming on Monday, right?

Finally, particularly strong confidence is displayed by speakers who put *sure* or *e* at the beginning of a declarative clause to produce what is a tag question in that it invites the addressee to confirm the speakers' expectations. (It also has the intonation of a question.) (Cf. (58), and note that (58a) is not equivalent to 'Are you sure that Harry supports Celtic?')

(58)(a)   Sure Harry supports Celtic?
   (b)   E Harry supports Celtic?

4.3.10   The definite article and possessive pronouns

A well-known characteristic of Scottish English is the use of *the* with nouns denoting institutions, certain illnesses, certain periods of time and with quantifiers such as *both* and *all*.

(59)(a)   the day [= today], the morn [= tomorrow], the now [= now]
   (b)   She has the hiccoughs/the shivers/the 'flu/the measles/the chickenpox.
   (c)   They are at the kirk [= at church]/at the school/in the jail/in the hospital/at the college.
   (d)   in the house [= at home], through the post [= by post], up the stair [= upstairs], down the stair, over the phone [= by phone]
   (e)   The bouncer throws the both of them out.
   (f)   Cathy helps Trisha . . . and the both of them get on really good.
   (g)   The hale three of them's back on it [= the whole three, all three].

Phrases such as *at the school* and *in the hospital* do not necessarily refer to a specific school or hospital as they would in standard English but are equivalent to *in school* and *in hospital*.

Examples of possessive pronouns are given in (60).

(60)(a) Look Cathy, I'm off for my dinner [= to have dinner].
   (b) After our tea we all went to our bed [= to bed - not a communal bed!]
   (c) went to France on my holidays [= on holiday].
   (d) . . . to get ready to go up to your work [= to work]

4.3.11 Comparatives

Where *more than* and *as much as* are followed by a clause, *what* intervenes between them and the clause, as in (61).

(61)(a) more than what you'd think actually
   (b) you've as much on your coat as what you have in your mouth

Comparative forms are used only before *than: Sue is bigger than Jane.* Elsewhere the superlative form is used, even in relation to two individuals or things: *Who is biggest, Sue or Jane?*

4.3.12 Gerunds and infinitives

In English generally some verbs take infinitives, as in (62a), while others take gerunds, as in (62b).

(62)(a) We hope to leave next week [not *we hope leaving . . .]
   (b) Bob resents spending money on books [not *Bob resents to spend . . .]

Other verbs can take either an infinitive or a gerund, as in (63).

(63) The children started to quarrel/quarrelling.

Some verbs − and nouns and adjectives − that can take either infinitives or gerunds in Scots are shown in (64).

(64)(a) It's difficult to know/knowing how to start this letter.
  (b) They always continue to work/working until the bell goes.
  (c) He started to talk/talking to his friend.
  (d) It was daft to leave/leaving the puppy in the house.
  (e) Try to eat less/eating less if you are putting on weight.

Tests administered to groups of Scottish and English secondary pupils and to Scottish and English secondary teachers allow the following comments. In non-standard English generally, the gerund is more frequent where there is a choice. For some examples both Scottish and English pupils had highly significant and significant numbers of gerunds, but for the examples in (64) the Scottish pupils had significant numbers of gerunds while the English pupils did not. Indeed, in a test with thirty examples some Scottish pupils used the gerund to the exclusion of the infinitive. Teachers greatly preferred infinitives, with English teachers showing a stronger preference than the Scottish teachers. There is a clash in this area between standard and non-standard English, and between Broad Scots and other varieties, but a mass of detail remains to be uncovered.

The marker of the infinitive in Broad Scots is not *to* but *for to*: *He's come for to collect the rent.* Some verbs that take infinitives in standard English are followed by *and* plus a verb phrase, as in (65).

(65)(a) try and do your homework by tomorrow [= try to do]
  (b) remember and bring her back by 12 o'clock
  (c) she tells us to mind and dae what we're tellt [. . . to remember to do what we're told]

MIND is the Scots equivalent of REMEMBER but they take the same type of complement.

LOOK and SEEM are regularly followed by *like* plus clause rather than *as if* plus clause: *It looks like they're no gonna come, It seems like they're all out.*

WANT and NEED are regularly followed by a past participle: *the car needs washed, She wants collected at four o'clock.* Standard English requires *to be washed/collected* or *washing/collecting.*

Infinitives can follow AWAY: *I'm away to ask her to dance.*

With the exception of *for to*, which is a great shibboleth, all the above usages are common in the informal speech of educated Scottish speakers.

4.3.13 Reflexives

The reflexive pronoun *myself* is frequently used in speech and writing where standard English requires just *me* or *I*.

(66)(a) He was just two years younger than myself.
  (b) There wasn't one policeman on duty at the time and if it hadn't been for myself, no evidence either.
  (c) Myself and Andy changed and ran onto the pitch.

4.3.14 Prepositions and adverbs

The prepositional system of Broad Scots has yet to be studied in detail, but the following points can be made.

(1) The typical prepositions in passive clauses are *from, frae/fae* [= from], *off (of)* and *with*. The latter is quite common in the language of educated speakers.

(67)(a) heh, ah'm gonna get killt fae ma maw [= I'm going to get killed by my Mum]
  (b) we were all petrified frae him
  (c) ah'm no feart fae gypsies [= I'm not frightened by gypsies]
  (d) ah'd rather hae no job than bein beat frae pillar tae post aff a that man [= I'd rather have no job than being beaten from pillar to post by that man]
  (e) ... except when it's their weans that get battert wi some other weans [= except when it's their kids that get battered by some other kids]
  (f) I was very impressed with the way they dressed
  (g) there was always a lot of shouting going on between carters getting jammed up wi coal lorries [= with coal lorries]
  (h) she was attacked with a Labrador, a big rusty-coloured dog

(2)   OFF generally replaces FROM expressing the source of something: *I got the book off Alec.* In standard English FROM expresses cause, as in *Many old people die from hypothermia.* In Broad Scots OFF replaces FROM with certain verbs and expressions, as in *I'm crapping myself off you* (uttered sarcastically) = [I'm crapping myself because of you]. A satisfactory study of OFF has yet to be done.

(3)   BY is avoided in its location sense, as in *by the fire.* Instead, AT, BESIDE, and NEXT TO are used. In its directional sense BY is infrequent, PAST being used instead: *They drove past the house on their way to the airport.* Attempts to elicit BY from undergraduates in examples such as *We went to Inverness___Stirling* elicited VIA.

(4)   IN and OUT do not need to be followed by TO or OF after verbs of movement: *She ran in the living room, . . . because she's just walked out the shop with it.* Cf. standard English *into the living room, out of the shop.*

(5)   The regular preposition with BORED and FED UP is OF, not WITH. The usage is frequent in Edinburgh, has been sighted in the pages of that Dundee institution 'The Beano' and has even been heard in radio interviews.

(6)   DOWN and UP do not require TO after verbs of movement: *We're going down the town, go down the shops* (Compare Chapter 3). After verbs of location they do not require AT: *One day I was down the beach, They were up the town yesterday.*

(7)   OUTSIDE is regularly followed by OF: *outside of the school*

(8)   Miscellaneous examples: *shout on someone* [= shout to someone], *over the phone* [= by phone], *through the post* [= by post], *wait on someone* [wait for someone], *fair on someone* [= fair to someone], *married on someone* [= married to someone]. Some of these are, of course, not peculiar to Scots.

4.4   Organization of discourse

Speakers combine sentences to form discourses and tailor them to suit the contributions of other speakers in a conversation. Scottish

English has a range of devices for catching the hearer's attention, putting items into prominence or focusing sharply upon them. The devices are different from those of the standard written language: different because they belong to speech and not writing.

First, speakers often announce the topic of a new chunk of discourse by means of a noun phrase followed by a complete clause containing a pronoun referring back to the noun phrase. This construction, exemplifed in (68), is not just a device whereby the speaker escapes from a syntactic tangle. It occurs frequently with simple noun phrases and with no pause between the noun phrase and the clause. The noun phrase may be introduced by *there's*, as in (68d).

(68)(a) it's not bad – ma Dad he doesn't say a lot
   (b) the driver he's really friendly – you get a good laugh with him
   (c) well another maths teacher that I dinnae get he must've corrected my papers
   (d) and there's one girl she's a real extrovert

Secondly, standard written English possesses what are called the cleft and pseudo-cleft constructions, exemplified in (69) and (70).

(69)(a) It was Bill who left.
   (b) It was to Stirling that she retired.
(70)(a) What I want is a large cup of coffee.
   (b) What you have done is wreck the plans.
   (c) What she does is to interrupt at every turn.

These constructions focus on certain words and phrases: *Bill* and *to Stirling* in (69), *a large cup of coffee, wreck the plans* and *interrupt at every turn* in (70). In colloquial Scots the pseudo-cleft construction in (70a) is infrequent and the construction in (70b,c) is very rare. More common is a construction in which the *what . . . is* part is followed by a whole clause, as in (71).

(71)(a) so what you had to do was you got a partner and you got a match . . .
   (b) but what you did in the evening you carried a sandwich or two . . .

In (71a) *what you had to do was* is followed by the clause *you got a partner . . .* In (71b) *what you did* does not even contain *was*. These features can be summed up by saying that the two parts of the construction are more closely integrated in the written language than in the spoken.

In contrast, the cleft construction is quite frequent, particularly in WH questions, as in (72).

(72)(a)   where is it he works again?
　　(b)   who is it that's been murdered?

Thirdly, various focusing devices are used to give prominence to items (or propositions) that the speaker wishes to introduce into the discourse. As an introducing device, SEE can be close to the verb SEE in its basic perception sense, as in (73a), but the connection grows more tenuous from (73a) to (73c).

(73)(a)   see those old houses . . . this area was all houses like that right round
　　(b)   A: ma cousin she got pregnant . . . the guy . . . done a bunk
　　　　　B: see it's daft − better living up wi the fella first to see if he's really gonna live wi ye
　　(c)   A: there's a car park
　　　　　B: aye − see I hate going in there

See introduces the Noun Phrase *the old houses* in (73a) and whole propositions in (73b,c). One problem of analysis is whether, e.g. *see those old houses* is an imperative or a question. In the map-task dialogues, where one participant is giving instructions and there is a lot of checking that information has been received and understood, examples such as *see the bridge below the forest* are always understood as questions: the other participant replies *uhuh* or *aye* or *right*. Analysing the construction as a command would leave us with the difficulty that SEE does not normally occur in the imperative. (But consider *see here! I've had enough of this nonsense!*)

The map-task dialogues reveal another property of SEE as an introducing device: it is used only when the speaker treats a landmark as being on both maps and therefore findable or given.

In syntactic terms, SEE always takes a definite noun phrase: *see the fast-flowing river* but not **see a fast-flowing river*. To introduce items that the speakers suspect might not be on both maps, or might have a different label, they use, e.g. *can you see a fast-flowing river?* or *do you see a fast-flowing river? Can you/do you see* can also introduce *definite* noun phrases: *can you see the castle?*

SEE can introduce and give prominence to entire clauses. Examples from the map-task dialogues are given in (74).

(74) A: right see if you come down straight down right see if you come round the left of the hills right
B: uh huh
A: see if you go straight down but not go straight to the aeroplane right see where the see where the pilot would go that wee bit

Macafee (1983: 48) cites *see you* as a type of vocative: *see you, you're just a pain in the neck*. Usually the comment following *see you* is pejorative.

In the map-task dialogues, items are introduced by KNOW: *know the bridge across the fast-flowing river*. As with SEE, these utterances are understood as questions, and contain only definite noun phrases. Thus **know a bridge across the fast-flowing river* is not possible.

KEN is the Broad Scots counterpart of KNOW. Unlike its German cognate KENNEN, KEN is quite general in meaning: you can KEN someone and KEN how to do something. *Ken* can introduce items into a discourse, or a complete new topic of conversation. It never combines with *you* or *ye* in this construction. Examples are given in (75).

(75)(a) ken John Ewan – he breeds spaniels
  (b) the estate up at Macmerry – ken there's a big estate there – it's got a gamekeeper
  (c) [after a long pause in the conversation] ken this wee lassie comes in with tea towels at ten to seven and I washed them – ken I'm wanting them boiled so they take a wee while you know

The second *ken* in (75c) illustrates another use of KEN – to introduce a proposition by way of explanation. Another example is (76).

(76) she's on the machine until they can get another kidney for her – ken to have a transplant

Propositions and properties of things or people are introduced and made prominent by *the thing is, thing is*, possibly with an adjective preceding *thing*, or with *thing* followed by a prepositional phrase, as in (77c).

(77)(a) but the thing is – at our age what is there what sort of facilities can you provide
   (b) thing is he's watching the man he's not watching the ball
   (c) the thing about school is that you can get them to relax
   (d) the only thing wi Beth – Beth's mean – she'll no gie ye two haufs for a one

Fourthly, LIKE occurs in all types of clause and in many positions. It typically promotes an item explaining a preceding piece of discourse or leading to an explanation. In interrogatives it concentrates a request for information on a particular point.

(78)(a) so like you were left with three teachers there? [the speaker is checking on information that has already been given by the addressee]
   (b) I ken whae he is like – he used to lecture in the first year to us
   (c) A: we get lectures there as well I've been on a chemistry one
       B: I've been on a chemistry one as well – that was a right bore the sex life of insects
       C: really in chemistry? I thought that would be in like biology
       B: no it was chemistry they kept giving us all the silly formulas
   (d) . . . sometimes I go there with my family you know it's really tremendous cause there's a wee kiddie's pool you

know where my wee girl can swim you know she has her wings like – she jumps right in . . .

Note *like* at the end of the clause is relates to in (78b,d), at the beginning of the clause in (78a) and in the middle of the clause, immediately before the noun it relates to, in (78c). In (78c) *like* is very close in meaning to *for example*.[2]

LIKE, SEE, KNOW and THE THING IS are all common in the informal spoken language of educated Scots, but KEN is avoided.

Conclusion

This chapter has tried to show that Scottish English, while sharing many grammatical features with other non-standard varieties of English, is distinguished from them by its specific mix of morphology, syntax and vocabulary. It has tried to show that the differences between standard and non-standard English are systematic and far-reaching. Clearly much work is still to be done on the grammar of Scots. For the moment, if this chapter makes it possible for facts to be introduced into public debate on non-standard language, much will have been achieved.

Note

1. This chapter would not even have been conceivable without the many illuminating discussions with Keith Brown that led to the SSRC-funded project on the syntax of Scottish English (Grant HR5152) in the University of Edinburgh between 1977 and 1980. My thanks go to Bill Campbell and Martin Millar, who recorded and transcribed a hundred hours of conversations, and to Sue Polson, who typed out the transcriptions and entered them on computer file. Norman Dryden and Irene Macleod of the Department of Linguistics, University of Edinburgh gave invaluable help with the computer analysis of the data. Many other people have discussed points with me and, wittingly and unwittingly, provided clues and insights. They are Alex Agutter, Jack Aitken, David Clement, John Kirk, Caroline Macafee, Jim and Lesley Milroy, Annette Sabban, Cynthia Shuken, George Thompson of Dalry, Galloway, Peter Trudgill and Regina Weinert.
2. My recent work on conversation indicates that clause-final LIKE counters possible objections or misunderstandings. Thus in 78(d)

the speaker was explaining: it's not that she can actually swim; she uses water-wings.

References

BROWN, E. K. and MILLER, J. E. (1980) Scottish English: End of Grant Report to the Social Science Research Council

BROWN, G., CURRIE, K. L. and KENWORTHY, J. (1980) *Questions of Intonation.* London: Croom Helm

GRANT, W. and MAIN-DIXON, J. (1921) *Manual of Modern Scots.* Cambridge: Cambridge University Press

LORIMER, W. L. (1983) *The New Testament in Scots.* Edinburgh: Southside Publishers

MACAFEE, C. (1983) *Glasgow.* Amsterdam: John Benjamins

MACAULAY, R. K. S. (1987) A microlinguistic study of the dialect of Ayr. In A. R. Thomas (ed.) *Methods in Dialectology.* Clevedon: Multilingual Matters

MACAULAY, R. K. S. (1991) Narrative skills of a Scottish coalminer

MILROY, J. and MILROY, L. (1978) Change and variation in an urban vernacular. In P. Trudgill (ed.), *Sociolinguistic Patterns in British English,* London: Edward Arnold, pp. 19–36

MURRAY, J. A. H. (1873) *The Dialect of the Southern Counties of Scotland.* London: The Philological Society

REID, E. (1976) Social and Stylistic Variation in the Speech of Some Edinburgh Schoolchildren. MLitt thesis, University of Edinburgh

ROMAINE, S. (1975) Linguistic Variability in the Speech of Some Edinburgh Schoolchildren. MLitt thesis, University of Edinburgh

WILSON, SIR JAMES (1915) *Lowland Scotch as Spoken in the Lower Strathearn District of Perthshire,* London: Oxford University Press

5 The grammar of Irish English

John Harris

5.1 Introduction

This chapter outlines some of the more saliently non-standard grammatical characteristics of English usage in Ireland.[1] The term *non-standard* here is not meant to carry any implications of linguistic inferiority. It simply refers to the fact that the features in question don't correspond to institutionalized norms. For example, they aren't codified in dictionaries and grammar books in the way that standard norms are. Contrary to a widely held belief, such lack of official sanction doesn't reflect random or 'careless' deviation from the standard. Non-standard speech is no less systematic or rule-governed than standard speech.

A simple example from Irish English should make this point clear. Standard English makes no overt distinction between singular and plural in second-person pronouns: *you* may refer to one or more than one person. In some dialects, particularly those spoken in Ireland, as well as others with Irish connections, we find the vernacular form *youse*. Now, it cannot be said that *youse* is simply a non-standard variant of standard *you*. This is because the latter form occurs in these dialects as well, but with a more restricted meaning. Unlike standard English, the grammars of the dialects in question overtly mark the singular-plural distinction in second-person pronouns: *you* is singular, *youse* is plural. We can summarize the differences between the two systems of subject pronouns (i.e. those that can occur as the subject of a sentence) as follows:

person	*Standard* sing.	plur.	*Irish English* sing.	plur.
1	*I*	*we*	*I*	*we*
2	*you*	*you*	*you*	*youse*
3	*he/she/it*	*they*	*he/she/it*	*they*

This is a straightforward illustration of the structural differences that can exist between vernacular and standard forms of English. Some of the differences between standard English and non-standard usage in Ireland which we discuss below are not quite so obvious. Nevertheless, they illustrate the same important point, namely that our appreciation of the extent of such structural divergence depends on our ability to uncover the internal regularities which underlie vernacular usage.

The majority of the population in Ireland speaks some form of non-standard English as a first language. The linguistic details vary from region to region: someone from Dublin, for instance, obviously speaks differently from a native of Belfast. Nevertheless, in spite of this regional variation, dialects of English in Ireland share a number of important linguistic features which distinguish them from dialects spoken elsewhere.

It's sometimes said that the type of English spoken in Ireland is a mixture of the language of Shakespeare and the Irish of the Gaelic earls. In spite of its obvious sentimentality, the adage does in fact contain an element of truth. Modern Irish English does indeed bear the marks of two major historical inputs. On the one hand, we have the various types of English and Scots that were brought to Ireland during the peak years of English and Scottish colonization in the sixteenth and seventeenth centuries. On the other, there is an early hybrid jargon which arose as a result of contact between the Irish and English languages. Contact jargons typically spring up during the initial stages of language shift; that is, in circumstances where an indigenous population, either in whole or in part, gives up its native language in favour of that of a colonial power. Simplifying greatly, we can characterize a contact jargon as a dialect in which the vocabulary of an 'external' language is grafted on to the grammar and pronunciation patterns of an indigenous language.

Different varieties of Irish English display the effects of these two main historical sources in varying proportions. The linguistic impact of the contact between Irish and English is most clearly seen in those areas where Irish continues to be spoken as a mother tongue or where it survived until recently. Elsewhere, and especially in eastern areas where English and Scottish settlement was concentrated, the direct influence of earlier forms of English and Scots is more in evidence.

Some idea of Irish English's mixed linguistic heritage may be gained by considering briefly the origins of three particular grammatical constructions. A well-known feature of Irish English is a construction consisting of *be after* and an *ing*-participle, as in

She's after selling the boat

This is something described as a 'hot-news' perfect; that is, it refers to an event that has taken place in the very recent past. (So a standard translation in this case might be something like 'She has just sold the boat'.) The construction is almost certainly a straight borrowing from Irish:

Tá sí   tréis an bád a dhíol
Be she after the boat selling

Another characteristic of Irish English is the optional omission of subject pronouns in relative clauses, e.g:[2]

I've a friend lives over there
('I've a friend who/that lives over there')

Exactly the same feature occurs in some regional dialects spoken in Scotland and England. It's more than likely that Irish English acquired it from the seventeenth-century ancestors of these dialects.

From a similar source comes the Irish English use of *for to* plus infinitive after certain verbs where the standard language has only *to*, e.g:

It wouldn't do for to say that[3]

This usage has a long history in English – and not just in vernacular varieties either. Besides showing up in a number of present-day non-standard dialects, it is attested in earlier forms of the literary language. There is plenty of evidence of it in Chaucer, for instance, and, as the following example shows, in Shakespeare:

> Forbid the sea for to obey the moon
> (*Winter's Tale*, 1.2.427)

This feature is in fact only one of many which illustrate the linguistically conservative nature of Irish English. Many of the non-standard grammatical characteristics to be examined below are retentions of features which were once general in English, including the literary language. Although these characteristics have now dropped out of standard usage, they continue to have general currency in vernaculars spoken all over the English-speaking world. In fact, when we compare the structural details of different dialects of English, it turns out that in many cases it is the standard that is the odd one out. This is because the standard has undergone a number of important linguistic changes over the years that have had little or no impact on vernacular varieties.[4]

In a chapter of this length, we cannot hope to do more than scratch the surface of Irish English word and sentence structure. Some may feel that there are important omissions or that there are particular aspects which should have been gone into in more detail. All I can do in such cases is refer the reader to the relevant literature. A list of suggested further readings is provided at the end of the chapter for this purpose.

As already pointed out, Irish English consists of a range of regional varieties which differ from one another in certain important respects. We have a fair idea about how pronunciation differences are distributed across Ireland, but our knowledge of the geographical distribution of grammatical differences is unfortunately much more limited.[5] Information about the regional dimensions involved (whether east-west, north-south, urban-rural, or whatever) is at this stage more or less impressionistic. In general, therefore, I have avoided attributing individual grammatical features to particular geographical domains, except in cases where reliable research indicates that we are on firmer ground. I welcome feedback from readers who may be able to put me right on any number of geographical or linguistic details.

Sections 5.2 and 5.3 deal with features of the Irish English noun phrase and verb group respectively. The manner in which elements of the verb group are harnessed to express relations of time is discussed in 5.4. Section 5.5, on the complex sentence, examines Irish English two-clause structures in which one clause is dependent on the other. Non-standard aspects of sentence negation and prepositional usage are treated in 5.6 and 5.7 respectively. Section 5.8, on discourse features, has to do with the use of grammatical devices for organizing the presentation of information in units larger than the sentence. Finally, in 5.9, we explore very briefly some of the potential educational problems posed by the existence of structural differences between Irish English and the standard language.

At every stage in the presentation, I've made full use of examples. Wherever possible, these are not concocted but are drawn from research based on actual recordings of natural speech. The sources are duly acknowledged in the notes. I've presented the examples throughout in more or less standard spelling, with little attempt to represent specific features of Irish English pronunciation. Except where ease of comprehension demands otherwise, I've omitted punctuation marks in order not to prejudice analysis of sentence constituent boundaries. For the sake of consistency, I have where necessary rewritten illustrative material drawn from the published literature in conformity with this format. In some cases, I've provided standard English translations (in quotation marks). As far as possible, I've tried to avoid the use of technical linguistic jargon. Some terms, such as **noun**, **clause** and **plural**, are used without comment, since they have general currency outside academic linguistics. In some cases, however, expository considerations make the introduction of specialist terminology more or less unavoidable. I provide brief explanations of such terms as we go along.

5.2 The noun phrase

5.2.1 Introduction

For present purposes, we may assume here that the grammatical unit **noun phrase** can be realized in one of three ways: as a noun (together with its satellite forms, such as *the*, *a*), as a pronoun, or as a whole clause functioning like a noun. (The last type of noun phrase is illustrated by the bold type words in *Cleaning the windows of skyscrapers can be dangerous*. In this case, the bold type phrase is functioning as the subject of the sentence, just as an ordinary noun can, cf. *Crocodiles can be dangerous.*) A noun can be modified by various satellite forms appearing to its left or right. Forms to the left include adjectives (e.g. *good food*) and determiners (e.g. articles such as *the*, and demonstratives such as *that*). Forms to the right include relative clauses, as in *the woman I met yesterday*. In this section, we'll review briefly some of the most saliently non-standard aspects of the Irish English noun phrase.

5.2.2   Articles

The system of article usage in Irish English differs in several respects from that of the standard **language**. The overall impression is that Irish English makes more extensive use of the definite article *the*. Let us examine briefly a number of illustrative contexts where this appears to be true.

In order to characterize accurately the differences between standard English and Irish English in this area of the grammar, we need to invoke the notions **generic reference** and **non-count**. Briefly, a noun is termed non-count if it denotes an entity which is viewed as an inseparable whole, e.g. *literature, information, integrity*. A noun is said to have generic reference when it refers to a class of entities rather than a specific entity. Thus *the cat* has specific reference in *The cat lapped up the milk* but generic reference in *The cat is a furry animal*. In standard English, non-count nouns usually occur with no article when they have generic reference. So in a sentence such as *She appreciates wine*, the noun *wine* can only refer to wine in general, not to a specific instance of it. On the other hand, in some types of Irish English (and, incidentally, in Scots) it's quite usual to find the definite article being used in this context, e.g:

> I'm tormented with the cold[6]
> He's a terrible man for the drink
> She's in bed with the flu
> The goodness is in it[7]

Another point at which the patterns of article usage in standard and Irish English diverge involves contexts where there exists a close semantic bond between a noun and a noun complement.

In *Davy is the culprit*, for instance, *the culprit* is the noun complement of *Davy*. As this example shows, standard English usually requires the definite article *the* with the noun complement if this refers to a specific entity. When the reference is not specific, however, standard usage requires indefinite *a/an*, as in *Davy is an idiot*. Some types of Irish English, in contrast, prefer *the* in the latter context, e.g:

> You're the quare singer[8]
> He's the wise boy[9]

In standard English, so-called pre-determiners such as *all (of), both (of), most of* (as in *most of the work*) are almost never preceded by an article. This is not the case in Irish English, as the following examples testify:

> I saw the both of them[10]
> We have the most of it killed now

There is a tendency in Irish English to use *the* in contexts where the standard language requires a possessive adjective (*my, your, his, her*, etc.). Some examples:

> He's not the same without the wife[11]
> How's the health?[12]
> It would take the arm off ye

Finally in this section, we may note cases where a possessive form in Irish English corresponds to zero in standard usage, e.g:

> I'm away to my bed
> Come on in for your dinner

5.2.3 Demonstratives

Several points about Irish English demonstratives may be noted here. First, as in many types of non-standard English, the plural form of *that* is regularly *them* as opposed to standard *those*, e.g:

> Them two fellas was hit

Secondly, many types of Irish English have a more sophisticated system of demonstratives than the standard language. Demonstrative forms in the latter only involve two degrees of distance: near to the speaker (*this/these*) and distant from the speaker (*that/those*). The equivalent system in some varieties of Irish English, on the other hand, has the means of expressing three degrees of distance. Besides *this/these* and *that/them*, there are the forms *yon* or *thon* (both singular or plural) which signal a greater degree of distance from the speaker (and, by implication, from the hearer) than *that/them*.

5.2.4   Plural of quantity nouns

Nouns which indicate quantities (of weight, measure, mass, cost, time, etc.) include such words as *pound, mile, foot, year*. In standard English the notion of plurality is expressed twice when these co-occur with numerals, once in the numeral itself, and again in the plural *s*-ending, e.g. *two miles, five years*. The redundancy is typically avoided in non-standard dialects, including Irish English, by omitting the plural ending in such contexts. Hence, for example, *two mile, five foot, four pound*, etc.

5.2.5   Pronouns

The pronoun system of standard English has no formal means of distinguishing second person singular from plural; both categories are indicated by *you*. As mentioned briefly in 5.1, however, Irish English makes the distinction explicit: singular *you/ye* versus plural *youse* (alternative spellings *yez/yiz*). The usefulness of this contrast is illustrated neatly in the following sentence recorded from a Belfast woman:

> So I said to our Jill and our Mary: 'Youse wash the dishes.' I might as well have said: 'You wash the dishes', for our Jill just got up and put her coat on and went out.[13]

Among the various forms that pronouns take in English, two in particular are important here. Subject pronouns, as the term suggests, are those which occur as the subject of a sentence: *I, you, he, she, it, we, they*. The so-called oblique forms (*me, you, him, her, it, us, them*) are those which, besides other functions, occur as sentence objects (as in *The dog bit him*), or after prepositions (as in *The idea came to him*). (Note that *you* and *it* don't have distinct subject and oblique forms.) In colloquial English, be it standard or non-standard, the oblique forms are also those that appear in isolation or after *it's*. (For example: *Who's there? – Me.*) Only in very formal or self-consciously correct usage do we find subject forms being used in the latter contexts. Thus, *It's me*, although frequently stigmatized, sounds more natural than *It is I*. Irish English follows the general colloquial pattern in this respect.

A general tendency in non-standard English is for the oblique form to be used as a subject pronoun when it is conjoined with another subject, e.g. *Me and Mary are good mates*. This is also the usual pattern in Irish English.

In standard English, the so-called reflexive pronouns (those ending in *-self/-selves*) can generally only be used when they are construed with a noun or pronoun in the same sentence. In *Monica considered herself lucky*, for instance, *herself* is construed with *Monica*. In certain types of Irish English, on the other hand, the corresponding pronoun forms can be used to refer to persons not mentioned elsewhere in the same sentence. Typically, the reference in such cases is implicit. That is, rather than the person being mentioned explicitly in the immediate linguistic context (for instance, in a preceding sentence), the reference draws on the shared knowledge of the speaker and hearer. Note that in each of the following sentences there is no noun phrase with which the *self*-pronoun can be construed:

> Herself will tell you
> Did you see himself?[14]

Compare these with the following from Shakespeare:

> Bid herself assay him
> (*Measure for Measure* I.2.171)

Some types of Irish English have plural demonstrative pronoun forms ending in *-un's (-ones): usun's, yousun's, themun's*, e.g:

> Yousun's can go now

5.2.6   Nominalization

Nominalization refers to the process whereby a word or phrase acquires a noun-like status it doesn't ordinarily have. For example, nominalizing the verb in *The Graf Spee was sunk* gives us *The sinking of the Graf Spee*. A nominalized form can thus be made to perform the sort of grammatical functions (e.g. subject or object) normally associated with ordinary nouns.

Nominalized forms in Irish English frequently appear in contexts where the standard language is more likely to have a verb. These may occur as subject complements (as it were, 'completing' the description of the subject), as in

> It's his own rearing[15]
> ('He reared it himself')

as objects, as in

> If I had the doing of it again, I'd do it different.[16]
> ('If I could do it again, I'd do it differently')

or in prepositional phrases, as in

> Is this the first of you arriving?
> ('Have you only just arrived?')
> I was at the leaving down of the first stone[17]
> ('I was there when the first stone was being laid')

5.2.7   Relative clauses

Relative clauses in spontaneous speech are almost exclusively of the **restrictive** type. That is, they provide information which helps specify the identity of the noun to which they are attached (as in *the woman I met yesterday*). So-called **parenthetic** relative clauses, which don't have this specifying function, are hardly ever found outside planned formal discourse (as in *The woman, who incidentally comes from Canada, has just left*). The following discussion deals only with restrictive relatives.

A relative clause can be thought of as a clause that is embedded in another clause, specifically in the noun phrase which it modifies. Thus in *That's the woman I saw yesterday*, the clause *I met yesterday* is embedded in the noun phrase *the woman* which appears in the main clause *That's the woman*. The forms which introduce relative clauses in standard English are: the subject relatives *who, which, that*; the object relatives *who(m), which, that*; and the possessive relative *whose*. Object relatives may be omitted, e.g. *the woman (who(m)/that) I met yesterday*.

The first thing we may note about relative clauses in Irish English is that the *wh*-relative forms are not particularly frequent, a characteristic shared with some other dialects. Instead, basic Irish English vernacular has available at least three devices for achieving relativization: a 'quasi-relative' clause formed with *and*, a *that* clause embedded in the main sentence in a way that differs strikingly from the standard pattern, and an embedded clause with no relative pronoun. A notable feature of all of these constructions is that they frequently contain 'shadow' pronouns which refer back to the main clause noun.

The *and*-relative in Irish English is illustrated by:

There was a woman and she made soda bread
('There was a woman who made soda bread')

At first sight, this looks pretty much like a simple co-ordinating structure, i.e. one where two clauses of equal status are conjoined. But certain factors to do with the pronunciation of such sentences suggest that they have a greater internal cohesion than simple co-ordination. For one thing, they are typically produced as a single breath group and with a unified intonation pattern. The most plausible analysis is that *and* plus a shadow pronoun (*she* in the above example) together constitute a grammatical device for achieving relativization.

Optional omission of object relatives is as characteristic of Irish English as it is of standard English. However, in Irish English and many other non-standard varieties, omission extends to subject relatives, as in

I've a friend lives over there.

Sometimes this pattern also occurs with a shadow pronoun, e.g:

> Any man had a thatched house he knew how to thatch
> ('Any man who had a thatched house knew how to thatch')

In the light of examples such as the following, it may be possible to say that omission also applies to possessive relatives in Irish English:

> This woman next door her man didn't get paid till Friday she'd a come in to see me
> ('This woman next door whose husband didn't get paid till Friday would've come in to see me')

However, it's not clear here whether we are dealing with a case of zero relative plus shadow *her* or whether *her* is functioning as a possessive relative in its own right. (Note also in this example the use of shadow *she* to mark the return to the main clause.)

That-relative clauses in Irish English seem in many ways to follow patterns of subordination rather than standard relativization. (By **subordination**, we mean the linking of two clauses such that one is dependent on the other.) In fact, we may treat *that* in such contexts on a par with the subordinating *that* which we get in non-relative sentences such as *We decided that it was time to go*. In sentences like

> I'd say a lot of things that they're not right either

two grammatical functions (relativization and the signalling of relative-clause subject), instead of being combined in one form as in the standard (i.e. *which* or *that*), are distributed over two forms (*that* and *they*). A similar pattern is observable with object relatives, e.g:

> I thought they would a put a steel door on that they couldn't have opened it

It's also observable in possessive relatives:

> Remember the man that's house got burnt down?

(Note that *that/that's* is analogous to *who/whose*.) The same pattern is found in cases where standard literary English requires prepositional relatives (such as *on whose, of which*), e.g:

> Some fella that the graveyard was on his land
> ('Some fellow on whose land the graveyard was')

> A herb that the root of it was boiled[18]

5.3   The verb group

5.3.1   Introduction

In this section, we focus on the constellation of forms which make up what is sometimes called the *verb group*, including the basic verb stem itself (e.g. *walk, take, sing*), verb endings (as in *walk+ed, walk+s walk+ing*), and auxiliaries like *have, be, will* (as in *have walked, am walking*). In particular, we will look at the following things. First, at different forms of the so-called 'strong' verbs, i.e. verbs whose past-tense and participle forms don't conform to the regular ('weak') *-ed* pattern. (In standard English, *walk/walked/walked* is weak, *sing/sang/sung* is strong.) Secondly, we examine the system of subject-verb concord; that is, the grammatical rules governing the form of verbs after different types of subject noun phrase. Thirdly, we look at some of the ways in which various combinations of elements in the Irish English verb group are used to express relations of time. Fourthly, we note some of the special imperative forms that occur in Irish English. And finally, we mention a number of isolated non-standard characteristics of the Irish English verb group.

5.3.2   Strong verbs

There are various ways of classifying the strong verbs of standard English. If we concentrate on the three categories of basic stem, past tense and past participle, we can identify three main groups:

(1)   verbs with three different forms,
(2)   those with two different forms, and
(3)   those with identical forms for all three categories.

Differences in form typically involve some change in the stem vowel, and sometimes a consonant change as well. Some examples of the three groups:

(1)   *do/did/done, give/gave/given*:
(2)   *come/came/come, buy/bought/bought*;
(3)   *hit/hit/hit, put/put/put*.

The strong verb system was much more complex and extensive in Old English times. Since then there has been a progressive erosion of the range of forms associated with each strong verb, while some originally strong verbs have become shifted into the weak category. The process, which affected literary and vernacular varieties alike, was well advanced by the eighteenth century. Since then, however, there has been a sporadic and partial reversal of the change in the standard language but not in non-standard dialects. The result is that the latter tend to have simpler strong verb systems than the modern standard; and this is no less true of Irish English. Typically, what we find is that many standard two- and three-form patterns correspond to non-standard one- and two-form patterns respectively. So, for instance, where modern standard English has *do/did/done* or *go/went/gone*, most non-standard dialects (including Irish English) have *do/done/done* and *go/went/went* (just as in earlier stages of the literary language). Standard *come/came/come* corresponds to non-standard *come/come/come*. Hence Irish English examples like

> I done the secretarial course
> He would a went on his own
> ('He would've gone on his own')

Compare the latter with Jane Austen's

> . . . the troubles we had went through
> (*Sense and Sensibility*)

The list of differences between standard and non-standard usage in this area of the verb system is quite extensive. For the sake of brevity, we confine ourselves to a few illustrative comparisons.

First, some Irish English verbs with identical past-tense and past-participle forms corresponding to the standard three-form format:

Irish English		Standard English		
bite	bit	bite	bit	bitten
hide	hid	hide	hid	hidden
sing	sung	sing	sang	sung
do	done	do	did	done
drink	drunk	drink	drank	drunk
break	broke	break	broke	broken
see	seen	see	saw	seen
take	took	take	took	taken
tear	tore	tear	tore	torn
grow	grew	grow	grew	grown
fall	fell	fall	fell	fallen
go	went	go	went	gone

Examples of Irish English verbs with identical forms for all three categories of base, past tense and past participle, corresponding to a standard two-form pattern, include: *run, come, give, beat, loss* (= standard *lose*).

Do can function either as a main verb or as an auxiliary. (Auxiliary verbs are those such as *do, have, be, can, will, may* which are subordinate to a main verb, e.g. She *can* sing, They *are* going.) The use of *do* as a main verb is illustrated in That's what he *does* for a living. Auxiliary *do* appears in negative sentences and questions where it supports a main verb, as in He *doesn't know*, or *Does he know?* (This pattern is often referred to as **do-support**.) It can also be used to substitute for a main verb, e.g. *Anne sang, and so did Tom*. In many non-standard dialects, including Irish English, the forms of *do* differ according to whether it has main-verb or auxiliary status. Thus, while the non-standard past tense of the main verb is regularly *done*, the form *did* occurs in auxiliary contexts. Compare the following:

He done it
He didn't do it
Did he do it?
He broke the window, so he did
(*. . . so he done)

(An asterisk placed against a sentence indicates that it contravenes grammatical rules, in this case the rules of most non-standard varieties of English.)

5.3.3   Subject-verb concord

The term **subject-verb concord** refers to the relationship between a subject and its verb whereby the number and person of the former determines the shape of the latter. The standard pattern is quite simple: present-tense verbs other than *be* take an *s*-ending if the subject is third person singular; otherwise they remain uninflected:

		singular	plural
person	1	*I run*	*we run*
	2	*you run*	*you run*
	3	*he/she/it runs*	*they run*

With *be*, we get the alternations *am/is/are* in the present tense and *was/were* in the past. In our survey of how Irish English differs from the standard in this area of the grammar, we'll focus on patterns of concord involving plural subjects.

Historically, we find three main types of verb-ending which mark subject-verb concord: *-eth* (which survives only in the most archaic usage, e.g. *he goeth*), *-(e)s* (the source of the modern *s*-inflection), and zero. The use of these three forms in different varieties has fluctuated over the centuries. In fact, the modern standard pattern of subject-verb concord was not stabilized until comparatively recently. What is noteworthy in the context of the present discussion is that the *-(e)s* verb-ending has a long history of being used with plural subjects. This pattern, which is evident in early literary texts, is retained in many present-day non-standard varieties, including Irish English. Hence, we find *the women knows* corresponding to standard *the women know*.

The basic Irish English concord pattern (leaving aside for the moment details of variability) is that, with third-person subjects, the *s*-ending occurs not only in the singular (as in the standard) but also in the plural. Thus we find both *the woman knows* and *the women knows*. The pattern extends to forms of *be: the women is/was*. The details are in fact much more complex than this. Most Irish English speakers don't use the non-standard s-ending categorically. But the extent to which they do appears to be sensitive to a range of grammatical (not to mention social) constraints which we're only just beginning to understand. Here we can only sketch some of the grammatical factors which govern the likelihood of a verb appearing with an s-ending after a plural subject.

One of the factors is the nature of the subject itself. Generally speaking, the s-ending (including *is/was* in the case of *be*) occurs freely with subjects which are full nouns (as opposed to pronouns), e.g:

> Them two fellas was hit
> ('Those two fellows were hit')
> Her grandchildren comes down

As far as we can make out, however, a bare plural pronoun almost never takes the s-ending. Thus, *they knows/is/was* is ungrammatical by the rules of Irish English. The same goes for first- and second-person plural pronouns: *we/youse/knows/is/was*. This distinguishes the dialect from some other types of non-standard English in which, for instance, *we was* is used. The third-person demonstrative plural forms *them* and *themuns* (see 5.2.5) do, on the other hand, occur with the s-inflection, e.g:

> Them's the words he used to me
> ('Those are the words he used to me')

S-inflections also show up after relative pronouns:

> Some of them that was released are all right
> ('Some of those that were released are all right')
> You get wee ones that screws things
> ('You get little ones that screw things')

The different behaviour of full-noun and pronoun subjects with respect to verb concord is clearly demonstrated in the following example:

> Them eggs is cracked, so they are[19]
> (*. . . so they is)

The most favourable context for a verbal s-ending to occur with a plural subject appears to be in questions where we get subject-verb inversion, e.g:

> Is my hands clean?

Finally, it is quite usual in Irish English to find the s-inflection with 'collective' noun phrases, which have plural meaning but contain no grammatically plural noun, e.g:

> The whole six of us was sitting . . .
> Most of the hard core's all older men

This phenomenon is by no means restricted to Irish English or vernacular English generally (cf. variation between *the government is* and *the government are* in standard usage).

5.3.4 'Historic present'

While we're on the subject of subject-verb concord, it's as well to mention another verb form which involves an s-ending. This is the so-called 'historic present', which is used to bring dramatic effect to the narration of past events, as in

> And I goes down and gets him by the neck

Strictly speaking, we should postpone discussion of this grammatical device until we examine the Irish English tense system in the next section. But it's appropriate to bring it up here in order to underline the fact that the narrative s-ending is quite independent of subject-verb concord. This is confirmed by the ability of the narrative s-inflection to occur in contexts where the 'empty' s-ending of subject-verb concord cannot, e.g. after first-person subjects, as in the above example.

5.3.5 Imperatives

Imperative forms of verbs are employed for the purposes of giving commands or making requests, as in Go *away!* or Bring *that bottle* *over here*. As these examples show, the imperative form of the verb in general English is indistinguishable from the infinitive. In Irish English, there is a tendency to use a **continuous** form in such contexts, i.e. a construction composed of *be* and an *ing*-participle:

> Be peeling them there
> Don't be talking[20]

In standard usage, the second-person pronoun is only implicit in imperatives. (It could be said that *you* is implied in, for instance, *Come here!*) In some types of Irish English, on the other hand, it's quite usual to find the pronoun being given explicit expression, as in

> Go you on!
> Don't you be staying out late now!

Compare this with Shakespeare's

> Come you to me at night
> (*The Merry Wives of Windsor*, 2.2.277)

Other types of imperatives in Irish English are constructed with modal auxiliaries, especially *may* or *can*, as in

> You may leave that there!
> ('Leave that there')

or, in some areas, with *let* or *leave*:

> Let you all go now!
> Let you not be making noise![21]

5.3.6   Miscellaneous non-standard verb forms

We conclude this section with a brief mention of several other characteristically non-standard forms which occur in the Irish English verb group.

amn't

In many types of Irish English, the contracted form of *am not* is regularly *amn't* (as in Scottish English) rather than *aren't*, e.g:

> I'm old enough to get in, amn't I?

will/shall

Some of the more conservative guides to standard British English usage insist that the auxiliary forms *shall* and *will* should be used in mutually exclusive environments: the former only after first-person subjects (e.g. *I shall go*), the latter after second- and third-person subjects (e.g. *they will go*). *Will* with first-person subjects in this type of English is said to indicate volition rather than simple prediction. In fact, the rule doesn't hold for many varieties of English, both standard and vernacular. In Irish English, as in most Scottish and American varieties, *shall* as a marker of prediction is almost nonexistent. Typically, *will* as an expression of prediction occurs with all personal subjects, including first person, without any necessary implication of volition (as in *I will go*).

A similar pattern is evident with conditional *should/would*. Formal English English usage requires *should* with first-person, *would* with second- and third-person subjects. In Scottish, American and Irish English, on the other hand, *would* tends to be used in all persons (e.g. *I would be grateful* versus formal English English *I should be grateful*). Whenever *should* does occur in these varieties, it almost always signifies obligation (as in *I should go but I can't be bothered*).

'Subjunctive' was/were

Older 'subjunctive' forms of *be* are common as conditionals in conservative types of Irish English. These are formally identical to simple-past *was/were* and occur in contexts where the modern standard language usually prefers *would/should be*, e.g:

> 'Twas better for her come down to earth[22]
> ('It would be better for her to come . . .')

The similarities with older literary English here are striking.

haven

A characteristic of some Dublin speech in the use of *haven* (pronounced with the same vowel as that in *have*) as an auxiliary with *shoulda* (from *should have?*). The form has positive meaning and is thus unrelated to negative *haven't* e.g:[23]

> I shoulda haven killed him
> ('I should have killed him')

5.4   The expression of time

5.4.1   Tense and aspect

The grammatical expression of time by means of different elements in the verb group is generally analysed into two important components: **tense** and **aspect**. Very broadly, tense has to do with the objective location of an event in time, for example in the past or the present. Aspect, on the other hand, has to do with the perspective adopted by the speaker with respect to the internal time structure of an event. The latter component thus provides information about such questions as the following: Is the event completed or still in progress? Is it a one-off affair or repeated? Is it instantaneous or prolonged? In English, the *ed*-ending is usually considered a tense category, in this case **past**. *He arrived*, for instance, clearly records an activity which occurred at some time prior to the moment of speaking. The *ed*-ending, however, doesn't necessarily have anything to say about the internal structure of the event. The construction *be* Verb+*ing* (as in *Mary is singing*), on the other hand, does; it is often referred to by the aspectual term **continuous**. In a sentence like *Mary was singing when Tom arrived*, the activity described in *was singing* was on-going when the event of Tom's arrival occurred. In this case, the verb group *was singing* carries both tense and aspect information. The form of the *be* element (*was*) indicates past tense; the combination of *be* and an *ing*-participle indicates continuous aspect.

The expression of tense and aspect in Irish English differs from the standard in several fundamental respects. We focus here on three areas of the verb group where this divergence is clearly in evidence.

5.4.2   The Irish English 'perfects'

The so-called present perfect form in standard English (as in *have walked*) is used to express a number of tense and aspect distinctions. There are four in particular that need to be examined here. In contrast to the standard pattern, speakers of basic Irish English vernacular tend to make these temporal distinctions grammatically explicit. Rather than employing the standard perfect, such speakers may make use of at least five other constructions.

Resultative

The term **resultative** refers to a verb-form which describes a past event with present relevance (e.g *Peggy has broken her leg*). Irish English has two resultative forms, one restricted to verbs which take an object (**transitive** verbs), the other to verbs which don't (**intransitive** verbs). The transitive construction is a 'split perfect' consisting of *have* plus a past participle placed after the object. For example, in

> I've it pronounced wrong

the *have* form (contracted to *'ve*) is separated from the participle *pronounced* by the object pronoun *it*.[24] The intransitive counterpart is formed with *be* plus a past participle. It tends to be restricted to verbs of change or motion, e.g:

> I'm not too long left

Hot-news

As the name suggests, hot-news describes an event that occurs immediately before the moment of speaking (e.g. *Peggy has just arrived*). To express hot-news, Irish English has the familiar *be after doing* construction already referred to in 5.1:

> I was after coming down the stairs
> ('I had just come down the stairs')

The form also occurs with noun phrases which don't contain verbs, as in

I'm only after my dinner
('I've just had dinner')

The immediate past reading of the construction distinguishes it
from the 'future-of-intention' use of *after* which we sometimes
find in colloquial British English (as in *He's after my job* = 'He
wants my job').

In many parts of Ireland, hot-news is the only meaning that the
be after doing construction can have. However, in what seems to
be a recent development in some areas (Dublin, for example), the
form has taken on a more broadly perfect sense. The result is that
it can be used to refer to longer time-scales, as illustrated by the
following:

All the week is after being cold[25]

Extended-now

This describes a situation initiated in the past and persisting
into the present (e.g. *I've known Peggy for some time*). Many
languages, including French, German and Irish, use a present-
tense form rather than some perfect-type construction to express
extended-now time. Irish English is similar to this respect. Thus
we find simple or continuous present forms in sentences like the
following, where standard usage would require the perfect:

I know his family all me life
('I've known his family all my life')
We're living here seventeen years
('We've been living here for seventeen years')

Indefinite since-time

This refers to an event or events occurring at (an) unspecified
point(s) in a period leading up to the present (e.g. *I've only met
Peggy twice*). To express this time relation, Irish English prefers
the simple past verb form, e.g:

I never saw a gun in my life nor never saw one fired
('I've never seen a gun in my life . . .')

In this respect, Irish English is somewhat similar to some types of American English. (Compare American *I already ate* with British standard *I've already eaten.*)

To summarize, in basic Irish English there are at least five forms which can do the work of the standard perfect: *have* – object – past participle; *be* – past participle; *be after* – *ing*-participle; present (simple or continuous); and simple past. Of these, the last two are obviously not non-standard in themselves. Rather it is the use to which they are put in this context that differs from the standard.

5.4.3   Habitual aspect

An important aspectual category in many of the world's languages is that of **habitual**. Briefly, as the name suggests, this refers to events which take place repeatedly over a period of time. In standard English, *used to* can be employed to express this temporal relation in past time, e.g. *He used to come home late every evening.* (In some types of Irish English, the equivalent form can be simply *used*, as in *He used come home late.*) However, the standard verb group has no non-past form which expresses habitual aspect exclusively. Habitual aspect obviously can be indicated by using the simple present form, e.g. *Joe goes to school every day.* But this is only one of a range of temporal functions that are potentially performed by the form. Basic Irish English vernacular is quite different in this respect. It has a number of verb-group devices which make the habitual-non-habitual distinction explicit.

One such device is habitual *be*. Its finite forms (i.e. when it occurs with a subject) are, depending on the dialect, *be/be's* or *do/does be*. (The former appears to be more typically northern.) It contrasts quite clearly with non-habitual *be* which has the general English finite forms *am/is/are*. Compare *He's sick now* (non-habitual) with *He be's sick often* (habitual). Some recorded examples:[26]

> Even when I be round there with friends I be scared
> He never be's sick or anything
> He does be late for dinner sometimes

With verbs other than *be*, the habitual is formed by *do* plus an infinitive, as in

He does plough the field for us
A lot of them does cut them on into June

(Note the non-standard subject-verb concord in the last example – see 5.3.3.) *Do* in such sentences is not necessarily stressed. The usage is thus quite unrelated to the stressed auxiliary *do* which is employed for emphatic purposes in English generally. (For instance, a response to *You don't know Jim of course* might be *But I DO know him* without any element of habitual aspect.) In fact, as the following example shows, habitual *do* or *be* in Irish English can co-occur with emphatic *do* anyway.

He's the kind of person that you would never know when he was drunk but he DOES be, if you know what I mean.

Moreover, habitual *do* in Irish English cannot be considered a mere extension of the general English rule of *do*-support which we discussed briefly in 5.3.2. Recall that this controls the occurrence of auxiliary *do* as a 'dummy' form supporting main verbs in negative and interrogative contexts (e.g. *He knows* versus *He doesn't know* and *Does he know?*). The independent status of habitual *do/be* in Irish English is confirmed by the fact that these occur freely with *do*-support, just as any main verb can, e.g:

It doesn't be much a week
We never be out, do we?

Habitual *be* or *do be* can be combined with *ing*-forms of main verbs to produce a 'habitual continuous' category. This indicates that the internal temporal structure of each event in a recurrent series is one of extended duration. For example:

They be shooting and fishing out at the forestry lakes
They do be fighting among other[27]
('. . . among themselves')

To summarize, basic Irish English vernacular has special forms of *be* which exclusively express habitual aspect (*he be's sick, he does be sick*). Habituals of other verbs are formed with *do* (*he does go*). In addition, there is a habitual continuous category (*he be's going, he does be going*).

5.4.4   Continuous forms of stative verbs

In grammatical analysis, a distinction is sometimes drawn between **dynamic** and **stative** categories of verb. Briefly, the former includes verbs which describe activities (like *drink, work*) or processes (like *grow, leave*). The latter includes verbs of inert perception and cognition (like *want, realize*) as well as relational verbs (like *own, resemble*). Typically in standard English, the continuous verb form can occur with dynamic but not stative verbs. (Thus *I'm working*, but not **I'm resembling my father.*) In Irish English, in contrast, stative verbs, particularly those of perception and cognition, appear quite extensively in the continuous, e.g:

> They're not believing it
> That's what I was wanting
> I was knowing your face[28]

5.5   Complex sentences

5.5.1   Subordination

For our purposes, we may define a complex sentence as one that exhibits subordination. (Recall our definition of subordination in 4.2.7 as the linking of two clauses such that one is dependent on the other.) Grammatical forms which overtly mark subordination (such as *because, that, if, although, whereas*) are generally termed **subordinators** or **subordinating conjunctions**. The full range of subordinators typically only occurs in written English. In colloquial speech, be it standard or non-standard, there are various alternative ways of introducing dependent clauses, many of which are also used in Irish English.

5.5.2   Subordinators

In types of Irish English showing most clearly the effects of Irish influence, we find phrasal constructions corresponding to single-word question forms in other varieties, e.g: *what way* 'how', *what reason* 'why', *what man* 'who', *what time* 'when', *what thing* 'what'. Related forms crop up as subordinators (e.g. *the time (that)* 'when'). Perhaps the most striking of these is *the way that*. Along with its variant forms *in a way, the way, the ways*, this generally introduces subordinate clauses of result or purpose, as in

> He put down his leg on it in a way he cut the leg off himself
> ('. . . with the result that . . .')[29]
> They made poteen away out on the hill the way you wouldn't know a bit about it
> Leave it in a way the cattle won't spill it[30]

A more widely used device for introducing clauses of purpose in Irish English is the subordinator *till*, e.g:

> Come here till I tell ye

The forms *from* and *whenever* in Irish English are frequently used as subordinators of time. In this function, *from* corresponds roughly to standard *since*, as in

> I know him from he was a wee fella
> ('I've known him since . . .')

In most types of English, *whenever* used with a past-tense verb implies repeated action. In characteristically northern Irish English, in contrast, the same form has no such implication; it generally refers only to a single event. In the following example, recorded from a Belfast speaker, *whenever* is clearly being used in a sense more or less equivalent to *when* in other types of English:

> My husband died whenever I was living in New Lodge Road

5.5.3   Subordinating *and*

And as means of linking clauses in standard usage is associated exclusively with co-ordinate structures, i.e. where one clause is not dependent on another (as in *It was raining, and Danny was feeling homesick*). In some types of Irish English (particularly southern and western), however, it can be used with a subject pronoun to introduce a non-finite subordinate clause (i.e. one which lacks a verb marked for tense). Typically, this occurs with an *ing*-participle, as in

> We were listening to them and them talking[31]
> ('. . . while they were talking')

The construction appears to be related to a more general Irish English pattern consisting of *and* plus verbless clause, as in

> I met him and the cattle with him[32]
> ('I met him driving cattle')

As these examples indicate, the construction can express a temporal relation. This is in fact its most usual function. Some more examples:

> He waved at me and he coming down the road[33]
> ('. . . as he was coming . . .')
> You put in your nose and us churning[34]
> ('You appeared while . . .')

Non-finite clauses introduced by *and*, however, have a potentially wide range of meanings, including, as the following example indicates, concessive (= standard 'although'):

> Ye'd wonder at that child being so stupid and the mother so clever[35]

A related non-finite clause structure is one formed with the infinitive form of the verb. In some cases, this clearly has subordinate status, as in

> Do you know anything at all about them you to bid that little?[36]
> ('. . . considering you bid . . .')

In other cases, however, such clauses occur in what can be analysed as co-ordinate structures, as in

> Close the gate then and not to open it after[37]

5.5.4   Verb complement clauses

The term verb **complement** generally applies to a grammatical unit which as it were 'completes' the action specified by the verb. The complement can be a subordinate clause, either finite (sometimes introduced by *that*, as in *Joe felt (that) he had succeeded*) or non-finite (as in *Joe knows how to swim*).

An archaic characteristic of Irish English, mentioned briefly in the opening section, is that it preserves an older English non-finite complement structure introduced by *for to*, e.g:

He was asked for to loosen the rope
It wouldn't do for to say that[38]

Generally speaking, modern standard usage requires simply *to* in such contexts. *For to* also occurs in Irish English adjective complements:

He'd be only too proud for to be speaking to you[39]

It's sometimes assumed that *for to* only introduces clauses of purpose. There are indeed examples of this usage:

I went to the shop for to buy some sweets[40]

Nevertheless, the previous examples show that this is only one of the functions performed by *for to*.

Another feature of Irish English is an extended use of the general English pattern whereby 'bare' infinitives (i.e. without *to*) can occur in complement clauses after certain verbs. This is of course the normal pattern with modal auxiliaries such as *can, must, may* (e.g. *he can swim*, not **he can to swim*. In standard English, *make, let* and, optionally, *help* are also of this type (e.g. *I helped him (to) move*). In Irish English, this category contains a number of additional verbs, including *order, compel, allow* (as in *She allowed him stay out late*).

5.5.6   Indirect questions

The indirect reporting of direct speech is achieved in standard English by means of a verb complement structure; specifically, by subordinating the words of the speaker to a main clause verb (such as *say, tell, announce*) and modifying the tense of the original verb(s) in particular ways. (Thus, '*It's time to go*'→ *She said (that) it was time to go.*) In standard usage, two additional operations are necessary for formulating indirect questions. First, the verb-subject inversion of the original question has to be undone. (So, *How can you think that?* becomes *He asked me how I could think that.*) Secondly, indirect versions of questions requiring yes or no answers must be introduced by *whether* or *if.* (e.g: '*Did you see her?*' → *He asked me if I had seen her*).

In Irish English, as in many types of non-standard English, the last two grammatical operations are not obligatory. Thus, with indirect WH-questions (i.e. those introduced by *what, why, how, when*, etc.), we find the subject-verb inversion of the original question retained, as in

He wanted to know how far was it to Lurgan

This is also true of yes-no questions which lack the subordinators *if* or *whether*:

He came to see would we set up a shop at the end of the road

5.6   Negation

5.6.1   Negative concord

There are various ways of negating a finite clause in standard English. The negative particle *not* (or a contracted form of it) can be placed to the right of an auxiliary verb (*we may go* → *we may not go*). In the case of full verbs, *not* is attached to a supporting *do*-form (*we go* → *we don't go*). Alternatively, a negative pronoun, determiner or adverb (such as *nobody, no, none (of), never*) may be used (e.g. *no one is coming*).

An important feature of standard English negatives is that only one of these operations may be performed to achieve the simple negation of a clause. Two negative forms appearing in the same clause are deemed to 'cancel each other out', thus producing an overall positive meaning (e.g. *Not many people have never been frightened* = 'Most people have been frightened').

This pattern is quite different from the one we encounter in most types of non-standard English, including Irish English, which exhibit the rule of **negative concord**. Briefly, this requires that any word appearing in a simple negative sentence must take a negative form if it can. That is, verbs, pronouns, determiners and adverbs must if possible agree in the marking of negation. Thus we get so-called 'double negatives' in sentences such as

I didn't see nobody
('I didn't see anybody')

I never said nothing
('I didn't say anything')

A better term would be 'multiple negation', since more than two negatives can appear in a sentence exhibiting negative concord, as in

She never lost no furniture nor nothing
('She didn't lose any furniture or anything')

(The previous two examples illustrate another general feature of non-standard English which also occurs in Irish English: the use of *never* as a combined negative and past-tense form.) The rule also operates with words such as *hardly, scarcely, barely*, which have a positive form but negative function, e.g:

They couldn't hardly get her into the tender
('They could hardly get . . .')

Negative concord is in fact a rule of some antiquity in English. Indeed, at one time it was current in the literary language, as the following from Sidney bears witness:

A vow . . . that I would never marry none . . .
(*Arcadia* 323)

It was eighteenth-century prescriptive grammarians who, on the basis of the pseudo-logical principle that two minuses make a plus, denounced the use of multiple negation in simple negative sentences. (Though quite why there should be any intrinsic connection between logic and grammar was never made particularly clear. Many of the world's languages, including standard literary ones, operate with rules which are very similar to non-standard English negative concord.)

5.6.2 Non-assertive forms

In English, there is a set of non-assertive forms which do not usually occur outside clauses involving negation, interrogation or conditional statements. These include determiners and pronouns such as *any, either* and adverbs such as *yet, at all* (e.g. *I've had some → I haven't had any; He's already left → He hasn't left yet*). Two points about the behaviour of these forms in Irish English may be noted here.

First, some non-assertive forms occur freely in positive clauses. *Yet* in such contexts generally means 'still', as in

> I used to go fishing there when I was a boy – and I do go yet

(Note the use of habitual *do* – see 5.4.3.) A well-known stereotypical feature of Irish English is the use of *at all* in a more extensive set of contexts than is possible in other dialects, e.g.:

> He's the fine boy at all

In this connection, we may also mention the use of positive *anymore* which usually means something like 'nowadays' or simply 'now', as in

> They're getting big boys anymore
> That's the way they do it anymore[41]

A second feature of non-assertive forms in Irish English concerns the indeterminate subject pronoun/determiner *any*. In standard English, the occurrence of this form is governed by a rule known as **negative attraction**. This stipulates that a negative particle which would otherwise appear to the right of a verb is 'attracted' to a subject pronoun/determiner if this has indefinite reference. On the basis of the normal word-order pattern (which we get with definite subjects, as in *she doesn't go*), we might expect something like *anybody doesn't go*. Instead, negative attraction gives us *nobody goes*. The rule is, however, not binding on some types of Irish English, where we encounter sentences such as

> Anyone doesn't go to mass there[42]
> ('No one goes . . .')

5.7 Prepositional usage

The non-standard use of prepositions in Irish English is a potentially vast topic. In conservative varieties especially, it is an area where the effects of Irish influence are very much in evidence. In order to do justice to the complexity of the facts, it is a topic that is better dealt with in an account of the Irish English lexicon. In other words, it has more to do with the meanings of individual words (the prepositions themselves) than with generally applicable rules of grammar. So we will limit ourselves here to a very brief discussion of a number of specific features which should at least give some idea of the extent to which conservative Irish English usage in this area differs from that of the standard. For much fuller discussions of prepositional usage in Irish English, the reader can refer to the relevant literature.[43]

In some cases, it's simply a matter of noting correspondences between different prepositions in the two varieties. For instance, many rural Irish English speakers use *with* in adverbial phrases of time where standard English requires *for*:

> He's dead now with many a year[44]
> ('He's been dead for many years')

Some Irish English prepositional forms simply don't occur in the standard language, although it's not difficult to find standard equivalents for them. *Over the head of*, for example, is sometimes used with the meaning 'because of' or 'on account of'. The northern forms *forbye* and *fornenst/fornent* (which derive from Scots) mean respectively 'in addition to' and 'opposite to/in relation to'.

In the majority of cases, however, comparison between standard and Irish English in this area of the grammar is a more complicated affair, due to a tendency in the latter to express in prepositional phrases meanings that in the standard are conveyed by other means, e.g. verbally, adjectivally or adverbially. Frequently, for instance, the 'logical' subject of an Irish English sentence is represented by a noun phrase governed by a preposition. Some examples:

> The money is with them
> ('They have plenty of money')
>
> She wasn't asked had she a mouth on her
> ('. . . whether she was hungry')
>
> There's great humour to him[45]
> ('He's very humorous')
>
> Would ye look at the state of him
> ('Consider what he looks like')
>
> Sure there was geese and hens by everyone that time[46]
> ('. . . everyone owned geese . . .')

Aspectual information which in standard English is generally expressed adverbially or in elements of the verb group is sometimes indicated in conservative Irish English by prepositional means. Continuous aspect, for example, is sometimes expressed in this way:

> It's at the rain
> ('It's raining')
> They made odious noise in the going out[47]
> ('They made a lot of noise while they were going out')

The hot-news perfect with *after* (see 5.4.2) is also of this type.

A more general characteristic of non-standard English which also occurs in Irish English is the use of *on* as a so-called 'preposition of disadvantage', as in

> Ye've lost me pen on me[48]

Another non-standard feature which is also current outside

Ireland is preposition chaining, in which complex directional and locational meanings are expressed by combining different prepositions (or particles derived from them) in sequence, as in

Come on out from in under the table

5.8 Discourse devices

5.8.1 Introduction

The term **discourse** applied to spoken language generally refers to a stretch of connected speech, larger than a sentence, which makes up a unified speech event, such as a conversational exchange or spoken narrative. In this section, we examine very briefly a number of grammatical devices in Irish English whose function it is to help organize the presentation of information in spoken discourse. We'll look specifically at some of the grammatical means available to Irish English speakers for focusing attention on particular sentence constituents and for making explicit the distinction between **given** and **new** information. (Briefly, given information is that which is already supplied by the previous context of speaking; new, as the term suggests, refers to information not previously provided.)

The initial unit of a clause is often referred to as the **theme**, which can be described as 'the communicative point of departure for the rest of the clause'.[49] Typically, the theme contains given information which is completed by new information presented in the remainder of the clause. However, by giving intonational prominence to clause-initial position, it's possible to make the theme the focal point of new information. In English statements, it is the clause subject that normally appears in this position. But speakers have recourse to a number of grammatical fronting operations which have the effect of shifting a sentence constituent out of its 'normal' or expected position and into the theme slot. One of these is **left-dislocation**, whereby the targeted constituent is simply fronted to theme position, e.g. *I'd call it daylight robbery* → *Daylight robbery I'd call it.* Another is **clefting**, whereby a clause is split into two portions, each with its own verb. One version of this produces a so-called *it*-cleft: the first subclause is introduced by *it is/was* followed by the fronted element; the second resembles a *that* relative clause. For example: *I saw Joe yesterday* → *It's Joe* *(that) I saw yesterday.* In some types of Irish English, these devices are used much more frequently than is usual in standard speech. Moreover, the grammatical conditions under which the operations are permitted to apply in Irish English differ in several important respects from standard usage.

5.8.2   Left-dislocation

In standard usage, detachment of an object or adverbial complement from its verb through left-dislocation tends to be disfavoured or sounds archaic. This sort of fronting is, however, quite common in many types of Irish English, e.g:

> A story now he told me when he was young
> Too much motors you'd be meeting
> In some building he is working[50]

A strikingly non-standard feature of left-dislocation in some varieties of Irish English is the tendency for a fronted noun phrase to leave a pronoun 'trace' or 'shadow' of itself in its 'normal' position. For instance:

> Anything you wanted you could a got it

with left-dislocation of the object noun phrase *anything you wanted* and shadow *it*. (The corresponding sentence without left-dislocation would be *You could a got anything you wanted.*) Similarly:

> That baby from it was born her mother had it

(Compare this with *Her mother had that baby since it was born.*) The same phenomenon appears to be involved in non-standard relative clause structures with shadow pronouns of the type discussed in 5.2.7. For example, in

> This girl I was actually travelling with, her mother is in hospital

we have left-dislocation of *this girl I was actually travelling with* plus shadow *her.* (Cf. the standard order, without fronting, *The mother of the girl I was actually travelling with is in hospital.*)

5.8.3   *it*-clefting

Irish English has fewer restrictions than standard English on the type of sentence constituent that can be fronted by means of *it*-clefting. For instance, in standard usage clefting is generally not permitted to break up subject complement structures (see 5.2.2). This constraint is not binding on Irish English, as the following sentences illustrate:

> It's flat it was
> It's asleep he is[51]

Unlike standard usage, Irish English also permits clefting of a verb phrase, as in

> It's looking for more land a lot of them are[52]
> Was it drinking she was?[53]
> It must be working for her he was

The fronting of the logical subject of an **existential** *there* sentence through clefting is generally not acceptable in standard English. (*There's a fly in my soup* is an example of this type of sentence, with *a fly* as logical subject. We wouldn't normally expect *It's a fly there is in my soup* in standard usage.) Not so in Irish English:

> It was a kind of a house built of strong timber was there one time[54]

(Note the non-standard absence of subject relative *that,* discussed in 5.2.7.)

As already noted, clefting generally serves the discourse function of presenting the fronted element as new or contrastive information. In Irish English, *it*-clefting can be used for an additional, rather different effect in cases where new information is imparted not just by the fronted constituent but by the sentence as a whole. In such cases, the scope of *it is* can be said to be the entire sentence, since the fronted element is not given any special intonational prominence. In the context in which the following example was recorded

> So it were Daniel O'Connell then fell into the house in Derrinane[55]

the constituent *Daniel O'Connell* received no contrastive stress. The function of introductory *it is/was/were* in such contexts seems to be to give expressive emphasis to the whole statement.

5.8.4   Other focusing devices

Our discussion of the last example is perhaps taking us away from our central concerns of grammatical description and more into the realm of discourse analysis. In fact, there is a whole area where the boundary between the two domains of enquiry becomes blurred. There are many other grammatical devices in Irish English for organizing discourse which we could have examined in detail. For instance, I've said nothing about the widespread use of rhetorical questions as a means of highlighting new information, as in

> And who was the doctor but the same young fellow[56]

Nor have we looked at the use of single-word grammatical devices which, in various ways, focus on a constituent or command the listener's attention, such as *like, sure*, or sentence-final *but*, as in

> Did you get to see him like?
> Sure it's not worth it
> It's all finished now but

or emphatic sentence tags of the form *so it is*, as in

> He done it, so he did
> It's raining, so it is

However, a detailed discussion of these and other discourse features would take us beyond the scope of this short chapter.

5.9 Conclusion

5.9.1 Grammatical 'simplicity'

From the foregoing, it should be clear that Irish English usage cannot be viewed as reflecting 'careless' or unsystematic deviation from standard linguistic norms. Close inspection of Irish English word and sentence structure reveals that it is governed by grammatical rules which differ systematically and in some cases quite fundamentally from equivalent rules in the standard language. Nor can the differences be assessed in terms of some overall measure of grammatical 'simplicity'. To be sure, it is possible, when comparing two linguistic systems, to identify specific areas where one system is formally simpler than the other, in the sense that it has fewer grammatical forms to express a given set of meanings. However, comparisons of this sort are likely to be a matter of swings and roundabouts. What one system lacks in formal complexity in some part of the grammar is likely to be compensated for in some other part. For instance, there is no doubt that, in terms of gross number of forms, Irish English has a simpler strong verb system than the standard (see 5.3.2). On the other hand, it's equally clear that Irish English has a more complex tense-aspect system than standard English (see 5.4).

It's important to note that formal simplicity in a particular area of a grammar doesn't imply a net reduction in the potential for expressing differences in meaning. In other words, we need to distinguish between the **structure** of a grammatical system (its make-up in terms of grammatical rules and forms) and its **function** (the way it operates to convey meaning). The point can be illustrated by considering for a moment some of the differences between the tense-aspect systems of Irish English and standard English. Suppose a speaker wishes to distinguish two sorts of time-frame for past events: one in which an event is located at some point that is temporally separated from the present ('then-time'); and another in which an event occurs at some unspecified time during a period leading up to the present. (We referred to the latter as indefinite since-time in 5.4.2.) In terms of verb group structure at least, standard English has the formal means for capturing this distinction; Irish English hasn't. In standard usage, then-time is indicated by a simple-past form (e.g. *I was there*), indefinite since-time by the perfect (e.g. *I've been* *there*). Speakers of basic Irish English tend to use the simple-past form for both temporal categories. (Hence the example *I never saw a gun in my life* cited in 5.4.2.) However, the absence of this particular formal contrast in the Irish English verb system obviously doesn't mean that Irish English speakers are unable to express the semantic distinction at all. The linguistic or real-world context of speaking will often furnish the details necessary to avoid any potential ambiguity. Moreover, the time relations in question can be expressed adverbially anyway. The word *yesterday* in *I was there yesterday*, for instance, unambiguously locates the event in then-time, just as, say, *twice during the past year* necessarily indicates since-time.

Habitual aspect illustrates the same point, except in this case it's the Irish English verb system that exhibits more formal contrasts than standard English. Although the standard language lacks anything directly equivalent to the special *be* and *do* habituals of Irish English, this obviously doesn't imply that habitual aspect cannot be expressed at all in that variety. The temporal relation can usually be unambiguously conveyed through a simple-present verb form, perhaps supplemented by adverbial means (as in *Tom goes to night-classes every Thursday*).

5.9.2 Educational implications

Nevertheless, it's important not to underestimate the practical effects of structural differences between varieties of the same language. This is particularly true when it comes to considering the sorts of communicative difficulties that potentially result from differences of this nature. Of special relevance in this context are the kinds of educational problems likely to be involved in the teaching of standard English to speakers of basic Irish English vernacular.[57]

Of necessity, most speakers of vernacular English have at least some receptive command of the standard language (for example, as a result of sustained exposure to the broadcast media). Many educationalists see it as one of the tasks of the education system to provide such individuals with the opportunity of extending this passive knowledge into full productive ability, at least as far as writing is concerned. There are some who would argue that those who do not have an active command of standard forms of language are likely to be at a disadvantage in modern society. The achievement of this goal of course doesn't depend on seeking to eradicate vernacular usage, an approach traditionally advocated in most of the English-speaking world. Experience in many other parts of the world confirms the value of teaching the standard language as an additional linguistic resource for use in writing and in formal social settings (such as education, public administration, the media), while acknowledging the independent status of vernaculars as vehicles of everyday communication and symbols of local or ethnic identity. This is, for example, the situation in German-speaking Switzerland where virtually the whole population acquires Swiss German dialect as a mother tongue and subsequently learns standard German as an additional language at school. Speakers use both varieties side-by-side for complementary social functions. Generally speaking, Swiss German is reserved for intimate and informal settings, and standard German for more formal purposes. Of course, such a policy is only likely to be of practical benefit if speakers of non-standard varieties consider that their chances of success in such areas as education and employment will be genuinely enhanced by acquiring the standard language. If such conditions are not present, attempts to teach the standard are likely to be futile and even humiliating to the learner.

Our review of the grammatical characteristics of Irish English allows us to identify specific areas of potential difficulty for the vernacular speaker who is seeking to gain competence in the standard language. It's reasonable to suppose that these will involve grammatical subsystems where there is a degree of structural mismatch between the two varieties. A mismatch of this sort can take one of two forms. On the one hand, the vernacular system may exhibit over-differentiation in relation to the standard. That is, the former may have a particular grammatical distinction that is not present in the latter. The Irish English habitual-non-habitual contrast is of this type. Other examples include *you* versus *youse* (see 5.2.5) and *that* versus *thon* (see 5.2.3), both of which correspond to single categories in the standard. On the other hand, the vernacular grammar may under-differentiate in relation to the standard. For example, as already noted, basic Irish English lacks the formal contrast between simple-past and perfect which can be used in standard English to differentiate then-time from indefinite since-time.

Each of these patterns poses its own problems for the teaching of standard English to vernacular speakers. On the face of it, over-differentiation on the part of the non-standard dialect shouldn't create too many difficulties. After all, all the vernacular speaker apparently has to do in such circumstances is learn to collapse a grammatical distinction that is present in his or her native system but not in the standard. It's not difficult to see, however, that a learner may be reluctant to suppress a grammatical contrast which has proved its communicative usefulness in vernacular speech. This factor probably goes at least part of the way towards explaining the persistence of over-differentiated non-standard features in circumstances where vernacular speakers are encouraged or required to use standard English. Loyalty to vernacular cultural (including linguistic) norms is likely to be another important factor determining the maintenance of dialect features in the face of standardizing pressures.

Under-differentiation on the part of the non-standard dialect is likely to pose greater problems. The learning task for the vernacular speaker here involves splitting a unitary non-standard category into two or more standard equivalents. The potential difficulty of this exercise is illustrated by the widespread phenomenon of linguistic **hypercorrection**. This describes a situation where a speaker, in seeking to use a socially prestigious linguistic form which is not present in his or her native system, overcompensates by extending its use to linguistic contexts where, by the rules of standard usage, it is inappropriate. A well-known example is the hypercorrect avoidance of *me* as an oblique pronoun form (see 5.2.5). In an attempt to emulate the prestigious use of *I* (as in *It is I*), some speakers frequently overcorrect by employing it in certain circumstances as an object pronoun as well (e.g. *between you and I*).

Another illustration is provided by the strong verb system. Generally speaking, as we saw in 5.3.2, non-standard dialects, including Irish English, under-differentiate *vis-à-vis* the standard in this area of the grammar. When seeking to emulate the prestige norm, some speakers hypercorrect by using standard simple-past strong verb forms as participles, e.g. *He shouldn't have drank it, she should've came earlier.*

For another example of hypercorrection by Irish English speakers, we may return to the distinction between the simple-past and perfect forms used in standard English to express then-time versus indefinite since-time. As already indicated, basic Irish English under-differentiates in this part of the system; the simple-past form performs both temporal functions. The mismatch is apparently responsible for the difficulties some Irish English speakers have in gaining full productive control of the standard perfect. An overgeneralized use of this form to indicate then-time is characteristic of hypercorrect usage in Ireland, e.g:

I've done a course two years ago
They've been here when we came

Against the background of such structural mismatches, overt correction of isolated Irish English vernacular forms as a method of teaching standard English is likely to be at best inefficient and at worst counterproductive. At any rate, the success of teaching standard English in such circumstances is likely to be diminished unless there is an appreciation on the part of the teacher of the wider grammatical subsystems within which the vernacular forms are embedded.

It is of course by no means universally accepted that structurally based techniques are an appropriate way of teaching the standard language (or a foreign language for that matter). Nevertheless, a sympathetic understanding on the part of the teacher of the systematic structural differences between standard and non-standard varieties is likely to have a beneficial effect on the educational performance of the vernacular-speaking child. The testimony of many teachers bears out the argument that much of the alienation experienced by pupils, particularly in inner-city schools, stems from the humiliation of being told that their mother tongue is inferior and wrong.[58] Research of the kind on which this chapter is based underlines the need to accept that the linguistic competence of speakers of non-standard vernaculars is no less complex or systematic than that underlying standard speech.

Notes

1. My thanks are due to Cliff Griffiths, Jim Milroy and Lesley Milroy for providing additional information as well as helpful comments on an earlier draft of this chapter. Not all of these people, it should be pointed out, share the opinions expressed in 5.9.2. Any mistakes are entirely due to me.

2. Unless otherwise credited, the indented examples are almost all culled from the tape-recorded archives of three projects, all funded by the UK Social Science Research Council: *Language variety and speech community in Belfast* (J. and L. Milroy 1977), *Sociolinguistic variation and linguistic change in Belfast* (J. Milroy et al. 1983) and the *Tape-Recorded Survey of Irish English Speech* (Barry 1981a).

3. Example from Henry 1957.

4. Accounts of the history of Irish English are to be found in Hogan 1927 and Kallen 1988. For an overview of the sociolinguistic status of English in Ireland, see Edwards 1984 and Harris 1991a.

5. The regional distribution of pronunciation differences in Irish English is discussed by, among others, Henry (1958), Gregg (1985), Barry (1981b) and Harris (1984a). Grammatical differences between rural and urban varieties are explored in Filppula 1991 and Harris 1991b.

6. Example from Todd 1975.

7. Example from Henry 1957.

8. Example from Todd 1975 ('quare' is colloquial Irish English for 'queer'; in the context here, it means something like 'remarkable, excellent').

9. Example from Henry 1957.

10. Example from Henry 1957.

11. Example from Todd 1975.

12. Example from Henry 1957.

13. Example from J. Milroy 1981.

14. Both examples from Henry 1957.

15. Example from Henry 1957.

16. Example from Henry 1957.

17. Example from Henry 1957.

18. Both examples from Henry 1957.

19. Example from J. Milroy 1981.

20. Both examples from Henry 1957.

21. Both examples from Henry 1957.

22. Example from Henry 1957.

23. I owe this information to Brenda Ní Shúilleabháin.

24. Except where indicated, all the examples in 5.4.2 are from Harris 1984b.

25. Example from Kallen 1991.
26. Except where noted, all examples in 5.4.3 are from Harris 1986.
27. Example from Henry 1957.
28. All examples from Henry 1957.
29. This and the following example from Lunny 1981.
30. Example from Henry 1957.
31. Example from Henry 1957.
32. Example from Henry 1957.
33. Example from Lunny 1981.
34. Example from Henry 1957.
35. Example from Ua Broin 1944.
36. Example from Henry 1957.
37. Example from Henry 1957.
38. Both examples from Henry 1957.
39. Example from Henry 1957.
40. Example from J. Milroy 1981.
41. Both examples from J. Milroy 1981.
42. Example from Lunny 1981.
43. For a particularly detailed treatment of Irish English prepositional usage, see Henry 1957.
44. Example from Lunny 1981.
45. This and the previous two examples from Henry 1957.
46. Example from Lunny 1981.
47. Both examples from Henry 1957.
48. Example from Todd 1975.
49. Quirk & Greenbaum 1973 (412).
50. All these examples from Filppula 1986.
51. Both these examples from Henry 1957.
52. Example from Filppula 1986.
53. This and the following example from Henry 1957.
54. Example from Filppula 1986.
55. Example from Filppula 1986.
56. Example from Henry 1957.
57. The educational implications of nonstandard English usage in Ireland are discussed in Harris 1989.
58. See, for example, Trudgill 1975 for a full discussion of this issue.

Further reading

Recently published works on Irish English which are both widely available and accessible to non-specialists include Joyce 1910, Ó Muirithe 1977 and Milroy 1981. Joyce's *English as we speak it in Ireland*, originally published in 1910, is one of the earliest accounts of Irish English. Given its popular orientation, it tends to be somewhat anecdotal, but its wealth of material on grammar, pronunciation and idiom makes it something of a classic. The convenient anthology edited by Ó Muirithe (1977) contains articles by a number of experts on such subjects as the history of Irish English, the role of Irish in its evolution and its use in literature. Milroy (1981) presents an up-to-date sociolinguistic account of Belfast, including an outline of a number of northern Irish English grammatical characteristics.

Those interested in pursuing the subject of Irish English word and sentence structure in more depth are recommended to seek out more specialist books and articles. The following presuppose some knowledge of technical linguistic terminology. By far the most detailed and comprehensive account of any single Irish English dialect is Henry's 1957 book on north Roscommon. Bliss (1979) presents a linguistic analysis of early Irish English texts which he uses to throw light on the historical development of the dialect. Three areas of Irish English syntax which have been subjected to particularly detailed linguistic analysis are topicalization (Filppula 1986; 1990), tense-aspect (Harris 1984b; 1986; Kallen 1989; 1990) and subject-verb concord (Policansky 1981). The collections edited by Ó Baoill (1985) and Harris et al. (1986) contain several articles on various features of Irish English grammar.

References

BARRY, M.V. (ed.) (1981a) *Aspects of English Dialects in Ireland.* Belfast: Institute of Irish Studies, Queen's University Belfast

BARRY, M.V. (1981b) The southern boundaries of northern Irish English speech. In Barry, M.V. (ed.) (1981a), pp. 52–95

BLISS, A.J. (1979) *Spoken English in Ireland 1600–1740.* Dublin: Dolmen

CHESHIRE, J. (ed.) (1991) *English Around the World: Sociolinguistic Perspectives.* Cambridge: Cambridge University Press

EDWARDS, J. (1984) Irish and English in Ireland. In Trudgill, P. (ed.) (1984), pp. 480–98

FILPPULA, M. (1986) *Some Aspects of Hiberno-English in a Functional Sentence Perspective.* University of Joensuu Publications in the Humanities, 7. Joensuu: University of Joensuu

FILPPULA, M. (1990) Substratum, superstratum, and universals in the genesis of Hiberno-English. *Irish University Review* **20:** 41–54

FILPPULA, M. (1991) Urban and rural varieties of Hiberno-English. In Cheshire, J. (ed.) (1991), pp. 51–60

GREGG, R.J. (1985) *The Scotch-Irish Dialect Boundaries in the Province of Ulster.* Ottawa: Canadian Federation for the Humanities

HARRIS, J. (1984a) English in the north of Ireland. In Trudgill, P. (ed.) (1984), pp. 115–35

HARRIS, J. (1984b) Syntactic variation and dialect divergence. *Journal of Linguistics* 20: 303–27

HARRIS, J. (1986) Expanding the superstrate: habitual aspect markers in Atlantic Englishes. *English World-Wide* 7: 171–99

HARRIS, J. (1989) Ireland. *Sociolinguistica 3, Dialekt und Schule in den europäischen Ländern*: 54–60

HARRIS, J. (1991a) Ireland. In Cheshire, J. (ed.) (1991), pp. 37–50

HARRIS, J. (1991b) Conservatism versus substratal transfer in Irish English. In P. Trudgill & J.K. Chambers (eds) *Dialects of English: Studies in Grammatical Variation*. London: Longman, pp. 192–213

HARRIS, J., D. LITTLE and D. SINGLETON (eds) (1986) *Perspectives on the English Language in Ireland: Proceedings of the First Symposium on Hiberno-English*. Dublin: CLCS, Trinity College Dublin

HENRY, P.L. (1957) *An Anglo-Irish Dialect of North Roscommon*. Dublin: University College Dublin

HENRY, P.L. (1958) A linguistic survey of Ireland: preliminary report. *Lochlann* 1: 49–208. Supplement to *Norsk Tidsskrift for Sprogwidenskap 5*

HOGAN, J.J. (1927) *The English Language in Ireland*. Dublin: Educational Company of Ireland

JOYCE, P.W. (1910) *English as we speak it in Ireland*. London: Longmans, Green and Co. (Reprinted 1979 with an introduction by T. Dolan. Portmarnock, Co. Dublin: Wolfhound.)

KALLEN, J.L. (1988) The English language in Ireland. *International Journal of Society and Language* 70: 127–42

KALLEN, J.L. (1989) Tense and aspect categories in Irish English. *English World-Wide* 10: 1–39

KALLEN, J.L. (1990) The Hiberno-English perfect: grammaticalisation revisited. *Irish University Review* 20: 120–36

KALLEN, J.L. (1991) Sociolinguistic variation and methodology: *after* as a Dublin variable. In Cheshire, J. (ed.) (1991), pp. 61–74

MILROY, J. (1981) *Accents of English: Belfast*. Belfast: Blackstaff

MILROY, J. and L. MILROY (1977) *Speech Community and Language Variety in Belfast*. Report to the Social Science Research Council (UK). Grant no. HR 3771

MILROY, J., L. MILROY, J. HARRIS, L. POLICANSKY, B. GUNN, and A. PITTS (1983) *Sociolinguistic Variation and Linguistic Change in Belfast*. Report to the Social Science Research Council (UK). Grant no. HR 5777

Ó BAOILL, D.P. (ed.) (1985) *Papers on Irish English*. Dublin: Cumann na Teangeolaíochta Feidhmí

Ó MUIRITHE, D. (ed.)(1977) *The English Language in Ireland.* Cork: Mercier

POLICANSKY, L. (1981) Grammatical variation in Belfast English. *Belfast Working Papers in Language and Linguistics* **6**: 37–66

QUIRK, R. and S. GREENBAUM (1973) *A University Grammar of English.* London: Longman

TODD, L. (1975) Base-form and substratum: two case studies of English in contact. Unpublished PhD thesis. Leeds: University of Leeds

TRUDGILL, P. (ed.) (1984) *English in the British Isles.* Cambridge: Cambridge University Press

TRUDGILL, P. (1975) *Accent, Dialect and the School.* London: Arnold

UA BROIN, L. (1944) A south-west Dublin glossary. *Béaloideas* **14**: 162–86

6 The grammar of Tyneside and Northumbrian English

Joan Beal

6.1 Introduction

The modern counties of Northumberland and Tyne and Wear, occupying as they do the extreme North-Eastern corner of England, are geographically closer to the Lowlands of Scotland than to the seat of government in Southern England. As we shall see this proximity to Scotland is reflected in the linguistic characteristics of the area. Indeed, the Northumbrian and Lowland Scots dialects share a common origin in the Anglian dialect of the early kingdom of Northumbria. This kingdom originally extended from Doncaster to the River Forth, with a division into the Northern sector of Bernicia and the Southern Deira marked by the River Tees. Thus, the same dialect of Old English was spoken on both sides of what is now the Scottish border, at least in the East of the country. In fact, the first part of the kingdom to undergo linguistic influences leading to a divergent development of the dialect was Deira: the Danish invasions of the eighth and ninth centuries affected the southern half of the kingdom far more than Bernicia, so that extensive Scandinavian influence is found in the dialects of what are now Yorkshire, Humberside and Cleveland far more than in those of Northumberland and Tyneside. The River Tees is still recognized as an important linguistic boundary: for instance, the definite article is not realized as a glottal stop north of the Tees ('down t'road') and the dropping of *h* was not found north of Darlington until relatively recently: it has now moved as far north as Sunderland.

The battle of Carham (1018) saw the division of Lothian from Northumbria, and its subsequent incorporation into Scotland. However, this Anglian-speaking region was to become the most influential part of the Scottish kingdom, and the kings of Scotland adopted its dialect, which eventually developed into Lowland Scots.

Northumbria, now confined to the area between the Tees and the Tweed, retained its independence under the Earls of Northumberland well beyond the Norman Conquest, and was not finally confirmed to the crown of England until 1242. The dialect of Northumberland likewise retained its independence, being little influenced by either the Celtic of the North and West, the Scandinavian of the Danelaw, or the Norman French of the South. When a standardized form of English began to develop in the fifteenth century, Northumberland was just about as far removed from the centre of standardization in London as it was geographically possible for a dialect region in England to be. To the sixteenth-century Londoner, Northumbrian sounded distinctive and outlandish, as can be seen from the reaction of the woman in William Bullein's (1578) *Dialogue Against the Fever Pestilence* to a beggar from Redesdale:

> What doest thou here in this Countrie? Me thinke thou art a Scot by thy tongue.

This comment shows that despite the separation of Lothian from Northumberland, and despite (or maybe because of) the fierce border raids referred to by the beggar in his reply to the woman, Northumbrian English in the sixteenth century continued to have a great deal more in common with Lowland Scots than with the London standard.

The reign of Elizabeth I saw the first significant influx of workers from the surrounding rural districts into the Newcastle area. The increasing use of coal at this time created a demand for labour, such that the men of Tynedale and Redesdale moved to the colliery districts to become miners and keelmen on the Tyne. R.O. Heslop (1892: xvi) saw this as an important influence on the sociolinguistic situation on Tyneside:

> To these dalesmen we owe the strong clansmanship of the colonies of pitmen and keelmen scattered along Tyneside and throughout

the colliery districts, where the dialect of Northumberland has been preserved with a vigour peculiar to these localities.

To this day, the mining districts of mid-Northumberland are strongholds of 'traditional' dialect; many of the syntactic features mentioned in the course of this chapter are more likely to be encountered in these districts than in the City of Newcastle.

The second major influx of immigrants into Newcastle (and the North-east generally) was to take place in the nineteenth century, when, particularly after 1840, the development of industry and technology in this area created a huge demand for labour. These developments coincided with the Irish potato famine so that a large proportion of the immigrant workers came from Ireland. House (1954: 47) writes that:

> In 1851, Newcastle, the most cosmopolitan of the north-eastern towns, had one person in every ten born in Ireland.

This immigration tailed off towards the end of the nineteenth century, but was to form the basis of a large and well-integrated Irish community in Newcastle. Cooter (1972: i) suggests that in the nineteenth century the North-east was 'roughly the fourth most important area in England for Irish immigration' after London, Liverpool and Manchester, but that the Irish in Newcastle encountered none of the hostility found in these other areas, and were allowed to 'thrive and prosper like nowhere else in England'.

Of equal significance to the Irish immigration into Newcastle in the nineteenth century was that from Scotland. In this case, the immigration did not tail off as sharply towards the end of the century. Indeed, movement from Scotland to Newcastle is still very common: the city has a thriving Caledonian society for the comfort of expatriates, and the coastal resorts of North Tyneside and Northumberland are subjected to an annual invasion during 'Glasgow Fortnight' in July. The strongest influence on the dialects of Tyneside and Northumberland is undoubtedly from Lowland Scots, but this can hardly be called an outside influence given the common origin of these dialects; it must rather be said that the continuing close relationship between Scots and Northumbrians has served to maintain and reinforce the linguistic similarities between their dialects. Influence from Irish English on the dialects of Tyneside and Northumberland has, to my knowledge, never been mentioned by any writer on the dialects concerned: however, given the size and integration of the Irish community, it cannot be discounted, and may serve to explain some features of Tyneside English which are shared with Irish dialects such as the second person plural pronoun *yous* (section 6.6.1).

In the twentieth century, the North-east has fallen dramatically from its position in the previous century as one of the richest areas of England to become one of the very poorest, having built its riches on the very industries which are now in decline – steel, shipbuilding and coalmining. The solidarity referred to above by Heslop has, however, been strengthened by hardship; members of mining communities such as those of mid-Northumberland have testified to a rekindling of 'community spirit' during the hardships of the 1984–5 strike. This, coupled with some feeling of resentment towards the wealthier South, has tended to reinforce the sense of regional identity felt by Tynesiders and Northumbrians. That a corresponding pride is taken in the local dialect can be seen from the number of popular publications on and in 'Geordie' available in Newcastle bookshops. However, this pride goes hand-in-glove with a feeling that the dialect is inferior to standard English. Most of the features described in this paper would be condemned by 'Geordies' as simply 'bad English': yet they are of ancient and respectable pedigree. Indeed, Heslop (1892: xx–xxi) describes certain syntactic features as typical of the Northumbrian dialect and laments the fact that 'the tendency to assimilate the form of the dialect with the current English of the schools is increasing'. One of these features is the use of the objective pronoun as part of a compound subject (section 6.6.1) as in:

Me and me marrow wis gannin ti work

In fact, this feature is not unique to Tyneside, but is found in most non-standard dialects of English. But what is interesting about Heslop's comment is that the feature is still common almost a hundred years later, and is still condemned in classrooms.

6.2 The grammar of Tyneside and Northumberland English

The following sections describe those features of Tyneside and Northumbrian grammar which differ from Standard English. It must be said at the outset, however, that the reader is unlikely to encounter anybody who will use all of these features all of the time. Sociolinguists such as Labov (1966) and Trudgill (1974) have shown that non-standard features are subject to variation of several kinds. First, geographical variation must be taken into account, especially in an area in which there is a stark contrast between the Tyneside conurbation, the small mining towns of mid-Northumberland, and the isolated rural communities of North Northumberland. In most cases, little is known about the exact geographical distribution of the features described, and in such cases I have used the designation *Tyneside* to cover Tyneside and Northumbrian. However, we do know that, for instance, double modals are more likely to be used in Northumberland than on Tyneside (6.3.3) and, conversely, that the intensifier *geet* is a fashionable feature of the coast and city (6.6.4). Secondly, social variation exists to the extent that the higher the social class a person belongs to, and the longer he or she has spent in full-time education, the more likely that speaker is to have been influenced by Standard English, and to avoid the localized features. This is a commonplace of sociolinguistic theory, but some of the features described below are used by speakers higher up the social and educational scale than might be expected. In conversation, I have heard double modals (6.3.3) and non-standard verb forms (6.3.1) from a teacher and a clerical worker respectively, in the following sentences:

(1)   We might could do with some more potatoes up here.
(2)   She had went in (to hospital) and they tret it.

It is unlikely that the speakers quoted here would have used these non-standard features in a formal situation, or when addressing a newcomer, since stylistic variation of this kind also affects the likelihood of the features described below being used on any occasion. To complicate matters further, all these kinds of variation interact: for instance, a person's level of education may determine whether a feature is used in writing as well as in speech, or in formal as well as informal situations. A vast amount of research would be needed in order to quantify the amount and type of variation for each feature, so for the time being I have presented these features as if they were invariable. It is important to remember that this is an idealization.

6.3   The verb phrase

6.3.1   Irregular Verbs

A considerable number of verbs show different patterns in Tyneside and Standard English respectively. In some cases, the same pattern can be found in other non-standard dialects: for instance, the 'reversal' of *saw* and *seen* with *I seen* as the past and *I have saw* as perfect is reported for a Southern dialect by Jenny Cheshire (1982), and is also familiar to me as a native of Cheshire. However, many more of these patterns are less widespread and may well be peculiar to Tyneside. There are, for instance, a number of verbs with participles ending in -*en* in this dialect, although the number of these still in use is less than that reported by Heslop (1892: xxi); *getten*; *forgetten*; and *putten* are the survivors. In some cases, such as that of the verb *treat*, the Tyneside pattern is irregular, with *tret* as the past, whilst the Standard English verb is regular, with *treated*. Furthermore, Tyneside has certain verb forms which are not used at all in standard English: *go*, for instance, may be substituted by the lexically distinct verb *gan*, which is obsolete in standard English, and the negative of *do*, particularly in tags, is often *divvent*. This latter form may also occur in the positive when it follows or precedes *divvent* in a tag, e.g.

(1)   Ye divvent knaa, div ye? (= standard 'You don't know, do you?)
(2)   Ye div, divvent ye?

The use of *div/divvent* is confined to the auxiliary verb *do* used in questions and negation: the verb *do* meaning 'to perform' is the same in Tyneside as in standard English. Thus:

I do all the work, divvent I?

A similar, though differently expressed, distinction between auxiliary and non-auxiliary uses of *do* is found in a Southern dialect by Cheshire (1982).

In order to give a full picture of the differences between the verb patterns of Tyneside and standard English, I have reproduced Table 6.1 from McDonald (1980: 28–9).

Table 6.1: Examples of the correspondence between base, past and past participle or irregular lexical verbs in Tyneside and Standard English

Tyneside			Standard		
Base	Past	Participle	Base	Past	Participle
speak	spoke	spoke	speak	spoke	spoken
break	broke	broke	break	broke	broken
bite	bit	bit	bite	bit	bitten
take	took	took	take	took	taken
fall	fell	fell	fall	fell	fallen
write	wrote	wrote	write	wrote	written
forget	forgot	forgot	forget	forgot	forgotten
		forgetten			
eat	ate	ate	eat	ate	eaten
	et	etten			
beat	beat	beat	beat	beat	beaten
give	give	give	give	gave	given
do	done	done	do	did	done
go	went	went	go	went	gone
see	seen	saw	see	saw	seen
ring	rang	rang	ring	rang	rung
sing	sang	sang	sing	sang	sung
shrink	shrank	shrank	shrink	shrank	shrunk
	shrunk			shrunk	
sink	sunk	sunk	sink	sank	sunk
come	come	came	come	came	come
run	run	ran	run	ran	run
spin	span	spun	spin	spun	spun
swing	swang	swung	swing	swung	swung
get	got	getten	get	got	got
treat	tret	tret	treat	treated	treated
put	put	putten	put	put	put
say	sayed	sayed	say	said	said

6.3.2   Concord

In standard English, the form of the verb with *-s*, e.g. *comes*; *goes*; *does*;, is only used with a third person singular subject, thus: *he comes*; *she goes*. Tyneside, by contrast, and in common with many other non-standard dialects, has *-s* forms with third person plural subjects. However, with the exception of the past tense form *was*, this pattern apparently occurs in Tyneside only where the subject is a noun rather than a pronoun. Examples from McDonald (1980: 12) are:

(1)   Her sisters is quite near.
(2)   Things has changed.
(3)   I daresay the pitmen maybe swears away among theirsels.
(4)   The carpets was soaked. They was soaking.

6.3.3   Modal Verbs

The use and nature of modal verbs in Tyneside is markedly different from that of standard English in several important ways.

First, *may* and *shall* are hardly ever used in Tyneside English (as also in Scots English), and have no important part to play in the grammar. As in many other non-standard dialects, *can* is used rather than *may* to express permission, but in Tyneside, even the sense of possibility normally expressed by *may* is carried by *might* instead, as in:

Mind, it looks as though it might rain, doesn't it?
(McDonald 1981: 284)

There is, therefore, no strictly grammatical need for *may* in Tyneside, as it has no function that cannot equally well be performed by *can* or *might*. If it is used at all, it is as an ultra-polite and formal stylistic variant of *can*. *Shall*, likewise, rarely occurs in Tyneside: for the expression of futurity, *will* or *'ll* are used. This is also true of most dialects of English, where *will* varies with *shall* even in standardized varieties. However, in most dialects, *shall* is used in first person questions, such as:

Shall I put the kettle on?

In Tyneside, as in Scots and Irish English, *will* is used even here, thus:

Will I put the kettle on?

Secondly, there is a rule of standard English that only one modal verb can appear in a single verb phrase. Thus:

He must do it.

is grammatical whilst

*He must can do it.

is not. Indeed, Standard English has developed a whole battery of 'quasi-modal' verbs to 'stand in' for modals where the meaning requires them but the above rule forbids them. The meaning of the above sentence would therefore be expressed in Standard English as:

He must be able to do it.

In Tyneside English, the rule inhibiting double modals does not apply so long as the second modal is *can* or *could*. Thus the asterisked sentence would conform to the rules of Tyneside English. These double modals are also found in Scots and some American dialects, but more combinations of modals are allowed in these dialects than in Tyneside. Furthermore, more combinations are allowed in the dialects of rural Northumberland than in those of urban Tyneside. For instance, the combination of *would* and *could* appears in the urban area – but only in a negative form – whilst in rural Northumberland the positive form may be found. Examples from McDonald (1981: 186–7) are:

(1)   I can't play on Friday. I work late. I *might could* get it changed, though.
(2)   The girls usually make me some (toasted sandwiches) but they *mustn't could have* made any today.
(3)   He *wouldn't could've* worked, even if you had asked him. (Tyneside)

(4)   A good machine clipper *would could* do it in half a day. (Northumberland)

Thirdly, in standard English, certain adverbs are placed *before* main verbs but *after* modals, thus:

I only asked.
I can only ask.

In Tyneside English, adverbs may be placed before *can* and *could*. Examples from McDonald (1981: 214) are:

(1)   That's what I say to people. If they only could walk a little bit, they should thank God.
(2)   She just can reach the gate.

Fourthly, in Tyneside, as in other non-standard dialects of English, *can* and *could* are used in perfective constructions where Standard English has *be able to*:

(1)   He cannot get a job since he's left school.
(2)   I says it's a bit of a disappointment, nurse. I thought I could've brought it back again.

(McDonald 1981: 215–6)

These sentences could be 'translated' into standard English respectively as:

(1)   He has not been able to get a job since he left school.
(2)   I thought I would have been able to bring it back again.

Fifthly, there are several cases in which a modal or quasi-modal verb has a meaning in Tyneside different from its standard English meaning or where a different modal is used to express the same meaning. It is important for the outsider to be aware of these differences; after all a double modal immediately strikes a non-Tynesider as odd, and alerts him to the need for careful interpretation, but where a familiar syntactic structure has a different meaning, it may turn out to be a 'false friend'. For example, in a sentence with the meaning 'the evidence forces me to conclude that . . . not', standard English would use *can't*, whilst Tyneside would use *mustn't*. Thus:

> The lift can't be working (standard)
> The lift mustn't be working (Tyneside)
> (see Chapter 4.3.5 for a similar usage in Scottish English.)

On the other hand, where standard English uses *mustn't* to mean 'it is necessary not to . . .', Tyneside uses *haven't got to*. Here, misunderstandings could easily arise: a Tynesider, saying:

> You haven't got to do that!

means, not that you are not obliged to do it, but that you are obliged *not* to do it!

Table 6.2

Meaning	Standard	Tyneside
The evidence forces me to conclude that . . . not	can't	mustn't
Necessary not to	mustn't	haven't go to
Not necessary	haven't got to don't have to	don't have to

Table 6.2 sums up these semantic differences. They are, however, largely confined to negative sentences as both Tyneside and Standard English would have the positive sentence:

> The lift must be working.

Modals in Tyneside English also have different forms from the corresponding verb-forms of standard English when used in negatives and tags, as we shall see in 6.3.4 and 6.4.

6.3.4   Negatives

The expression of negation in Tyneside English differs from that in standard English in the following respects.

never

In standard English, *never* means 'not on any occasion'. In Tyneside, as in many other non-standard dialects, it does not have this specific meaning, but is merely an emphatic negative. An example from McDonald (1980: 13) is:

> The women were waiting for the men to play cards
> but the men never turned up so the women sent
> Ruby out to look for them.

Multiple Negation

The practice of negating more than one element in a phrase has been eradicated from standard English over the last two hundred years or so on the linguistically spurious grounds that 'two negatives make a positive'. However, in Tyneside, as in most other non-standard dialects, multiple negation is still common. Indeed, we shall see in section 6.3.5 (tags) that the double negative at times has a distinct and important function in Tyneside English. Examples of double negatives from McDonald (1980: 13) are:

(1)   You couldn't say nothing bad about it.
(2)   You bring it up or I won't have none.

Failure of Negative Attraction

In standard English there is a rule, known as 'negative attraction', whereby, if a sentence has an indefinite element such as *any, either, ever*, and is negated, the negative particle is 'attracted' to that indefinite element. Thus *not . . . ever* becomes *never, not . . . any* becomes *no* and so on. In Tyneside English, this rule does not always apply, as can be seen in the following examples:

(1)   Everyone didn't want to hear them.
(2)   Another house wasn't to be seen for miles around.
       (McDonald 1985)

Harris (1985: 305) points out the same syntactic feature in Irish English, and attributes it to interference from the syntactic patterns of Irish. However, the feature certainly occurs in Tyneside, and may possibly as the result of Irish influence, be more widespread in other non-standard dialects of English than has hitherto been acknowledged (see also 5.5.2, above).

Uncontracted Negatives

In standard English, all modal and auxiliary verbs have contracted negative forms, with the corresponding uncontracted forms being reserved for emphatic or formal usage. Thus:

> Don't touch that!
> *Do not* touch that! (emphatic)

> He won't eat his greens.
> He *will not* eat his greens! (emphatic)

> They shan't pass.
> They shall not pass! (formal/emphatic)

> I can't tell a lie.
> I cannot tell a lie. (formal)

In Tyneside English, parallel to Scots *cannae* the uncontracted form: *cannot*, is the normal negative of *can*. For the other modal verbs and the auxiliaries *have*, *do* and *be*, the uncontracted form is used in the negative interrogative. As was the case with double negation, the use of uncontracted negatives has a specific function in tags, as we shall see in the next section. Examples of these uncontracted forms are:

> He cannot get a job.
> Ha(ve) you not got it?

> Is he not there?
> Does he not want a one?

The negative of *will* is also different from that of Standard English. Tyneside has two alternatives to Standard English *won't*: either *'ll not*, or a rarer and more archaic negative *winnet*. Examples are:

> He'll not come tomorrow.
> I winnet empty the pedal bin.

> (McDonald 1981: 126)

6.3.5　Verb phrase complementation

Certain types of complementation are found in Tyneside that do not occur in standard English.

For to + infinitive

In Tyneside, as in Scots and Irish dialects the infinitive may be introduced by *for to* where Standard English has *to*, especially where it has the sense *in order to*. Examples are:

(1)　The firemen were putting on breathing apparatus for to go into the house.
(2)　The pair of them tried to contact Debbie for to tell her the news about the baby.

(McDonald 1985)

In standard English, this construction only survives in archaic usage, such as in folk songs, but it is still in use in Tyneside, Scots, Irish and some American dialects (cf. Chapters 4 and 5).

Verbs of necessity

After verbs of necessity, such as *need* and *want*, standard English has either a passive infinitive or a form ending in *-ing*. Tyneside, by contrast, uses the past participle here. Thus, standard English

> My hair needs to be washed
> My hair needs washing

would be in Tyneside English

> My hair needs washed.

This feature is also found in Scots and Irish English (cf Chapter 4, above).

Certain conditioning clause operators

Certain conditioning clause operators are used in Tyneside but not in standard English. These are *being as* and *with*. Examples are:

He can't come, being as he's working.
With the wife being ill, I'll have to look after her.
(Pellowe et al. 1972: 46)

6.3.6   Other non-standard verbal patterns

Had have + past participle

Where Standard English uses *had* + *past participle* in conditional clauses, Tyneside along with other non-standard dialects uses *had have* + *past participle*. An example of this is:

> She might just have getten the same sort of job if she had have stayed at school.
>
> (McDonald 1985)

The *have* is often reduced – as also in Scots – to *a* (cf Chapter 4).

Reversal of been and being

It would appear that, for some Tyneside speakers, the functions of *been* and *being* as used in standard English are reversed. This could have arisen from neutralization of the contrast between the two in speech, where both would be pronounced [biːən], but the following examples are from *written* Tyneside English:

(1)   I also played in the muck where my granddad had being digging.
(2)   I think old people should not be kept alive because the death of the person is just been prolonged.

(McDonald 1985)

Both these examples are from the usage of adolescents and therefore may be 'mistakes'. However, since the two forms sound identical in speech, it is difficult to tell how widespread this reversal is.

6.4   Interrogative tags

In standard English, there are two main types of interrogative tag: either a negative tag follows a positive declarative clause, or a positive tag follows a negative clause. Examples of these would be:

> He is coming, *isn't he?*
> He isn't coming, *is he?*

Positive tags following positive statements are rare in Standard English, and, according to Quirk and Greenbaum (1973: 195) indicate, either by a rising tone or by being preceded by *oh* or *so*, that the speaker has arrived at a conclusion by inference. Their example is:

> So that's your little game, is it?

In Tyneside English, positive tags following positive statements are more common, and are used to ask for information concerning the statement. Furthermore, positive tags may follow positive questions, a combination which only occurs in standard English by way of afterthought or repetition. Examples are:

> Are you next door to each other are you?
> You could say it could you?
>
> (McDonald 1981: 325–6)

In these Tyneside examples, there is no pause before the tag.

Negative tags following negative statements are virtually non-existent in standard English. In Tyneside English, however, there are two patterns in which this combination arises. Here, the non-standard features of double negation and uncontracted negatives are used to differentiate the two patterns, which have contrasting functions. The two patterns are:

(1)   A negative clause followed by *auxiliary + subject + not*. This pattern is used when information is sought.

(2)   A negative clause followed by *auxiliary + n't + subject + not*. This pattern is used when confirmation of the negative is sought.

Examples of these would be:

(1)   She can't come, can she not?
(2)   She can't come, can't she not?

The *auxiliary* + *n't* + *subject* + *not* pattern is also used in negative questions, where the speaker knows very well that the answer is 'no', but requires confirmation, possibly to settle a dispute with a third party. It is often used by children appealing to adult arbitration. An example would be:

Can't he not swim?

A similar contrast occurs between two patterns for negative tags following positive clauses in Tyneside English. Here, the two patterns are:

(1)   *Auxiliary* + *subject* + *not*, asking for information
(2)   *Auxiliary* + *n't* + *subject*, asking for confirmation

Examples of these would be:

(1)   She can come, can she not?
(2)   She can come, can't she?

Such fine distinctions between questions asking for information and those asking for confirmation are absent from the syntax of standard English, where the different expectations are signalled by stress and intonation patterns. The double negative in *can't he not?* and the uncontracted negative in *can she not?* would possibly be condemned by outsiders as 'bad English', yet they are essential features of a tag system which is syntactically more complex than that of Standard English. The possibilities of this system are summed up in Table 6.3.

Table 6.3

Information	Negative + auxiliary + subject + not
	Positive + auxiliary + subject
	Positive + auxiliary + subject + not
Confirmation	Negative + auxiliary + n't + subject + not
	Positive + auxiliary + n't + subject

6.5 Interrogatives

In standard English, direct and indirect questions have different word order, thus:

'Can I go home early?' she asked?

would contrast with:

She asked whether she could go home early.

In the indirect question, there is no inversion of subject and auxiliary; *whether* is inserted to introduce the indirect question, and the auxiliary is in the past tense.

In Tyneside English, as in Scots and Irish (cf. Chapters 4 and 5), the auxiliary and subject are inverted in indirect as well as direct questions, and no *whether* is inserted. An example of this is:

She once asked me did it interfere with me.

(McDonald 1980: 15)

Here, the past tense signals the indirect question but the word order is that of a direct question.

A further example from McDonald shows the same pattern in an indirect question introduced by *what*:

When he discovered I wasn't at school he wanted to know what was the matter.

(McDonald 1980: 15)

6.6   The noun phrase

6.6.1   Pronouns

Personal pronouns

The personal pronouns of Tyneside English are so different from those of Standard English, that it is best to set out the differences in tabular form (Table 6.4, below). What is most noteworthy about the Tyneside system is that it has distinctive forms for the subjective, objective and plural of the second person pronoun, whereas standard English has to make do with *you* for all these functions. Moreover, the functions of *we* and *us* are reversed in Tyneside as compared to standard English.

Table 6.4

	Subject		Object		Possessive	
	St	Ty	St	Ty	St	Ty
1sg	I	I	me	us	my	me
pl	we	us	us	we	our	wor
2sg	you	ye	you	you	your	your
pl	you	yous	you	yous/yees	your	your
3sgm	he	he	him	him	his	his
f	she	she	her	her	her	her
n	it	it	it	it	its	its
pl	they	they	them	them	their	their

For some younger speakers, *yous* has been generalised as the local form of the second person, and may be used to address one person. Other speakers, however, maintain the distinctions set out above. Examples of Tyneside usage are:

(1)   Ye can get lost, Kevin!
(2)   Give us me ball!
(3)   Us'll do it.
(4)   Wor Charlie said yous could come.
(5)   Give it we!
(6)   They beat we four nil!

Parts of this table are found in other dialects: for instance *yous* as a plural is found in Scots, Irish and Liverpool dialects, whilst *us* as first person singular object is common throughout the North (and possibly further afield). However, the table as a whole shows an overall pattern unique to Tyneside.

Reflexives

In standard English, reflexives are formed by adding *self/selves* to the possessive forms of the first and second person pronouns, but to the objective form of the third person pronouns. Tyneside English is more consistent in this respect, adding *self/selves* to the possessive form in every case. Table 6.5 sets out this contrast.

Table 6.5

Standard	Tyneside
myself	meself
ourselves	worselves
yourself	yourself
yourselves	yourselves
himself	hisself
herself	herself
itself	itself
themselves	theirselves

Objective pronoun in subject position

In compound subjects, the objective pronoun may be used as the subject in Tyneside English. This feature is common in other non-standard dialects, and, as we have already noted (6.6.1) was common in Northumbrian English in the nineteenth century. Examples are:

(1)   Me and my brother Martin went on a trip.
(2)   One day him and his dad made a hot air balloon.
(3)   Her and her friend were looking at a programme.

(McDonald 1980: 16)

Demonstratives

In Tyneside, as in other non-standard dialects, *them* is used as a demonstrative for distant reference with a plural noun. In such cases, standard English would have *those*. Thus, standard English:

> I like those books.

corresponds to Tyneside:

> I like them books.

Relatives

The use of relative pronouns in Tyneside English differs from that in standard English in several ways. Firstly, *which* may occur with a personal antecedent, whereas in Standard English it would only occur after an impersonal referent. An example from present-day Tyneside is:

> The ladies which accompanied him had curly hair.
> (McDonald 1980: 20)

This use of *which* is found in other non-standard dialects, and may be a hypercorrect form, arising from a feeling that *which* is superior to the more informal *that*. Secondly, the non-standard relative pronoun *what* is used in Tyneside English. This is in fact very common in non-standard English, to the point of being a stereotype, as is witnessed by the catchphrase of the comedian Ernie Wise:

> My new play what I wrote.

In Tyneside English, the antecedent of *what* may be either personal or impersonal, as can be seen from the following examples:

(1)   The coats what the men wore were very long.
(2)   It cannot be anyone else but you what's left that bath dirty.
(McDonald 1980: 20)

Finally, in standard English the relative pronoun may be deleted if it is the object of the clause, thus:

The man I served yesterday came back to complain.

is quite grammatical. However, if the relative is the subject of the relative clause it cannot be deleted in standard English, so that:

*The man served me yesterday was a clumsy idiot.

would not be grammatical. That such sentences were formerly found in educated standard English can be seen from Shakespeare's (*Measure for Measure*, II.ii.34):

I have a brother is condemned to die.

The construction persists in Tyneside English, as in Scots and Irish dialects but only after clauses containing the verb *to be* and a complement:

Leck is a young boy was coming home from school.
(McDonald 1980: 20)

In spoken Tyneside English, the above sentence would have a pause before *was*, which would be pronounced fully stressed.

6.6.2   Replacive 'one'

In standard English *one* can be used to substitute for a noun. It only occurs with the indefinite article if an adjective intervenes. Thus:

Q Would you like a drink?
A Yes, but just a little one.

In Tyneside English, *one* is preceded by *a* whether an adjective intervenes or not:

My ideal job is a receptionist. I would like to be a one because it is a job where you meet people.
(McDonald 1980: 21)

6.6.3   Number

In Tyneside English, nouns of quantity often have plurals without -*s*. Such 'zero plurals' occur for some nouns of quantity in standard English, e.g. *ten stone*; *three foot*; *five ton*, but the list is longer for Tyneside, including units of time and money as can be seen from the following examples:

(1) His temporary visa was now six month out of date.
(2) I lived there for ten year.
(3) If you take early retirement, they'll pay you twenty three pound a week to retire.

> (McDonald 1980: 22)

6.6.4   Adjectival constructions

Double comparatives and superlatives

These, like double negatives, have been eradicated from standard English since about the eighteenth century. However, they persist in Tyneside and other non-standard dialects of English, as can be seen from the following examples:

> She's got the most loveliest clothes.
>
> (McDonald 1980: 22)

> I think alcohol is much more safer, kind of relaxing if took in small quantities.
>
> (McDonald 1985)

Intensifiers

Some intensifiers used in Tyneside would not be found in Standard English.

(1) That

Where standard English would have *so ... that*, Tyneside, along with other non-standard dialects, has *that* alone. An example is:

> I was that excited I didn't know what to say.

In standard English this would be:

I was so excited I didn't know what to say.

(McDonald 1985)

(2) Geet

An intensifier possibly unique to Tyneside is *geet*. I have never seen this written, but it is pronounced [gi:ʔ]. In meaning, it corresponds to Standard English *really*; Yorkshire *right* and Northern *dead* (the latter is also used on Tyneside). An example would be:

> This is geet hard, Sir. [Tyneside]
> This is dead hard, Sir. [Northern]
> This is right hard, Sir. [Yorkshire]
> This is really hard, Sir. [Standard]

The word is most often heard in the highly localized term of approbation *geet lush*, a term which as recently as ten years ago was perceived as being specifically localized to the coastal areas of North Tyneside, but which is now in vogue amongst the young people of Newcastle. The only possible etymological explanation I can think of for *geet* is that it derives from the Scots *gey*, which was in turn borrowed from French. An example of the Scots usage would be:

> It's gey dreich the day (*dreich* means 'damp and dismal')

Scots /ei/ would correspond to Tyneside /i:/, and, since glotalization of final voiceless stops is common in Tyneside, an underlying /t/ may have been added by inference. The 'Scots connection' is highly plausible given the coastal origins of the term, since there is contact with Scottish fishermen in the port of North Shields.

6.7   Sentence-final elements

6.7.1   Pronouns

In Tyneside English, the subject of a sentence may be taken up again at the end of the sentence. In this position, an objective pronoun is used. By contrast, other dialects, such as Yorkshire, would repeat the subject pronoun and verb. Examples of Tyneside usage are:

> They're useless, them.
> My skirt's too short, this.
> I could just go a toasted sandwich, me. (Here *go* means 'have' or 'enjoy'.)

6.7.2 But

In Tyneside, as in Scots and Irish dialects, *but* not only functions as a conjunction at the beginning of a clause, as in standard English, but can also stand at the end, where it is equivalent in meaning to standard English *though*. An example of this is:

> I'll manage but
>
> (Pellowe *et al.* 1972: 42)

6.8 Prepositions

Some prepositions have different uses in Tyneside and standard English. The Tyneside prepositions and their standard English equivalents are set out in Table 6.6. Most non-standard dialects of English have prepositional usages which are different from the standard, but these usages seem to be distinct in each dialect.

Table 6.6

Tyneside	Standard
off	from/by
on	about
at	in (place)
on	at (time)
used with	used to
by	of (agent)

Examples are:

He is forever getting hit off my parents.

The pilot did as best he could to keep the radio informed on where the plane was going to land.

Ten people had already died by the fumes.

In May, Mam, Dad, Michelle and I are going to a place called Estartit at the Costa Brava.

You should get yourself out more, especially on a weekend.

(McDonald 1985)

6.9 Conclusion

It is evident that Tyneside English has several syntactic features that are common to most, if not all, the non-standard dialects of English. Many of these are features that were previously found in standard English, but were eradicated as a consequence of the codifying activities of the eighteenth-century grammarians. The double negative and double comparative and superlative constructions are examples of this. Many more features are shared by Tyneside, Scots and Irish dialects, bearing witness to the common linguistic heritage and influence from immigration referred to in the Introduction. Tyneside also has its unique features, such as the verb forms *tret, divent, getten, forgetten* and *putten*, and the system of tags outlined in section 4. The complexity and regularity of the tag systems show particularly clearly that far from being a simple and slovenly 'poor relation', Tyneside, like other non-standard dialects, is as much a complex rule-based linguistic system as standard English.

References

BULLEIN, WILLIAM (1578) *A Dialogue Bothe Pleasaunte and Pietifull, Wherein is a Goodly Regiment Against the Fever Pestilence.* London: Early English Text Society (Extra Series No. LII)

CHESHIRE, JENNY (1982) *Variation in an English Dialect: A Sociolinguistic Study.* Cambridge: Cambridge University Press

COOTER, ROBERT (1972) The Irish in County Durham and Newcastle c. 1840–1880. University of Durham: Unpublished MA Thesis

HARRIS, JOHN (1985) Syntactic Variation and Dialect Divergence. *Journal of Linguistics* **21**:2

HESLOP, OLIVER (1892) *Northumberland Words*. London: English Dialect Society

HOUSE, J.W. (1954) *North Eastern England. Population Movements and the Landscape Since the Early Nineteenth Century*. Newcastle: Department of Geography, King's College

LABOV, W. (1966) *The Social Stratification of English in New York City*. Washington, DC: Center for Applied Linguistics

McDONALD, CHRISTINE (1980) Some Contrasts in Teachers' and Pupils' Language and Aspects of their Relevance in the Classroom. University of Newcastle: Unpublished Graduate Certificate of Education Dissertation

McDONALD, CHRISTINE (1981) Variation in the Use of Modal Verbs with Special Reference to Tyneside English. University of Newcastle: Unpublished PhD Thesis

McDONALD, CHRISTINE (1985) Notes on Local Syntax. Mimeo

PELLOWE, J., NIXON, G., and McNEANY, V. (1972) Defining the Dimensionality of a Linguistic Variety Space. University of Newcastle. Unpublished Draft of Paper for Colloquium on Urban Speech Surveying

QUIRK, RANDOLPH and GREENBAUM, SIDNEY (1973) *A University Grammar of English*. London: Longman

TRUDGILL, P. (1974) *The Social Differentiation of English in Norwich*. Cambridge: Cambridge University Press.

7 The grammar of southern British English

Viv Edwards

7.1 Dialect grammar and south-eastern English dialects

Traditionally those linguists who took an interest in dialect paid most attention to pronunciation and vocabulary. The interest in grammar has in fact been a very recent development and one which arguably has more implications for education than either pronunciation or vocabulary. It is true, for instance, that regional pronunciation is reflected in children's spelling and any teacher in the south-east will be familiar with spellings such as *fink* for *think* and *pole* for *pool*. Yet the fact remains that the pronunciation of standard English has changed so much over the centuries that present-day orthography does not favour the speakers of any particular dialect.

With regard to regional vocabulary, we may note that items such as *bunk* (to play truant) or *chin* (to hit on the chin) tend to be relatively quickly 'edited out' as children develop a sense of the differences between speech and writing, and a feeling for what is appropriate in different situations. Those regionalisms that do remain tend to be overlooked, or even appreciated as lending a certain local colour. The same is not true, however, of grammar. Although the grammatical differences between standard English and south-eastern English are relatively few in number, they are highly stigmatized and often provoke strong criticism from teachers and others.

In the pages which follow we will attempt to redress the

imbalance in the discussion of dialect, by focusing on the grammar rather than the pronunciation of south-eastern non-standard speech. In order to appreciate present-day non-standard speech we shall look briefly at the historical development of English dialects, and the emergence of a standard language. Then we shall consider the importance of London for south-eastern dialects and the history of low status of south-eastern speech, before going on to describe its main grammatical characteristics. Finally, an appendix of two short texts (a narrative and a contribution to a group discussion both by south eastern dialect speakers) will, it is hoped, dispel many of the current stereotypes of non-standard dialect as a limited and linguistically inferior form of speech.

If we are to appreciate the reasons for the differences between the standard and non-standard dialects of English spoken in the south-east of England today, it is very helpful to briefly consider the history of the English language. Three main tribes – the Angles and Saxons and the Jutes – were responsible for the colonization of what we now know as England. The various Germanic dialects spoken by these tribes differed from one another in many important ways, and this sharp difference between dialects, in writing as well as speech, seems to have continued in the Middle English period (approximately 1100 to 1450).

London lay at the intersection of three of the ancient kingdoms – the Mercian, West Saxon and Kentish. Over the years, a mixed dialect containing regional features of those who drifted to the London area gradually became fixed. The emergence of a standard language has in many ways reduced the difference between the various dialects. Certainly they no longer have autonomous writing systems, and dialect speakers attempt to write in standard English. None the less, the influence of the original dialects is still to be found in present-day varieties of English.

The main reason for recognizing that a south-east dialect region exists stems from the social and economic interdependence of London and the surrounding areas. In earlier centuries the speech of the capital was moulded by the synthesis of the south-eastern dialects of the original inhabitants and the east midlands dialects of the newcomers from the surrounding counties to the north. The population movement over the centuries has exerted such a strong levelling force on speech that some observers have doubted whether a distinctively non-standard south-eastern speech actually exists. The famous linguist A.J. Ellis, himself a north Londoner, wrote in 1890 that 'all London north of the Thames . . . is essentially a place where dialect could not grow up because of the large mass of changing and more or less educated population'.

More recently, in the early 1950s, Eugen Dieth, another eminent linguist, expressed doubts as to whether any Cockney remained. But as part of the Leeds University Survey of English Dialects, Peter Wright was sent to record systematically the dialects of South Hackney in the East End, Harmondsworth in Middlesex, Nettleswell in Essex, Walton-on-the-Hill in Surrey and Farningham in Kent. His findings left little doubt that south-eastern dialects remain distinct from the standard and are likely to continue to do so.

In the years since the First World War the influence of London speech has been working outwards. Large population movements from the capital to new housing developments in Dagenham, Basildon and Milton Keynes have greatly increased the influence of London speech. The extension of railway and underground lines, making it possible for people to live outside the capital and commute to work, has had a similar effect. Many people evacuated to what was then the 'country' during the Second World War never returned.

Strong demographic, political and economic forces ensure that London remains the most important linguistic centre in the south-east, and most writers who have set out to study south-eastern speech have made the capital their focus. While there is a great deal of variation in the south-eastern region as a whole and even within London, it would seem that the main differences are on the level of pronunciation, and the non-standard grammar of the region is remarkably homogeneous. However, the fact that this grammar is homogeneous in no way implies that it is invariant. The proportion of standard and non-standard features varies from person to person and even within the same person's speech according to topic and situation so that, for instance, non-standard features appear more frequently in informal conversations with family and friends than in more formal encounters with teachers and employers.

7.1.1   The low status of south-eastern dialects

All non-standard speech has low status but it is interesting to note that non-standard south-eastern speech is particularly stigmatized. This would appear to be the case not only today but also in the past.[1] The language of the upper classes in London, whose speech formed the basis for standard English remained distinct from that of the ordinary Londoner who originally spoke the south-eastern dialect from which present day Cockney is descended. It is important to remember that, from earliest times, differences between the standard and south-eastern dialects have been inextricably linked with social status differences. These status differences must presumably have been even sharper and more noticeable in London and the south-east, because of the presence of the court, than they were elsewhere in the country.

When Edgar in King Lear takes on the guise of 'base peasant' he switches to the Kentish dialect. Early in the nineteenth century Egan described the Cockney as 'brought into life within the sound of Bow bell – pert and conceited, yet truly ignorant, they generally discover (i.e. 'reveal') themselves by their mode of speech, notwithstanding they have frequent opportunities of hearing the best language'. In 1909, the London County Council report on the teaching of English in the elementary schools is no more complimentary:

> When a boy or girl in Devonshire, Lincolnshire, or Yorkshire is taught to acquire the constructions of the King's English at the expense of his native forms of speech, there is a balance of loss and gain in the process. But with the pupil in the London elementary school this is not the case. There is no London dialect of reputable antecedents and origin which is a heritage for him to surrender in school. The Cockney mode of speech, with its unpleasant twang, is a modern corruption without legitimate credentials, as is unworthy of being the speech of any person in the capital city of the Empire.

As recently as 1974 it was possible to read an account of how John Stevens, the son of a London docker and a highly competent student teacher, discovered to his own personal cost that the prejudice against south-eastern speech was alive and well. He was told that his application for a job as lecturer in Woolwich

College of Further Education had been unsuccessful because of the 'grammatical and other faults' in his spoken English, a 'failing' which needed to be 'eradicated' in the interest of his professional future (see note 1 again).

Thus, while it might be expected that, because south eastern dialects are more closely related to standard English than other British dialects they would be less heavily stigmatized, this would not appear to be the case either today or in the past. It is possible to demonstrate a hierarchy of public preferences in which standard English spoken with Received Pronunciation (sometimes called BBC or Queen's English) is judged to be of highest status, followed by rural speech and then urban varieties. Devon or Norfolk or Cumbrian speech is considered to be 'dialect' and is generally felt to be 'quaint' and 'attractive', while 'Brummie', 'Scouse' and 'Cockney' are dismissed as 'bad English' and considered 'harsh', 'ugly' and 'unattractive'. Nearness to the standard in no way ensures higher status for south-eastern speech than other British dialects; as we have seen, the opposite appears to be the case.

Language scholars, however, prefer to describe regional dialects in terms of their own internal structure, and generally agree that any superiority attributed to the standard can be explained in terms of the social status of standard speakers rather than intrinsic linguistic qualities. There is, however, a long tradition of explaining dialect grammar in terms of 'deviation' rather than 'difference'. Dialect forms are labelled 'ungrammatical' by standard speakers and dismissed as 'irritating' and 'unorthodox'. It is true that they do not always follow the rules of standard English, but they have their own internal rule system which is no less effective or logical. Dialect forms may be non-standard but they are in no way sub-standard (on 'non-standard' and 'sub-standard', see further Chapter 1).

Even those writers who recognize the validity of the internal rules of south-eastern speech sometimes fall into the trap of trivialization. The comments which they make, some of which are used to introduce the various grammatical features discussed below, often have the effect of making the Cockney, whose speech forms the focus for their work, seem a comic figure. South-eastern speakers can be amusing in the same way as other dialect speakers, including those who use standard English; but humour is a characteristic of individual speakers and not of the dialect they speak.

Features of south-eastern non-standard grammar are best seen as having developed independently and so should be described in their own terms rather than as 'corruptions' or 'deviations' from the standard. The Germanic dialects of the Angles, Saxons and Jutes were highly inflected 'synthetic' languages which have gradually changed over a period of fifteen hundred years into 'analytic' languages with very few vestiges of inflection. To some extent, this change is still in progress and is reflected in much of the variation to be found in south-eastern and other British dialects.

Other areas of difference between standard and regional dialects are the direct result of the standardizing and codifying activities of such eighteenth-century grammarians as Lowth, who attempted to fix a single set of uniquely correct forms for English. As a result, the modern standard departs from the native English patterns common in writers like Shakespeare and Milton before the eighteenth century, and still to be found in British dialects.

7.2   South-eastern English grammar

7.2.1   Introduction

Our knowledge of the *grammar* of south eastern, and indeed other British dialects, is limited because of the traditional emphasis on pronunciation and vocabulary. The only systematic study of grammar undertaken in the south east is Jenny Cheshire's *Variation in an English Dialect: a Sociolinguistic Study*, which is based on the dialect spoken in the Berkshire town of Reading. Other sources of information on south-eastern speech include older works like Matthews' *Cockney Past and Present* (1938) and Franklyn's *Survey of London Life and Language* (1953) which, because they were written several decades ago, are unlikely to accurately reflect present-day speech in the region. Studies like North's comparative account of two West Kent dialects or Wright's *Cockney Dialect and Slang* devote most attention to pronunciation or vocabulary.

There is enough information in the more recent studies, however to construct a fairly coherent picture of the non-standard dialects spoken in the south-east. The description which follows does not claim to be a complete or definitive account, but it does represent a useful starting point for those interested in the non-standard grammar of the region.

7.2.2 Past tenses

> Most educated Londoners become rather weary of this persistent Cockney habit of mixing past tenses and past participles, but it is well-rooted in the dialect.
>
> (Matthews 1938)

> Past and present tense, participle, and preterite are devastated in Cockney grammar.
>
> (Franklyn 1953)

Standard English forms past tenses in two main ways. In the majority of cases the so-called 'weak verbs' add -ed to the stem (as in walk *ed*; she row *ed*; it rott *ed*). In a small number of cases 'strong' verbs achieve the same end by changing the vowel in the stem (e.g. he *swam*; she *ran*). Whereas in present-day English weak verbs greatly outnumber strong verbs, this was not always so. In West Saxon, for instance, about five-sixths of the recorded verbs were strong verbs which often marked tenses with as many as five distinct vowel changes, and also marked changes between singular and plural in this way.

The movement away from the strong verb pattern is more generalized in south-eastern and other British dialects than it is in standard English, so that forms like *growed*, *throwed*, and *builded* are not uncommon. There is, however, considerable variation in the form which this movement takes. On some occasions, the present tense form is identical with both past tense and past participle (see Table 7.1).

Table 7.1

Present	Past	Past participle
come	come	come
give	give	give
run	run	run

On other occasions the past tense is extended to the past participle so that we find examples like *I've forgot* and *he's drove it away* (see Table 7.2).

Table 7.2

Present	Past	Past participle
drive	drove	drove
forget	forgot	forgot
speak	spoke	spoke
steal	stole	stole
take	took	took
do	done	done

It is interesting to note that this two-way pattern is stigmatized only in strong verbs which change the vowel in their stem and is accepted as regular in the weak verbs which add -ed (e.g. I love; I loved; I have loved). It is also noteworthy that the two-way pattern was extremely common in the sixteenth and seventeenth centuries when forms such as 'the food was stole' and 'the letter was wrote' were perfectly acceptable. During the eighteenth century, however, prescriptive grammarians decided that the three way division into present, past and participle, which followed a Latin model, should be the norm, and the two-way pattern has gradually become more stigmatized ever since.

The enormous variations which are to be found in the past tenses and past participles of common verbs like *know*, *break*, *eat*, and *see* point very clearly to a process of linguistic change which is still in progress (see Table 7.3).

Table 7.3

Present	Past	Past participle
know	knowed/knew	knowned/known
break	breaked/broke	broke/broken
eat	eat/ate	eaten/ate
see	seen/seed	seen/seed

It is interesting to note that this process of change is also affecting the standard, although to a lesser extent. Many educated speakers hesistate over whether they should say 'he *swum*' or 'he *swam*' and 'I *drunk*, or 'I *drank*'.

7.2.3 Present tense verb forms

Variation in present tense verb forms is another indication of a very different linguistic past. Many languages use pronouns for emphasis only and indicate whether the subject of the verb is singular or plural, and whether it is first, second or third person, by means of verb endings. In Spanish, for instance, we find the following:

and*o*	I walk
and*as*	you (singular) walk
and*a*	he/she walks
and*amos*	we walk
and*ais*	you (plural) walk
and*an*	they walk

In Anglo-Saxon dialects, the number of verb endings is less than in languages like Spanish: we find -*e*, for 'I', -*est* for 'you' singular, -*eth* for 'he' and -*ath* for all plural forms. Thus, for example, the verb *fremman* to perform takes the following forms:

fremm*e*	I perform
frem*est*	you (singular) perform
frem*eth*	he/she performs
fremm*ath*	we/you/they perform

In present-day standard English the only remnant of this system of verb endings is in the third person singular -*s*, as in 'he walks', 'she runs'. It is interesting to note that in East Anglia and many parts of the world where varieties of English are spoken, the loss of verb-endings is complete and only the pronoun remains to indicate person; thus, forms like *he go, she see* and *it stop* are common. There is thus a progressive tendency in English for person and number to be marked in the pronoun rather than in the verb stem, whereas in languages like Spanish these distinctions can be marked exclusively in the verb stem.

The south-east and certainly other regions have achieved the same end in rather a different way, generalizing the -s form to all persons and giving the following paradigm:

I goes
You goes
He, she, it goes
We goes
You goes
They goes

Historically, the first records of this -s ending for all persons are found in the Northumbrian dialect of Old and Middle English. It spread later to the midlands dialects and there is also some evidence of this pattern in the speech of standard English speakers up until the middle of the seventeenth century. There are reports of -s endings in many parts of the English speaking world today, particularly in narratives, reflecting this historical spread, but it is not clear how general the practice is within the south-east. It is reported by one writer as dying out in London, but remains a strong feature of Reading speech:

I gets out of the car and walks down the street for a few yards before I sees them boys coming towards me.

This generalization of third person -s to other persons is also associated with the verb 'to be'. Forms like 'you was', 'they was' and 'them blokes is coming' are common throughout the south east and indeed many other parts of the country. 'Were' can also be heard occasionally with first and third person singular subjects (I, he, she, it, the man, etc.), especially in negative sentences:

Best one of the lot, weren't I?
He were going to make a big fuss about that.

It is important to point out, however, that despite the generalization of -s in present tense verb forms, there are also constraints on its use. Cheshire's study of Reading, for instance, shows that -s forms are far more likely to occur when the speaker uses slang verbs like *leg it* or *bunk* than with standard English verbs. She also shows that the form of the verb is influenced by the complement which follows it. When tense is *not* marked in the complement, as in:

I fancies *going over Caversham.*

there is a much greater likelihood of finding the *-s* ending than when tense *is* marked, as in the following example:

I believe that there is life after death.

Here the present tense is marked in the verb form *is*.

7.2.4 The irregular verbs HAVE and DO

The picture concerning the irregular verbs *have* and *do* is very interesting inasmuch as the non-standard dialect tends to operate in this area of the grammar in a more complex way than the standard. In standard English the only changes in these verbs are determined by person and number (see Table 7.4).

Table 7.4

I have	I do
you have	you do
he/she/it has	he/she/it does
we have	we do
you have	you do
they have	they do

In south-eastern dialects there is evidence that the form of the verb depends not only on person and number but on the grammatical function of the verb. *Have* and *do* both behave in two quite distinct ways related to two different functions. Their first function is as full verbs:

I *have* a good relationship with the school.
I *do* a lot of reading.

Their second function is as auxiliaries, that is when they are dependent on and attached to another verb:

> I *have* been here on a number of occasions.
> I *do* like that music.

In south eastern non-standard English *has* can occur with all persons, but only when functioning as a full verb, as opposed to an auxiliary verb. Thus it is possible to hear examples such as the following:

> We *has* a great time down there.
> I *has* the answer for that.

but not

> *We *has* been doing that for ages.
> *I *has* seen that before.

In these two ungrammatical sentences (in the sense that they are not constructed in accordance with the rules of the dialect grammar) *has* functions as an auxiliary attached to the main verbs *do* and *see*. The situation for *do* is more complex still. The only analysis of this verb in the south-east has been undertaken by Jenny Cheshire in the town of Reading, Berkshire. Reading is on the very edge of what we are defining as the south-east, and it is unclear how widespread this pattern is in the rest of the region. But in Reading, at least, three non-standard forms alternate with the standard. The first, *do*, functions as an auxiliary:

> He gives her more time than he do her sister.
> She makes a fuss about nothing, she do.

The second and third forms occur when *do* functions as a main verb. *Does* is used for all persons *except* the third person singular:

> Every time we *does* anything wrong, he sticks you.
> That's what I *does* anyway, I just ignores them.

while *dos* (pronounced *dooze*) is used mainly for the third person singular:

> All the headmaster *dos* now is make you stand in the corner
> One bloke stays at home and *dos* the house-cleaning and all that.

7.3   Negation

> The mathematical axiom that multiplication of negatives
> results in positives has never recommended itself to Cockneys
> (Matthews 1938)

7.3.1   Multiple negation

The use of double negatives or, more correctly, multiple negatives is extremely widespread. In fact, standard English is the only British dialect which does not express negation in this way. The abhorrence for the multiple negative is relatively recent. Chaucer, Shakespeare and Pope used multiple negatives without fear of criticism but in the last two hundred years or so, this feature has been singled out for special censure. An argument based on mathematics is frequently invoked: two negatives make a positive. Thus, it is argued that the 'logical' meaning of *I don't want none* is *I want some*. It is possible to counter this argument in a number of ways. From a commonsense position, the child who insists that she doesn't want none leaves little latitude for misunderstanding. Even if the listener is a standard English speaker, the child's intention is quite clear. It also seems inconsistent to apply the 'two negatives make a positive' argument to non-standard English while accepting without comment the French 'je *ne* vois *rien*' or the Spanish '*no* he visto *nada*'. A further, and perhaps more telling observation, however, is that three negatives are just as unacceptable as two. Thus, applying the mathematical principle, three negatives make a negative, sentences such as

> He couldn't find none nowhere.

should therefore be perfectly acceptable. However, this is not the case.

7.3.2 Ain't

> People complain about this widespread Cockney liking for
> ain't, but the thinking Cockney replies that he has to keep
> saying it, especially for asking questions, because it's so
> darned helpful.
>
> (Franklyn 1953)

Any discussion of negation must include *ain't*. *Ain't* is the
present tense negative form of the verb *to be*. Thus we find:

> I ain't telling you
> You ain't coming
> It ain't there

It also functions as a negative when *have* is used as an auxiliary
verb:

> I ain't seen her
> He ain't found it

7.3.3 Never

> Perhaps of a less hoary antiquity, but no less deep seated in
> the cockney idiom, is *never* for 'did not'.
>
> (Franklyn 1953)

In standard English *never* generally expresses the idea of 'not on
any occasion' as in:

> I never go to that part of town
> I have several nice hats but I never wear them

In south-eastern and certain other non-standard dialects, however, *never* can also be used as a past tense negative in the same
way as 'didn't' but only when it refers to one specific occasion.
Thus we find examples like:

> She said that last week but she never this morning
> I saw you do that!
> No I never!

7.4   Relative pronouns

'Along with the need to speak quickly before someone else
butts in, confusion over these pronouns may well be the
reason why so often they disappear'

(Wright 1980)

The situation concerning the development of relative pronouns
in English is extremely complex. In present day standard English
the relative pronoun can take five different forms. *Who* is used
to refer to people, *which* to things and *that* to both people and
things. Additionally, *who* can be inflected for case – *whose* to
show possession, and *whom* to show that the pronoun functions
as the object of the sentence. However, *whom* is now restricted to
formal writing and seldom occurs in speech:

> The car *which* went
> The car *that* went
> The man *that* went
> The man *who* went
> The man *whom* I saw
> The man *whose* car I borrowed

The relative pronoun can also be omitted, but only when it
functions as the object of the relative clause. Thus it is possible
to say:

> The man *I saw* (corresponding to 'I saw *the man*')

but not

> *I gave him the pen *writes best* (corresponding to '*the pen*
> writes best')

These standard English relative constructions occur in south
eastern non-standard speech alongside *what* and, in some parts
of the region, *as*. Both of these forms can be used to refer to people
and things:

> The girl *what's* coming over
> The car *what* I saw

The boy *as* I asked
The food *as* I bought

However, the relative pronoun can be omitted in dialect speech not only in object position as in standard English but also in subject position as in the following examples:

There's a train goes through without stopping.
It ain't the best ones finish first.

Readers might like to refer to the second paragraph of the first extract in the Appendix where the following sentence appears:

They're still building them high rise flats *are going up all over the place.*

Again, we find that the relative pronoun, functioning as subject, has been omitted. This pattern appears in a number of British dialects (see particularly Miller's account of relative pronouns in Scots English in section 4.3.3), and there is no reason to suppose that it should be explained in terms of confusion, or the need to speak quickly, as is suggested in the quotation at the beginning of this section.

7.5   Personal and reflexive pronouns

The Cockney employs many variants from the normal pronouns

(Matthews 1938)

There are two main areas of difference between south eastern non-standard and standard English pronouns. The first contains the use, as subject of the sentence, of emphatic personal pronouns in south eastern non-standard English. These pronouns take the same form as standard pronouns in *non-subject* position:

Him and *her* are the ones you should pick.
Them what you like should come.

The dialect thus has the possibility of contrasting emphatic and non-emphatic pronouns in subject position in a way that the standard cannot do. The second area of difference can be seen in reflexive pronouns, which are formed by adding the endings *-self* or *-selves*. In standard English these endings occur with the possessive pronouns in the case of *my, your* and *our* (*myself, yourself/selves, ourselves*) and the object pronoun in the case of *him, her, it* and *them* (*herself, itself, themselves*). In south eastern and many other non-standard dialects, however, this system has been regularized and all reflexive pronouns are formed by adding *self* to the possessive. It should be remembered that the English pronoun system was once much more fully inflected than it is today, and this is yet another area where a non-standard dialect has accelerated changes which are already present in the language.

meself	ourselves
yourself	yourselves
hisself	theirselves
herself	.
itself	

Thus we find examples such as:

He builded that boat *hisself*.
They want it for *theirselves*.
We ought to do it *ourself*.

Other variants which deserve comment include the use of *me* for *my*

I give it to me brother.

This gives rise quite regularly to the reflexive pronoun *meself*, as in:

I don't think much of that *meself*.

The use of *us* for *me*, as in:

Give us a look.

might also be noted at this point, although it is possible to argue that this latter case is a feature of colloquial style rather than of non-standard dialect. There are, however, restrictions on the distribution of plural forms for reference to the singular. Thus, while it is possible to use *us* for *me*, the corresponding use of *we* for *I* does not occur.

7.6 Adjectives and adverbs

Standard English forms many adverbs by adding -*ly* to the related adjectives.

Table 7.5

Adjective	Adverb
happy	happily
quick	quickly
right	rightly
sweet	sweetly

In most non-standard varieties, including south-eastern dialects, the standard English adjective form serves both functions.

Bring it here quick.
You're doing that a bit too slow.
She was talking very quiet.
He done it good.

This same tendency can, of course, be found to some extent in educated informal speech.

7.6.1 Comparatives and superlatives

Cockneys often indulge in unorthodox comparatives and superlatives.

(Matthews 1938)

Standard English forms comparatives and superlatives by adding -*er*/-*est* or *more*/*most* to adjectives (see Table 7.6). This, however,

Table 7.6

nice	nicer	nicest
happy	happier	happiest
wonderful	more wonderful	most wonderful
beautiful	more beautiful	most beautiful

was not always the case and the works of earlier English writers abound with examples of *-er/-est* used in conjunction with *more/most*, as in 'This was the most unkindest cut of all' in Shakespeare's *Julius Caesar*. These methods of forming comparatives and superlatives are very common in non-standard dialects and are a widespread feature of south-eastern speech:

> I couldn't have asked for a more nicer friend.
> That was the most horriblest experience of my life.

Comparative forms of *bad* also differ from the standard pattern on occasions and it is possible to find examples such as:

> That programme is even *worser* than the one on the other side.
> He's *badder* than his brother.

7.7   Demonstratives

In standard English we find the following system of demonstratives which is marked for nearness *versus* distance and also for number:

this	these
that	those

In south-eastern English we find the same distinctions expressed in a slightly different way; there are two alternative forms for each of the singular demonstratives (*this*, *that*), and the plural of *that* is *them*:

this/this here	these
that/that there	them

and we find examples like:

> This here jacket cost a bomb.
> I saw them boys just a minute ago.

7.8   Verb particles and prepositions

Prepositions are treated equally roughly.

(Franklyn 1953)

There is a good deal of variation between the standard and non-standard dialects in the choice of verb particle in prepositional verbs. Certain complex verb particles consisting of more than one word are reduced to simple particles consisting of one word:

> I looked *out* the window.
> I told him to get *out* the house.

The converse is also true and simple verb particles in the standard can become complex in the non-standard dialect:

> We got *off of* the bus

There is a great deal of variation in the use of prepositions:

> They've got seven weeks *off of* school this summer.
> We leave it there *of a* night.
> I saw it *at* London.
> We've been here just *on* three weeks.
> Everybody *down* our street is going tomorrow.
> He asked the three *on* us.
> I'm going *up* the park/the baths/the pictures.

Choice of prepositions in a given context varies enormously from one language to another. In French, for instance, one puts the key *on* ('sur') not *in* the door and one talks *at* ('au') and not *on* the phone. Given the notoriously arbitrary way in which languages handle this area, it is not at all surprising that there should be a good deal of variation between standard and non-standard dialects. Considerable variation in the choice of prepositions is reported in the other accounts in this volume, which outline the grammars of Irish, Scots and Tyneside English.

7.9 Nouns of measurement

Like many non-standard dialects, south-eastern varieties do not add -s to nouns of measurement where, of course, plural marking is semantically redundant. Thus forms like:

> two hundred mile
> six foot
> five pound

are common.

7.10 Conclusion

A number of points have recurred in this discussion of non-standard south-eastern grammar. Very often dialect forms have a long historical pedigree and standard forms are innovatory; sometimes they are the exception to far more general tendencies in the language as a whole. The stigma which is attached to south-eastern dialect also has deep historical roots which can be understood more correctly in terms of the relative social status of dialect and standard speakers in the region than in terms of any inherent linguistic characteristics. Finally, and of fundamental importance to an appreciation of the nature of non-standard grammar, it is important to emphasize that dialects are internally consistent and rule governed, and not, as is commonly believed, the product of sloppiness or illogicality.

Note

1. The following quotations attest to the low esteem in which 'Cockney' has been held from 1791 until recently.

(a) Cockneys have the disadvantage of being more disgraced by their peculiarities than any other people. The grand difference between the metropolis and the provinces is that people of education in London are generally free from the vices of the vulgar; but the best-educated people in the provinces, if constantly resident there, are sure to be tinctured with the dialect of the county in which they live. Hence it is that the vulgar pronunciation of London, though not half so erroneous as that of Scotland, Ireland, or any of the provinces, is, to a person of correct taste, a thousand times more offensive and disgusting.

(Walker 1791)

(b) Cockney is the characteristic speech of 'the greatest city of the greatest empire that the world has known'. But Cockney is such a pariah that not even the philologists have a good word for it. They deny it the status of a dialect and describe it as vulgar speech based upon error and misunderstanding.

(Matthews 1938: x)

(c)   April 1, 1974
Dear Mr Stevens,
You may not recognise the name but I was Chairman of the Panel which interviewed you on March 27 for the vacancy as Lecturer Grade 1 in Sociology at Woolwich College for Further Education when no one was appointed.

I am writing to give you some personal advice which I hope you will accept in the spirit it is given, to help a young man whom most of us felt had much to offer if one failing can be eradicated.

We were generally impressed by your written statement and you interviewed well except that we were all very worried by grammatical and other faults in your spoken English. It is not a question of accent but of grammar and aspirates, looseness of which we felt may be harmful for pupils and inhibit full cooperation with colleagues, this being a college where there is full harmony. I hope that on reflection you will appreciate this viewpoint and take steps to remedy the failing as we feel this would greatly assist your future in the profession.
Yours sincerely,
K.F. Valpy

(quoted in *Language and Class Workshop 2*,
Falling Wall Press, p. 19).

Appendix

Some examples of South-eastern non-standard English
(1) *Dialect and debate*
The following extract was recorded by Sue Shrapnel and appears in *Language and Class Workshop* 2, edited by Harold Rosen. The speaker is a member of a group which started as a Rent Action Group and developed into a women's group formed to tackle other problems on a housing estate with only one small playgroup, a community centre which was empty most of the day, and pubs.

> We think that we're bad enough done to, but I feel awful sorry for them girls – young girls, of eighteen, nineteen, twenty – stuck in them high-rise maisonettes, seven floors high; and half of them don't even know their next-door neighbours, they never see a soul them girls up there. I feel really sorry for them. And they're not built – you know, it's only recently they've starting building houses again at the back of this estate, they're still building them high rise flats are going up all over the place; they're going up in places where we didn't think they should have put them – I mean, where's the sense of putting a young couple, with a three year old toddler, and a young baby of nine months, on the top floor of a block of maisonettes? A two-year-old toddler – as soon as that door's open the kid's out and away; you just can't – I mean your own common sense tells you, if you let a child outside the front door on one of them high rise flats; you can – your imagination runs riot with you and you think of all the things that can happen. They could take a tumble down, they could fall off the verandah, they can get stuck in lifts – that's what frightens them up there.
>
> And as far as we're concerned no-one's ever been near us to talk about the problems. It was left to the women themselves to talk to one another and recognize that the problem's there, nobody else. You get a lot of people coming up and doing surveys– not up here, but I know that it's done by different organizations. They do their survey, and they get all the statistics, and they make a report, but that's it, finished, nothing ever comes of it. Nothing constructive is ever done afterwards. It's just put in the files, and you get files and files and files of statistics – Tower Hill's no special case; Cantril Farm's a carbon copy, and Skelmersdale's another good example, and they're within spitting distance of one another. What about the people that live in them areas?

(2) War time narrative recorded by E. Sivertsen and reported in *Cockney phonology*

There's one thing stands out in my memory. Er – it was on a Saturday night. I can remember it as plain as anything.

Er – suddenly the warning went and – no sooner the warning went, so the bombs started dropping. Well, I – I turned the light out, and I pulled the curtain aside and looked out the back window. So I turned round and said to my husband, 'Oh, Jack', I said, 'it's raining fire'. So – so he said, 'What's wrong with you? Gone mad?' So I said, 'Yes, come and have a look, quick!' So he looked. He didn't say nothing. So I opened the front door and running up the street. So I said, 'Look, quick! The streets alight'. So I said, 'Isn't it terrible!' So he come in, and just as he come in I saw one fall right down, right the side of our window. Right in the corner of our window it was. And – the moment it fell, the flames shot up, quite six feet high. My husband and the man next door and my intended son-in-law rushed round and put sand on it, and eventually they got it out. Well, he come in, and – he come in, and he went ba- then he went back again, and he said, 'I want to make sure it's out'. So he bent over it – Well, just as he went to make sure it was out, so this thing blasted and he got the whole full blast. It was marvellous that he wasn't killed instantly. Well anyway, the two men running round the Mildmay for first aid. And – while they was round the Mildmay for first aid – of course they was dropping the heavy stuff as well – a bang come at the door. Er – 'All you people get out within ten minutes because there's a land mine dropped on St Hilda's. St Hilda's is a – belongs to Cheltenham College. And – so of course, they said, 'If you don't get out within ten minutes it might go up and you'll all go up.' So my sister come running round and – we found our bags and our belongings, and we all started walking up Bethnal Green Road. I looked this side and that side, and everywhere you looked so it was fires. But the thing struck me most was – as the men was putting out the fires everything seemed so quiet and silent. They seemed not, seem to be making no noise. They was just putting them out quite naturally. And – and then – as we was going along we started singing – well, I started singing, 'Fire, fire, fire! Get a bucket of water! There's a fire down below'. We used to sing that round St Hilda's. So – anyway just at that minute, I looked up and I give out one shriek. So my sister said, 'What's wrong with her?' So I said, 'Look! Quick!' So she said, – 'That won't hurt you'. So – I said, 'Oh,' I said, 'it will'. So – I said, 'What is it?' So she said, 'Oh its only the –' The picture post had caught fire, and that hoarding right the top had got loose and the wind had carried it right up in the air, and it was spinning round and round and round, and to my imagination I thought it was a German bomb – German parachute coming down, and that's what terrified me. So of course they all roared alaughing, and we laughed and laughed till we got to the rest centre. Well, the woman in there, I think she thought we'd all gone crackers, because everybody else was crying, and all us lot laughing. So – well anyway, the lady took down our names and addresses, and – and our identification numbers. So she said. So she said, 'Do you want something to eat and drink?' So we said yes, but we didn't.

References and Further Reading

AYLWIN, B. (1973) *A Load of Cockney Cobblers (London's Rhyming Slang Interpreted)*. Edinburgh: Johnston and Bacon

BOWYER, R (1973) A Study of the Social Accents in a South London Suburb. Unpublished MA thesis, University of Leeds

DODSON, M. and SACZEK, R. (1972) *Dictionary of Cockney Slang and Rhyming Slang*. London: Hedgehog Enterprises

FRANKLYN, J. (1953) *The Cockney: a Survey of London Life and Language*. London: André Deutsch

FRANKLYN, J. (1961) *Dictionary of Rhyming Slang*, 2nd edn. London: Routledge.

JONES, J. (1971) *Rhyming Cockney Slang*. London: Abson Wick

LAWRENCE, J. (1975) *Rabbit and Pork: Rhyming Talk*. London: Hamish Hamilton Children's Books

LEITH, R. (1971) Dialectology in London. Unpublished MA thesis, University of York

MATTHEWS, W. (1938) *Cockney Past and Present*. London: Routledge

SIVERTSEN, E. (1960) *Cockney Phonology. Studies in English 8*. Oslo: Oslo University Press

WALKER, J. (1791) *A Critical Pronouncing Dictionary* London: Robinson and Cadell

WEEKLEY, E. (1930) *Adjectives and Other Words*.

WRIGHT, P. (1980) *Cockney Dialect and Slang*. London: Batsford

Appendix to Part II: Glossary of grammatical terms

Jim Miller (with additions by Jim Milroy)

ASPECT *Jane was eating a cake* presents Jane in the process of eating, whereas *Jane ate a cake* presents the action as complete. The contrast between *was eating* and *ate* is referred to as ASPECT. What is important in many instances is how the speaker views the action, what aspect the speaker provices. *Was eating* presents the action in progress and is called the progressive form of the verb. *Ate* is the simple form.

AUXILIARY VERB In *Susan might have been helping Edmund,* *helping* is called the main verb. This reflects the fact that the major bits of meaning conveyed by the sentence are that there is an action of helping involving Susan and Edmund. The speaker can add subsidiary or auxiliary bits of meaning: the action can be presented as possible – hence *might*, or as having been in the past – hence *have*, or as being in progress rather than as complete – hence, *been*. The verbs conveying these auxiliary pieces of meaning are called auxiliary verbs, the relevant verbs in English being CAN, MAY, MIGHT, WILL, SHALL, COULD, MUST, SHOULD, WOULD, BE, HAVE, DO. These verbs have two important properties:

(1) They take *not* or *n't* – *He can't swim, She didn't help.* Cf. the incorrect *She helped not.*

(2) They can occur at the beginning of questions: *Can he swim?,* *Did she help?* but not **Helped she?*

CLEFT SENTENCE CONSTRUCTION *It was Lydia who married Wickham* is a cleft sentence. The label *cleft* reflects the view that the basic sentence *Lydia married Wickham* is cleft in two. *Lydia* is put in one clause along with *It is* and *married Wickham* is put into another clause with *who*. The construction emphasizes that Lydia and not somebody else married Wickham.

COMPLEMENT *The baby put* is not complete because PUT requires other words or phrases after it: e.g. *The baby put the* *bricks into the bath.* Words or phrases that are required to make a sentence complete by filling out or complementing (the meaning of) the verb are said to be the complement of the verb.

CONDITIONAL CLAUSE *If Angus comes to the party, Fiona will go home* conveys the message that Fiona's going home is conditional, or depends, on another event, Angus' coming to the party. The event on which Fiona's going home is conditional is presented by the *if* clause, which is called a conditional clause. (Note: not all clauses introduced by IF are conditional clauses. See INDIRECT QUESTION.)

CONJUNCTION Words such as *and, but,* and *or* join other words – *Bill and Ben, bloody but unbowed,* phrases – *in France or in Britain,* or clauses – *Angus arrived and Fiona left.* These joining words are conjunctions.

DOUBLE NEGATIVES These are now non-standard in English. They are represented by sentences such as *I didn't see nobody.* As there can be more than two negatives in such sequences, *multiple negation* is the preferred term. Harris (section 5.6.1) uses the term *negative concord.*

INDIRECT OBJECT In *Celia lent John her car, John* is said to be the indirect object. John is affected by the action but not as directly as the car, which is the direct object.

INDIRECT QUESTION see INTERROGATIVE

INTERROGATIVE Sentences that convey questions are interrogative. Speakers can ask two sorts of questions:

(1) They can ask about whole events – *Did Sheila pass the exam?* Because such questions can be answered *yes* or *no,* they are called yes-no questions. (Alternatively, polar questions.)
(2) They can ask about particular people or things involved in an event: *Who passed the exam?*

Because this type of interrogative usually begins with a word such as *who, where, why,* they are known as WH interrogatives.

The examples above are direct questions, but speakers can put questions indirectly, as in *I was wondering if/whether Sheila passed the exam.* In direct WH questions the order of words is WH word + auxiliary verb subject noun. In indirect questions, at least in standard written English, the order is WH word + subject noun + main verb, as in *She asked what you bought.*

IRREGULAR VERBS See regular verbs.

MODAL VERB MAY, MIGHT, CAN, WILL, SHOULD, SHALL, COULD, WOULD, MUST are the central modal verbs of English. They express modality, i.e. whether the speaker presents an event or state as possible or necessary, or whether the speaker expresses a desire to do something. They have no forms in *-ing* – cf. *playing* but not **musting* – and no forms ending in *-s* – *plays* but not **musts*. They have the general properties of auxiliary verbs (q.v.).

NEGATION *Angus did not come to the party* is used to assert that an event – Angus' coming to the party – did not occur. *Not* expresses negation and the negation applies to the whole event, or to the whole clause. In *Fiona is unhappy* and *Not Angus but Alasdair came to the party*, *un* – and *not* express negation, but the negation applies to single words – *happy, Angus* – or to individual participants in the event.

PERFECT TENSE see TENSE

PROGRESSIVE see ASPECT

PSEUDO-CLEFT *What Fiona bought was a book* is a pseudo-cleft sentence. The basic sentence – *Fiona bought a book* – is cleft, but in contrast with the cleft construction (q.v.) the subject and the verb are put together in one group together with *what* and *a book*, the direct object, is combined with *was*. Pseudo-cleft sentences are used to emphasise particular words or phrases. The pseudo-cleft is also called the WH cleft.

QUANTIFIER/QUANTIFYING WORDS ALL, SOME, EACH, EVERY, MANY, MORE, FEW are called quantifiers because they express quantity (but not numerosity). They present particular problems for syntax and semantics.

REGULAR VERBS These are verbs such as *walk/walked*, which form their past tense by the addition of *-ed*, or *-d* to the stem. Irregular verbs are those that do not conform to this rule, such as *drive/drove, cut/cut*. See also strong verbs and weak verbs.

RELATIVE CLAUSES   In *The athlete who won the gold medal was unknown* the clause *who won the gold medal* provides information relative to the athlete. In syntactic terms, it modifies *athlete.* Such clauses are called relative clauses and there are two types in English. One is introduced by WH words such as WHO and WHICH, called relative pronouns, while others are introduced by THAT: *The pictures that fetched enormous prices were fakes.* THAT is regarded by many analysts not as a relative pronoun but as a conjunction joining two clauses.

STRONG VERBS   Historically, strong verbs are verbs which form their past tense by a change of vowel, rather than by addition of *-ed,* or *-d,* to the stem. They are normally included among 'irregular' verbs (q.v.) Examples: *drive/drove; drink/drank; eat/ate.*

TAG QUESTIONS   *Angus can swim, can't he* consists of a declarative clause *Angus can swim,* expressing an assertion, and *can't he,* a piece of interrogative syntax expressing a question. This question is tagged on to the main clause, hence its name 'tag question'. The tag consists of the first auxiliary verb in the main clause plus a pronoun. Failing an auxiliary, DO is used: *Angus drinks beer, doesn't he?*

TENSE   *Fiona is leaving* contrasts with *Fiona was leaving.* The former places the event in present time, the latter – in past time. *Is* is said to be in the present tense, *was* – in the past tense.

    In *Fiona has left* or *Fiona has visited Paris, has left* and *has visited* are said to be the perfect tense of LEAVE and VISIT. The perfect tense indicates that an event took place in the past but is relevant to the present time. *Fiona has left* is likely to be used to answer a question such as *Where's Fiona? Fiona has visited Paris* may answer a question such as *Who knows the name of the biggest museum in Paris* – Fiona does because of her visit to Paris.

WEAK VERBS   Historically, weak verbs are verbs which form their past tense by the addition of *-ed,* or *-d* to the stem. Examples are: *walk/walked, fade/faded.* They contrast with strong verbs (q.v.). In the course of history, some originally weak verbs have come to resemble 'strong' verbs, q.v. An example is *hide/hid.* With strong verbs, these are usually included amongst 'irregular' verbs.

Part III

Resources

8 A directory of English dialect resources: the English Counties

Viv Edwards

8.1 Introduction

The starting point for the compilation of the directory was the
Survey of British Dialect Grammar, a project based at Birkbeck
College, University of London, and funded by the Economic and
Social Research Council. Work on the project left no doubt that
dialect continues to be a source of fascination for a wide range
of people – for academics who believe that the description of
dialect is as important to linguistic theory as standard English; for
teachers who feel that education should acknowledge and build on
children's speech, rather than criticizing and rejecting it; for writers
and performers who find dialect a versatile vehicle for their work;
for the large body of lay people who identify with regional speech
and want to find out more.

Work on the project also made it clear that there was a very
great need for a central source of information on dialect resources.
This directory attempts to cater for the various groups of people
who are interested in dialect by compiling as comprehensive a
range as possible of books and commercially available sound
recordings, and by pointing readers in the right direction to find
out more about the particular English dialect which interests
them.

Books on dialect

The sheer quantity of dialect material is such that certain decisions needed to be made at the outset about what could realistically be included in the directory. The first decision affected geographical scope: only English dialect materials are listed; Scots or Lallans, Anglo-Welsh and Hiberno-English resources must, perforce, form the subject of a companion volume; so, too, must any references to Celtic dialects of Welsh, Gaelic and Irish.

The next decision concerned the nature of the written material which would be included. The extremely large numbers of articles which have been written on the subject would fill several volumes and so it seemed reasonable to restrict the scope to books. Writing on and in dialect has been commonplace for several hundred years, but is particularly concentrated in the nineteenth and twentieth centuries, and entries for books have therefore been confined to this period. Many of the older books are extremely rare and only those known to be available through the various county library services have been included. Only published materials have been included with one major exception: higher degree theses have been written on a very wide range of regional dialects and, in many cases, are the only source of information on a particular area.

Readers wishing to consult books on dialect are best advised, in the first instance, to contact their county library to discuss their particular needs. Generally speaking, there are no special dialect collections, and works on, and in, dialect are usually located in local studies collections. The scope of these local studies collections varies considerably from county to county. In some cases there is an extensive network throughout the county which includes many individual collections of note. In other cases, local branches hold very few works in dialect and the best source of information is the county library. In all cases, however, it is unlikely that the local branches will hold much material which is not also held centrally. Addresses and telephone numbers for the main local studies collection for each county are listed in the directory.

In addition to county and branch libraries, dialect material can also sometimes be found in the records or archives offices for each county. Readers are advised to consult The Royal Commission on Historical Manuscripts, *Record Repositories in Great Britain* (London: HMSO, 1987) to find the location of the office for the county which they are researching.

Sound recordings

The directory also lists commercially available recordings in the form of records, compact discs, sound cassettes and video cassettes. In a small number of cases, recordings which were not produced commercially or which are now extremely difficult to obtain are included: when it is known that such recordings are held in the local studies collection of a library, this information is indicated in the text.

The National Sound Archive is currently engaged in the immense task of comprehensively cataloguing commercially produced recordings of speech. In the absence of a published central source, there will inevitably be serious gaps in the information listed in the directory. The inclusion of sound recordings, however, serves as a marker for their importance as a dialect resource and goes at least some way towards remedying the dearth of information in this area. Whereas progress has been slow in the cataloguing of individual recordings, information is now available on the various sound collections nationwide. The *Directory of Recorded Sound Resources* (Weerasinghe, 1988) lists over 480 collections of both privately made and rare commercial recordings in the UK, many of which include dialect speech.

The burgeoning of interest in oral history provides another source of sound recordings. Although the primary focus of oral history groups is historical rather than dialect, a great deal of their material is recorded from dialect speakers. Readers who wish to pursue this line of inquiry further should either consult their county library to find if there is a local oral history group or contact the Oral History Society (see page 253). It may also be of interest that local studies librarians are always happy to receive donations of sound recordings from individuals.

Societies, Organizations and Centres

The continuing interest in dialect is reflected in the various societies found throughout the country. Sometimes the *raison d'être* of the society is the wish to enjoy and find out more about the local dialect; sometimes the focus is on a particular dialect writer; sometimes the attention to dialect is part of a broader interest in the region as a whole. There are also various regional centres and folk museums which show an active interest in dialect.

A note on organization

Material in the directory is organized along regional and county lines. It follows the same pattern set out in the *Survey of English Dialects* carried out between 1962 and 1971 by Harold Orton and his colleagues at the University of Leeds. Smaller geographical area such as the Black Country, Lakeland and the Cotswolds are indicated within these larger regions, and there is a further division into counties.

For each county, there are listings of books, followed by details of local studies collections, sound recordings and societies. The county boundaries employed, however, are those which were in existence before local government reorganization in 1974. In cataloguing resources which often date back a hundred years and more, it was simply too confusing to attempt to make material fit into the new county classification. Large cities other than London, such as Liverpool, Manchester and Birmingham, are listed according to the county to which they belonged prior to reorganization.

8.2   English dialects

Books

ANDERSON, P. (1987) *A Structural Atlas of the English Dialects.* London: Croom Helm
BLAKE, N.F. (1981) *Non-Standard Language in English Literature.* Oxford: Blackwell
BROOK, G.L. (1963) *English Dialects.* London: Deutsch.
CHAMBERS, J. and TRUDGILL, P. (1980) *Dialectology.* Cambridge: Cambridge University Press
CHESHIRE, J., EDWARDS, V., MÜNSTERMANN, H. and WELTENS, B. (1989) *Dialect and Education: Some European Perspectives.* Clevedon, Avon: Multilingual Matters
COLEMAN, S.J. (1962) *Dialects, Jargon and Slang.* London: Folklore Academy
EDWARDS, V., TRUDGILL, P. and WELTENS, B. (1984) *The Grammar of English Dialect: A Survey of Research.* London: Economic and Social Research Council
ELLIS, A.J. (1889) *Early English Pronunciation, Part V: The Existing Phonology of the English Dialects.* London: Trübner
ELLIS, A.J. (1890) *English Dialects: Their Sounds and Homes.* London: English Dialect Society

ELLIS, S. (1969) *Studies in Honour of Harold Orton on the Occasion of his Seventieth Birthday*. Leeds: School of English, University of Leeds

ELLIS, S. (1971) *Tape Recording of Local Dialect*. London: National Council of Social Service for the Standing Conference for Local History

ENGLISH DIALECT SOCIETY PUBLICATIONS (1974) Nos 1–80, first published 1873–1876, this edition Vaduz: Kraus Reprint Ltd

GROSE, F. (1968) *A Provisional Glossary, with a Collection of Local Proverbs, and Popular Superstitions*. Menston: Scolar Publishing

HUGHES, A. and TRUDGILL, P. (1987) *English Accents and Dialects. An introduction of Social and Regional Varieties of British English*, 2nd edn, London: Edward Arnold

KENNEDY, P. (ed.) (1973) *The Folksongs of Britain*. London: Cassell.

KIRK, J.M., SANDERSON, S. and WIDDOWSON, J.D.A. (eds) (1985) *Studies in Linguistic Geography: the Dialects of English In Britain and Ireland* London: Croom Helm

KOLB, E., GLAUSER, B., EILMER, W. and STAMM, R. (1979) *Atlas of English Sounds*. Bern: Francke

LANGUAGE AND CLASS WORKSHOP (1974) *Language and Class Workshop*. London: Falling Wall Press.

LLEWELLYN, S. (1986) *Yacky Dar Moy Bewty! A Phrasebook for the Regions of Britain (with Irish supplement)*. London: Grafton

MOLIN, D.H. (1984) *Actor's Encyclopaedia of Dialects*. New York: Sterling Poole Blandford

O'DONNELL, W.R. and TODD, L. (1980) *Variety in Contemporary English*. London: Allen & Unwin

ORTON, H. (1969) *Survey of English Dialects, (A): Introduction*. Leeds: E.J. Arnold for University of Leeds

ORTON, H. and WRIGHT, N. (1974) *A Word Geography of England*. London: Seminar Press

ORTON, H., SANDERSON, S. and WIDDOWSON, J. (1978) *The Linguistic Atlas of England*. London: Croom Helm

PETYT, M. (1980) *The Study of Dialect: an Introduction to Dialectology*. London: Deutsch

PHILLIPPS, K.C. (1986) *Language and Class in Victorian England*. Oxford: Blackwell

TRUDGILL, P. and CHAMBERS, J.C. (1990) *Dialect of English*. London: Longman

TRUDGILL, P. (1975) *Accent, Dialect and the School*. London: Edward Arnold

TRUDGILL, P. (ed.) (1978) *Sociolinguistic Patterns in British English*. London: Edward Arnold

TRUDGILL, P. (1983) *On Dialect: Social and Geographical Perspectives*. Oxford: Blackwell.

TRUDGILL, P. (1990) *The Dialects of England.* Oxford: Blackwell

UPTON, C., SANDERSON, S. and WIDDOWSON, J. (1987) *Word Maps: A Dialect Atlas of England* London: Croom Helm

WAKELIN, M.F. (ed.) (1972) *Patterns in the Folk Speech of the British Isles.* London: Athlone Press

WAKELIN, M.F. (1972) *English Dialects: An Introduction.* London: Athlone Press

WAKELIN, M.F. (1985) *Discovering English Dialects,* 2nd edn. Aylesbury: Shire

WEERASINGHE, L. (ed.) (1988) *Directory of Recorded Sound Resources in the United Kingdom.* London: The British Library

WRIGHT, J. (1905) *The English Dialect Dictionary.* Oxford: H. Frowde.

WRIGHT, J. (1905) *English Dialect Grammar,* Vol. VI, *The English Dialect Dictionary;* also as a separate edition, Oxford: H. Frowde

Records and cassettes

English Accents and Dialects
ISBN 0 7131 6507 3
A. Hughes and P. Trudgill, London: Edward Arnold

Accents of English
ISBN 0 521 24648/2
John Wells, BBC and Cambridge University Press

All Round England and Back Again
English customs and traditions through the seasons
Saydisc SDL 332 (record); CSDL 332 (cassette)

Sound collections

The British Library National Sound Archives
29 Exhibition Road, London SW7 2AS. Tel 071 589 6603

The British Library National Sound Archive holds nearly half a million discs of all kinds and over 35,000 hours of recorded tape. The archive has, over the last 35 years, gathered and preserved a collection which reflects the development of recorded sound from early wax cylinders to modern compact discs. Through voluntary deposit the archive attempts to acquire one copy of each disc commercially issued in the United Kingdom; it makes its own recordings at outside venues and encourages the deposit of private collections.

The archive records selectively from BBC broadcasts, keeps duplicate copies of BBC Sound Archives material and holds BBC transcription discs. The listening service offers public access to such material. The archive aims to be comprehensive with special responsibility to British recording and includes popular music of all kinds, oral history, sound effects and documentary material. A separate department of Language and Dialect was created in 1986. Part of the brief of this department is to hold as comprehensive a collection as possible of recordings of varieties of English from the UK and other countries where English is spoken either as a mother tongue or as a second language. The curator's activities currently include documenting and accessioning material which the National Sound Archive already holds; establishing links with other organizations, archives and libraries; and collecting unpublished material, especially that made in the course of academic research.

The National Sound Archive offers:

(1) A free listening service, available by appointment only to any member of the public from 10.30 to 5.30 Monday to Friday with late opening to 9.00 on Thursdays.

(2) A comprehensive library containing printed material, microfilm and microfiche relating to sound recording (catalogues, discographies, periodicals, reference volumes, etc.). The library is open from 10.00 to 4.30 Monday to Friday with late opening to 9.00 on Thursdays. No appointment is necessary, nor any reader's ticket.

(3) An information service which can help with preliminary research to locate particular recordings and can advise on their availability and on manufacturers' or distributors' addresses.

(4) An archival service for deposits of privately recorded tapes.

Centres

The Centre for English Cultural Tradition and Language
University of Sheffield, S10 2TN. Tel: 0742 768555

The Centre was founded in 1964 as an archive and interpretative unit concerned with all aspects of cultural tradition and language. Through voluntary help and in association with the University of

Sheffield, the Centre has achieved international recognition yet retains strong local and regional ties.
The Centre's aims are:

(1) To draw attention to our traditional heritage through publications, courses, lectures, displays and exhibitions and preserve and study cultural tradition and language at all levels.

(2) To encourage and undertake the collecting and recording of traditional culture and language through individuals, societies and organizations, colleges and schools.

(3) To maintain and develop permanent archives for the study of traditional culture, language and crafts.

(4) To provide a forum for the exchange of ideas and information between individuals and with other archives, libraries, record offices, museums and kindred institutions and organizations.

(5) To make collected material on English cultural traditions available to a wider audience, including not only folklorists but other researchers in related disciplines and other users.

Publications include *Lore and Language*, an international journal with a wide range of contributions from folklore, linguistics, anthropology, sociology, psychology, history (especially oral history) and literary studies; and a *Newsletter* which contains information on events, exhibitions, talks, courses, conferences, etc.

The Centre for Oral Traditions
16 Brunswick Square, Gloucester GL1 1UG.
Tel: 0452 415110.

Folktracks and Soundpost Publications was set up in 1969 in order to record, preserve and disseminate field tapes (authentic location recordings) of what are called 'oral traditions', i.e. passed on by word of mouth in both speech and music. There are now over 300 programmes of sounds and instrumental music as well as storytelling, samples of language and dialect speech and Mummers plays.
Folktracks Cassettes came into being in 1975 when Peter Kennedy began to compile audio cassettes chapter by chapter to go

with the book which he edited, *The Folksongs of Britain* (Cassell: 1973). Peter had been granted a fellowship by the Trustees of Dartington Hall, Totnes, Devon both to lecture in all departments of the College of Art and Folk Studies and to build a resource centre of folk traditions for use by the college and community. The Centre is currently situated in Gloucester and includes the Folktracks traditions library which is open daily by appointment for students and researchers. There is a useful collections of specialist books as well as audio and video recordings.

Societies

The Oral History Society
National Sound Archive, 29 Exhibition Road, London SW7 2AS. Tel: 071 589 6603

The Oral History Society aims:

(1) To enrich history by giving voices to lives which are often undocumented or hidden.
(2) To allow active participation by people in writing their own histories.
(3) To bring status and value to the lives of the oldest members of our communities.
(4) To bring old and young together through the sharing and contrasting of experiences.
(5) To broaden and deepen many areas of the educational curriculum from the youngest infant class through colleges and universities to the various branches of adult education
(6) To unlock the door to the rich and poetic world of oral tradition and vernacular speech, dialect and languages
(7) To preserve the past for the future through sound recordings which are collected in local and national archives.
(8) To unite historians across the world in the common activity of recording the past through memory.

The Oral History Society has 800 members in over 20 countries. It holds meetings on special themes in London, Manchester, Bradford and Edinburgh. It also organizes practical workshops on Reminiscence Therapy or on Reminiscence Drama. It publishes two journals: *Oral History* twice-yearly, and *Life Stories* annually.

8.3 The Northern Counties and the Isle of Man

Books

BROCKETT, J.T. (ed.) (1846) *A Glossary of North Country Words*, 3rd edn, 2 vols. Newcastle upon Tyne: Emerson Charnley

KOLB, E. (1966) *Phonological Atlas of the Northern Region: The Six Northern Counties, North Lincolnshire and the Isle of Man.* Bern: Francke Verlag

ORTON, H. and HALLIDAY, W. (1963) *The Basic Material (B), Vol. 1: The Six Northern Counties, and the Isle of Man.* Leeds: Edward Arnold for the University of Leeds

PEACOCK, R.B. (1869) *A Glossary of the Hundred of Lonsdale, North and South of the Sands, Together with an Essay on Some Leading Characteristics of the Dialect Spoken in the Six Northern Counties of England.* London

WALTON, C.R. (1949) *Selection of Songs and Ballads of Northern England.* Newcastle upon Tyne: T. & G. Allan

Records and Cassettes

King William – Kid's Play: England 2
44 Children's singing games from Cumbria, Lancashire and Yorkshire
Folktracks Cassettes 60–195

Bow-legged Chicken – Kid's Play: England 3
44 Children's singing games from Castleford, Chorley, Garforth, Leyland and Nelson schools
Folktracks Cassettes 60–196

Raspberry Jam – Kid's Play: England 4
80 Children's singing games from Keswick, Leyland and Workington
Folktracks Cassettes 60–197

As She Is Spoke: 1
Dialect: North of England
Folktracks Cassettes 60–451

'Blaydon Races' and Other North Country Songs
Owen Brannigan
HMV 7EP 7050

North Countrie Folk Songs
Owen Brannigan
HMV C 3868; HMV C 3976; HMV 7EG 8578

Sound collections

North West Sound Archive
Old Stewards Office, Castle Grounds, Clitheroe Castle, Clitheroe, Lancashire. Tel: 0200 27897.

The North West Sound Archive is a collection of over 12,500 tape recordings covering many aspects of the history, tradition, culture, industry and current issues of the North West. The Archive is based at Clitheroe Castle where facilities include an archive store, offices, a recording studio and a listening area for the public. Details of the service and its computerized information service are available on request. In order to make this valuable resource more accessible to the general public, a selection of over 350 recordings from the Archive can be obtained via the Greater Manchester Records Office.

Dialect Database. During 1985 the North West Sound Archive, in association with Lancashire Libraries, various societies and individuals, set out to systematically collect technical and dialect words from the region. Thousands of such words were collected and published in a volume entitled *Sounds Gradely.* The archive hopes eventually to produce a cassette which will be of use to theatre groups performing Lancashire plays and to form a Lancashire Dialect Centre where recordings of Lancashire speech can be heard.

Lakeland (Cumberland, Westmorland, Lancashire North of the Sands)

Books

DENWOOD, E.R. and DENWOOD, M. (eds) (1946) *Oor Mak O'Toak: An Anthology of Lakeland Dialect Poems, 1746–1946.* Carlisle: Lakeland Dialect Society
DENWOOD, M. and THOMPSON, T.W. (eds) (1950) *A Lafter O'Farleys in T'Dialect O' Lakeland: An Anthology of Lakeland Dialect Prose.* Carlisle: Lakeland Dialect Society
ELLWOOD, REV. T. (1985) *Lakeland and Iceland, being a Glossary of Words in the Dialect of Cumberland, Westmorland and North Lancashire which seem Allied or Identical with the Icelandic or Norse.* Frowde: English Dialect Society

FERGUSON, R. (1856) *The Northmen in Cumberland and Westmorland.* Carlisle: R. & J. Steel

KIRKBY, B. (1975) *Lakeland Words: A Collection of Dialect Words and Phrases, as used in Cumberland and Westmorland, with Illustrative Sentences in the North Westmorland Dialect.* Wakefield: E.P. Publishing

MORRIS, J.P. (1869) *A Glossary of the Words and Phrases of Furness (North Lancashire) with Illustrative Quotations, Principally from the old Northern Writers* Carlisle: G. & T. Coward

PEACOCK, R.B. (1869) *A Glossary of the Dialect of the Hundred of Lonsdale, North and South of the Sands in the County of Lancaster.* London: Asher & Co. for the Philological Society

SMITH, J.R. (1839) *Westmorland and Cumberland Dialects* Smith

SPARKE, A. (1907) *A Bibliography of Dialect Literature of Cumberland and Westmorland and Lancashire North of the Sands* Kendal: Wilson

SULLIVAN, J. (1857) *Cumberland, Westmorland, Ancient and Modern: the People, Dialect, Superstitions and Customs* Whitaker: Kendal, Hudson

Cassettes

The Sound of his Horn
Lakeland songs, dances, customs and stories
Folktracks cassettes 90–120

Nay Not a Bit On't
Lake District Traditions
Folktracks cassettes 45–410

Societies

Lakeland Dialect Society
Hon. Sec.: Irving Graham, Knox Croft, Thornby, Wigton, Cumbria CA7 0HQ.

Founded in 1939, the aims of the Society are to encourage interest in dialect speech, in the writing of dialect verse, prose and drama; to stimulate the publication of dialect literature and the production of dialect plays; to study the origins and history of dialect, folklore, folk songs and local customs and traditions.

The Society meets at roughly quarterly intervals on Saturday afternoons at venues throughout Cumbria. Every second year the Society hold a dialect service in a church somewhere in the county. The service is conducted throughout in dialect: lessons are translated and read in dialect and hymns are either translated or composed in dialect.

Publications: *Annual Journal of the Lakeland Dialect Society* compiled from writings of members of the Society and *Lakeland Dialect Society Newsletter*, containing news and views, as well as dialect articles.

Cumberland

Books

ANON. (1933) *Robert Anderson, the Cumberland Bard, Born 1770–Died 1833 Centenary Celebration Souvenir*. Carlisle: Charles Thurnam & Sons Ltd

ANDERSON, R. et al. (1870) *Ballads in the Cumberland Dialect*. Cockermouth: I. Evening

ARMSTRONG, A.M. et al. (1950–1952) *The Place Names of Cumberland*. Publications of the English Place Names Society XX to XX11 Cambridge: Cambridge University Press

BELL, J.G. (1851) *A Glossary of Provincial Words Used in the County of Cumberland* London

BIRKETT, E. (1953) *Martha and Methoosaleh*. Carlisle: Charles Thurnam & Sons Ltd (Printers)

BRILIOTH, B. (1913) *A Grammar of The Dialect Of Lorton (Cumberland), Historical and Descriptive with an Appendix on the Scandinavian Element, Dialect Specimens and a Glossary* London: Oxford University Press

CARRICK, T.W. (1952) *Willy Carrick's Cummerlan Teals*. Carlisle: Charles Thurnam & Sons Ltd

COOPER, I. (1979) *Pinning T' Teal On A Cuddy*. Whitehaven: George Todd & Sons (Printers)

COOPER, I. (1976) *Hess Thoo Iver Seen A Cuddy: Cumbrian teals i' rhyme*. Cleator Moor and Workington: Bethwaites

DENWOOD, J. (1950) *Twinters Wedding*. London: Fore Publications

DENWOOD, J. (1933) *Rosely Hill Fair*. London: Jarrolds

DICKINSON, W. (1878) *The Dialect of Cumberland*. London: Trübner & Co

DICKINSON, W. (1859) *A Glossary of the Words and Phrases of Cumberland*. Russell: Whitehaven, Callander & Dixon

DICKINSON, W. and PREVOST, E.W. (1900) *A Glossary of the Words and Phrases Pertaining to the Dialect of Cumberland, with a Short Digest of the Phonology and Grammar of the Dialect by S. Dickinson Brown* (first supplement 1905, second supplement 1924) Carlisle: B.A. Thurnam & Son

FARRALL, T. (1975?) *Betty Wilson's Cummerland Teals.* First published Carlisle: James C. Mason, this edition Charles Thurnam & Sons Ltd

FASHOLA, J. (1969) *The Influence of Received Pronunciation on a West Cumbrian Speaker of Provincial Standard English* M.Phil, School of Oriental and African Studies, University of London

FERGUSON, R. (1887) *The Dialect of Cumberland with a Chapter on its Place Names.* Carlisle: Steel

FISHER, E. (1979) *Cumbrian Dialect Tales.* Whitehaven: George Todd & Son (Printers)

T' *Cumbrian Dialect*

Ya day ah thowt ah'd amuse meself
wid t'dictionary off oor shelf
Tu finnd oot t'meanins uf 'laal' un 'browt'
but t'dictionary laarnt mu nowt.
So these few wurds ah've written here
shud help uther folk frae far un near
Tu understand oor dielect wurd
– explainin things thu've nivver hurd!

Ethel Fisher, *Cumbrian Dialect Tales 1*

FISHER, E. (1988) *Cumbrian Dialect Tales 2.* Available from Ethel Fisher, 39 Main Road, Seaton, Workington, Cumbria CA14 1HU

GIBSON, A.C. (1910) *Folk Speech of Cumberland and Some Districts Adjacent, Being Short Stories and Rhymes in the Dialects of the West Border Counties.* First published Carlisle: Coward and London: John Russell Smith

GILPIN, S. (ed.) (1893) *Cumberland Ballads by Robert Anderson.* London: Bemrose & Son and Carlisle: G. & T. Coward

GREGSON, K. (1980) *Cumbrian Songs and Ballads.* Clapham via Lancaster: Dalesman

HEATHERINGTON, G. (n.d.) *Miscellaneous Thoughts.* Penrith: Reeds Ltd. (Printers)

LIMON, J. (1951?) *Ya Mak Ma Laff.* Cockermouth: Brash Bros. Ltd.

METCALFE, E. (1987) *By Lake and Fell: Cumbrian Dialect Verse.* Appleby Business Services (Printers)

PREVOST, E.W. (1905) *A Supplement to the Glossary of the Dialect of Cumberland, with a Grammar by S. Dickson Brown.* Carlisle: Thurnam & Son

PREVOST, E.W. (1924) *Second Supplement to the Glossary of the Dialect of Cumberland.* Carlisle: Thurnam & Son

REANEY, P.H. (1927) *A Grammar of the Dialect of Penrith (Cumberland): Descriptive and Historical with Specimens and a Glossary.* Manchester: Manchester University Press

RICHARDSON, J. (1876) *Cumberland Talk, Being Short Tales and Rhymes in the Dialect of that County.* London: John Russell Smith and Carlisle: George Coward

ROBERTS, R. (1984) *Summat Ah've Sed: Cumbrian Dialect Verse.* Penrith: Airey & Stevenson (Printers)

RYDLAND, K. (1978) *Vowel System and Lexical Phoneme Patterns in South-East Cumbria: A Study in Structural Dialectology.* PhD thesis, University of Bergen (Norway)

SARGISSON, J. (1881) *Joe Scoap's Jurneh Through Three Wardles (in the Cumberland dialect).* Whitehaven: Smith Brothers (Printers)

STURSBERG, M. (1970) *The Stressed Vowels in the Dialects of Longtown, Abbey Town and Husonby (Cumberland): a Structural Approach.* Diss. (Swiss PhD). University of Basle

THOMLINSON, W.J. (n.d.) *Mostly Sentimental and Broadly Speaking.* Penrith: Reeds Ltd. (Printers)

WRIGHT, P. (1978) *Cumbrian Chat: How It Is Spoke.* Clapham via Lancaster: Dalesman

WRIGHT, P. (1979) *Cumbrian Dialect.* Clapham via Lancaster: Dalesman

Local studies collection

Carlisle County Library, 11 Globe Lane, Carlisle CA3 8NX. Tel: 0228 24166)

Cassettes

Bessy Brown Bags
Children talking about Easter Pace Egg customs
Folktracks Cassettes 30–108

Dip Zoo Macazoo
Kids Play: England 1
Folktracks Cassettes 30–194

Westmorland

Books

BOWNESS, W. (n.d.) *Rustic Studies in the Westmorland Dialect and Other Poems.* T. Wilson (printers)

CLARK, T., BOWNESS, W. and SOUTHEY, R. (1897) *Specimens of the Dialect of Westmorland*. Kendal: Pollitt (Printers)

HIRST, T.O. (1906) *A Grammar of the Dialect of Kendal (Westmorland) Descriptive and Historical with Specimens and a Glossary*. Heidelberg: Carl Winter.

KIRKBY, B. (1900) *Granite Chips and Clints, or Westmorland in Words*. Kendal: T. Wilson (Printers)

SMITH, A.H. (1967) *The Place Names of Westmorland* Publications of the English Place Names Society XL11-XL111. Cambridge: Cambridge University Press

WILLIAMS, G. (ed.) (1983) *Westmorland aw' sooarts: the Dialect Writings of J.C. Robinson Selected and Edited for the Society*. Penrith: Airey & Stevenson for the Lakeland Dialect Society

Local studies collection

Kendal Public Library, Stricklandgate, Kendal LA9 4PY. Tel: 0539 720254

Lancashire

Books

ACKWORTH, J. (1907) *The Partners*. London: Robert Culley

ACKWORTH, J. (1897) *Beckside Lights*. London: Charles Kelly

ANON. (1975) *Just Sithabod: Dialect Verse from Lancashire Life*. Manchester: Whitehorn Press

ASHTON, T. (*pseud.*) (CLARKE, A.) (1922) *Tum Fowt Sketches*. Bolton: Pendlebury & Sons

ASHTON, T. (*pseud.*) (CLARKE, A.) (n.d.) *The Spriggs Sketches*. Bolton: Pendlebury & Sons

ASHTON, T. (*pseud.*) et al. (1933a) *Lancashire Smilers: Readings and Recitations No. 1*. Blackpool: Palatine Books

ASHTON, T. (pseud.) et al. (1933b) *Lancashire Smilers: Readings and Recitations No. 2*. Blackpool: Palatine Books

BAMFORD, S. (1854) *The Dialect of South Lancashire or Tim Bobbin's Tummus and Meary, with his Rhymes and an Enlarged Glossary of Words and Phrases Chiefly Used by the Rural Population of the Manufacturing Districts of South Lancashire*, 2nd edn. London: John Russell Smith

BARON, J. (1988) *Bits o' Broad Lancashire: Poems in the Dialect*. Manchester: John Heywood

BARON, J. (1906) *Cuckoo Fowt Chronicles, Humorous Sketches in the Dialect*. Rochdale: J.D. Howarth

BARON, J. (1907) *A Lankashir Dickshonary*, 4th edn. Blackburn: Advance Press.

BEARMAN, L. (1977) *Poems in the Lancashire Dialect*. Clapham via Lancaster: Dalesman

BENNETT, J. (1960) *A Lancashire Miscellany of Dialect Verse*. Oldham: Hirst, Kidd & Rennie Ltd.

BERRY, J. P. (ed.) (1984) *Verse and Prose in Standard English and Dialect, 75th Anniversary Edition*. Preston: Lancashire Authors' Association

BERRY, J.P. (ed.) (1979) *Verse and Prose in Standard English and Dialect*. Preston: Lancashire Authors' Association

BRIERLEY, B. (n.d.) *Lancashire Wit and Humour*. Oldham: W.E. Clegg

BRIERLEY, B. (1881) *Daisy Nook Sketches*. Manchester: Abel Heywood & Son

BRIERLEY, B. (1884) *Treadlepin Fold, The New Borough, A Fight for Love, Little Dodey's Christmas, Beginning the World*. Manchester: Abel Heywood & Son

BRIERLEY, B. (1884) *The Chronicles of Waverlow*. Manchester: Abel Heywood & Son

BRIERLEY, B. (1884) *Marlocks of Merriton and Red Windows Hall*. Manchester: Abel Heywood & Son

BRIERLEY, B. (1885) *Abo-o' th'-Yate in Yankeeland: The Results of Two Trips to America*. Manchester: Abel Heywood & Son

BRIERLEY, B. (1885) *Out of Work, Our Old Nook and The Fratchingtons of Fratchingthorpe*. Manchester: Abel Heywood & Son

BRIERLEY, B. (1885) *Irkdale*. Manchester: Abel Heywood & Son

BRIERLEY, B. (1886) *Cast Upon the World: The Story of a Waif*. Manchester: Abel Heywood & Son

BRIERLEY, B. (1886) *Cotters of Mossburn*. Manchester: Abel Heywood & Son

BRIERLEY, B. (1893) *Tales and Sketches of Lancashire Life*. Manchester: John Heywood & Son

BRIERLEY, B. (1911) *Ab-o' th'-Yate's Lancashire Reciter*. Oldham: W.E. Clegg

BRIERLEY, B. (n.d.) *Ab-o' th'-Yate and the Lord Mayor of London at Blackpool*. Manchester: Abel Heywood & Son

BRIERLEY, B. (n.d.) *Sam o'Ducky's Courtship*. Manchester: Abel Heywood & Son

BRIERLEY, B. (n.d.) *Drop't on at Blackpool by Ab-o' th'-Yate*. Manchester: Abel Heywood & Son

BRIERLEY, B. (n.d.) *Gooin' to Cyprus: Companion to 'Jingo' by Ab-o' th'-Yate*. Manchester: Abel Heywood & Son

BRIERLEY, B. (n.d.) *Fair Trade or Picky-Pockety by Ab-o' th'-Yate*. Manchester: John Heywood & Son

BRIERLEY, B. (n.d.) *Adventures at Blackpool by Ab-o' th'-Yate.* Manchester: John Heywood & Son

BRIERLEY, B. (n.d.) *Billy Softly's Kesmas Dinner.* Manchester: Abel Heywood & Son

BRIERLEY, B. (n.d.) *Bits O'Fun for Lancashire Firesides: a Selection of Prose and Verse.* Manchester: Abel Heywood & Son

BRIERLEY, B. (n.d.) *Bundle O'Fents From A Lancashire Loom, Suitable for Penny Readings, Being Selections from the Writings of Ben Brierley.* Manchester: Abel Heywood & Son

BRIERLEY, B. (n.d.) *Gradely Bow Eaut by Ab-o' th'-Yate.* Manchester: Abel Heywood & Son

BRIERLEY, B. (n.d.) *'Jingo' and the Bear, ot Th'Great Feight between Ben at Isaac's alias 'Owd Dizzy' and Alick O'Nick's, alias 'The Young Bear' by Ab-o' th'-Yate.* Manchester: Heywood & Son

BROOKS, J.B. (n.d.) *Th' Good News Accordin' to Mark, Arrang't an' thranscrib't fer Northerners i'th Lankisher Dialect.* J.B. Brooks, 1 Bickerton Road, Headington, Oxford

BROOKS, J.B. (n.d.) *Chaucer's Cock and Other Fables in Lancashire Dialect.* J.R. Brooks, 41 Eden Drive, Headington, Oxford

BROOKS, J.B. (n.d.) *Ecclesiastes in Lancashire Dialect.* J.R. Brooks, 41 Eden Drive, Headington, Oxford

BROOKS, J.B. (n.d.) *Noah Th' Boat Builder.* Oxford: Church Army Press

CLARE, B. (1978) *Recollections: Lancashire Dialect Poetry.* Westhoughton: Excelsior Press

CLARE, B. (1980) *Just Tell Mi.* Bolton: Brian Clare (for accompanying cassette, see *Cassettes and Compact discs* below)

CLARK, M.C. (ed.) (1966) *Mary's Miscellany; Prose and Verse by Lancashire Writers.* Accrington: Bridge Press

CLARKE, A. (1893) *Bill an' Bet Shriggs' visit t' Princess May, t'Duke of York, an' her Majesty t'Queen, an' t'presents they took t'young couple.* Manchester: Abel Heywood & Son

CLARKE, A. (1897) *Bill Spriggs Goes A-mindin' (In T'spinnin Reaum), also Patsy Filligan's Mustard Plaster.* Bolton: Pendlebury & Sons

CLARKE, A. (1897) *Bill Spriggs in T'weivin Shed as a Tackler.* Bolton: Pendlebury & Sons

CLARKE, A. (1904) *Smilers: Being Lancashire Sketches.* Liverpool: Tinling & Co.

CLARKE, A. (1906) *Bill Spriggs Turns Th'Tables: a Dialogue for Two Characters.* Bolton: Pendlebury & Sons

CLARKE, A. (1907) *More Smilers: Being Lancashire Tales and Sketches.* Blackpool: Teddy Ashton

CLARKE, A. (1911) *Extra Smilers: The Adventures of General Spriggs* and '*Ginger*', also the *Kock-Krow Cycling Club and Other Sketches*. Blackpool: Teddy Ashton

CLARKE A. (1911) *Filligan Smilers: Being Patsy Filligan's Letters and Adventures*. Blackpool: Teddy Ashton

CLARKE, A. (1913) *More Smilers: Being the Droll Adventures of Bill an' Bet Spriggs and Jud Nowls and Sarah Ann in Paris*. Blackpool: Teddy Ashton

CLARKE, A. (1913) *Teddy Ashton's Gradely Guide to Blackpool, Containing Gradely Advice as well as Gradely Fun*. Blackpool: Teddy Ashton

CLARKE, A. (1928) *Teddy Ashton's Lancashire Poems*. Blackpool: Palatine Books

CLEGG, J.T. (1895) *David's Loom: a Story of Rochdale life in the Early Years of the Nineteenth Century*. London: Longmans, Green & Co.

CLEGG, J.T. (1895) *The Works of John Trafford Clegg: Stories, Sketches and Rhymes, Chiefly in the Rochdale Dialect*, 2 vols. Rochdale: James Clegg

CRAVEN, H. (1972) *A Bacup Miscellany: Prose and Verse by Local Writers Past and Present*. Bacup: Borough of Bacup Amenities Committee

CRONSHAW, J. (1908) *Dingle Cottage: a Lancashire Story with Poems and Sketches*. Manchester: Herbert Eva & Co.

CUNLIFFE, H. (1886) *A Glossary of Rochdale with Rossendale Words and Phrases*. Manchester: John Heywood

CURRIER, E. (1984) *Dinin' Eaut and Other Stories*. Bolton: Bolton Metropolitan Borough College, Writing Development Project

DOBSON, B. (1981) *Clattering Clogs*. Staining, Blackpool: The Landy Publishing Company

DOBSON, B. (n.d.) *Concerning Clogs*. Clapman: Dalesman

DOBSON, B. (1973) *Lancashire Nicknames and Sayings*. Clapman: Dalesman

DOBSON, B. (ed.) (n.d.) *Woven in Lancashire: Some Lancashire Dialect Poems*. Blackpool: Lady Publishing Co. for Fylde Folk Festival

DRONSFIELD, J. (ed.) (1885) *Ab-o' th'-Yate Sketches and Other Short Stories*, 3 vol. Oldham: Clegg

DUNNE, T. and ENTWISTLE, P. (1981) *Bolton Festival Book of Dialect and Local Poetry*. Bolton: Metropolitan Arts Department

DUTTON, D. (1978) *Lanky Spoken Here: A Guide to the Lancashire Dialect*. Walton on Thames: M. & J. Hobbs and London: Michael Joseph

FITTON, S. (1929) *Gradely Lancashire*. Stalybridge: Whittaker & Sons

FORD, E. (1984) *Ten Ut' Best: A Collection of Dialect Verse*. E. Ford

FORD, E. (1987) *Lancashire Tales of Mirth*. Clapham via Lancaster: Dalesman

HARDMAN, S. (1922) *Around the Fire: a Collection of Stories in Dialect and Literary English.* Manchester: Sherratt & Hughes

HARGREAVES, A. (1904) *A Grammar of the Dialect of Adlington, Lancashire.* Heidelberg: Carl Winter's Universitätsbuchhandlung

HARLAND, J. (ed.) (1865) *Ballads and Songs of Lancashire.* London: Whittaker

HAYES, C. (1976) *Opening Doors: a Collection of Verse.* C. Hayes

HEYWOOD, A. (n.d.) *Heywood's Samples of Lancashire Prose and Verse.* Manchester: Abel Heywood & Son

HOLLINGWORTH, B. (1977) *Songs of the People.* Manchester: Manchester University Press

HOWCROFT, A.J. (1922) *Tales of a Pennine People.* Oldham: H.C. Lee, Whitehead & Co. for the author

HUMPHRIES, E. (n.d.) *Wigan Fair.* Wigan: Wigan Pier Publications

HUNT, J. (1959) *A Grammar of the Dialect of Heywood, Lancashire.* Unpublished MA thesis, Leeds University

HUNTER, S.A. (1967) *Lucille and Other Poems (including Lancashire Dialect).* Oldham: S.A. Hunter

JACKSON, N. (1930) *Lays from Lancashire.* London: T. Werner Laurie Ltd

JONES, J.L. (1975) *Jimmy Jones's Tyldesley.* Tyldesley: George Smith & Son

KERSHAW, H. (1958) *Lancashire Sings Again: a Collection of Original Verses.* Rochdale: Harvey Kershaw

KERSHAW, H. (1963) *Lancashire Sings Again, First Encore: a Further Collection of Dialect Verses.* Rochdale: Harvey Kershaw

KNOWLES, G. (1974) *Scouse: the Urban Dialect of Liverpool.* Unpublished PhD thesis, University of Leeds

LAHEE, M.R. (1910) *Owd Neddy Fitton's Visit to Th'Earl O'Derby: a True Lancashire Sketch,* 33rd edn, first published 1859. Manchester: John Heywood

LAYCOCK, S. (1883) *Lancashire Songs, Poems, Tales and Recitations.* Manchester: John Heywood

LAYCOCK, S. (n.d.) *Lancashire Poems, Tales and Recitations.* Manchester: John Heywood

LEE, H. (1893) *Bit O'Things.* Manchester: John Heywood

LEECH, M. (1985) *Skrikin' wi Laughin': Easily Digested Lancashire Dialect Poetry.* Maureen Leech and the Lamp Community Bookshop with assistance from North West Arts

MATHER, J.M. (1995) *Lancashire Idylls.* London: Frederick Warne

MILLS, F. (n.d.) *Popular Sketch Book.* Oldham: Felix Mills

NEWBIGGING, (1900) *Lancashire Humour.* London: J.M. Dent

NODAL, J.H. and MILNER, G. (1972) *A Glossary of the Lancashire Dialect.* Bath: Cedric Chivers.

NORTH WEST SOUND ARCHIVE (1986) *Sounds Gradely: a Collection of Dialect and Other Useful Words Used in Lancashire Folk Speech*. Clitheroe: North West Sound Archive

OLDHAM CHRONICLE (1960) *A Lancashire Miscellany of Dialect Verse*. Oldham: Hirst, Kidd & Rennie

OWD LINTHRIN BANT (1981) *Bits of Local History*, 2nd edn. Radcliffe: Radcliffe Local History Society

POMFRET, J. (ed.) (1964) *Summat From Home: Lancashire Poems and Stories*. Nelson, Lancs: Gerrard

POMFRET, J. (ed.) (1969) *Lancashire Evergreens: a Hundred Favourite Old Poems*. Nelson, Lancs: Gerrard

POMFRET, J. (ed.) (1969) *Nowt So Queer: New Lancashire Verse and Prose*. Nelson, Lancs: Gerrard

PEARCE, E. (1919–25) *Red Rose Leaves: a Collection of Prose and Verse by Members of the Lancashire Authors' Association*. 10 vols. Accrington: Fulcher Robinson

PROUD, D. (1968–9) North Lancashire Speech in the Nineteen Sixties. Unpublished PhD thesis, University of Lancaster

RAWCLIFFE, R. and RAWCLIFFE, J. (1891) *Pebbles Fro' Ribbleside*. Blackburn: J. & G. Toulmin

RUDKIN, E. (1973) *Lancashire Folklore*. First published Belton's Gainesborough, 1936; this edition Wakefield: EP Publishing

SALVESON, P. (ed.) (1985) *Teddy Ashton's Lancashire Scrapbook – Selections*. Bolton: Bolton People's History Group, available from Paul Salveson, North West Labour History Group, 6 Alfred Street, Farnworth, Bolton BL4 7JT

SCHILLING, J. (1906) *A Grammar of the Dialect of Oldham, Lancs*. Darmstadt

SHAW, F., SPEIGL, F. and KELLY, S. (1966) *Lern Yerself Scouse: How to Talk Proper in Liverpool*. Scouse Publishing

SHORROCKS, G. (1980) A Grammar of the Dialect of Farnworth and District. Ph.D thesis, Sheffield University, published in microform and xerographic form by University Microfilms International, reference no. 81–70,023

SPARTH, J. (1965) *A Flower i' t'Ditch: Poems in the Lancashire Dialect*. Accrington: Kathleen Pilkington

SPEIGL, F. (1966) *Lern Yerself Scouse, or – the ABC of Scouse*, vol. 2 Liverpool: Scouse Press, reprinted 1970 and 1979

STATON, J.T. (1852–3) *Th'Milisho Papers Wi Obadiah Hezekiah Jeremiah Jodrill, a Full Private in Heet Majesty's Thard Lankishire Milisho: beein a Batch O'Letters to his at Cuzzen Joe Fernuth 1852–3* Manchester: Abel Heywood.

STATON, J.T. (1857) *Bobby Shuttle un his Wife Sayroh's Visit to*

Manchester, un to th'Greight Hert Treasures Eggsibishun, at Owd Trafford. Manchester: John Heywood

STATON, J.T. (1859) *Missis Caustic's Hearthstone Lectures with Occasional Notes by Job her Husband.* Manchester: Abel Heywood

STATON, J.T. (1859) *The Song of Solomon in the Lancashire Dialect, as Spoken at Bolton, from the Authorized English Version.* Manchester: John Heywood

STATON, J.T. (1861) *Aynuck O'Red's un his Pretty Dowter Sally, or Ambishun un its Rewards: a Legend Suitable for any Toime, un Belonging to th'Same Category us th'Cocklone Ghost.* Manchester: John Heywood

STATON, J.T. (1863) *The Rivals: a Humerous Dialogue, also Going for the Census! a Comic Tale.* Manchester: John Heywood

STATON, J.T. (1863) *The Wife Hunters: a New Comic Sketch for Representation at Social and Family Gatherings.* Manchester: John Heywood

STATON, J.T. (1864) *The Bachelor's Wants: a Comic Bagatelle,* 2nd edn. Bolton: J. Staton

STATON, J.T. (1865) *Kestor un Betty: or the Adventures un Mischoances un a Yewood Felly, i'th'Coarse un a Hunt after Some Goose Eggs, for a Lad ut wur Afficted wi'th'Pappilarieties.* Manchester: John Heywood

STATON, J.T. (1867) *Th'Visit to th'Greight Parris Eggsbishun of Bobby Shuttle un his Wife Sayroh.* Manchester: Abel Heywood

STATON, J.T. (1868) *Bobby Shuttle un his Wife Sayroh at th'Darrun Eggsibishun: Descroibin Wot They Seed, Wot They Yerd, Un Wot They Enkeawtert.* Manchester: John Heywood

STATON, J.T. (1869) *Bobby Shuttle un his Wife Sayroh's visit to th'Mechanics Institushun Eggsibishun at Bowtun.* Manchester: John Heywood

STATON, J.T. (1869) *Owd Wisdom's Lankishire Awmenack for th' Yer 1861.* Manchester: John Heywood

STATON, J.T. (1871) *Rays fro' th'Loominary: A Selection of Comic Lancashire Tales, Adapted for Public Reading or Reciting.* Manchester: John Heywood

STATON, J.T. (c. 1873) *Bobby Shuttle un his Wife Sayroh wi th'Prince un Princess O Wales at Bowtun on Whit Thursday, June 5, 1873; wi a Toothrey Facts un Notions abeawt th'New Tean Haw, un th'Opening Festivities.* Manchester: John Heywood

STATON, J.T. (1874) *Th'Lond-Tillers Lock-Eawt: Bobby Shuttle wi'th Demonstrationists at Manchester, Saturday, June 20th, 1874.* Manchester: John Heywood

STATON, J.T. (1901) *Luddites and Blackfaces or 'Th'Brunnin O'Westhoftun Factory': A Reissue of the Story Published in the 'Bowtun Luminary'.* Westhoughton: R. Clough

STATON, J.T. (n.d.) *Owd Wisdom's Lankishire Awmenack for th' Yer 1860.* Bolton: J.T. Staton

STATON, J.T. (n.d.) *Pay Your Own Debts: a New Temperance Drama in Two Parts, Designed for Representation at Social Festivities.* Manchester: John Heywood

STATON, J.T. (n.d.) *Wiggles the Wiseacre: a Comic Dramatic Sketch.* Manchester: John Heywood

STATON, J.T. (n.d.) *Lancashire Laughs and Fireside Physic: a Series of Sketches adapted for Readings.* Manchester: Abel Heywood

SWANN, J.R. (1924) *Lancashire Authors A Series of Biographical Sketches.* St Annes: J. Robertson & Co. Ltd.

TAYLOR, F.E. (1901) *The Folk Speech of South Lancashire.* Manchester: John Heywood

THOMASON, M. (1959) *'Baa Baronet 'and 'Maggie – a Fast Piece': Two Stories.* Leigh: Leigh Chronicle Printing Co.

THOMASON, M. (1961) *The Poetry of Mart Thomason.* Leigh: Alice Maud Prescott

THOMPSON, T. (1934) *Lancashire Mettle.* London: George Allen & Unwin

THOMPSON, T. (1938) *Lancashire Fun.* London: George Allen & Unwin

THOMPSON, T. (1940) *Lancashire Pride.* London: George Allen & Unwin

THOMPSON, T. (1943) *Lancashire Rampant.* London: George Allen & Unwin

THOMPSON, T. (1945) *Lancashire Lather.* London: George Allen & Unwin

THOMPSON, T. (1947) *Lancashire Lure.* London: George Allen & Unwin

THOMPSON, T. (1951) *Lancashire Laughter.* London: George Allen & Unwin

THROP, J. (1987) *Poems From Lancashire Life.* Clapham via Lancaster: Dalesman

VICINUS, M. (1984) *The Ambiguities of Self-Help: Concerning the Life and Work of the Lancashire Dialect Writer Edwin Waugh.* Littleborough: George Kelsall

WALMESLEY, L. (n.d.) *Lancashire History.* Blackburn: L. Walmesley

WAUGH, E. (1855) *Sketches of Lancashire Life and Localities.* London: Whittaker & Co.

WAUGH, E. (n.d.) *Lancashire Sketches: Second Series.* Manchester: John Heywood

WAUGH, E. (n.d.) *Tufts of Heather,* 2 vols. Manchester: John Heywood

WAUGH, E. (n.d.) *Poems and Songs.* Oldham: G.G. Walersley

WAUGH, E. (n.d.) *Besom Ben Stories*. Manchester: John Heywood
WAUGH, E. (n.d.) *Chimney Corner*. Manchester: John Heywood
WELSBY, M. (1903) *Tales and Talks*. Rochdale: Joyful News Book
    Depot
WHITTAKER, G.H. (ed.) (1936) *A Lancashire Garland of Dialect Prose
    and Verse*. Stalybridge: George Whittaker & Sons
WOOD, B. (n.d.) *Amusing Lancashire Readings*. Bury: T. Compton &
    Co.
WOOD, B. (n.d.) *Lancashire Sketches, Recitations, Etc*. Bury: The Times
    Office
WRIGHT, P. (1986) *The Lanky Twang – How It Is Spoke*. Clapham via
    Lancaster: Dalesman
WRIGHT, P. (1982) *The Lancashireman's Dictionary*. Clapham via
    Lancaster: Dalesman
WRIGHT, P. (1976) *Lancashire Dialect*. Clapham via Lancaster: Dalesman
WRIGHT, P. (1954) *Grammar of the Dialect of Fleetwood, Descriptive
    and Historical*. Unpublished PhD thesis, University of Leeds
WRIGLEY, A. (1937) *Those Were The Days*. Stalybridge: George
    Whittaker & Sons
WRIGLEY, A. (1942) *Lancashire Idylls*. London: George Allen &
    Unwin
WRIGLEY, A. (1940) *Old Lancashire Words and Folksayings*. Stalybridge:
    George Whittaker & Sons
YATES, M. (1923) *A Lancashire Anthology*. Liverpool: The University
    of Liverpool Ltd and London: Hodder & Stoughton

Local studies collections

Headquarters Library, 143 Corporation Street, Preston, PR1 2TB.
Tel: 0772 264021

Brown, Picton and Hornby Libraries, William Brown Street,
Liverpool L3 8EW. Tel: 051 225 5429

Central Library, St Peter's Square, Manchester M2 5PD. Tel: 061
234 1972
Houses Broadside Ballad Collection. Acquired before 1879, the
collection includes about 2000 broadsides mounted in 13 volumes.
They include many printed in the provinces, particularly Manchester.

Cassettes and compact discs

Lancashire Miscellany. Verse and Prose
Lancashire Authors' Association (cassette)

Sounds 800
Celebration of Local Artistes to commemorate Clitheroe's 1186-1986 heritage (cassette)

Caught in Time: the Memories of North West England Captured in Sound
NW Sound Archive & Philips & Du Pont Optical UK (compact disc)
All available from the North West Sound Archive, Regional Sound Heritage Centre, Castle Grounds, Clitheroe Castle, Clitheroe, Lancs.

Just Tell Mi
Lancashire Dialect Poetry

Recollections
Lancashire Dialect Poetry

Both available from Brian Clare, Lancashire Dialect and Humour, 71 Park Road, Westhaughton, Bolton.

Societies

Lancashire Authors' Association
General Secretary: Eric Holt, 'Heatherslade', 5 Quaker Fields, Westhoughton, Bolton BL5 2BJ. Tel: 0942 816785

Founded in 1909 for writers or lovers of Lancashire literature and history. The objects of the Association are to foster and stimulate public interest in all phases and forms of Lancashire literature by organizing lectures on the words of past and present Lancashire authors; by getting their works placed in public libraries; by organizing visits to places of literary and historical interest; by furthering the study and preservation of Lancashire dialect; by original compositions; by providing entertainments at which the programme shall consist principally of Lancashire songs, recitations, etc.; and by adopting any other methods calculated to promote the welfare of Lancashire literature, history and fellowship.

Publications: *The Record*, the official quarterly journal of the association; *Red Rose Magazine*, an annual collation of members' work. Annual competitions for original compositions in verse and prose in dialect and standard English. The association's library is housed in the Lancashire Library Headquarters, Corporation Street, Preston.

The former Lancashire Dialect Society has now amalgamated with the Lancashire Authors' Association

Northumbria (True Northumberland – Tweed to Tyneside)

Books

BELL, J. (ed.) (1812) *Rhymes of Northern Bards, Being a Curious Collection of Old and New Songs and Poems, Peculiar to the Counties of Newcastle upon Tyne, Northumberland and Durham.* Newcastle Upon Tyne: M. Angus

COOK, A. (1894) *A Glossary of the Old Northumbrian Gospels.* Halle: Max Niemeyer

GEESON, C. (1969) *A Northumberland and Durham Word Book: The Living Dialect, Including a Glossary with Etymologies and Illustrative Quotations, of Living Dialect Words.* Newcastle upon Tyne: H. Hill

HESLOP, R. (1892–4) *Northumberland Words: a Glossary of Words Used in the County of Northumberland and on the Tyneside.* London: English Dialect Society

HESLOP, R. (1896) *A Bibliographical List of Works Illustrative of the Dialect of Northumberland.* London: English Dialect Society

LOGAN, R. (1945) *People and Places of Northumberland.* Amble: Richard Logan

MORPETH NORTHUMBRIAN GATHERING COMMITTEE (1971) *Northumbrian Anthology No. 1.* Morpeth: Morpeth Northumbrian Gathering Committee

MORPETH NORTHUMBRIAN GATHERING COMMITTEE (1972) *Northumbrian Anthology No 2.* Morpeth: Morpeth Northumbrian Gathering Committee

PAHLSSON, C. (1972) *The Northumbrian Burr: a Sociolingistic Study.* Lund: Gleerup

REED, F.J. (1977) *Cumen and Gannin: New Poems in the Northumbrian Dialect.* Whitley Bay: Erdesdun

ROBSON, J.P. (1860) *The Book of Ruth in the Northumberland Dialect.* London: George Barclay

ROBSON, J.P. (1860) *The Song of Solomon in the Northumberland Dialect.* London: George Barclay
WARKENTYNE, H.J. (1965) *The Phonology of the Dialect of Hexham in Northumberland.* Unpublished M.Phil thesis, University College, London

Local studies collection

County Central Library, The Willows, Morpeth, Northumberland NE61 1TA.
Tel: 0670 512385/6/7

Records and Cassettes

Chevy Chase
Northumbrian Minstrelsy
Folktracks Cassettes 45–330

Brannigan's Northumbria
Owen Brannigan
MWM 1007

Dreams of Northumbria
Jean and Basil Clough
Beltona LBA 66

The High Level Ranters:
Northumberland Forever Topic 12TS425
The Lads of Northumbria Trailer LER 2007

Northumbrian Folk
BBC Records REC 1185

Northumbrian Garland
Louis Killen
Topic TOP 75

Cullercoats Fish Lass and Other Northumbrian Songs
Fred Lawson
MANOR M510

Northumbrian Voice
Fred Reed
White Meadow 01

Songs of Northumbria
Dennis Weatherley
Decca Eclipse ECS 2099

Folksongs of Northumbria
Owen Brannigan
HMV 7EG 8551

The Lambton Worm
Hedgehog Pie
Rubber TUB12

Societies

Northumbrian Language Society
Mrs. K.M. Bibby-Wilson, 27 Wallace Street, Spital Tongues, Newcastle upon Tyne NE2 4AU. Tel. 091 232 4329

The Northumbrian Language Society was formed in 1983. Meetings are held every two months at Hexham and periodically at Morpeth, with guest speakers and performers. *The Reed Neet* is held on April 30th, the birth date of Fred Reed, internationally acclaimed poet and the Society's first Vice-President, and is preceded by the Society's Annual meeting. It is a celebration of the life and work of Fred Reed, featuring the traditional pie and peas supper, the Muckle Stotty Cyek, formal toasts and informal entertainment. *The Yule Meet* is the Society's Christmas get–together, a 'merry neet' of music, poetry, studies and festive fare. *The Hot Trod Roadshow* is an evening of songs, stories, history, music and verse to increase awareness of the language and recruit members, besides providing an enjoyable entertainment.

The Society is also engaged in a *Dialect Survey*, an on-going study of the nature, origins and health of the Northumbrian language and its local variations. Research is carried out by local volunteers. Competitions for dialect poetry and prose, by adults and children, are run in conjunction with the annual Morpeth Northumbrian Gathering.

Northumbriana Magazine appears two or three times a year and publishes the results of the Dialect Survey and many of the entries to the Morpeth Gathering writing competition. Other projects include a bibliography of manuscripts and books in and about

Northumbrian; production of a schools' information pack; and future publication of booklets and larger volumes.

Tyneside

Books

ARMSTRONG, T. (1968) *Tommy Armstrong, the Great Balladeer of the Coalfields: the words of his songs on Topic Record 12T122*, London: Topic Records

BARRASS, A. (1897) *The Pitman's Social Neet*. Consett: J. Dent

BEWICK, T. (1850) *The Howdy and the Upgetting: two tales of sixty years sin seyne in the Tyneside dialect*. London: The Admirers of Native Merit

DOBSON, S. (1969) *Larn Yersel' Geordie*. Newcastle upon Tyne: Frank Graham

DOBSON, S. (1970) *Advanced Geordie Palaver*. Newcastle upon Tyne: Frank Graham

DOBSON, S. (1970) *Hist'ry o' the Geordies*. Newcastle upon Tyne: Frank Graham

DOBSON, S. (1970) *Hadrian and the Geordie Waall*. Newcastle upon Tyne: Frank Graham

DOBSON, S. (1971) *Stotty Cake Row*. Newcastle upon Tyne: Frank Graham

DOBSON, S. (1971) *Supergeordie: Scott Dobson's Xmas Book*. Newcastle upon Tyne: Frank Graham

DOBSON, S. (1972) *Aad Geordie's Almanack*. Newcastle upon Tyne: Frank Graham

DOBSON, S. (1973) *A Light Hearted Guide to Geordieland*. Newcastle upon Tyne: Frank Graham

DOBSON, S. (1974) *The Geordie Dictionary*. Newcastle upon Tyne: Frank Graham.

DOBSON, S. (1976) *The Geordie Book of Horror*. Newcastle upon Tyne: Frank Graham

DOBSON, S. (1978) *Geordie Recitations, Songs and Party Pieces*, with music by E. Boswell. Newcastle upon Tyne: Frank Graham

DOBSON, S. (1980) *Geordie 900*. Newcastle upon Tyne: Frank Graham

DOBSON, S. and IRWIN, D. (1971) *Geordie on the Beer . . . or That Demon Drink*. Newcastle upon Tyne: Frank Graham

DUNBAR, W. (1874) *Local and Other Songs, Recitations and Conundrums*. Newcastle upon Tyne: Stevenson & Dryden

EDINGTON, J.S. (1863) *Billy Purvis's Benefit, the Keelman's Grand Remonstrance, and Other Pieces*. North Shields: Alexander Clifford

ELLIOT, REV. A. (1971) *The Geordie Bible*. Newcastle upon Tyne: Frank Graham

ELLIOT, REV. A. (1974) *A Geordie Life of Jesus*. Newcastle upon Tyne: Frank Graham

ELLIOT, REV. A. (1977) *The New Geordie Bible*. Newcastle upon Tyne: Frank Graham

ELLIOT, REV. A. (1983) *The Geordie Genesis*. Newcastle upon Tyne: Frank Graham

FALLAW, H.F. (1915) *The Tyneside Tongue*. Gateshead

FORSTER, J.G. (1860) *The Song of Solomon in the Newcastle Dialect*. London: George Barclay

GRAHAM, F. (ed.) (1965) *Tyneside Songs*. Newcastle upon Tyne: Harold Hill

GRAHAM, F. (1970) *Tyneside Songster*. Newcastle upon Tyne: F. Graham

GRAHAM, F. (ed.) (1971) *The Geordie Song Book*. Newcastle upon Tyne: Frank Graham

GRAHAM, F. (ed.) (1977) *The Geordie Netty and Guide: a Short History and Guide*. Newcastle upon Tyne: Frank Graham

GRAHAM, F. (ed.) (1978) *Geordie Songs, Jokes and Recitations*. Newcastle upon Tyne: Frank Graham

GRAHAM, F. (ed.) (1979) *The New Geordie Dictionary*. Newcastle upon Tyne: Frank Graham

GREENWELL, G.C. (1971) *A Glossary of Terms Used in the Coal Trade of Northumberland and Durham*. First published London: Bemrose & Sons, 1888 Facsimile edition, Newcastle upon Tyne: Frank Graham

HASWELL, R. (*pseud.* Murphy, J.) (1975) *Fifty Famous Rhymes and Recitations Consarnin Geordie Broon of Blackworth: Omnibus Edition*. Whitley Bay: Deakin Printers

HOWIE, P. (n.d.) *The Geordie Cook Book*. Newcastle upon Tyne: Frank Graham

IRWIN, D. (1975) *100 Geordie Jokes*. Newcastle upon Tyne: Frank Graham

IRWIN, D. (1976) *The Geordie Laff Inn*. Newcastle upon Tyne: Frank Graham

IRWIN, D. and DOBSON, S. (1970) *Geordie at the Club*. Newcastle upon Tyne: Frank Graham

IRWIN, D. and DOBSON, S. (1970) *The Geordie Joke Book*. Newcastle upon Tyne: Frank Graham

IRWIN, D. and DOBSON, S. (1970) *Geordie Laffs*. Newcastle upon Tyne: Frank Graham

IRWIN, D. and DOBSON, S. (1980) *The Geordie Book of Beer*. Newcastle upon Tyne: Frank Graham

IRWIN, D. (1973) *Geordie on the Beer*. Newcastle upon Tyne: Frank Graham

JAMES, M.C. (1898) *Sum Tyneside Sangs: a Collection of Prize Songs, etc., in the Tyneside Dialect*. Newcastle upon Tyne: Andrew Reid

LINGFORD J. (1949) *Lingford's High Level Tyneside Song Book*. Bishop Auckland: Joseph Lingford & Son

MACDONALD, C. (1981) Variation in the Use of Modal Verbs with Special Reference to Tyneside English. Unpublished PhD thesis, University of Newcastle upon Tyne

MARSHALL, T. (1829) *A Collection of Original Local Songs*. Newcastle upon Tyne: William Fordyce

ROBSON, J.P. (1849) *Songs of the Bards of the Tyne: a Choice Selection of Original Songs Chiefly in the Newcastle Dialect*. Newcastle upon Tyne: T. France

ROBSON, W.J. (1925) *The Adventures of Jackie Robson Monologues in the Tyneside Dialect*. Newcastle upon Tyne: R. Robinson

SANVID, D.S. (pseud. Dorfy) (1956) *Aaal Tegithor Ageyn: A New Collection of Dialect Stories and Poems*. South Shields: Shields Gazette

SANVID, D.S. (pseud. Dorfy) (1964) *Watt Cheor?: a Collection of Readings and Recitations in Tyneside Dialect*. South Shields: Shields Gazette

SANVID, D.S. (pseud. Dorfy) (1970) *A Basinful o'Geordie*. Newcastle upon Tyne: Harold Hill & Son

SANVID, D.S. (pseud. Dorfy) (1964) *Mair Geordie Taalks: Readings and Recitations in Tyneside Dialect*. Newcastle upon Tyne: Harold Hill & Son

SELKIRK, J. (ed.) (1853) *Selkirk's Collection of Songs and Ballads for the People: Original and Select*. Newcastle upon Tyne: J. Selkirk

SKELTON, M. (1976) A Phonological Study of Two Newcastle Ideiolects. Unpublished MA thesis, University of Leeds

SMITH, J.E. (1923) *Tyneside Dialect Poems on Topical Subjects*. Newcastle upon Tyne: Northumberland Press

THOMPSON, T. et al. (1827) *A Collection of Songs, Comic, Satirical and Descriptive, chiefly in the Newcastle Dialect and Illustrative of the Language and Manners of the Common People on the Banks of the Tyne and Neighbourhood*. Newcastle upon Tyne: J. Marshall

TODD, G. (1977) *Todd's Geordie Words and Phrases: an Aid to Communication on Tyneside and Thereabouts*. Newcastle upon Tyne: Frank Graham

VEITCH, N. (1936) *The Lang Pack: a Tale of the North Tyne*. Birmingham: Play Publishers

WALKER, D. (1973) *Geordie's Court*. Cambridge: Rivers Press (originally broadcast as a six part serial by BBC Radio Durham)

WILSON, T. (1872) *The Pitman's Pay and Other Poems With a Memoir of the Author.* London: G. Routledge

WARRINGTON, C.E. CATCHESIDE (ed.) (1917) *Tyneside Stories and Recitations.* Newcastle: J.G. Windows

YEOMAN, J. (1960) *Shields Sayings, a Manner of Speech Proverbial Phrases and Idioms.* South Shields: J. Greenwood and Sons

Local studies collection

Central Library, Newcastle upon Tyne NE99 1DX. Tel: 091 2610691

Records and Cassettes

Howay the Lads, it's Newcastle United!
Barrie Brothers
Magpie IS/BB/10003A

Geordie Songs
Owen Brannigan
HMV 7EP 7050

Owen Brannigan's Tyneside
Owen Brannigan
Decca SKL 5153

When the Boat Comes in
Barrie Sisters
Mawson and Wareham MWM1021

Home Newcastle and Takin' the Time
Busker
EMI 5235

Very Canny
Canny Fettle
Tradition TSR 023

Canny Newcassel: ballads and songs
Topic 12TS219

Songs of the Tyne
Consett Citizens Choir
Delyse ECB 3169

Wor Geordie
Bob Davenport
Topic TOP83

The Waters of Tyne and Bladon Races
Dunelea Singers
Manor M512

Mike Elliot:
At Last It's Mike Elliot Rubber RUB044
Out of the Brown Rubber RUB025

Voices of the Tyne
Felling Male Voice Choir
MWM 1028

Geordie Sings
Alec Forrester
Windmill

Geordie Pride
Mortonsound MTN 3114

Alex Glasgow:
Alex Glasgow Sings Geordie Songs EMI 7EG 8978
Joe Lives MWM 1003
Mix Me a Folk Song HMV CLP 1746
Now and Then MWM 1011
Songs of Alex Glasgow 1 MWM 1006
Songs of Alex Glasgow 2 MWM 1009
Songs of Alex Glasgow 3 Rubber RUB030
Northern Drift MWM 1018

Johnny Handle:
The Collier Lad Topic 12TS270
Stottin Doon the Waal Topic TOP78

High Level Ranters:
The Bonnie Pit Laddie Topic 12TS 271/2

Border Spirit Topic 12TS 5343
Four in a Bar Topic 12TS 388
High Level Trailer LER 2030
Keep Your Feet Still Geordie Hinnie Trailer LER 2020
A Mile to Ride Trailer LER 2037
The New High Level Ranters Topic 12TS 425
Ranting Lads Topic 12T8297

George House and Mike Neville:
Geordierama MWM 1005S
Larn Yersel Geordie MWM 1004
New Improved Geordierama MWM 1016
Son of Geordie MWM 1004

Michael Hunt:
The Blaydon Races Decca Eclipse ECM 2037
Water of Tyne Decca LK 4902

Coaldust Ballads
The Ian Campbell Folk Group
TRA 123

Keelers and Colliers
Documentary recording of mining life and conditions
Folktracks cassette 45-409

Tommy Armstrong of Tyneside
Louis Killen
Topic Records 12T122

Louis Killen and Johnny Handle:
Along the Coaly Tyne Topic 12T189
The Collier's Rant Topic TOP73

Bonny Tyneside and the Legend of the Lambton Worm
Fred Lawson
Manor M501

Fog on the Tyne
Lindisfarne
CAS 1050

Aall Tegithor Like the Foaks o'Shields
Jim Mageean and Anni and Others
GVR 223

A Neet Wi' the Geordies at 'Balmbra's Music Hall'
Decca Eclipse ECS 2073

The Cliff of Old Tynemouth and Divvent Bang the Door
The Northumbrian Serenaders
Manor M5S7

Bobby Pattison's Talk of the Tyne
Bobby Pattinson
Bullseye BLP010

Alan Price:
Andy Cappa KRY4
Geordie Roots and Branches MWM-SPI
The Trimdon Grange Explosion Deram DM263

Pitwork, Politics and Poetry
Jock Purdon
Lynx Studios PL P001

Elsie Marley and Other Local Songs
William S. Robinson
Manor M508

Banks of the Tyne
Carolyn Robson
Dingle's Records DIN 316

*Take Off Your Head and Listen Anthology of Music and Songs
being performed in Tyneside Clubs*
Rubber LP001

Bobby Thompson:
The Bobby Thompson Laugh-in Rubber Records RUB 038
The Little Waster Rubber Records RUB 032

Wot Cheor Geordie!
MWM SP4A

Durham

Books

ANON, (1849) *A Glossary of Provincial Words Used in Teesdale in the County of Durham*. London: J.R. Smith

BELL, J. (ed.) (1812) *Rhymes of Northern Bards, Being a Curious Collection of Old and New Songs and Poems, Peculiar to the Counties of Newcastle-upon-Tyne, Northumberland and Durham*. Newcastle upon Tyne

BLENKINSOP, R.W. (1931) *Teesdale Dialect*. Barnard Castle: Teesdale Mercury Press

DOUGLASS, D. (1973) *Pit Talk in County Durham: A Glossary of Miner's Talk Together with Memories of Wardley Colliery, Pit Songs and Piliking*. London: Routledge & Kegan Paul

EGGLESTONE, W.M. (1886) *Weardale Names of Field and Fell: An Etymological and Historical Inquiry into the Names of Places in County Durham*. Stanhope

GEESON, C. (1969) *A Northumberland and Durham Word Book: The Living Dialect, including a Glossary with Etymologies and Illustrative Quotations of Living Dialect Words*. Newcastle upon Tyne: H. Hill

GRAHAM, J.J. (1939) *Weardale Past and Present*. Gateshead: Northumberland Press

GREENWELL, G.C. (1971) *A Glossary of Terms Used in the Coal Trade of Northumberland and Durham*. First published London: Bemrose & Sons, 1888, facsimile edition Newcastle upon Tyne: Frank Graham

NICHOLSON, W.E. (1888) *A Glossary of Terms Used in the Coal Trade of Northumberland and Durham*. Newcastle upon Tyne: Andrew Reid

ORTON, H. (1936) *The Phonology of a South Durham Dialect*. London: Kegan Paul.

PALGRAVE, F.M.T. (1896) *A List of Words and Phrases in Everyday Use by the Natives of Hetton-Le-Hole*. London: English Dialect Society

VIKAR, A. (1922) *Contributions to the History of the Durham Dialects: an Orthographical Investigation*. Malmö. (In the stock of Durham University Library)

WORKERS' EDUCATION ASSOCIATION (n.d.) *Accents on the North East: Dialect Jottings*. Darlington: Workers' Education Association, Bennett House, 14 Horsemarket, Darlington DL1 5PT (A cassette tape of local dialect speakers recorded while producing this booklet is kept at Bennett House, Darlington)

Local studies collection

Durham County Library, South Street, Durham DH1 4QS. Tel: 091 3864003

Records and cassettes

The Green Banks of Grain
Graham Miles sings rural songs of sport and love from Teesside
Folktracks Cassettes 90–221

Smokestack Land
Graham Miles singing industrial ballads from Cleveland and Teesside
Folktracks Cassettes 90–222

The Ironmasters
Graham Miles singing industrial ballads from Cleveland and Teesside
Folktracks Cassettes 45–225

Yorkshire

Books

ADDY, S.O. (1888) *A Glossary of Words Used in the Neighbourhood of Sheffield; Including a Selection of Local Games, and Some Notices of Folklore, Games and Customs*. London: Trübner, for the English Dialect Society

AHIER, P. (1943) *The Legends and Traditions of Huddersfield and District*, 2 vols. Huddersfield: Advertiser Press

ANON. (1824) *Horae Momenta Cravenae or the Craven Dialect, Exemplified by Two Dialogues between Farmer Giles and his Neighbour Bridget, to which is Annexed a Copious Glossary by a Native of Craven.* Leeds: Robinson & Hernaman

ANON. (1828) *The Dialect of Craven in the West Riding of the County of York with a Glossary Illustrated by Authorities from Ancient English and Scottish Writers and Exemplified by Two Familiar Dialogues by a Native of Craven,* 2nd edn. London: W.M. Crofts

ANON. (1855) *Glossary of Yorkshire Words and Phrases, Collected in Whitby and the Neighbourhood.* London: J.R. Smith

ANON. (1860) *Dictionary of the Dialect of Batley.* Bartley: J. Fearnsides

ANON. (1862) *The Dialect of Leeds and its Neighbourhood.* London: John Russell Smith

ANON. (1986) *Reet Yorkshire Treat.* Clapham via Lancaster: Dalesman

ANON. (n.d.) *Specimens of the Yorkshire Dialect in Various Dialogues, Tales and Songs, to which is added Aud Isaac, a Poem Composed of Facts and Similitudes.* Otley: Yorkshire Joint Stock Publishing & Stationery Co.

ANDERSON, P. (ed.) (1980) *Yorkshire at Work: a Selection of Articles Reprinted from Transactions of the Yorkshire Dialect Society.* Leeds: Yorkshire Dialect Society

ATKINSON, J.C. (1868) *A Glossary of Cleveland Dialect: Explanatory, Derivative and Critical.* London: J.R. Smith

BANKS, W.S. (1865) *List of Provincial Words in Use at Wakefield in Yorkshire.* London: John Russell Smith

BEAUMONT, W. (n.d.) *Rhymes in the North Country Humour.* No publishing details.

BEAUMONT, W. (1972) *Ben Briggs and Other Rhymes.* Huddersfield: Advertiser Press

BLACKHAH, T. (1867) *Songs and Poems Written in Nidderdale Dialect.* London and Pately Bridge

BLACKHAH, T. (1867) *Oliver Banks; or St Thomas's Bounty.* Pately Bridge

BLAKEBOROUGH, R. (1899) *T'Hunt O'Yatton Brigg: A Legend of Cleveland, Also a Collection of Rare Old Songs and Two Humorous Sketches All Written in the Cleveland Dialect,* 2nd edn. Stockton: Yorkshire Publishing Press

BROWN, F. (n.d.) *The Muse Went Weaving.* Youlgrave: HUB Pubs and Yorkshire Dialect Society

BRUFF, H.J.L. (ed.) (1937) *Dialect Poems and Prose.* York

BURNETT, W.H. (1877) *Songs and Sketches in Broad Yorkshire from the Writings of Castillo, Mrs. G.M. Tweedle, Reed, Lewis and Others* Middlesborough: Burnett & Hood

BYWATER, A. (1877) *Sheffield Dialect*, 3rd edn. Wakefield: W. Nicholson & Sons

CARLILL, J.A. (1908) *Woz 'Lo: Humorous Sketches and Rhymes Mostly in East Yorkshire Dialect*. Hull: F. Smith & Son

CARR, W. (1828) *The Dialect of Craven*, 2 vols, 2nd edn. London

CAUVERT, O. (1871) *Sladdburn Faar!* Skipton

COWLEY, B. (ed.) (1963) *An East Yorkshire Anthology, Dialect Verses from York and the Wolds, the Vale of Pickering and the Sea*. Keighley: Yorkshire Dialect Society

COWLEY, B. (ed.) (1963) *Cleveland Anthology*. Leeds: Yorkshire Dialect Society

COOKRIDGE, J.M. (1967) *Owd Yorkshire Relish*. Ilfracombe: A.H. Stockwell

COWLEY, W. (ed.) (1970) *Dialect Verse from the Ridings*. Leeds: Yorkshire Dialect Society

COWLING, G.H. (1925) *Yorkshire Dialect Reciter*. London: Folk Press

CUDWORTH, W. (1906) *Yorkshire Speyks and Bradford Dialect Sketches*. Bradford: Clough, Smith, Mathews & Brooke

De ROBINSON, G. (n.d.) *Humour from the Ridings. Chulton Parva Chronicles*. York: Yorkshire Dialect Society

DUNCAN, P. (c1880) *Penny Readings and Recitations in Prose*. Wakefield: W. Nicholson & Sons

DYER, S. (1970) *Dialect of the West Riding of Yorkshire: A Short History of Leeds and Other Towns*. Wakefield: S.R. Publishers

DYSON, B.R. (1960) Dialect of the Upper Holme Valley. Unpublished MA thesis, University of Leeds

DYSON, B. and ELLIS, S. (eds) (1974) *Yorkshire Pudding Olmenack: a Mixture of Early Yorkshire Almanacs* Leeds: School of English, University of Leeds for the Yorkshire Dialect Society

EASTHER, A. (1883) *A Glossary of the Dialect of Almondbury and Huddersfield*. London: Trübner for the English Dialect Society

ENGLAND, G. (ed.) (1983) *Words Throo' T' Shuttle Ee: An Anthology of Industrial Dialect Verse from Victorian South and West Yorkshire*. Ilkley: Yorkshire Dialect Society

GEE, H.L. (1962) *Yorkshire Wit and Humour*. London: Epworth Press

GLAUSER, B. (198?) *The Phonology of Present-Day Grassington Speech (North Yorkshire)* Bern: Francke

GLOVER, K. (1977) *Yorkshire Brass: Dialect Poetry and Reminiscences*. K. Glover

HAIGH, W.E. (1928) *A New Glossary of the Dialect of the Huddersfield District*. London: Oxford University Press

HALLIDAY, W.J. (ed.) (1943) *Yorkshire Dialect Poems 1914–1943*, 2nd edn. Leeds: Yorkshire Dialect Society

HALLIDAY, W.J. (1947) *The Yorkshire Dialect Society 1897–1947: Fifty Years of Dialect Progress.* Kendal: Yorkshire Dialect Society

HALLIDAY, W.J. (ed.) (1967) *York Minister Screen: Being a Specimen of Yorkshire Dialect As Spoken in the North Riding.* First printed Malton (1833), this edition Leeds: Yorkshire Dialect Society.

HALLIDAY, W.J. and UMPLEBY, A.S. (1949) *The White Rose Garland of Yorkshire Dialect Verse and Local Folk-Lore Rhymes.* London: J.M. Dent & Sons

---

The Bill's O' Jack's Grace
Spoken at a 'Churn' Supper

Neaw then, o yoh naybors, yoh'r fere op o' th'itch
Wi yoh'r een o breet un yoh'r meauths o twitch, –
Toh smack ut these pies un puddins soh rich
Aw hopw yoh'll get filled as full as a fitch,
Un brast eaut yoh'r singlets – every button un stitch!
But win first thank the Lord ut provides us wi'sich;
Neaw then, lads, wire in, yoh cannot heyt toh mich!

Aamon Wrigley, in England, G. (ed.) (1983) p.12

HAMPSON, W. (1911) *Tykes Abrooad.* Wakefield: W. Nicholson and Sons Ltd

HAMPSON, W. (1916) *Private Job Muggleston.* London: W. Nicholson and Sons Ltd

HARTLEY, J. (c. 1873 to c. 1953) *Original Illuminated Clock Almanack in the Yorkshire Dialect.* Wakefield: W. Nicholson & Sons Ltd

HARLAND, J. (1873) *Glossary of Words Used in Swaledale, Yorkshire.* London: Trübner for the English Dialect Society

HARTLEY, J. (1876) *Yorkshire Puddin'.* London & Wakefield: W. Nicholson and Sons Ltd

HARTLEY, J. (1892) *Grimes Visit to th' Queen: A Royal Time Among royalties.* London: W. Nicholson and Sons Ltd

HARTLEY, J. (n.d.) *Yorkshire Ditties.* London & Wakefield: W. Nicholson and Sons Ltd.

HARTLEY, J. (n.d.) *Yorkshire Lyrics.* London & Wakefield: W. Nicholson and Sons Ltd

HARTLEY, J. (n.d.) *Yorkshire Tales: Amusing Sketches of Yorkshire Life in the Yorkshire Dialect.* London & Wakefield: W. Nicholson and Sons Ltd

HARTLEY, J. (n.d.) *Yorkshire Sketches.* Wakefield: W. Nicholson and Sons Ltd

HARTLEY, J. (n.d.) *Seets i' Lundun.* Wakefield: W. Nicholson and Sons Ltd

HARTLEY, J. (n.d.) *Seets i' Blackpool, Fleetwood, Lytham and Southport, as seen by Sammywell Grimes an' his wife Mally on their holiday trip, wi' a few incidents an' accidents 'at occurred.* London: W. Nicholson and Sons Ltd

HARTLEY, J. (n.d.) *Grimes and Mally Laikin' i' Lakeland.* London: W. Nicholson and Sons Ltd

HARTLEY, J. (n.d.) *Mally an' Me: a reflection of humorous and pathetic incidents from the life of Sammywell Grimes and his wife Molly.* Wakefield: W. Nicholson and Sons Ltd.

HEDEVIND, B. (1967) *The Dialect of Dentdale in the West Riding of Yorkshire.* Studia Anglistica Uppsaliensia 5

HORBURY FREE PRESS (1874) *Illustrated Almanac for 1874.* Wakefield: Free Press

HUNTER, J. (1984) *The Hallamshire Glossary.* First published London: William Pickering, 1829, this edition, Sheffield: CECTAL and the Hunter Archaeological Society

JACKSON, G. (1979) *Poems Form The Yorkshire Dales.* Clapham via Lancaster: Dalesman

LAYCOCK, S. (c. 1893) *Warblins fra an Owd Songster.* London: Simpkin, Marshall, Hamilton, Kent & Co.

MALHAM-DEMBLEBY, J. (1912) *Original Tales and Ballads in the Yorkshire Dialect: Known as Inglis, the Language of the Angles and the Northumbrian Dialect Spoken Today in Yorkshire and in Early Times from South Yorkshire to Aberdeen.* London: Walter Scott Publishing Co.

MELCHERS, G. (1972) *Studies in Yorkshire Dialects.* Stockholm Theses in English 9. Stockholm: University of Stockholm

METCALFE, J. (n.d.) *Bunderley Boggard and Other Plays in Yorkshire Dialect.* London: Heath Cranton

MITCHELL, A. and WADDELL, S. (1987) *Teach Thissen Tyke.* First edition, Newcastle upon Tyne: Frank Graham (1971), this edition Clapham via Lancaster: Dalesman

MITCHELL, A. (1987) *Yorkshire Jokes.* Clapham via Lancaster: Dalesman

MITCHELL, A. and WADDELL, S. (1987) *Teach Thissen Tyke.* First edition, Newcastle upon Tyne: Frank Graham (1971), this edition Clapham via Lancaster: Dalesman

MITCHELL, A. and WADDELL, S. (1987) *Teach Thissen Tyke.* First edition Newcastle upon Tyne: Frank Graham (1971), this edition Clapham via Lancaster: Dalesman

MOORMAN, F.W. (1917) *Yorkshire Dialect Poems (1673–1913) and Traditional Poems*. 2nd edn, London: Sidgwick & Jackson.

MOORMAN, F.W. (1920) *More Tales of the Ridings*. London: Elkin Mathews.

MORRIS, M.C.F. (1911) *Yorkshire Folk Talk with Characteristics of Those Who Speak it in the North and East Ridings*. 2nd edn. London: A. Brown & Sons.

NICHOLSON, J. (1889) *The Folk Speech of East Yorkshire*. Hull: A. Brown & Sons.

PLEASE, SIR A.E. (1928) *A Dictionary of the Dialect of the North Riding of Yorkshire with Comments by John Fairfax-Blakeborough*. Whitby: Horne & Son

PETYT, K.M. (1970) *Emily Brontë and the Haworth Dialect: A Study of the Dialect Speech in 'Wuthering Heights'*. Menston: Scolar Press for the Yorkshire Dialect Society

PETYT, K.M. (1985) *Dialect and Accent in Industrial West Yorkshire*. Amsterdam: John Benjamins

RATCLIFFE, D.U. (1946) *Under T'Hawthorn: Yorkshire Dialect Lyrics*. London: Frederick Muller

RATCLIFFE, D.U. (1956) *Over Hill Over Dale*. London

RATCLIFFE, D.U. (1960) *Yorkshire Lyrics*. London & Edinburgh: Thomas Nelson for the Yorkshire Dialect Society

ROBINSON, F.K. (1855) *A Glossary of Yorkshire Words and Phrases Collected in Whitby and Neighbourhood*. London: J.R. Smith

ROSS, F. (1877) *Glossary of Words used in Holderness in the East Riding of Yorkshire*. London: Trübner for the English Dialect Society

SMITH, K.E. (1979) *The Dialect Muse*. Wetherby: Ruined Cottage

SMITH, K.E. (1982) *West Yorkshire Dialect Poets*. Wilsden: Dialect Books

SMITH, K.E. (1987) *Dialect Poets of the Dales*. Wilsden, Bradford: Dialect Books

SPEAKMAN, C. (ed.) (1981) *A Yorkshire Dales Anthology*. London

SPENCER, R. (1890) *Field Flowers and Yorkshire Dialect Poems*. Batley: J. Spencer Newsome

STOCKTON, N. (1986) *East Riding Dialect Dictionary*. Driffield: East Riding Dialect Society

STUART, D. (1976) *Craven Yorkshire Dialect*. Illinois Institute of Technology, Chicago. See also *Dissertation Abstracts International* 38: 234A

TAYLOR, G. (1934) *T' Second Time of Asking (A One Act Play)*. Holmfirth: George Taylor

TAYLOR, R.C. (1975) *A Descriptive and Historical Study of the Phonology of the Dialect of Lumb-in-Rossendale*. Unpublished MA thesis, University Of Manchester

THOMPSON, W.H. (1890) *The Speech of Holderness and East Yorkshire*. Hull: A. Brown & Sons

THWAITE, J. (1946) *Wensleydale Dialect Rhymes*. Clapham: Dalesman

TIDHOLM, H. (1979) *The Dialect of Egton in North Yorkshire*. Göteborg: Bokmaskinen

TODDLE, T. (1866) *Tommy Toddle's Comic Almanac fur all t'fowks in warld an' rahnd abaght*. Leeds: Newton Hirtsy, London: Simpkin Marshall, Manchester: J. Heywood

TOOTH, E.E. (1970) *A Comparative Phonology Between Tunstall and Longton*. Unpublished MA thesis, University of Leeds

TREDDLEHOYLE, T. (c.1845–c.1905) *The Bairnsla Foaks' Annual and Pogmoor Olmenack*. Leeds: Alice Mann

TURNER, B. (1912) *Dialect and Other Pieces from a Yorkshire Loom*. London: St. Catherine Press

TWEDDLE, G.M. (1869) *Rhymes to Illustrate the North Yorkshire Dialect*. North of England Tractates No. 4 Stokesley: Tweddell and Sons

TWEDDLE, G.M. (1873) *Aud Gab O'Steers: How He Tried to Sweetheart Betty Moss: a Trew Teeale Related in the North Yorkshire Dialect*. North of England Tractates No. 13 Stokesley: Tweddell and Sons

TWEDDLE, G.M. (1892) *Rhymes and Sketches to Illustrate the Cleveland Dialect*, 2nd edn. Stokesley: Tweddell and Sons

TWISLETON, T. (1867) *Splinters Stuck Off Winskill Rock*. Settle: Edmondson & Wilson

TWISLETON, T. (1907) *Poems in the Craven Dialect*. Settle: Edmondson & Wilson

UMPLEBY, A.S. (1937) *A Boddin' O'Cowls: Verses in the Cleveland Dialect Depicting the Life and Character of the Farming and Fisherfolk of North-East Yorkshire*. Cambridge: The Cambridge University Yorkshire Society

WADDINGTON-FEATHER, J. (1970) *Yorkshire Dialect*. Clapham via Lancaster: Dalesman

WADSWORTH, K. (1987) *Talkin' Brooad*. Hebden Bridge: Littlewood Press

WADE, G. (1964) *An Anthology of West Riding Dialect Verse*. Kendal: Yorkshire Dialect Society

WADE, G. (1966) *The Golden Galloway*. Driffield

WHOMERSLEY, D. (1981) *'Sheffieldish' a Beginner's Phrase-book*. Sheffield: Sheffield City Council

WIDDOWSON, J.D.A. (1965–6) *A Pronouncing Glossary of the Dialect of Filey in the East Riding of Yorkshire*. MA thesis, University of Leeds

WILCOCK, J. (1869 and 1870) *Illustrated Family Almanack*. Wakefield: J. Wilcock

WRIGHT, J. (1892) *A Grammar of The Dialect of Windhill in the West Riding of Yorkshire*. London: English Dialect Society
WRIGHT, P. (1980) *The Yorkshire Man's Dictionary.* Clapman: Dalesman

---

One pitch dark neet a trombone player wor comin across o t fields throo Dick Hudson's to Baildon, an he kept blawin a nooat on his trombone to keep his courage up. All at once he heeard anuther rawtin noise. He thowt it wor sumbdy else wi a trombone, but, as a matter o fact, it wor a mad bull. He blew his paything ageean, an t answer com back ageean, cloise tuv his lug. T next move he wor flyin ower t wall. He sat whear he let, an he shahted ta t chap ower wall, "Thar a coward! Ah'll tell thee that! An Ah'll tell thi summat else – tha may be varry strong, bud tha'rt noa musician!"

(De Robinson (ed.) (n.d.) *Humour From the Ridings*, p. 15)

WRIGHT, P. (1973) *The Yorkshire Yammer: How It Is Spoke.* Clapman via Lancaster: Dalesman
YORKSHIRE DIALECT SOCIETY (1921) *A Little Book of Yorkshire Dialect or Original Tales and Verses in Dialect.* York: Waddington for the Yorkshire Dialect Society
YORKSHIRE DIALECT SOCIETY (1967) *Yorkshire Dialect Prose, 1st series,* 2nd edn. Leeds: Yorkshire Dialect Society
YORKSHIRE DIALECT SOCIETY (1967) *Yorkshire Dialect Prose, 2nd series,* 2nd edn. Leeds: Yorkshire Dialect Society

Local studies collections

Central Library, Calverley Street, Leeds LS1 3AB. Tel: 0532 478274

Library Headquarters, Balne Lane, Wakefield WF2 0DQ Tel: 0924 295376

Central Library, Princess Alexandra Walk, Huddersfield, HG1 2SU Tel: 0484 513808

Central Library, Princes Way, Bradford, BD1 1NN Tel: 0274 753600

Central Library, Northgate, Halifax HX1 1UN Tel: 0422 357257

Northallerton Library, 1 Thirsk Road, Northallerton DL6 1PT Tel: 0609 776271

Central Library, Vernon Road, Scarborough YO11 2NN. Tel: 0723 364285

Central Library, Victorian Avenue, Harrogate HG1 1EG. Tel: 0423 502744

County Library, Museum Street, York Y01 2DS. Tel: 0904 655631

County Library, Victoria Square, Middlesborough, Cleveland TS1 2AY Tel: 0642 248155

Central Library, Albion Street, Kingston-upon-Hull Tel: 0482 224040)

Central Library, Surrey Street, Sheffield S1 1XZ Tel: 0742 734711

Central Library, Shambles Street, Barnsley S70 2JF Tel: 0226 733241

The Brian O'Malley Central Library and Arts Centre, Walker Place, Rotherham S65 1JH Tel: 0709 382121

Central Library, Waterdale, Doncaster DN1 3JE Tel: 0302 734305

Records and Cassettes

First o t'Sort
LP of readings in dialect verse and prose, recorded at the Yorkshire Dialect Society's meeting at the Ilkley Literature Festival. Available from the Librarian, YDS, School of English, the University, Leeds, LS2 9JT.

Come In, Old Toss Pot
Customs, costumes and Easter eggs from the village of Dent, West Yorks
Folktracks cassettes 30–109

The Streets of Leeds
Local songs, customs, street cries, children's games collected by Rowland Kellett
Folktracks cassettes 60–209

Two Jolly Miners
George Hoyland and Louis Wroe, two Sheffield 'sword dance'
musicians describe their dance, sing, play tunes and talk about
local customs
Folktracks Cassettes 60–212

Brass Nuts
George Tremain
Folktracks Cassettes 30–329

Smokestack Land
Graham Miles singing industrial ballads from Cleveland and
Teesside
Folktracks Cassettes 90–222

The Ironmasters
Graham Miles singing industrial ballads from Cleveland and
Teesside
Folktracks Cassettes 45–225

Research projects

Tape Recorded Survey of Yorkshire Speech
The College of Ripon & York St John, Lord Mayor's Walk, York
Y03 7EX. Tel: 0904 656771

The Tape Recorded Survey of Yorkshire Speech is an ongoing
research project based at the College of Ripon & St John. The
research has several related strands, involving the geographical
and sociolinguistic investigation of regional phonology, grammar
and lexis. An archive of recordings is held at the college.

Societies

Yorkshire Dialect Society
Hon. Sec.: Mr. Stanley Ellis, Fairfields, Weeton Lane, Weeton,
LS17 0AN

The Yorkshire Dialect Society was founded in Bradford in 1897.
Its real beginnings, however, were in a Committee formed three
years earlier by Professor Joseph Wright, 'having for its object
the collecting of further Yorkshire material for the English Dialect
Directory'. Interest in the Society was immediate, and has never
slackened.

The Society began with scholarly aims which it continues to promote. One of its quarterly meetings is usually devoted to a lecture on some academic dialect or language topic, and over the years the Society's annual *Transactions* have contained many papers which have made important contributions to English dialect studies.

The other principal interest is the fostering and promotion of Yorkshire dialect speech and literature, and there is a very lively response to these among members. Members include many gifted dialect writers and reciters and both of the Society's publications – the *Summer Bulletin* and the *Transactions* – often contain pieces of original dialect prose and verse. The Society also publishes a wide range of anthologies of dialect literature. The Society's library is housed at the School of English, The University, Leeds LS2 9JT. Publications of the YDS can also be ordered from the Librarian at this address.

East Riding Dialect Society
Hon. Sec.: Brian Spencer, 39 East Dale Road, Melton, North Ferriby, HU14 3HS., Tel. 0482 632905

The Society was formed in 1984 with the aim of preserving the East Riding dialect and to promote public interest in the dialect and its history through meetings, study groups and collaboration with other bodies with similar aims. Regular meetings are held with guest speakers and prose and verse readings from all parts of the East Riding. The Society produces a quarterly newsletter, to which members are invited to contribute their own dialect writing.

8.4 The West Midlands Counties

Books

ORTON, H. and BARRY, M. (1969) *Survey of English Dialects (B) Basic Material, Vol. 2: The West Midland Counties, Parts 1–3*. Leeds: Edward Arnold for the University of Leeds
NORTHALL, G.F. (1965) *Folk-Phrases of Four Counties (Glouc., Staffs., Warw., Worc.), Gathered from Unpublished MSS. and Oral Traditions*. Vaduz: Kraus Reprint Ltd

Cheshire

Books

ANDERSON, P. (1977) The Dialect of Eaton-by-Tarporley (Cheshire): a Descriptive and Historical Grammar, 2 vols. Unpublished PhD thesis, University of Leeds

DARLINGTON, T. (1887) *The Folk Speech of South Cheshire*. London: Trübner & Co. for the English Dialect Society

FLYNN, K. (1975) A Grammar of the Dialect of Moulton (Cheshire). 2 vols. MPhil thesis, University of Leeds

HOLLAND, R. (1884) *A Glossary of Words Used in the County of Cheshire*. London: English Dialect Society

LEIGH, E. (1973) *A Glossary of Words Used in the Dialect of Cheshire*. Wakefield: E.P. Publishing

NEWBROOK, M. (1986) *Sociolinguistic Reflexes of Dialect Interference in West Wirral*. London: Peter Lang

PAINTING, V. (1976) The Lore and Language of Schoolchildren of South Cheshire. Unpublished MA thesis, University College Swansea

WRIGHT, P. (1974) *The Cheshire Chatter: How It Is Spoke*. Clapham, N. Yorks: Dalesman

Local studies collection

Libraries and Museum Department, 91 Holle Road, Chester CH2 3NG. Tel: 0244 312935

Sound and video cassettes

Step In, Wild Horse
Cheshire Soulcakers, collecting food, drink and hopefully money from pubs, farms and big houses on the last day of October. Folktracks Cassettes 60–107 and Video Cassette V6

Derbyshire

Books

ANDREWS, W. (1877) *A Collection of Derbyshire Rhymes*. Buxton: J.C. Bates

BACON, H. (1976) *They's Non So Many On Us Left*. H. Bacon

FROGATT, D. (1977) *Poor Owd Tup: A Killamarsh Anthology*. Killamarsh: Killamarsh Amenities and Community Association

MILWARD, R. (1982) *A Glossary of Household, Farming and Trade Terms from Probate Inventories*. Chesterfield: Derbyshire Record Society

PEGGE, S. (1965) *Two Collections of Derbicisms, Containing Words and Phrases in a Great Measure Peculiar to the Natives and Inhabitants of the County of Derby*. First printed 1896, London: English Dialect Society, 2nd edn, Vaduz: Kraus Reprint.

ROBINSON, J.B. (1870) *Owd Sammy Twitcher's Second Visit tu't Great Exibishun e Darby wi' Jim*. Derby: Robinson

ROBINSON, J.B. (1870) *Owd Sammy Twitcher's Crismas Bowk for the Year 1870*. Derby: Robinson

ROBINSON, J.B. (1881) *Owd Sammy Twitcher's visit tut Royal Aggeracultural Show e Darby wi His Son Jim*. Bemrose & Sons

ROBINSON, J.B. (n.d.) *Owd Sammy Twitcher's Visit tu't Watter Cure Establishment at Matlock Bank*. Derby: J.B. Robinson

SCOLLINS, R. (1978) *An Almost Totally Insane Derbyshire Look at British History in Pictures*. Ilkeston: Scollins & Titford

SCOLLINS, R. and TITFORD, J. (1976) *Ey up, mi duck! Part One: An Affectionate Look at the Speech, History and Folklore of Ilkeston, Derbyshire and the Erewash Valley*. Ilkeston: Scollins & Titford

SCOLLINS, R. and TITFORD, J. (1977) *Ey up, mi duck! Part Two: An Affectionate Look at the Speech, History and Folklore of Ilkeston, Derbyshire and the Erewash Valley*. Ilkeston: Scollins & Titford

SCOLLINS, R. and TITFORD, J. (1977) *Ey up, mi duck! Part Three: An Affectionate Look at the Speech, History and Folklore of Ilkeston, Derbyshire and the Erewash Valley*. Ilkeston: Scollins & Titford

STORR, J. (1977) *Survey of the Dialect of Selston in the Erewash Valley*. MA thesis, University of Leeds

WATSON, O.V. (1976) *Weak i' th' Yedd: Childhood Days in the Mining Village of Marlpool during and just after the 1914–18 War*. Ripley: Brittain

WRIGHT, P. (1986) *The Derbyshire Drawl: How It Is Spoke*. Clapham, N. Yorks: Dalesman

Local studies collections

Derby Central Library, The Wardwick, Derby DE1 1HS. Tel: 0332 2931111)

Holdings include information on local mumming plays and on the dialect poem 'The Derby Tup' and a series of plays written by Dr. L. du Garde Peach between 1957 and 1967, all of which were performed in Hucklow Village Theatre.

Records and cassettes

Muckram Wakes
John and Susie Adams and Helen and Roger Watson
Leader Sound Ltd, 1976; Trailer LER 2093

The Young May Moon
Ram's Bottom
Traditional Sound Recordings, 1981: TSR 038

Oak-Apple Day
Castleton Garland
Folktracks Video Cassette V14

Shropshire

Books

INSALL, J. (n.d.) *All Friends Around The Wrekin*. Jack Insall
JACKS, D. (1967–68) *The Living Dialect of Stokesay, Shropshire. The
    Mercian Defensive Earthworks on the Kerry Hill Ridgeway (Shropshire
    and Montgomeryshire) to the West of Offa's Dyke*. MPhil thesis,
    University of Leeds
JACKSON, G.F. (1879) *Shropshire Word-Book: A glossary of Archaic
    and Provincial Words*. London: Trübner and Co for the English Dialect
    Society
JENKIN, A.E. (1982) *Titterstone Clee Hills: Everyday Life, Industrial
    History and Dialect* (with cassette) A.E. Jenkin, Bower House, Orleton,
    Ludlow SY8 4HR
KILFORD, V. (1981) *Shropshire Words and Dialect*. Telford: V. Kilford,
    2 Edward Tce., Trench Road, Telford, Salop, TF2 6PJ

Local studies collection

Local Studies Department, Castle Gates, Shrewsbury, SY1 2AS.
Tel: 0743 361058

Kidderminster Reference Library, Market Street, Kidderminster
DY10 1AD. Tel: 0562 752832
(Covers Worcestershire in general, with particular emphasis on the
north-western area, together with the nearer parts of Shropshire,
Staffordshire and the West Midlands.

Black country (Dudley, Sandwell, Walsall, Wolverhampton)

Books

BIDDULPH, J. (1986) *A Short Grammar of Black Country*. Pontypridd: Languages Information Centre

BLACK COUNTRY SOCIETY (1973) *The Coming of the Kingdom – Nine Readings from the Authorized Version of the Bible in the Dialect of the Black Country read by Members of the Society at Slater Street Methodist Church, Darlaston, 22nd December, 1973*. Tipton: Black Country Society

FLETCHER, K. (1979) *The Old Testament in the Dialect of the Black Country, Part I*. Tipton: Black Country Society

FLETCHER, K. (1979) *The Old Testament in the Dialect of the Black Country, Part II*. Tipton: Black Country Society

JONES, J.W. (1974) *Factory and Fireside*. Tipton: Black Country Society

JONES, J.W. (1972) *From Under The Smoke: a Selection of the Poems and Black Country Ballads*. Halesowen: Black Country Society

JONES, J.W. and FLETCHER, K. (1986) *Jim and Kate*. Tipton: Black Country Society

LANGLEY, T. (1980) *Tales of Puddinbag*. Tipton: Black Country Society

LYONS, A. (1901) *Black Country Sketches*. London: Elliot Stock

MANLEY, S. (1971) *The Black Country Dialect in the Cradley Heath Area*. Unpublished MA thesis, University of Leeds

MURRAY, D.C. (1973) *Cap Fullo' Nails*. Tipton: Black Country Society

PARKER, D. (1983) *Aynuk's Black Country Joke Book*. Wolverhampton: Broadside

PARSONS, H. (1968) *Black Country Stories*. Halesowen: Black Country Society

RAVEN, J. (1978) *Black Country Word, Book One*. Wolverhampton: Broadside

RAVEN, J. (1978) *Black Country Word, Book Two*. Wolverhampton: Broadside

RAVEN, J. (1978) *Aynuk's Fust Black Country Waerd Book*. Wolverhampton: Broadside

RAVEN, J. (1978) *Tales from Aynuk's Black Country*. Wolverhampton: Broadside

RAVEN, J. (1979) *Aynuk' Secund Black Country Waerd Buk*. Wolverhampton: Broadside

RAVEN, J. (1977) *The Urban and Industrial Songs of the Black Country and Birmingham with extensive local history*. Wolverhampton: Broadside

GENESIS
(Chapter 1)

Ter start evvrythin' off, God med the wairld. Mind yo' 'e cudn't see ennythin' cuz it wuz all dark, soo 'e sed, "Let's a' sum lite" and the lite cum, an 'e wor arf plasied wi' it, soo 'e called it Day, an' the darkniss 'e called Nite.

The nex' day God med the clowds an' the sky an' called it 'Evv'n.

The thaird day 'e purra lorra wairter rahnd the plairse an' called it the say. The dry land 'e called airth an'; 'e med sum trees and bushis an' plantid um on it.

On the fowerth day 'e med sum lites – tew big uns an' alorra little uns. 'E purrum all in the sky an' sed, "One o' yow lites is the mewn an' yown gorra shine at nite, an' th'uther is the sun an' yown gorra shine in the day, an all yow little uns um gunna be called stars an' yow con shine at nite wi' the mewn ter mek a bit mower lite when it's dark.

The fifth day 'e med alorro diffrunt things. 'E med bairds, sum ter stop on the wairter an' sum ter fly arahnd an' stop on the land. 'E alsoo med sum fishis, all syziz frum a jackbannuk tew a wairle.

Then on the sixth day 'e med th' animuls, them wot live in the jungul, an' them wot dow. like cats, dogs an' 'ossiz. 'E med bobowlers an' all th' uther insects, an' wairms, an' all things wot crape.

Then 'e med a mon in 'iz oon imij ahter the dust. God breethed inter this mon an' the mon cum alive, an 'e nairmed 'im Adam.

Translation by Kate Fletcher,
The Old Testament in the Dialect of the Black Country, p. 4)

RAVEN, J. (1986) *Stories, Customs, Superstitions, Tales, Legends and Folklore of the Black Country and Staffordshire*. Wolverhampton: Broadside

RAVEN, M. and RAVEN, J. (1967) *A Good Christmas Box*. Wolverhampton: Broadside

SHAW, T.V. (1930) *A Glossary of Black Country Words and Phrases.* Birmingham: Cornish Brothers

SOUTHALL, D. (1983) *Verses on Tay Towels.* Kingswinford: Black Country Society

SOUTHALL, D. (1984) *Verses on Tay Clothes.* Kingswinford: Black Country Society

TOTTEN, M. and RAVEN, J. *The Nailmakers: Black Country Society.* Wolverhampton: Broadside

Local studies collections

Central Library, Lichfield Street, Walsall WS1 1TR. Tel: 0922 650069

Central Library, Snow Hill, Wolverhampton WV1 3AX. Tel: 0902 312025

Central Library, St. James' Road, Dudley DY1 1HR. Tel: 0384 453557

Sandwell Central Library, High Street, West Bromwich B70 8DZ. Tel: 021-569 3381

Records and Cassettes

Black Country Night Out, Vol. 1
Tommy Mundon, Jon Raven, Dolly Allen, Harry Harrison, Brian Clift
LP BRO 120; CASS: KBRO 120

Black Country Night Out, Vol. 1
Tommy Mundon, Jon Raven, Dolly Allen, Harry Harrison, Brian Clift
LP BRO 122; CASS: KBRO 122

Dolly Allen
Dolly Allen, Black Country comedienne
LP BRO 129; CASS: KBRO 129

Off The Cuff
Harry Harrison, poet, humourist, raconteur and all round entertainer
LP BRO 130; CASS: KBRO 130

An Evening With The Original Black Country Night Out Show
Tommy Mundon, Jon Raven, Dolly Allen, Harry Harrison, Brian Clift
LP: BRO 132; CASS: KBRO 132

The Best of the Black Country Night Out Show
Tommy Mundon, Jon Raven, Dolly Allen, Harry Harrison, Brian Clift
LP: LJES 001: CASS: KLJES 001

All available from record shops or *Broadside Records*, Studley House, 68 Limes Road, Tettenhall, Wolverhampton WV6 8RB.

Societies

Black Country Society
Hon. Sec: Mrs. P. Purcell, 15 Claydon Road, Wallheath, Kingswinford, W. Midlands DY6 0HR. Tel. 0384 293656

The Black County Society was formed in January, 1967. In the years since its formation it has steadily grown to be acknowledged locally and nationally as one of the most important voices representing the people of the area as a whole. As a result of its work, the region now has a regular local publication, *The Blackcountryman*, a flourishing group with its own identity, and a readiness to inform those in authority of its wishes. While continuing to publish serious studies of the past of the Black Country, the Society also organizes many events to encourage contemporary artists and sportsmen and plays a major part in the future planning of the region in cooperation with local and county authorities. The Society is open to all regardless of race or political or religious belief and devotes itself only to the good of the people of the Black Country.

Staffordshire

Books

GIBSON, P.H. (n.d.) Studies in the Linguistic Geography of Staffordshire. Unpublished MA thesis, University of Leeds
HEATH, C.D. (1980) *The Pronunciation of English in Cannock, Staffordshire: A Socio-linguistic Survey of an Urban Speech-Community.* Publications of the Philological Society, XXIV. Oxford: Basil Blackwell

LEVITT, J. (1968) *North Staffordshire Speech*. Keele: Department of Adult Education, University of Keele

NICHOLS, R. (1934) *Dialect Words and Phrases used in the Staffordshire Potteries*. Knightley, Madeley, Crewe

POOLE, C.H. (1880) *Attempt towards a Glossary of the Archaic and Provincial Words of the County of Stafford*. Stratford-upon-Avon: St Gregory's Press for the author

POOLE, C.H. and MILLER, M.H. (1968) *Staffordshire Dialect Glossaries with an introduction by John Levitt*. Stoke-on-Trent: Stoke-on-Trent City Libraries

POVEY, A. and RIDLER, A. (1973) *Arfur Tow Crate in Staffy Cher: A Humorous Guide to Potteries Dialect*. Stoke-on-Trent: Novel Productions

POVEY, A. and RIDLER, A. (1986) *The Second Book of Arfur Crate in Staffy Cher: Another Humorous Look at Potteries Dialect*. Stoke-on-Trent: Novel Productions

RAVEN, J. (1986) *Stories, Customs, Superstitions, Tales, Legends and Folklore of the Black Country and Staffordshire*. Wolverhampton: Broadside

SCOTT, A. (1972) *The First Book of Jabez (Stories in North Staffordshire Dialect)*. Audley, Stoke-on-Trent: A. Scott

SCOTT, A. (1973) *The Second Book of Jabez (Stories in North Staffordshire Dialect)*. Audley, Stoke-on-Trent: A. Scott

SCOTT, A. (1978) *The Third Book of Jabez (Stories in North Staffordshire Dialect)* Audley, Stoke-on-Trent: A. Scott

WILSON, D. (1970/71) The Phonology and Accidence of the Dialect of the North Staffordshire Potteries and a Glossary of Staffordshire Dialect Words. MA thesis, University of Birmingham

WILSON, D. (1974) *Staffordshire Dialect Words: A Historical Survey*. Stafford: Moorland Publishing Company

Local studies collection

City Central Library, Bethesda Street, Hanley, Stoke-on-Trent, ST1 3RS. Tel: 0782 285773

Walsall Library and Museum Services Department, Central Library, Lichfield Street, Walsall, West Midlands WS1 1TR. Tel: 0922 650069

Central Library, Snow Hill, Wolverhampton WV1 3AX. Tel: 0902 312025

Sandwell Central Library, High Street, West Bromwich B70 8DZ. Tel: 021–569 4904

Kidderminster Reference Library, Market Street, Kidderminster
DY10 1AD. Tel: 0562 824500
(Covers Worcestershire in general, with particular emphasis on the
north-western area, together with the nearer parts of Shropshire,
Staffordshire and the West Midlands.)

Records and cassettes

The Horn Dance
An ancient processional ritual performed every year in September
at Abbots Bromley
Folktracks Cassettes 30–110

The Processional Dance
Horn Dancers and Morris
Folktracks Video Cassette V9

The Jabez Album: Stories in the North Staffordshire Dialect
Written and performed by W.A. Bloor; recorded by dk PRO-
AUDIO, 24 Westlands Ave, Newcastle-under-Lyme, Staffs.

Herefordshire

Books

BONAPARTE, PRINCE LOUIS LUCIEN (1877) *On the Dialects
of Monmouthshire, Herefordshire, Worcestershire, Gloucestershire,
Berkshire, Oxfordshire, South Warwickshire, South Northamptonshire
Buckinghamshire, Hertfordshire, Middlesex and Surrey with a New
Classification of the English Dialects.* London: English Dialect Society
HAGGARD, A. (1972) *Dialect and Local Usages of Herefordshire.*
London: Grower Books
LEEDS, W. (1985) *Herefordshire Speech: The Southwest Midland Dialect
as Spoken in Herefordshire and Its Environs.* Kimbolton: Arch.
WATERS, I. (1982) *Folklore and Dialect of the Lower Wye Valley.* First
printed 1973, Chepstow: Chepstow Society

Cassettes

Blow the Windy Morning
Emily Bishop
Folktracks Cassettes 60–129

Worcestershire

Books

BERKELEY, M. and JENKINS, C. (1932) *A Worcestershire Word Book.* Worcester: Worcestershire Federation of Women's Institutes

BONAPARTE, PRINCE LOUIS LUCIEN (1877) *On the Dialects of Monmouthshire, Herefordshire, Worcestershire, Gloucestershire, Berkshire, Oxfordshire, South Warwickshire, South Northamptonshire, Buckinghamshire, Hertfordshire, Middlesex and Surrey with a New Classification of the English Dialects.* London: English Dialect Society

CHAMBERLAIN, Mrs. (1882) *A Glossary of West Worcestershire Words.* London: English Dialect Society

JONES, L.M. (1972) *Customs and Folklore of Worcestershire.* London: Estragon

LAWSON, R. (1884) *Upton-On-Severn Words and Phrases* London: Trübner for the English Dialect Society

NORTHALL, G.F. (1965) *Folk-Phrases of Four Counties (Glouc., Staffs., Warw., Worc.), Gathered from Unpublished MSS. and Oral Traditions.* Vaduz: Kraus Reprint Ltd.

SALISBURY, J. (1893) *A Glossary of Words Used in S.E. Worcestershire.* J. Salisbury

TOMKINSON, K. (1981) *Words of Old Worcestershire.* Kidderminster: Kenneth Thompson

Local studies collections

Worcester City Library, Foregate Street, Worcester WR1 1DT.
Tel: 0905 765314
(Covers the old county of Worcestershire and the City of Worcester.)

Kidderminster Reference Library, Market Street, Kidderminster DY10 1AD.
Tel: 0562 824500
(Covers Worcestershire in general, with particular emphasis on the north-western area, together with the nearer parts of Shropshire, Staffordshire and the West Midlands.)

Warwickshire

Books

BONAPARTE, PRINCE LOUIS LUCIEN (1877) *On the Dialects*

of Monmouthshire, Herefordshire, Worcestershire, Gloucestershire, Berkshire, Oxfordshire, South Warwickshire, South Northamptonshire, Buckinghamshire, Hertfordshire, Middlesex and Surrey with a New Classification of the English Dialects. London: English Dialect Society

COLLINS, H. (1964) A Phonology of the Dialect of Southern Warwickshire. Unpublished PhD thesis, University of Yale, cf. Dissertation Abstracts 25: 5266–67

TENNANT, R. (1982) The Book of Brum, or, 'Mikeya selfa tum': Random Thoughts on the Dialect and Accent of the Second City (Brumslag). Sutton Coldfield: Westwood

TENNANT, R. (1983) Aware Din Urea: A Second Book of Brum. Sutton Coldfield: Westwood

Special collections

The Reference Library, Chamberlain Square, Birmingham B3 3HQ. Tel: 021 235 4220

The Local Studies Department contains material on Birmingham, Black Country, Staffordshire and West Midlands dialects. Tel: 021 235 4220

The Archives Department has dialect material, including radio programmes, in the form of tapes and transcripts of the Charles Parker archive. Tel: 021 235 4217

The Music Library has a small number of dialect recordings. Tel: 021 235 2482

The Language and Literature Department has a small number of ballads and poems in dialect and quite various books on dialect grammar. Tel: 021 235 4227

Warwickshire Library, Barrack Street, Warwick CV34 4TH. Tel: 0926 493431

Monmouthshire

Books

BONAPARTE, PRINCE LOUIS LUCIEN (1877) On the Dialects of Monmouthshire, Herefordshire, Worcestershire, Gloucestershire, Berkshire, Oxfordshire, South Warwickshire, South Northamptonshire, Buckinghamshire, Hertfordshire, Middlesex and Surrey with a New Classification of the English Dialects. London: English Dialect Society

GLADWELL, A. (1973) Patterns in Distribution: an Intensive Study of the Dialect and Tradition in Rural and Industrial Monmouthshire. Unpublished PhD thesis, University College, Swansea

PARRY, D. (1964) Studies in the Linguistic Geography of Radnorshire, Breconshire, Monmouthshire and Glamorganshire. MA thesis, University of Leeds

WATERS, I. (1973) *Chepstow Talk.* I. Waters

Local studies collection

Central Library, John Frost Square, Newport NP9 1PA. Tel: 0633 265539

Cotswolds (Gloucestershire and parts of, Somerset, Wiltshire, Oxfordshire, Worcestershire and Warwickshire)

Records

Down to Earth
Eighty-six year old Mrs Emily Elliot in 1962 recalls the life of the poor at the turn of the century
CSDL 247

Forest Talk
Forest of Dean Humour with Winifred Foley, Keith Morgan, Harry Beddington and Dick Brice in verse, prose and song
CSDL 316

Cotswold Craftsmen
Recollections of thatching, cider-making, wheel-wrighting, hurdle making, working with oxen, Gloucester cheese, the Cotswold roof, wall and sheep
CSDL 247

Cotswold Voices
George & Dorcas Juggins tell all about snuff-taking, their courting days; Bert Butler recalls bath nights, 'oss mucking and a lot more
CSDL 267

While I work
Songs and humour of the Cotswolds
CSDL 300

All from Saydisc records, Chipping Manor, The Chipping, Wotton-under-Edge, GL12 7AD.

Gloucestershire

Books

BARTH, E. (1968) The Dialect of Naunton (Gloucestershire). Dissertation (Swiss Ph.D) University of Zurich

BONAPARTE, PRINCE LOUIS LUCIEN (1877) *On the Dialects of Monmouthshire, Herefordshire, Worcestershire, Gloucestershire, Berkshire, Oxfordshire, South Warwickshire, South Northamptonshire, Buckinghamshire, Hertfordshire, Middlesex and Surrey with a New Classification of the English Dialects.* London: English Dialect Society

HALL, G.E. (n.d.) *William Wurkman's Wit and Wisdom: Sketches in the Gloucestershire Dialect*, 2nd edn. Stroud News: Stroud

HARGREAVES, A. (1904) *A Grammar of the Dialect of Adlington (Gloucs).* Heidelberg

JOHNS, S.U. (ed.) (n.d.) *Forest Folk: Poems by Marina Lambert, Illustrations and Stories by W.B. Johns.* Lydney, Glos: M.D. Jenkins (printers for the authors)

MORGAN, K. (1978) *The 'Azards O' Chimuck Szwippin.* Coleford: Douglas McLean, Forest Bookshop

NORTHALL, G.F. (1965) *Folk-Phrases of Four Counties (Glouc., Staffs., Warw., Worc.), Gathered from Unpublished MSS. and Oral Traditions.* Vaduz: Kraus Reprint Ltd

PRICE, M.D.K. (1972) *Songs, Stories and a Mummer's Play from Gloucestershire.* Cheltenham: W.L. Langsbury, Tivoli

MORETON, Lord (ed.) (1890) *Glossary of Dialect and Archaic Words Used in the County of Gloucester, collected and compiled by J. Drummond Robertson.* London: English Dialect Society

Local studies collections

Gloucester Library, Brunswick Road, Gloucester GL1 1HT. Tel: 0452 426977)

Central Library, College Green, Bristol BS1 5TL. Tel: 0272 276121) Newspaper cuttings on dialect of Bristol, Gloucestershire and Somersetshire (Mounted Material 427).

The 'Azards o' Chimuck Szwippin

'Ast ever swep a chimuck
Ta earn theeself a bob?
Old 'Arry 'ave an' 'im da know
The 'azards o' thic job
The neighbour's 'ad some soot down
The biggest pile 'er'd seen.
So 'er decides ta fetch a mon
Ta szwip thic blighter clean.
"Er goes across to 'Arry's
Ta ex 'im if 'e knew
Of any mon wi' 'hout ta spare
Ta come an' szwip 'er flue.
Old 'Arry thought a minute
'Bout the merits of the job,
An' come ta the decision
That 'e could use a bob.
"I'll szwip thee chimuck far tha"
Old 'Arry volunteered,
"Thou give I couple 'a 'ours
An' I'll 'ave thic blighter cleared
Im shouted ta the neighbour
Ta take a look out back.
An' tell 'im when the brush wus through
Above the chimney stack
'Er stood outside about an hour
But nothing did appear.
Tho' 'Arry'd used up thirty rods
The top were no'where near.

(From K.W. Morgan's
The 'Azards O' Chimuck Szwippin, p. 35)

Cassettes

Marshfield Paperboys
Christmas Mummers from a village on the Gloucestershire-Wiltshire border
Folktracks Cassettes 30–104

The Old Stable Jacket
Traditions of Glos-shire
Folktracks Cassettes 45–415

All Brought Up on Cider
Traditions of Glos-shire 2
Folktracks Cassettes 45–416

Oxfordshire

Books

BONAPARTE, PRINCE LOUIS LUCIEN (1877) *On the Dialects of Monmouthshire, Herfordshire, Worcestershire, Gloucestershire, Berkshire, Oxfordshire, South Warwickshire, South Northamptonshire, Buckinghamshire, Hertfordshire, Middlesex and Surrey with a New Classification of the English Dialects.* London: English Dialect Society

Local studies collection

Central Library, Westgate, Oxford OX1 1DJ. Tel: 0865 815749)

Cassettes

Country Gardens
William Kimber talks on a wide range of topics including dancing, local customs, May Day and Mummers
Folktracks cassette 90–083

Constant Billy
William Wells, Fool, dancer and fiddler to the Morris troupe at Brampton-in-the-Bush
Folktracks cassette 90–084

8.5   The East Midland Counties and East Anglia

Books

ORTON, H. and TILLING, P. (1971) *Survey of English Dialects (B) Basic Material, Vol. 3, Parts 1–3: The East Midland Counties and East Anglia.* Leeds. E.J. Arnold for the University of Leeds

Cassettes

As She is Spoke 2
Dialect: Midlands and East
Folktracks Cassettes 60–452

Nottinghamshire

Books

GRANGER, M. (1974) *Far Above Rubies: a Short Story in the Idiom of the Trent Villages*. M. Granger
WATSON, O.V. (1975) *Strong i' th' arm: the Rhymes of a Marlpool Miner*. Marlpool: the author
WRIGHT, P. (1986) *The Notts Natter: How It is Spoke*. Clapman, Lancaster: Dalesman.

Local studies collection

County Library, Angel Row, Nottingham NG1 6HP. Tel: 0602 412121

Lincolnshire

Books

BROGDEN, J.E. (1866) *Provincial Words and Expressions Current in Lincolnshire*. London: Robert Hardwicke
BROWN, J. (1862) *The Rural Fete or Zeb. Gosling's Description of the Gala in Scrivelsby Park: a Lincolnshire Tale in the Dialect of the County*. Horncastle: Harrison
BROWN, J. (1980) *Literae Laureatae; or a Selection from the Poetical Writings in Lincolnshire Language ... with Introduction, Life and Explanatory Notes by J. Conway Walter*. Horncastle: W.K. Morton
BROWN, R. (1968–9) *A Grammar of the Dialect of Great Hale, Lincolnshire*, 2 vols. Unpublished M.Phil, University of Leeds
CAMPION, G. (1976) *Lincolnshire Dialects*. Boston, Lincs: Richard Kay
COLE, E.E.G. (1886) *A Glossary of Words used in South-West Lincolnshire*. London: Trübner & Co. for the English Dialect Society
DOBSON, F. (1964) *Life and Laughter in Lincolnshire Dialect and Other Poems*. Louth: Atkinson & Wilcox
DOBSON, F. (1971) *Lincolnshire Laughs Ageean! Dialect in Prose and Poem*. Lincolnshire: L.S.G. Printers Ltd.
DUDLEY, E.S. (1965) *Lovely Lincolnshire Poems for Everybody and Festival Tests*. Barton-on-Humber: Mrs E.S. Dudley
GILBERT, B. (1911) *Lincolnshire Lays*. Horncastle: W.K. Morton & Sons
GILBERT, B. (1915) *Gone to the War, and Other Poems in the Lincolnshire Dialect*. Lincoln: J.W. Ruddock

GOOD, J. (1973) *A Glossary or Collection of Words, Phrases, Place Names, Superstitions etc. Current in East Lincolnshire.* Skegness: Skegness Publicity Service, 41 Lumley Road, Skegness, Lincs. PE25 3LL

MALKINSON, S. (1934) *Jonathan Trumpitt Spins the Yarn.* Lincoln: Chronicle and Leader

MALKINSON, Rev S. (1935) *Jonathan Trumpitt Tells the Tale!* Lincoln: Chronicle and Leader

MALKINSON, Rev S. (1936) *Jonathan Trumpitt Speaks His Mind.* Lincolnshire: Lincolnshire Chronicle and Leader

OXLEY, J. (1940) *The Lyndsey Dialect.* London: Titus Wilson

PEACOCK, E. (1889) *A Glossary of Words Used in the Wapentakes of Manley and Corringham, Lincolnshire,* 2nd edn. London: Trübner & Co., for the English Dialect Society

PEACOCK, M. (1886) *Tales and Rhymes in the Lindsey Folk-Speech.* Brigg: George Jackson/London: Geo. Bell

PEACOCK, M. (1889) *Taales fra Linkisheere.* Brigg, George, Jackson & Son/London: Simpkin, Marshall

ROBSON, F. (1964) *Life and Laughter in Lincolnshire Dialect and Other Poems.* Louth: Atkinson & Wilcox

RAWNSLEY, W.F. (1914) *Highways and Byways in Lincolnshire.* London: Macmillan

SUTTON, E. (1881) *North Lincolnshire Words.* London: Trübner & Co. for the English Dialect Society

Local studies collection

Central Reference Library, Freeschool Lane, Lincoln LN2 1EZ. Tel: 0522 549160

Records and cassettes

Two Poems in Lincolnshire Dialect by Alfred Tennyson
Read by Edward Champion
Lincolnshire Association (now called Lincolnshire and Humberside Arts) LA/1, 1969

Three Poems in Lincolnshire Dialect by Alfred Tennyson
Read by Edward Champion, 1969
Lincolnshire Association (now called Lincolnshire and Humberside Arts) LA/2, 1969

Two Poems in Lincolnshire Dialect by Alfred Tennyson
Read by Edith Burgess

Lincolnshire Association (now called Lincolnshire and Humberside Arts) LA/3, 1970

In comes I, Tom Fool
Lincolnshire Plough Plays
Folktracks Cassettes 60–105

Brigg Fair
Mary Taylor
Folktracks Cassettes 45–135

Fred Dobson in Dialect
Lincolnshire County Council Recreational Services

Unto Brigg Fair
Folk music recorded by Vicky Clayton, John Conolly, Brian Dawson and Maureen Sutton Lincolnshire County Council Recreational Services

Reflections in Lincolnshire and the Fens
Paul Eady and Bob Brooker, Lindum 1988

All available from the Museum of Lincolnshire Life, Burton Road, Lincoln LN1 3LY

Museums

Museum of Lincolnshire Life, Burton Road, Lincoln. Tel: 0522 528448
Recordings of Lincolnshire Dialect are held in the museum's archives and dialect records and cassettes are on sale in the Museum shop.

Leicestershire and Rutland

Books

EVANS, A.B. and EVANS, S. (1881) *Leicestershire Words, Phrases and Proverbs*, First printed London: Pickering, 1848, 2nd edn. London: Trübner & Co. for the English Dialect Society
FORSTER, W. (ed.) (1969) *Pit-talk: A Survey of Terms Used by Miners in the South Midlands*. Leicester: University of Leicester
HIND LEYS LOCAL HISTORY GROUP (1981) *Padgeowling*. Hind Leys LHG

RUTLAND LOCAL HISTORY SOCIETY (1977) *Dialect in Rutland: A dictionary of Rutland Words*. Oakham: RLHS
WORDSWORTH, C. (1891) *Rutland Words*. London: English Dialect Society

Local studies collection

Leicestershire Collection, Leicestershire Libraries and Information Service, Information Centre, Bishop Street, Leicester LE1 6AA. Tel: 0533 556699

Northamptonshire

Books

BAKER, A.E. (1854) *Glossary of Northamptonshire Words and Phrases* 2 vols. London: J.R. Smith
BONAPARTE, PRINCE LOUIS LUCIEN (1877) *On the Dialects of Monmouthshire, Herefordshire, Worcestershire, Gloucestershire, Berkshire, Oxfordshire, South Warwickshire, South Northamptonshire, Buckinghamshire, Hertfordshire, Middlesex and Surrey with a New Classification of the English Dialects*. London: English Dialect Society
NORMAN, R.W. (n.d.) *Keep Laughing With Air Ada: A Selection of Cartoons, Conversation Pieces and Rhymes by R.W.N. in Aid of the Rushden St John Ambulance Motor Ambulance Appeal*. Rushden, Northants: St John Ambulance
STERNBERG, T. (1971) *The Dialect and Folk-lore of Northamptonshire*. First published London: J.R. Smith (1851), this edition Wakefield: S.R. Publishers

Local studies collection

Central Library, Abington Street, Northampton NN11 2BA. Tel: 0604 26771/2

Cambridgeshire

Books

BEAUCHAMP, A.C. (1977) *A Study of the Chatteris Dialect*. Brighton: Richard Coates, Arts E333, University of Sussex, Falmer, Brighton BN1 9QN
HUDDLESTON, N.A. (1957) *Lore and Laughter of South Cambridgeshire*. St Tibbs, for N.A. Hudleston

STRATTON, B. (1978) *A Study of Phonological Variables in Cambridge*. Brighton: Richard Coates, Arts E333, University of Sussex, Falmer, Brighton BN1 9QN

Local studies collection

Central Library, 7 Lion Yard, Cambridge CB2 3QD. Tel: 0223 65252

East Anglia

Books

FORBY, R. (1970) *The Vocabulary of East Anglia*. London 1830, facsimile reproduction Newton Abbot: David and Charles

NALL, J.G. (1866) *An Etymological and Comparative Glossary of the Dialect and Provincialisms of East Anglia*

ORTON, H. (1971) *Survey of English Dialects (B), Vol. 3: The East Midland Counties and East Anglia, Parts 1–3*. Leeds: E.J. Arnold for the University of Leeds

RYE, W. (1895) *Glossary of Words Used in East Anglia, Founded on that of Forby*. London: H. Frowde, OUP for the English Dialect Society

SKEAT, W.W. (ed.) (1879) *East Anglian Words*. Reprinted Glossaries XX. London: English Dialect Society

Records and cassettes

Rum owd folk: Some East Anglian characters
James Wentworth Day
331/3 sound disc, 1977

East Anglian Pageant
Folklore, Dialect, Music, Humour, Stories from East Anglia's Past
331/3 sound disc, 1977

Norfolk

Books

MARDLE, J. (1973) *Broad Norfolk*. Norwich: Wensum Books

TRUDGILL, P. (1979) *The Social Differentiation of English in Norwich*. London: Cambridge University Press

TRUDGILL, P. (1980) *A Sociolinguistic Study of Linguistic Change in Urban East Anglia*. End of-Grant-Report HR 2672 to the Social Science Research Council

Local studies collection

Central Library, Bethel Street, Norwich NR2 1NJ Tel: 0603 611277

Records and cassettes

Dinner is Served: interview with a Norwich farmer
BBC disc, 78 r.p.m., 12th October, 1935

Talk about Norwich-Over-The-Water in the 1920s in the Norwich dialect
Ted Snelling, 1974; 20 min. cassette

Talk about Norwich-Over-The-Water in the 1950s in the Norwich dialect
Ted Snelling, 1974; 45 min. cassette
All in the holdings of the Central Library, Bethel Street, Norwich NR2 1NJ

Seventeen Come Sunday
Harry Cox
Folktracks cassettes 60–032

Jack on the Rocks
Harry Cox
Folktracks cassettes 60–033

The Barley Straw
Harry Cox
Folktracks cassettes 60–034

Rabbit Pie
Fred Rooke
Folktracks cassette 60–044

The Smacksman
Tom Brown
Folktracks Cassette 60–133

The Great Meat Pie
Tom Brown
Folktracks Cassette 60–134

Over the Dogger Bank
Sam Larner
Folktracks Cassette 60–139

Rig-A-Jig-Jig
Norfolk village music and talk
Folktracks Cassette 30–328

Suffolk

Books

BUSBY, W. and WASE, F.W. (1914) *Hodge Podge; or a Suffolk Medley*. Halesworth
CLAXTON, A.O.D. (1981) *The Suffolk Dialect of the Twentieth Century*. Ipswich: N. Adland, 1968, reprinted as *Suffolk Dialect*. Woodbridge, Suffolk: Boydell Press
COOPER, E.R. (1932) *Mardles from Suffolk: Tales of the South Folk*. Cranton
KÖKERITZ, H. (1932) *The Phonology of the Suffolk Dialect*. Uppsala
GROOME, F.H. (1895) *Two Suffolk Friends*. Edinburgh: Blackwood
JOBSON, A. (1944) *Suffolk Yesterdays*. London: Heath Cranton
MOOR (1970) *Suffolk Words and Phrases*. First published 1823; this edition Newton Abbot: David and Charles
PARTRIDGE, C. (1925) *Prose and Poetry by 'Silly Suffolk'*. Ipswich
SKEAT, W.W. (ed.) (1879) *Suffolk Words*. Reprinted Glossaries XXI London: English Dialect Society

Local studies collection

Arts and Libraries Dept., St Andrew's House, County Hall, Ipswich IP4 2JS. Tel: 0473 230000

Records, video cassettes and sound cassettes

Down at the 'Old Ship'
Saturday Night sing-song at Blaxhall, Suffolk in 1953
Folktracks cassette 60–036

The Foggy Dew
Suffolk and Essex Singers
Folktracks cassette 60–040

The Knife in the Window
7 Suffolk Singers
Folktracks cassette 60–099

The Barley Mow
Suffolk pub-singing and stepping
Folktracks Video Cassette V5

Bedfordshire

Books

BURGON, J.W. (1868) *Provincialisms of West Bedfordshire: Glossary of Words and Phrases.* Bedford: Bedfordshire Times and Independent

SHAW, D.H. (1958) A Comparative Study (Descriptive and Historical) of the Dialect of Bedfordshire, Based Upon a Survey Conducted in Five widely Spread areas of the County. Unpublished PhD thesis, Kings College, University of London

WATSON, E.W. (1917) Dialect of Sutton, Beds. (Supplementary to Wright's Dialect Dictionary) *Modern Languages Review* 12: 354–6

Local studies collection

Bedford Central Library, Harpur Street, Bedford MK 40 1PG. Tel: 0234 350931

Buckinghamshire

Books

BONAPARTE, PRINCE LOUIS LUCIEN (1877) *On the Dialects of Monmouthshire, Worcestershire, Gloucestershire, Berkshire, Oxfordshire, South Warwickshire, Herefordshire, South Northamptonshire, Buckinghamshire, Hertfordshire, Middlesex and Surrey with a New Classification of the English Dialects.* London: English Dialect Society

HARMAN, H. (1970) *Buckinghamshire Dialect.* Wakefield: S.R. Publishers

Local studies collection

Central Library, Walton Street, Aylesbury HP20 1UU. Tel: 0296 383206

Essex

Books

BENHAM, C. (1895) *Essex Ballads*. Colchester: Benham & Co.
CLARK, C. (1856) *September; or Sport on Sporting! by Doggerel Drydog of Totham*. Great Totham: Charles Clark
CLARK, C. (n.d.) *A Doctor's Doings; or the entrapped heiress of Witham*. Totham: Charles Clark
CRANMER-BYNG, H. (1934) *Dialect and Songs of Essex*. Colchester: Benham & Co.
GEPP, E. (1969) *An Essex Dialect Dictionary*. First published London: Routledge, 1923, this edition Wakefield: S.R. Publishers
SLAUGHTER, B. (1981) *Essex and Suffolk Alphabet*. B. Slaughter, 6 Park Lane, Bulmer
SMITH, C. (1978) *The Fading Essex Dialect*. Hornchurch: Hobby Horse

Local studies collection

Colchester Central Library, Trinity Square, Colchester CO1 1JB. Tel: 0206 562243

Cassettes

The Foggy Dew
Suffolk and Essex Singers
Folktracks cassette 60–040

Hertfordshire

Books

BONAPARTE, PRINCE LOUIS LUCIEN (1877) *On the Dialects of Monmouthshire, Herefordshire, Worcestershire, Gloucestershire, Berkshire, Oxfordshire, South Warwickshire, South Northamptonshire, Buckinghamshire, Hertfordshire, Middlesex and Surrey with a New Classification of the English Dialects*. London: English Dialect Society
CARBURY, LADY M. and GREY, E. (1948) *Hertfordshire Heritage: Ourselves and Our Words*. London: John Green
CUSSANS, J.E. (1870–81) *A History of Hertfordshire* (esp. vol. 3, pp. 320–21 on Hertfordshire words). London: Chatto and Windus
GREY, E. (1934) *Cottage Life in a Hertfordshire Village*. London: Fisher, Knight & Co. (see pp. 40–43)

NELSEY, R.A. (1986) *Remember Markyate, Flamstead and Trowley.*
Buckingham: Barracuda Books
NIXON, D.B. (1977) *Walk Soft in the Fold.* London: Chatto &
Windus

Local studies collection

Local Studies Collection, Hertfordshire Library Service, County
Hall, Hertford SG13 8EJ. Tel: 0992 556624

London, Middlesex and Surrey

Books

AYLWIN, R. (1973) *A Load of Cockney Cobblers.* Edinburgh: Johnston
and Bacon
BARKER, R. (1979) *Fletcher's Book of Rhyming Slang.* London: Pan
BALTROP, R. and WOLVERIDGE, J. (1980) *The Muvver Tongue.*
London: Journeyman
BEAKEN, M. (1971) A Study of the Phonological Development in a
Primary School Population of East London. Unpublished PhD thesis,
University of London
BONAPARTE, PRINCE LOUIS LUCIEN (1877) *On the Dialects
of Monmouthshire, Herefordshire, Worcestershire, Gloucestershire,
Berkshire, Oxfordshire, South Warwickshire, South Northamptonshire,
Buckinghamshire, Hertfordshire, Middlesex and Surrey with a New
Classification of the English Dialects.* London: English Dialect Society
BOWYER, R. (1973) A Study of the Social Accents in a South London
Suburb. Unpublished MPhil dissertation, University of Leeds
DODSON, M. and SACZEK, R. (1972) *A Dictionary of Cockney Slang
and Rhyming Slang.* London: Hedgehog Enterprises
FRANKLYN, J. (1975) *A Dictionary of Rhyming Slang.* London:
Routledge and Kegan Paul
HURFORD, J. (1969) *The Speech of One Family: A Phonetic Comparison
of the Three Generations in a Family of East Londoners.* Unpublished
PhD thesis, University of London
JONES, J. (1984) *Rhyming Cockney Slang.* Bristol: Abson
KENDALL, S. (1969) *Up the Frog: the Road to Cockney Rhyming Slang.*
London: Wolfe
LAWRENCE, J. (1975) *Rabbit and Pork, Rhyming Talk.* London:
Hamilton
LEITH, R. (1971) Dialectology in London. Unpublished MA thesis,
University of Leeds

LEITH, R. (1973) The Traditional Phonology of North London Speech. Unpublished M.Phil thesis, University of Leeds

MATTHEWS, W. (1972) *Cockney Past and Present: A Short History of the Dialect of London*, 2nd edn. London: Routledge and K. Paul

SIVERTSEN, E. (1960) *Cockney Phonology*. Oslo: Oslo University Press

WRIGHT, P. (1981) *Cockney Dialect and Slang*. London: Batsford

Local studies collections

London Library, 14 St James Square, London SW1Y 4LG. Tel: 071 930 7705/6)

County Library HQ, West Street, Dorking, Surrey RH4 1DE. Tel: 0306 884444)

Middlesex University. Tel. 081 368 1299)

Cassettes

Little Johnny Brown
'Lucky' Luckhurst with songs, stories, street-lore of London life
Folktracks Cassettes 45–131

Knees Up, Mother Brown
'Lucky' Luckhurst with songs, stories, street-lore of London life
Folktracks Cassettes 60–132

Somebody Under the Bed
Kids Play: Home Counties
Folktracks Cassettes 30–202

The Four Horse Chara'
John Foreman performs London Music Hall songs
Folktracks Cassettes 30–210

8.6 The Southern Counties

Books

ORTON, H. (ed.) (1967) *Survey of English Dialects (B), Vol. 4: The Southern Counties, Part 1–3*, London: E.J. Arnold for the University of Leeds

BONAPARTE, PRINCE L.L. (1877) *On the Dialects of Eleven Southern and South Western Counties*. London: English Dialect Society

KURATH, H. and LOWMAN, G. Jr. (1974) *The Dialectal Structure of Southern England: Phonological Evidence.* Publication of the American Dialect Society 54

The South West

Books

AGRIKLER (*pseud.*) (Edwards, J.) (1872) *Rhymes in the West of England Dialect*, 2nd edn. Bristol: Leech and Taylor
BURTON, S.H. (ed.) (1975) *A West Country Anthology.* London: Hale
COCK, D.J. (1980) *Jan Stewer: A Westcountry Biography.* Bradford-on-Avon: Moonraker
DAVEY, C. (1983) *West Country Place-Names and What They Mean.* Bristol: Abson
HARRIS, W.G. (1931) *Old Words and Old Ways: A Book of Westcountry Ballads and Poems.* Tiverton: Gregory & Son
HARRIS, W.G. (1901) *Sketches of the West Countree.* Exeter: Besley & Dalgleish
HARRIS, W.G. (1910?) *Down Along O' We: Westcountry Sketches, Stories, and Verses.* Tiverton: Gregory & Son; Exeter: S. Drayton & Sons
HARRIS, W.G. (1923) *Zummerset Volk and Devonshire Diversions.* Tiverton: Gregory & Son: Torquay: Gregory & Scott
HARTIER, O. and HARTIER, M. (1896?) *Home Brewed from the West Country.* London: Simpkin, Marshall, Hamilton, Kent & Co.; Exeter: Henry S. Eland
OUTIS (pseud.) (1875) *Poems, Humorous and Philosophical . . . with which are included Rhymes in the West of England Dialect by Agrikler.* Bristol: J. Wright & Co.
PHILLIPS, K.C. (1976) *Westcountry Words and Ways.* Newton Abbot: David and Charles
PULMAN, G. (1853) *Rustic Sketches: Being Rhymes on Angling and Other Subjects Illustrative of Rural Life, etc. in the Dialect of the West of England, with Notes and a Glossary* London: John Gray Bell
PULMAN, G. (1853) *Rustic Sketches: Being Rhymes and 'Skits' on Angling and Other Subjects, in One of the South-western Dialects,* 3rd edn. London: John Russell Smith
ROBINSON, D. (1973) *Stand by for Blasting.* Abson, Wick: Bristol
SLOW, E. (1899) *Humorous West Countrie Tales.* Salisbury: R. R. Edwards
WAKELIN, M. (1986) *The South West of England.* Varieties of English Around the World 15, Amsterdam: John Benjamins

Local studies collection

Westcountry Studies Library, Castle Street, Exeter EX4 3PQ.
Tel: 0392 384216

Records and cassettes

Mainsail Haul
Songs, shanties and yarns from West country sailor Paddy Walsh
Folktracks Cassettes 60–206

Thatcher's Talk
2 craftsmen talking
Folktracks Cassettes 30–411

Tregeagle's Ghost
West Country folklore
Folktracks Cassettes 60–412

As She Is Spoke 3
Dialect: South and West
Folktracks Cassettes 60–453

My Old Chap
The poems of Norman Goodland
Record SDL 320; cassette CSDL 320
Saydisc records, Chipping Manor, The Chipping, Wotton-under-Edge, Glos. GL12 7AD

Somersetshire

Books

BURROWS, RAY 'BUGS' (1980) *Bide Awhile Wi'I: Somerset Dialect Poems*. Castle Carey: Castle Carey Press
CLARK, R. (1975) *Somerset Anthology: Twenty-Four Pieces Edited by Percy Lovell*. York: William Sessions
COX, J.S. (ed.) (1970) *Somerset Dialect Poems*. First published in the 'Graphic and Historical Illustrator', 1832 Guernsey: Toucan Press.
COX, J.S. (1974) *An Ilchester Word List and Some Folklore Notes: a Glossary of Words, Phrases and Rhymes used at Ilchester and Recorded before 1925*. St Peter Port: Toucan Press.
COX, J.S. and STEVENS, J. (1983) *More Ilchester Words, Sayings and Some Folklore Notes, Early 19th to Early 20th Century*. St Peter Port: Toucan Press

DOWTY, A.A. (1889) *'Zummerzet' Rhymes: Poems by 'Jan' and 'Tommy Nutty'*. 2nd edn, Houlston.

ELWORTHY, F.T. (1875–88) *The Dialect of West Somerset and East Devon*. London: English Dialect Society

ELWORTHY, F.T. (1886) *The West Somerset Word Book: a Glossary of Dialectical and Archaic Words and Phrases Used in the West of Somerset and East Devon*. London: Trübner

GARTON, J.A. (1936) *Glowing Embers from a Somerset Hearth*. Wells: Clare

GASS, D.J. (1922) *Down-along Talks by 'Dan'l Grainger'*. Somerset Folk Press

GASS, D.J. (1926) *More Down-along Talks by 'Dan'l Grainger'*. Somerset Folk Press

GREGORY, R.R.C. (1922) *Poems in Dialect*. Somerset Folk Press

HALL, M. and CROMWELL, A. (1984) *Bristol: Swanna Look Rown . . . Er Wot?* Bristol: Er Wot Publications

HALLIWELL-PHILLIPS, J.O. (ed.) (1843) *A Collection of Pieces in the Dialect of Zummerzet*. London: J. Russell Smith

HODGER, B. (pseud.) (1924) *Down Whoäme*, Somerset Folk Press

HUMPHRIES, S. (1981) *Hooligans or Rebels? An Oral History of Working-Class Childhood and Youth 1889–1939*. London: Routledge & Kegan Paul

JENNINGS, J. (1825) *Observations on Some of the Dialects of the West of England, Particularly Somersetshire*. First printed London: Baldwin, Cradock & Joy, 1825, 2nd edn, revised and enlarged, London: John Russell Smith

JENNINGS, J. (1869) *The Dialect of the West of England, Particularly Somersetshire with a glossary of words now in use there; also with Poems and Other Pieces Exemplifying the Dialect*, 2nd edn. London: Smith

JONES, W.M. (1928) *Jarge Balsh Goes to Lunnon; The Zexton o'Zpringvield; and 'Zummat o' Nothing'*. London: Folk Press

JONES, W.M. (1930) *Somerset Songs and Verse*. London: Folk Press

JONES, W.M. (1967) *Our Village Parliament*. Frome: P. Ellenbray

JONES, W.M. (1967) *Jarge Balsh at Bristol Zoo*. Frome: P. Ellenbray

JONES, W.M. (1967) *Somerset Songs and Verse*. Frome: P. Ellenbray

JONES, W.M. (1967) *Discovering Somerset and Jarge Balsh. Jarge Balsh at the Frome Cheese Show. Jarge Balsh goes to Lunnon*. Frome: P. Ellenbray

KRUISINGA, E. (1905) *A Grammar of the Dialect of West Somerset*. Bonn: P. Hanstein

LEE, T. (1985) *Grease and Grime*. Bristol: Broadsides

LEE, T. (1978) *Shush – Mum's Writing*. Bristol: Broadsides

MACKIE, J. (1925) *Dialect Poems and a Play*. Somerset Folk Press
PAUL, A.D. (1916) *'I've Huard um Zay': Somerset dialect dialogue and other poems*. Bristol: Bristol Times and Mirror
PICARDA, G. de (1976) *Zongs vrom a Zummerzet Wine-Zellar*. Wells: G. de Picarda
PULMAN, G.P.R. (1853) *Rustic Sketches*. John Gray Bell
RAYMOND, W. (1921) *Selected Poems in Somerset Dialect*. Somerset Folk Press
RAYMOND, W. (1923) *Two Men o'Mendip: A Play in Four Acts*. Somerset Folk Press
ROBSON, D. (1970) *Krek Waiter's Peak Bristle: A Guide to What the Natives Say and Mean in the Heart of the Wess Vinglun*. Bristol: Abson
ROBSON, D. (1972) *Bristle Rides Again: A Third Guide to What the Natives Say and Mean in the Heart of the Wess Vinglun*. Bristol: Abson Books
ROBSON, D. (1973) *Sick Sundered Yers of Bristle, 1373–1974*. Bristol: Abson
ROBSON, D. (1982) *Son of Bristle, A Second Guide to What the Natives Say and Mean in the Heart of the Wess Vinglun*. Bristol: Abson
ROGERS, N. (1979) *Wessex Dialect*. Bradford-on-Avon: Moonraker Press
STEWER, J. (Pseud) (COLES, A.J.) (1949) *On the Moor of a Night*. Taunton: Barnicoots Ltd., Wessex Press
WARBURG, J. and LORANT, T. (1985) *The Grockles' Guide: An Illustrated Miscellany of Words and Phrases of Interest and Use to 'Voreigners' in Somerset*. Wells: Thorn
WATSON, W. G. W. (1922) *The Land of Summer*. Somerset Folk Press
WATSON, W.G.W. (1924) *Somerset Life and Character*. Somerset Folk Press
WILLIAMS, W.P. and WILLIAMS, A.J. (1873) *A Glossary of Provincial Words and Phrases in use in Somersetshire*. London: Longmans, Green, Reader & Dyer
WILSON, H. (1912) *A Somerset Sketch-Book*. Dent
WOOD, F.H. (1922) *Tales of the Polden Hills*. Somerset Folk Press

Local studies collection   -

Central Library, College Green, Bristol BS1 5TL. Tel: (0272) 276121
Newspaper cuttings on dialect of Bristol, Gloucestershire and Somerset (Mounted Material) 427)

Local History Library, The Castle, Castle Green, Taunton TA1 4AD. Tel: 0823 288871

Video cassettes, records and sound cassettes

33SD 245 *Sounds of Bristol: A Portrait of Bristol in Sounds, Dialect and Song*
33SD 279 *Isambard Kingdom Brunel and Other Comical Saga'ls from our Area'l*
33SD 259 *George Woodruff Live*

33SD 260 *Old Pete's Christmas Story*
Saydisc Specialized Recordings Ltd, Ingelstone Common, Badminton, Glos. GL9 1BX

The Sailor's Horse
May Day Festival, Minehead
Folktracks Cassettes 60–216 and Video Cassette V2

Herchard of Taunton Dene
Village music from Somerset
Folktracks Cassettes 60–405

Somerset Farm Talk
Ernest Shire
Folktracks Cassettes 60–414

Wiltshire

Books

AKERMAN, J. (1842) *Glossary of Provincial Words and Phrases in Use in Wiltshire*. London: J.R. Smith
AKERMAN, J. (1850) *Spring Tide or The Angler and his Friends*. London: Richard Bentley
AKERMAN, J. (1853) *Wiltshire Tales*. London: J.R. Smith
CHANDLER, J. (ed.) (1982) *Figgetty pooden: the Dialect Verse of Edward Slow*. Trowbridge: Wiltshire Library and Museum Service
DARTNELL, A. and GODDARD, D. (1893) *Glossary of Words Used in the County of Wiltshire*. London: English Dialect Society
GURNEY, P. (*pseud.* Smith, C.S.) (1985) *Shepherds' Lore*. Gloucester: Alan Sutton Publishing. Available from the Wiltshire Folk Life Society

JONES, M. and DILLON, P. (1987) *Dialect in Wiltshire and its Historical, Topographical and Natural Science Contexts*. Trowbridge: Wiltshire County Council, Library and Museum Service

KJEDERQVIST, J. (1903) *The Dialect of Pewsey (Wiltshire)*. London

MORRISON, J. (n.d.) *Wiltshire Folksongs*. Available from the Wiltshire Folk Life Society

ROGERS, N. (1979) *Wessex Dialect*. Bradford-on-Avon: Moonraker Press

SLOW, E. (1881) *Wiltshire Rhymes: A Series of Poems in the Wiltshire Dialects*. 2nd edn. London: Simpkin, Marshall

SLOW, E. (1899) *Humorous Wiltshire Rhymes*. Salisbury: R.R. Edwards

SLOW, E. (1899) *The Wiltshire Moonraker's Edition of West Countrie Rhymes*. Salisbury: R.R. Edwards

Cassettes

Marshfield Paperboys
Christmas Mummers from a village on the Gloucestershire-Wiltshire border
Folktracks cassetes 30–104

The Vly on the Turmuts
Wiltshire Village Music
Folktracks cassettes 45–406

Societies

Wiltshire Folk Life Society
The Great Barn, Avebury, Marlborough, Wiltshire

The Society was founded in 1975 to stimulate interest in Wiltshire life, culture, and history. Activities are focused on the Centre for the Interpretation of Wiltshire Life at the Great Barn, Avebury. The Great Barn has been restored by the Society and now houses its collection and records as well as a Study Centre and restaurant. The Society engages in practical research on aspects of Wiltshire life, including dialect, from the seventeenth century to the recent past. Displays and exhibitions are mounted at the Great Barn and meetings held throughout the county.

Wiltshire Folklife, the journal of the Society, is published twice a year and distributed free to members.

Wiltshire Archaeological and Natural History Society
41 Long Street, Devizes SN10 1NS. Tel: 0380 727369
The Society was formed in 1853 to 'protect the Antiquities' of
Wiltshire. That object has always been interpreted broadly enough
to include matters of dialect and folklore.
The Society's Library contains the most comprehensive collection
of books on Wiltshire in existence. In addition to its own journal,
the *Wiltshire Archaeological and Natural History Magazine*,
published since 1854, it stocks journals of other county societies.
It also has an extensive pamphlet collection and indexed press
cuttings from local and national newspapers since about 1850.
Opening hours: Tuesdays to Saturdays 10.00 a.m. to 1.00 p.m.
and 2.00 p.m. to 5.00 p.m. (4.00 p.m. in winter). The library is
closed throughout the month of January, on public holidays and
occasionally at other times without notice. Visitors and researchers
should confirm beforehand.

Local studies collection

Headquarters Local Studies Library, Wiltshire Library and
Museum Headquarters, Bythesea Road, Trowbridge BA14 8BS.
Tel: 0225 753641

Berkshire

Books

BONAPARTE, PRINCE LOUIS LUCIEN (1877) *On the Dialects
of Monmouthshire, Herefordshire, Worcestershire, Gloucestershire,
Berkshire, Oxfordshire, South Warwickshire, South Northamptonshire,
Buckinghamshire, Hertfordshire, Middlesex and Surrey with a New
Classification of the English Dialects*. London: English Dialect Society
CHESHIRE, J. (1982) *Variation in an English Dialect: A Sociolinguistic
Study*. Cambridge: Cambridge University Press
LOWSLEY, B. (1988) *Glossary of Berkshire Words and Phrases*. London:
Trübner & Co.

Local studies collections

Central Library, Abbey Square, Reading RG1 3BQ. Tel: 0734
509241

Kent

Books

BAKER, D. (1932) *Guide to Tunbridge Wells, Wid Summat Bout de Town Hall Writ and Prented in de Old Kentish Dialect*. J. Richards

BUCKINGHAM, C. (1973) *Dick and Sal at Canterbury Fair: An Early Nineteenth Century Poem in the Kentish Dialect of the Period*. Whitstable: Shoestring Press

MAJOR, A. (1981) *A New Directory of Kent Dialect*. Rainham: Meresborough Books

MASTERS, J.W. (1830) *'Dick and Sal' or J'ack and Joanses Fair'*: a *Doggerel Poem*, 3rd edn. Dover: Z. Warren

NORTH, D. (1979) Two West Kent Dialects: A Comparative Philological Study of the Dialects of Hever and Chiddingstone, Kent. Unpublished MA thesis, University of Leeds

PARISH, W.D. and SHAW, W.A. (1889) *A Dictionary of the Kentish Dialect and Provincialisms in Use in the County of Kent*. First published London: English Dialect Society, 1887, this edition Lewes: Farncombe & Co.

PEGGE, S. (1874) *An Alphabet of Kenticisms . . . to Which is Added a Collection of Proverbs and Old Sayings*. London: K.A.S.

SANDERS, F.W.T. (1935) *Kentish (Wealdon) Dialect*. Chatham: F.W.T. Sanders

SANDERS, F.W.T. (1950) *The Dialect of Kent*. Chatham: F.W.T. Sanders

SKEAT, W.W. (ed.) (1881) *Words Used in the Isle of Thanet by J. Lewis (Reprinted Glossaries)*. London: English Dialect Society

Local studies collection

County Library, Springfield, Maidstone, Kent ME14 2LH. Tel: 0622 671411

Cassettes

The Wealden Folk
Graeme Miles
Folktracks Cassettes 60–231

Cornwall

Books

BATTEN, B. (1984) *Old Newlyn Speech*. Newlyn: B. Batten

BENNETT, C. (1903) *A Cornish 'Bussa' and Eight Other Cornish Tales, in Prose and Verse*. 3rd edn. Truro: Netherton & North

COURTNEY, M.A. and COUCH, T.Q. (1880) *A Glossary of Words in Use in Cornwall: West Cornwall*. London: Trübner and Co.

DADDOW, D. (1875) *Cornish Comicalities in Prose and Verse*. Truro: James R. Netherton

DANIEL, H.J. (c. 1870?) *A Batch of Humorous Tales and Sketches*. Devonport: W. Wood and London: Houlston & Sons

DANIEL, H.J. (c. 1870?) *The Cornish Thalia; Being Original Comic Poems, Illustrative of The Cornish Dialect*. Devonport: W. Wood and London: Houlston & Wright

DANIEL, H.J. (c. 1870?) *A Companion for the Cornish Thalia; Being Original Humorous Pieces in the Cornish and Devonshire Dialects*. Devonport: W. Wood

DANIEL, H.J. (1870?) *Mary Anne in Retirement*. Devonport: W. Wood

DANIEL, H.J. (1870?) *Mary Anne in the Hands of the Philistines*. Devonport: W. Wood

DANIEL, H.J. (1870?) *Mary Anne's Career (continued) and Cousin Jack's Adventures*. Devonport: W. Wood and London: John Russell Smith

DANIEL, H.J. (1870?) *Mary Anne's Experiences*. Devonport: W. Wood and London: Houlston & Sons

DANIEL, H.J. (1870?) *Mary Anne's Sunday Out*. Devonport: W. Wood

DANIEL, H.J. (1870?) *Mary Anne's Trip up the Tamar*. Devonport: W. Wood

DANIEL, H.J. (1870?) *Mary Anne's Wedding*. Devonport: W. Wood

DANIEL, H.J. (1870?) *Mirth for Long Evenings*. Devonport: W. Wood and London: Houlston & Wright

DANIEL, H.J. (1870?) *The Muse in Motley or a Wallet of Whimsies*. Devonport: W. Wood and London: Houlston & Wright

DANIEL, H.J. (1870?) *Mirth for 'One and All'; or Comic Tales and Sketches*. Devonport: W. Wood and London: Houlston & Wright

DANIEL, H.J. (1870?) *A New Budget of Cornish Poems*. Devonport: W. Wood and London: Houlston & Wright

DANIEL, H.J. (1870?) *Pickings from my Portfolio; Comprising Cornish, Comic and Other Humorous Pieces*. Devonport: W. Wood and London: Houlston & Wright

DANIEL, H.J. (1871) *Wit and Humour; or Fun and Frolic*. Devonport: W. Wood and London: Houlston & Wright

DEXTER, T.F.G. (1926) *Cornish Names*. London: Longman

FORFAR, W.B. (1885) *Cornish Poems and Selections form Pentowan*. Truro: Netherton & Worth.

FULLER, J.B. (1870?) *Jack Junk and Caroline Jane of Stoke*. Devonport: W. Wood

GERVIS, M. (ed.) (1846) *Original Cornish Ballads; Chiefly Founded on Stories, Humorously told by Mr. Tregellas*. London: Simpkin & Marshall and Penryn: T. Whitehorn

HENWOOD, G. and DANIEL, H.J. (c. 1870?) *A Gret Mine Conference: The Gwennap Boys The Preeten Cappen; The Fox Outwitted by a Cook. A Legend of St Germans; A Dialogue About India, China, Railways and Unions; The Poor Man and His Parish Church*. Devonport: W. Wood; London: John Russell Smith

ISABELL, J. (1898) *Eight Cornish Temperance Tales in the Cornish Dialect*, 2nd edn. Truro: Netherton & Worth.

JAGO, F. (1882) *The Ancient Language and Dialect of Cornwall, with an Enlarged Glossary of Cornish Provincial Words*. Truro: Netherton & Worth

JAMES, B. (1979) *Cornish Faist*, Redruth: Truran Publications

JAMES, G. (1978) Variables in Relative Clause Structure in a Dialect of English. Unpublished MPhil thesis, University of Reading

LEAN, H. (1951) *A Collection of Short Cornish Dialect Stories*. Cambourne: H. Lean

LEAN, H. (1951) *A Continuation of Short Cornish Dialect Stories*. Cambourne: H. Lean

LEAN, H. (1951) *A Continuation of Short Cornish Dialect Stories*. (Book 4). Cambourne: H. Lean

LEAN, H. (1951) *A Continuation of Short Cornish Dialect Stories*, (Book 5). Cambourne: H. Lean

LEAN, H. (1952) *Book Three of Short Cornish Dialect Stories*. Cambourne: H. Lean

NEWALL, T. (1935) *Echoes from Carn, Cove and Cromlech by Nicky Trevaylor*. St Ives: James Lanham for the Federation of Old Cornish Societies

NOALL, R.J. (1934) *Cornish Patriotic and Dialect Songs*. St Ives: W. & J. Jacobs

NANCE, R.M. (1923) *A Glossary of Celtic Words in Cornish Dialect*. Royal Cornwall Polytechnic Society

NORTH, D.J. (1983) *Studies in Anglo-Cornish Phonology: Aspects of the History and Geography of English Pronunciation in Cornwall*. Redruth: Institute of Cornish Studies

NORTH, D.J. and SHARPE, A. (1980) *A Word-Geography of Cornwall*. Redruth: Institute of Cornish Studies

PASMORE, W.S. (1890?) *Captain O. Takes to Keeping a Coach*. Exeter: H. Besley & Son

PASMORE, W.S. (1890?) *I do's It Vor Exercise*. Exeter: H. Besley & Son

PASMORE, W.S. (1890?) *Old Stories of Devon and Cornwall*. Exeter: Henry S. Eland

PASMORE, W.S. (1890?) *The Mock Berryin', Sir Thomas Fry, and the Botus Fleming Overseers.* Exeter: H. Besley & Son

PASMORE, W.S. (1890?) *The Song of the Pressgang.* Exeter: H. Besley & Son

PASMORE, W.S. (1890?) *The Story of the Coachwheels,* 2nd edn. Exeter: H. Besley & Son

PASMORE, W.S. (1890?) *The Story of the Cornish Jury,* 2nd edn. Exeter: H. Besley & Son

PASMORE, W.S. (1890?) *The Story of the Tavystock Local Fencibles; and Jope.* Exeter: H. Besley & Son

PASMORE, W.S. (1890?) *Wat be thoose Boogles Blowin' Vor?* Exeter: H. Besley & Son

PASMORE, W.S. (1900) *Tales of Devon and Cornwall,* 3rd edn. Exeter: Besley & Dalgleish

ROGERS, F.R.S. (1954) *Cornish Dialect Words and Phrases,* Sutton: Sutton Press.

SANDYS, W. (1846) *Specimens of Cornish Provincial Dialect Collected and Arranged by Uncle Jan Treenoodle* [sic]. London: John Russell Smith

SHARPE, A. and THOMAS, C. (1979) *The Institute's Cornish Dialect Project Progress Report on the First Nine Month's Work, July 1978 to March 1979.* Redruth: Institute of Cornish Studies

THOMAS, J. (1895) *Randigal Rhymes.* Penzance

TREGELLAS, J.T. (1846) *Original Cornish Ballads; Chiefly Founded on Stories Humorously Told by Mr Tregellas.* London: Simpkin and Marshall; Penryn: T. Whitehorn

TREGELLAS, J.T. (1854) *The Adventures of Rozzy Paul and Zacky Martin; the S. Agnes Bear Hunt; and The Perran Cherry Beam: Three Comic Cornish poems,* 3rd edn. Penzance: F.T. Vibert (bookseller)

TRENHAILE, J. (1954) *Dolly Pentreath, and Other Humorous Cornish Tales, in Verse* Devonport: W. Wood; London: Piper, Stephenson & Spence

TREGELLAS, J.T. (1855) *Hackey and Markey: Being the Adventures of Hacky Daniel and Marky Retchatts, Two Cornish Miners,* 2nd edn. Penzance: F.T. Vibert

TREGELLAS, J.T. (1858) *The Amusing Adventures of Josee Cock, the Perran Cockfighter; the Author's Address to Captain Peard, Rozzy Paul, Zacky Martin and Others; Billy May's Letter; and The True Tale of Titus Teague, of Wheal Bury Downs,* 3rd edn. London: J.C. Hotten; Penzance: F.T. Vibert; Plymouth: W. Brendon

TREGELLAS, J.T. (1868) *Peeps into the Haunts and Homes of the Rural Population of Cornwall.* Truro: James R. Netherton

TREGELLAS, J.T. (1895?) *Cornish Tales in Prose and Verse.* First published Truro: James R. Netherton, this edition Truro: Netherton & Worth

WAKELIN, M.F. (1975) *Language and History in Cornwall.* Leicester: Leicester University Press

WEST, C. (1865) *A New Budget of Cornish Poems.* Cambourne: T.T. Whear

WHEAR, T.T. (1863) *Jimmy Trebilcock; or, the Humorous Adventures of a Cornish Miner at the Great Exhibition.* Cambourne: printed by T.T. Whear

Local studies collection

County Local Studies Library, Clinton Road, Redruth TR15 2QE. Tel: 0209 216760

Video cassettes and sound cassettes

Going up Cambourne Hill
Folksongs from Cornwall
Folktrack Cassettes 60–010

Boscastle Bow Wow
Charlie Jose & Co.
Folktrack Cassettes 60–096

The Holy Grail
Matthew Spring
Folktrack Cassettes 14–128

Oss Oss Wee Oss
Padstow May Day Festival
Folktrack Cassettes 60–215 and Video cassette V3

The Old Grey Duck
Songs of Cornwall 1
Folktrack Cassettes 60–217

The Cluster of Nuts
Songs of Cornwall 2
Folktracks Cassettes 60–218

Hal-an-Tow
Helston, May 18th
Folktracks Video Cassette V15

Institutes

The Institute of Cornish Studies
Trevithick Centre, Trevenson Road, Pool, Redruth, Cornwall
TR15 3PL. Tel: 0209 712203

The Institute of Cornish Studies is jointly funded by Cornwall
County Council and the University of Exeter to provide a focal
point for the University's activities in Cornwall and to disseminate
learning on Cornwall to the world at large. Its facilities include:

(1)   An historical index of every place name in the county.
(2)   A comprehensive collection of newspaper articles since 1975
      (plus some earlier material on a wide range of Cornish
      topics.
(3)   A collection of tape recordings and index of dialect words

The Institute organizes seminars for teachers who wish to incorporate
Cornish Studies in their work. A handbook, *Cornish Studies for
Cornish Schools*, has been prepared.

Devonshire

Books

BAIRD, H. (1880?) *The Song of Solomon in the Devonshire Dialect, from
the Authorized Version*. London: George Barclay.
BAIRD, H. (1850) *Letters in the Devonshire Dialect by Nathan Hogg*,
2nd edn. Exeter: Curson & Sons; Torquay: Elliot & Wreford

**Nathan Hogg's Letters
tu es Brither Jan.**

THA HOSSMINSHIP.

Exeter, April 12, 1846

Deer Jan,

    I vrites, as I agreed,
Ta tell thur aul thit I've a zeed;
An girtly I've a bin amused,
Vur tu zich zights I bant a used.
Tha tother night I went ta zee

Tha hossminship, Lor what a spree!
I thort as how I shude a dide
Way laffing, an a split ma zide.
Tu chaps urn'd in za limp as ails
A turning auver taps an tails,
An valling down way zich a wack,
I thort thay must a brauk thare back;
I ax'd a chap a zitting thare
How 'twas thit thay cude doo za quare . . .

(from H. Baird, 1858)

BAIRD, H. (1858) *Poetical Letters tu es Brither Jan, and a Witch Story . . . in the Devonshire dialect by Nathan Hogg*, 3rd edn. London: John Russell Smith; Exeter: S. Drayton & Sons

BAIRD, H. (1863) *The Gospel of Saint Matthew, Translated into Western English as Spoken in Devonshire*. London: Strangeways & Walden

BAIRD, H. (1863) *A Second Series of Poems, Including 'Mucksy Lane', a Ghost Story in the Devonshire Dialect by Nathan Hogg*. London: John Russell Smith; Exeter: Curson, T.W. Roberts, Drayton, Wheaton

BAIRD, H. (1864) *A New Series of Poems, Including 'Mucksy Lane', a Ghost Story in the Devonshire Dialect by Nathan Hogg*. London: John Russell Smith; Exeter: Curson, T.W. Roberts, Drayton, Wheaton

CHOPE R.P. (1891) *The Dialect of Hartland, Devonshire*. London: Kegan, Paul, French, Trübner

COLES, A.J. (pseud. Jan Stewer) (1905) *Jan Stewer's Demshur Buke*. Exeter: Besley & Dalgleish

COLES, A.J. (pseud. Jan Stewer) (1905–08) *Our Weekly Dialect Story: in the Carrier's Van told by Jan Stewer*. Exeter: Devon and Exeter Gazette (Collection of cuttings from the Devon and Exeter Gazette)

COLES, A.J. (pseud. Jan Stewer) (1906) *In a Devonshire Carrier's Van: Tales Told in the Devon Dialect by Jan Stewer*. Plymouth: Western Morning News

COLES, A.J. (pseud. Jan Stewer) (1920?) *Jan Stewer at Home and Abroad*. Plymouth: Western Morning News

COLES, A.J. (pseud. Jan Stewer) (1928) *Rules and Regillations of the New Milk and Dairies Order according to Jan Stewer*. Exeter: Besley & Copp

COLES, A.J. (pseud. Jan Stewer) (1949) *On the Moor of a Night by Jan Stewer*. London: Westaway Books

COLES, A.J. (pseud. Jan Stewer) (1950) *A Parcel of Old Crams*. First published London: Herbert Jenkins, this edition Gloucester: Alan Sutton

COLES, A.J. (pseud. Jan Stewer) (1950) *Ole Biskit by Jan Stewer*. First published Exeter: Besley & Copp, this edition London: Westaway Books

COLES, A.J. (pseud. Jan Stewer) (1951) *Yap by Jan Stewer*. First published London: Herbert Jenkins, this edition London: Westaway Books

COLES, A.J. (pseud. Jan Stewer) (1952) *The Shop with Two Windows*. London: Westaway Books

COLES, A.J. (pseud. Jan Stewer) (1952) *Lias and Betty by Jan Stewer*. First published London: Herbert Jenkins, this edition London: Westaway Books

COLES, A.J. (pseud. Jan Stewer) (1980) *In Chimley Corner by Jan Stewer*. First published London: Herbert Jenkins, this edition Gloucester: Alan Sutton

COLES, A.J. (pseud. Jan Stewer) (1980) *A Parcel of Ol' Crams by Jan Stewer*. First published 1930, this edition Gloucester: Alan Sutton

CROMPTON, R. (1890?) *'Thicky Furrut': a Devonshire Poaching Story*. Exeter: W. Chudley & Son

DANIEL, H.J. (c. 1870?) *A Companion for the Cornish Thalia; Being Original Humorous Pieces in the Cornish and Devonshire Dialects*. Devonport: W. Wood

DEVONSHIRE ASSOCIATION (1909) *Devonshire Verbal Provincialisms as Collected by Members of the Devonshire Association*. Tiverton: Gregory & Son (printers)

DOWNES, J. (1986) *A Dictionary of Devon Dialect*. Padstow: Tabb House

DYMOND, R. (ed.) (1902) *Letters and Poems tu es brither Jan, in the Devonshire Dialect by Nathan Hogg'*. 7th edn. Exeter: S. Drayton & Sons

GOTTO, E.R. (pseud. Uncle Tom Cobleigh) (1900–1906) *The Talk at Uncle Tom Cobleigh's Club by Uncle Tom Cobleigh and Jan Stewer*. (Volume of newspaper cuttings from the Devon and Exeter Daily Gazette, 2 March 1900–23rd February 1906)

GOTTO, E.R. (pseud. Uncle Tom Cobleigh) (1900?) *Sum vunny Demshur Tellins by Uncle Tom Cobleigh*. Exeter: Henry Eland

GWATKIN, MRS. (ed.) (1839) *Devonshire Dialogue, to Which is Added a Glossary, for the Most Part by the Late Rev. John Phillips* London: G.B. Whitaker, W. Smith; Plymouth: Edward Nettleton

HARE, W. (1892) *Brither Jan's Visit ta tha Crismiss Pantymine: a Poetic Epistle in the Devonshire Dialect, with Other Effusions*, 4th edn. Exeter: printed at the Devon Weekly Times Office

HARRIS, M. (1967) *The Phonology and Grammar of the Dialect of South Zeal, Devonshire*. Unpublished PhD thesis, University of Leeds

MARTEN, C. (1973) *The Devonshire Dialect, Being a Collection of Reminiscences, Anecdotes, Customs and Traditions in which the Devonshire Dialect is Shown to be an Important Part of the Devonshire People, with Occasional References to the Counties of Dorset, Somerset and Cornwall.* Exeter: Clement Martin Publications

O'NEILL, H.C. (1893) *Told in the Dimpses.* London: Gibbings & Co.

PALMER, MRS. (1869?) *Devonshire Courtship, in Four Parts, to which is Added a Glossary.* Devonport: W. Wood; London: Houlston & Wright

HEWITT, S. (1892) *The Peasant Speech of Devon and Other Matters Connected Therewith.* London: Elliot Stock

JURY, S. (1980) *Devonshire Songs and Chatter.* Exeter: Joseph Banks & Sons

KEATS, G. (pseud. Zack) (1898) *Life is Life and Other Tales and Episodes* 2nd edn. Edinburgh, London: William Blackwood

PALMER, MRS (1837) *A Dialogue in the Devonshire Dialect (in three parts) by a Lady; to which is Added a Glossary by J.F. Palmer.* London: Longman, Rees, Orme, Brown & Longman; Exeter: P. Hannaford

PASMORE, W.S. (1890?) *Old Stories of Devon and Cornwall.* Exeter: Henry S. Eland

PERCIVAL, A. (1926) *They'm tellin' me; or, In the Heart of the Moors.* London: Mills & Boon

PULMAN, G. (1842) *Rustic Sketches: Being Poems on Angling, Humorous and Descriptive, in the Dialect of East Devon, with a Glossary and Notes by Piscator.* Taunton: printed by W. Bragg

PULMAN, G. (1860) *The Song of Solomon in the East Devonshire Dialect, From the Authorized Version.* London: Strangeways & Walden

REYNOLDS, S. WOOLLEY, B. and WOOLLEY, T. (1911) *Seems so! A Working Class View of Politics.* London: Macmillan

ROCK. W.F. (1867) *Jim and Nell: a Dramatic Poem in the Dialect of North Devon by a Devonshire Man.* London: printed for private circulation by Unwin Brothers

RUGG, D. (1983) *Across Cobble Stones.* Padstow: Tabb House

RUGG, D. (1983) *Zum Tales Vrum Debn.* Derrick Rugg

SHERRACOMBE, W. (1932) *Hearts and Diamonds.* London: Heath Cranton

SHERRACOMBE, W. (1937) *Devonshire Fold: Stories from Remote Villages, Farms and Hills.* London: Heath Cranton

SHRIMP, S. (1876?) *Jottings and Doings in the Devonshire Dialect by Jean Shrimp and her 'old man'.* Topsham: printed and published by R. Richards

SHRIMP, S. (1873) *The Tops'em Almanac, for 1873 Edited and Carefully*

Revised by Jean Shrimp and her 'old man'. Topsham: printed and published (for Sarah Shrimp) by R. Richards

STUART, J.G. (1903) *Jan Pumroy on Prayer: a Vew of his Zarmons Prayched Auver at Tiddicombe-on-the-Moor*. London: Charles H. Kelly

UGLOW, S. (1912) *Down to the Varm*. Tiverton: Gregory & Son

WEEKES, W. (1906) *Bits of Broad Devon*, 4th edn. Exeter: William Pollard & Co.

WEEKES, W. (1921) *'Twas Ordained and Other Devonshire Sketches*. Exeter: William Pollard & Co.

WEEKES, W. (1926) *Devonshire Yarns*, new edn. Exeter: William Pollard & Co.

WREFORD, R. (1900?) *Jan Clattery and Other Tales*. Tiverton: Gregory & Son

Local studies collection

Westcountry Studies Library, Castle Street, Exeter EX4 3PQ. Tel: 0392 384216

Cassettes

'Aive Down Your Prong
Devonshire Dialect 1
Folktracks Cassettes 45–401

A Morty Unlucky ol Chap!
Devonshire Dialect 2
Folktracks Cassettes 45–402

Did Ee Ever Yur Tell?
Devonshire Dialect 3
Folktracks Cassettes 45–403

Frawzies an' Scrumpy!
Devonshire Dialect 4
Folktracks Cassettes 45–404

The Old Country Squire
Devon Village Music
Folktracks Cassettes 45–407

Barracombe Lee and Widecombe Fair
An album of songs, tunes, customs and stories
Folktracks cassettes 60–086

The Ladies Breast-Knot
Fred Pidgeon on old-time music
Folktracks cassettes 60–087

Kingsbridge Fair
South Devon Song Contest
Folktracks Cassettes 60–088

One, Two, Three A-loopah
Kids Play, Devon, recorded in Sidbury village school
Folktracks Cassettes 30–201

A Taste of Tongue Pie
Recitations in Devon Dialect by Jan Stewer
Folktracks Cassettes 30–413

Dorset

Books

ADAMS, M., HOOPEL, M. and WOODMASON, T. (1969) *A Collection of Devonshire Dialect Words in use or 'Called to Mind' by Bigbury Families and Friends.* Bigbury: Bigbury Women's Institute

ATTWELL, J. (1987) *Dorset Dialect Days.* Sherborne: Dorset Publishing

BARNES, W. (1980) *Poems in the Dorset Dialect.* Oxford: Atlantis Press

BARNES, W. (1970) *A Glossary of the Dorset Dialect with a Grammar of its Shapening and Wording.* First printed, Dorchester: Case, 1886; this edition St Peter Port: Toucan Press

BARNES, W. (1859) *The Song of Solomon in The Dorset Dialect, from the Authorized English Version,* London: George Barclay

BARNES, W. (1859) *Hwomely Rhymes. A Second Collection of Poems in The Dorset Dialect.* London: John Russell Smith

BARNES, W. (1863) *A Grammar and Glossary of the Dorset Dialect with the History, Outspreading and Bearings of South-Western English.* Berlin: A. Asher & Co. for the Philological Society

BARNES, W. (1864) *Poems in the Dorset Dialect.* Boston, Mass: Crosby & Nichols

BARNES, W. (1879) *Poems of Rural Life in The Dorset Dialect: Three Collections and a Glossary.* London: C. Kegan Paul & Co.

BARNES, W. (1879) *Poems of Rural Life in the Dorset Dialect.* London: Kegan Paul

BELL, J.G. (1851) *A Glossary of Provincial Words Used in the County of Dorset.* London: C.B. Demaine

CARTER, H.S. (1926) *'Wha's Ma'r Wi' Poole?' and Other Conversational Scraps Overheard on Constitution Hill.* Looker

DUGDALE, G. (ed.) (1949) *Poems Grave and Gay.* Dorchester: Longmans

GRIGSON, G. (ed.) (1950) *Selected Poems of William Barnes, 1880–1886.* London: Routledge & Kegan Paul

HARDY, T. (ed.) (1908) *Select Poems of William Barnes.* London: Henry Frowde

KNOTT, O. (1954) *More About Dorset.* Dorchester: The Friary Press

KNOTT, O. (1952) *Down Dorset Way.* Dorchester: Longmans

NYE, R. (ed.) (1972) *William Barnes: A Selection of his Poems.* Oxford: Carcanet Press

PARRIDGE, W. (1981) *Poems from William Barnes.* Sutton Mandeville: Perdix Press

YOUNG, R. ('Rabin Hill') (1867) *Killing the Fat Pig.* Yeovil: Western Gazette and Flying Post

YOUNG, R. ('Rabin Hill') (1867) *Rabin Hill's Excursion to Weston-Super-Mare to See the Opening of the New Pier.* Yeovil: Western Gazette and Flying Post

YOUNG, R. ('Rabin Hill') (1910) *Poems in the Dorset Dialect by Robert Young.* ('Rabin Hill') Dorchester: Dorset County Chronicle Printing Works

YOUNG, R. ('Rabin Hill') (n.d.) *An Eclogue in the Dorset Dialect in Two Parts.* Blandford: J.H. Bartlett, Express Office

WIDEN, B. (1949) *Studies on the Dorset Dialect.* London: Williams & Norgate

Local studies collection

County Library, Colliton Park, Dorchester DT1 1XJ. Tel: 0305 251000

Video cassettes and sound cassettes

Up to the Rigs
Charlie Wills
Folktracks Cassettes 60–097

Dorset Singers and Work Songs
Stone quarry/Charlie Wills
Folktracks Cassette V10

Walk In, St George
Christmas Mummers in Symonsbury and Eype, near Bridport
Folktracks Cassettes 60–101 and Video Cassette V4

Knock, Ream and Bash
Portland Stone Quarrymen
Folktracks cassettes 30–203

The Greenwood Tree
Dorset Village Music
Folktracks cassettes 60–408

Societies

William Barnes Society
Hon. Sec.: Jill Bryant, 51 Binghams Road, Crossways, Dorchester, DT2 8BW. Tel. Warmwell 853338

William Barnes (1801–1886) is perhaps best known as a writer of Dorset dialect poetry though he published many poems in standard English too. His poetry was admired by Tennyson and is thought to have been influential in the writings of both Gerard Manley Hopkins and Thomas Hardy. The humour and pathos of his readings of his own dialect poetry delighted audiences in Dorset and beyond. The Society was founded in 1983 to provide a forum in which admirers can share fellowship and pleasure in his work. The Society's aims are those of promoting an interest in Barnes' work and also of recording examples of Dorset dialect reading. Meetings take place quarterly and, in addition, visits are organized to places of interest associated with the poet.

Society of Dorset Men
Hon. Sec.: Gordon Hine, 1 Bleke Street, Shaftesbury, Dorset SP7 8QA. Tel. 0747 52408

The Society of Dorset Men dates back to 1904. The objects of the Society are to promote good fellowship among Dorset Men, wherever they may reside, to foster love of county and pride in its history and traditions. The Society publishes a Year Book containing contributions on county life, its towns and villages, some of which contain material in dialect. Members include a group called the Yetties, who have the work of William Barnes and Hardy in their repertoire.

Hampshire and the Isle of Wight

Books

COPE, W.H. (1883) *A Glossary of Hampshire Words and Phrases.*
London: Trübner & Co.
LONG, W.H. (1931) *A Dictionary of the Isle of Wight Dialect.* First
printed by Brannon & Co., 1886, 2nd edn, Barrell
WILSON, Sir J. (1913) *The Dialect of the New Forest in Hampshire, as
Spoken in the Village of Burley.* Oxford: Oxford University Press

Local studies collection

Local Studies Library, Winchester Library, Jewry Street, Winchester,
SO23 8BY. Tel: 0962 841408

Cassettes

Three Maidens A-Milking
Folksongs from Hampshire
Folktracks Cassettes 60–426

Sussex

Books

CLADPOLE, J. (pseud. Richards, J.) (1934) *De Good News According
to Mark.* Tunbridge Wells: James Richards
CLADPOLE, J. (pseud. Richards, J.) (1935) *De Sermons of Amos.*
Tunbridge Wells: James Richards
CLADPOLE, J. (pseud. Richards, J.) (1935) *De Letter of James.*
Tunbridge Wells: James Richards
CLADPOLE, J. (pseud. Richards, J.) (1936) *De Love Letters of Old John.*
Tunbridge Wells: James Richards
CLADPOLE, J. (pseud. Richards, J.) (1936) *A Word Picter of Two Sons
by Saver of Nazareth, Commonly Called 'The Parable of the Prodigal
Son'.* Tunbridge Wells: James Richards
CLADPOLE, J. (pseud. Richards, J.) (1936) *De Story of Ruth, a Gall
from de Country.* Tunbridge Wells: James Richards
CLADPOLE, J. (pseud. Richards, J.) (1937) *De Shepherd Psalm.*
Tunbridge Wells: James Richards
CLADPOLE, J. (pseud. Richards, J.) (1938) *Bits from de Old Book:
Being One or More Bits From Each of de Sixty Six Books of De Bible.*
Tunbridge Wells: James Richards

COOPER, W.D. (1853) *A Glossary of the Provincialisms in Use in the County of Sussex*, 2nd edn. Brighton: W. Fleet, Herald Office

LOWER, R. (1850) *Tom Cladpole's Jurney to Lunnun*. Lewes: Farncombe & Co.

LOWER, R. (1860) *The Song of Solomon in the Dialect of Sussex*. London: George Barclay

LOWER, R. (1872) *Jan Cladpole's Trip to 'Merricur'*. Lewes: Farncombe & Co., East Sussex News

RICHARDS, J. (pseud. Jim Cladpole) (1927) *Firle Beacon*. Tunbridge Wells: James Richards

PARISH, W.D. (1957) *A Dictionary of the Sussex Dialect and Collection of Provincialisms in Use in the County of Sussex*. Expanded, augmented and illustrated by Helena Hall, together with some Sussex Sayings and Crafts (1967) Bexhill, Sussex: Gardners

Local studies collections

Brighton Central Library, Church Street, Brighton, East Sussex BN1 1UE. Tel: 0273 601197

Chichester Central Library, Tower Street, Chichester, West Sussex PO19 1QJ. Tel: 0243 777350)

Video cassettes and sound cassettes

Come All You Old Britons
The Copper Family: songs and talk about music and traditions
Folktracks Cassettes 90–238

Adam and Eve
The Copper Family
Folktracks Cassettes 90–239

Shepherds of the Downs
The Cooper Family
Folktracks Video Cassette V12

Rolling in the Dew
Folksongs from Sussex
Folktracks Cassettes 60–427

Index to Parts I and II

accessibility hierarchy, *see* relative
  clauses
adverbs, 108, 131–2
ain't, 73, 227
Anderson, Anne, 100
aspect, *see* tense
attitudes to language, 54–5,
  102–4, 139, 217–19, 234–5 *see*
  also stigmatized forms

Bourne, J, 15, 25, 36
Brown, E K, 100
Bullock Report, The, 55
Burchfield, Robert, 71
Burgess, T, 37
Bybee, Joan, 78

Cameron, Deborah, 15, 25, 36
Centre for Urban and Regional
  Development Studies (CURDS),
  60–3, 79, 96
Champion, T, 61
Chandler, P, 36
Cheshire, Jenny, 11, 20, 22, 23,
  28, 29, 35, 38, 49, 54, 55, 56,
  61, 67, 73, 192, 193, 225–6
Clark, R, 36, 50
class research projects on
  variation, 30–1, 36–7, 47–9
Collins, P, 46
comparatives, 129, 209, 231–2
Comrie, Bernard, 69
Coombes, M, 61
Cooter, Robert, 189

correction(s), 28–30, 39–42
  ineffectiveness of...40–1
correctness, 4–5
Coupland, Nicolas, 14, 63, 67, 75,
  77, 82
Cox Report (DES, 1989), The, 17,
  25, 36, 39–40, 50
Crystal, David, 35
Cullum, J, 21

Dannequin, C, 21
definite article, 128–9, 144–6
demonstrative adjectives
  demonstrative *them*, 65–6, 108
  distribution of...in North-west
  England, 81
dialect levelling, 53–83
dialect writing, 46–7, 101
Dieth, Eugen, 216
discourse organisation, 132–7,
  173–7
DO auxiliary, 78, 79, 224–6
done as past tense, 77–9, 106,
  224–6 *see also* verb forms in
  non-standard English
double negative, *see* multiple
  negation
Downes, William, 15

educational policy, 34, 106 *see*
  also language in education
Edwards, John, 54
Edwards, Viv, 35, 37, 38, 53, 54,
  55, 56, 57, 68, 75

Eisikovits, E, 70
elaboration of function, 5, 6
Ellis, A J, 216
errors, 28–30

Fairclough, Norman, 17, 25, 36
functional regions, 61–2, 79

Garrod, Simon, 100
gerunds, 129
Giles, Howard, 42
give me it, 73–5
Graddol, David, 15
grammaticality, 8, 9
Grant, W, 101, 120
Greenbaum, Sidney, 202

Handscombe, R J, 23
Harris, John, 53, 196
Hawkins, E, 55, 56
Heslop, R O, 188, 190, 192
history of non-standard dialects;
    101–2, 139–40, 187–90,
    214–16
Holmes, Janet, 22
House, J W, 189
Hughes, Arthur, 12, 63, 67, 68,
    70, 73, 74, 75, 77

inequality, 31
infinitives, 129–30
    with *for to*, 167, 200
intensifiers, 209–10
interrogatives,
    direct..., 125–6
    indirect..., 126–8, 167–8, 204
    tag..., 73, 203–4
it-clefting, 175–6

Jones, A P, 55, 56

Keenan, Edward, 69
Kirk, John, 74

Labov, William, 67, 191
language development
    ...in older children, 21–4
    ...in writing, 22–2
language in education, 25–31,
    104–6, 178–81
language maintenance, 5
language testing, *see* linguistic
    assessment
Lass, Roger, 69
left-dislocation, 174–5
legitimization, 6
linguistic assessment, 24–5, 83,
    104–6
linguistic awareness, 21–2, 37, 49,
    55–6
linguistic diversity
    reactions to ..., 38–42
Linguistic Minorities Project, 37
linguistic repertoire,
    of children, 25–6
literacy
    effects of ..., 7–9, 12
Lorimer, W L, 101

Macafee, Caroline, 57, 100, 109,
    111, 115
Macaulay, Ronald K S, 45, 100
McDonald, Christine, 193–212
Main-Dixon, J, 101, 120
matched guise experiments, 42, 44
Matthews, William, 235
metropolitan regions, 61–2
Miller, James, 100
Milroy, James, 25, 35, 53, 69, 103
Milroy, Lesley, 25, 35, 53, 103
modal verbs, 116–121, 194–7
Moder, C L, 78
morphology (of Scots) 106–8
multiple negation, 75–6, 168–70,
    198–200, 226–7
Murray, James A H, 102, 112

National Curriculum, The, 25, 34, 36, 49, 50
negation
    in Scots, 114–16
    see also multiple negation, never as negator
negative concord, see multiple negation
never as negator, 67–8, 198
nominalization (in Irish English), 148
non-assertive forms, 170–1
non-standard English, passim
    concept of..., 99–100, 177–8
    regional distribution of ... 82–3
    shared non-standard forms, 63–75
    variation in..., 11–14, 23–4
    see also history of non-standard dialects, stigmatized forms
norms, behavioural, 20
number agreement, 109, 154–6, 194

Orton, Harold, 57, 80

peer groups, 20–1, 44
Perera, Katherine, 23
personal identity, 18, 44–6
Petyt, Malcolm, 70
plural marking, 107
    absence of...in non-standard English, 66–7, 109–10, 146, 209, 234
Powesland, P, 42
prepositions,
    ...in non-standard English, 77, 132, 171–3, 211–17, 233–4
prescription, 5, 71
prestige, 31, 45
pronouns,
    demonstrative ..., 147, 207

personal ..., 108, 139–40, 146–7, 205–7, 211, 229–30
    possessive ..., 128–9
    reflexive ..., 77, 131, 147, 229–30
    see also relative pronouns

questionnaire(s), 37, 38, 57–9
    for Survey of British Dialect Grammar, 87–95
quick as adverb, 72–3
Quirk, Randolph, 19, 69, 70, 202

Received Pronunciation, 10, 42, 46
regional forms, passim
    attitudes to..., 14–17, 42–4, 44–6
    children's ..., 23–6, 30
    distribution of non-standard was and were, 79–81
    social significance of ..., 17–18
    see also attitudes to language, non-standard English
Reid, Euan, 100
relative clauses, 10–14, 148–51
    accessibility hierarchy for..., 69–70
relative pronouns, 18–19, 68–70, 207–9, 228–9
    what as relative pronoun, 68–70
Romaine, Suzanne, 21, 69
Rosen, Harold, 37, 236
Ryan, Ellen Bouchard, 42

sat and stood following BE auxiliary, 70–1
should of, 66
Sivertsen, Eva, 236–8
social dialects, 63, 82–3
social identity, 18, 38, 44–6

socio-economic class, effects of...
    12–13
speech, grammar of ... 7–9
standard English, history of...
    9–10
Standard Grade examinations (in
    Scotland), 104–5
standard language,
    acceptance of ..., 5
    codification of ..., 5, 6, 8, 16,
        139
    diffusion of ..., 5
    selection of..., 5
standardization, 3–6, 8, 10, 82
    ideology of ..., 10, 14–15
    stages of ..., 5–6
stigmatized forms, 39
Stubbs, Michael, 25, 36
subject-verb concord, see number
    agreement
subordinate conjunctions, 164
sub-standard (as distinct from
    non-standard), 3–4
Survey of British Dialect
    Grammar, The, 35–50, 53–83,
    regional coverage of..., 59–63,
        96
    see also questionnaire(s)
Survey of English Dialects, The,
    57, 59, 74–5, 80–1
Swann, Joan, 15

tense, 121–4
    ...and aspect in Irish English,
        159–64, 220–4
    'historic present', 156

there's (there was) with plural
    subject, 70
Trudgill, Peter, 12, 13, 35, 39, 42
    45, 63, 67, 68, 70, 73, 74, 76,
    77, 191

uniformity, 3–4
urban dialects, 53, 63–75

variability, suppression of ...4
variation as structured, 18–20,
    25–6
verb complement clauses, 167,
    200
verb forms in non-standard
    English, 106, 151–4, 157–9,
    192–4, 201, 220–6

Walker, J, 234–5
we was, 71–2
Welsh English, 14
Weltens, Bert, 35, 53, 54, 57, 68,
    75, 77
Whittle, Pamela, 53–96
Williams, A, 29
Wilson, James, 101, 102, 120
Winch, C, 25, 36

youse, 139–40
    distribution of ... in North-west
        England, 81